Danny Dorling has been a Professor of Human Geography at the University of Sheffield since 2003. He will take up the Halford Mackinder Professorship in Geography at the University of Oxford in autumn 2013. He is also Adjunct Professor in the Department of Geography, University of Canterbury, New Zealand, Visiting Professor, Department of Sociology, Goldsmiths, University of London, and Visiting Professor in the Department of Social Medicine, University of Bristol, UK. He is an Academician of the Academy of the Learned Societies in the Social Sciences, and Honorary President of the Society of Cartographers. In 2009 he was awarded the Gold Award of the Geographical Association and the Back Award of the Royal Geographical Society for his work on national and international public policy. He has worked both with the British government and the World Health Organization and is frequently asked to comment on current issues on TV and the radio. He has published more than twenty-five books, most recently *Injustice: Why Social Inequality Exists*, which was described by Richard Wilkinson and Kate Pickett, authors of *The Spirit Level*, as 'provid[ing] the brain-cleaning software we need to begin creating a happier society.' He lives in Sheffield with his family.

Also by Danny Dorling

Population 10 Billion

Danny Dorling

Constable • London

*To Richard, to help him get to sleep at night and to
Kate, who knows everything will be alright in the end,
and that if it is not alright then it is not the end.*

CONSTABLE
First published in Great Britain in 2013 by Constable.

A copy of the British Library Cataloguing in Publication
Data is available from the British Library

ISBN 978-1-78033-491-2 (paperback)
ISBN 978-178033-878-1 (ebook)

Printed and bound in Great Britain

3 5 7 9 10 8 6 4 2

Constable
An imprint of Constable & Robinson
100 Victoria Embankment
London EC4Y 0DY

An Hachette UK Company

www.hachette.co.uk

www.constablerobinson.com

CONTENTS

CHAPTER 1

INTRODUCTION: STOP WORRYING

On a mountain halfway between Reno and Rome,
We have a machine in a Plexiglas dome
Which listens and looks into everyone's home.

Theodor Seuss Geisel,
Dr Seuss's Sleep Book, 1962[1]

The machine in the Plexiglas dome is not found in a mountain; it is a small computer on a desk in an obscure room in that New York slab of hope that is the UN skyscraper. Inside the slab, on 3 May 2011, the United Nations Department of Economic and Social Affairs published a revision to global population estimates, and what was revealed was something of a surprise.[2]

Before May 2011, the latest global estimates had suggested that world population would peak at 9.1 billion in 2100, and then fall to 8.5 billion by 2150. In contrast, the 2011 revision suggested that 9.1 billion humans would all be alive at the same time much earlier – maybe by 2050 or before – and that by 2100 there would be 10.1 billion of us, with our numbers still rising in a century's time.

Initially the world's press did not react in horror at the news that we could soon be ten billion. Population forecasts are incredibly fickle numbers, and the long-term

1

prognosis was still for imminent global stability. What had happened was that the news had come in from some place – for now let's call it the County of Keck[3] – suggesting that a few (million) more babies were being born than had previously been the case, and a few less folk were dying.

Just a tiny change in fertility can be magnified in a century to an extra billion human beings. A tiny change in the other direction, a few (million) more people using condoms, and there will be fewer than eight billion of us in the near future. But how much does it matter? What difference does an extra billion, or a billion fewer, people make? Should we be concerned that the global human population count is currently on target to top ten billion, or are there more important things to worry about?

This book suggests that the actual number of people on the planet is, to an important extent, incidental to the impact humans have on both the environment and each other. It also suggests that many people are coming to understand this – which is why the news of an expected extra billion humans within three score years and ten did not result in panic. Instead, it's not how many of us there are but how we live that will matter most.

There are many signs that we may well collectively be choosing more often to live sustainably, not least in how we are already controlling our numbers. This is a book for pragmatists. It is about how ten billion people can live well on this planet. I do not argue that they will; just that enough evidence exists to suggest it is possible. So here is a story about that possibility. It is based on many facts, but it will almost certainly turn out to be a fiction of one kind or another. We can never know what will happen, but that is no excuse for not being interested in the future, nor for failing to try to influence it.

The story that follows is broken up into chapters marking

the point at which each billion human milestone was passed, or is expected to be reached. Within each chapter I have tried to place those contemporary debates most pertinent to that number of people. Chapter 2 considers the very long time it took to get human numbers up to five billion, and how even then some still claimed there were too many people. Chapter 3 takes us up to the year 2000, six billion people and concerns of disorder and peak consumption. Chapter 4 moves forward only to 2011, seven billion people and, among many issues, concerns for future energy supplies. That is the end of the first half of the book; the rest is speculation.

Chapter 5 considers the years up to 2025, to there being eight billion of us; it raises concerns about food and water, but also presents new thinking that we may be collectively becoming clever enough to organize ourselves better. Chapter 6 takes us forward to 2045, to nine billion people and questions of border controls and economic inequality. Chapter 7 is as far ahead as we venture, to the ten billion projected at the end of the century, and asks what they might then be living without, but also how they might be better-off than us. Finally, Chapter 8 casts a little doubt over whether there ever will be that many of us alive at the same time, and gives a long list of reasons to be hopeful about the future. The remainder of this chapter, like most of the book, is about competing and constructing stories. It concerns how we come to believe, and is about how changing some of our beliefs might be the key to our collective survival.

Discovering a new world

> 'Story telling is not in our genes or evolutionary history, but it is the essence of what makes us human.'
>
> David Canter, Professor of Psychology, 2012[4]

Human beings progress by telling stories. One event can result in a great variety of stories being told about it. Sometimes those stories differ greatly. Which stories are picked up and repeated and which are dropped and forgotten often determines how we progress. Our history, knowledge and understanding are all the collections of the few stories that survive. This includes the stories we tell each other about the future. And how the future will turn out depends partly, possibly largely, on which stories we collectively choose to believe.

Some stories are designed to spread fear and concern. This may be because the story-teller feels there is a need to raise some tensions. They might feel that facts are being overlooked, or that their point of view is not being taken seriously enough. To get attention, people sometimes tell stories to shock their listeners. For instance, one recent story refers to an apparently otherwise mild-mannered Cambridge University academic recommending that we should teach our children how to use guns so that, in the apparently inevitable forthcoming population Armageddon, they will have a better chance of survival.

Stories of us descending into a *Lord of the Flies*[5] world are frightening; they are totemic warnings: 'Fail to act now and we are all doomed.' They suggest that if we do not act in the way the protagonist would wish us and everyone else to act, the consequences will be dire, with our genes, our offspring, doomed to some kind of survival of the least empathetic. The only survivors will be those who find killing easy; what some call 'the fittest'.

For each generation the warnings are updated, although encouragingly, there are now caveats about the fallacies of such warnings; today the message of the book *The Hunger Games*[6] is taught in schools where I live in England more as a warning to beware selfish adults than as a prophecy that soon hunger will spread. At school I was made to read *Lord of the Flies* to try, I guess, to make me fearful of anarchy or tribalism.

Just as there are stories that we are all doomed, so too are there stories that all will be fine as long as we leave everything up to a few especially able, if often a little selfish, adults. Currently this trend is led by those who occasionally describe themselves as rational optimists.

Self-titled 'rational optimists' tend to claim that it is human nature to compete and to trade, to want above all to profit at the expense of others. They often use what they present as Darwinian arguments which suggest that people reached this point naturally, not realizing how people have evolved to become less selfish as they work in larger groups, and that only a minority of humans are quite as selfishly driven as the so-called rational optimists are. Rational optimists suggest that people will find a set of solutions to their problems driven by greed above all else. Pragmatists should doubt this.

The story-tellers of rational optimism like to try to paint themselves as sensible but cheerful folk. One, Matt Ridley, has argued forcefully along rational optimist lines.[7] His story suggests that it is mostly people trying to become rich ('wealth creators') who help others along the way, even if they cause a little hardship as they do so. Matt is the 5th Viscount Ridley. His family made its fortune by owning coal mines in northern England in Victorian times. He himself was chairman of the bank Northern Rock at the time of its collapse, the collapse that triggered the financial crash in Europe. Given his background and business failures, it is not hard to mock his views, but they need to be taken seriously because they are part of the current mantra of many at the top of the tree.

Matt's brother-in-law, Owen Paterson, was made

Environment Secretary by the British prime minister in September 2012. Owen thinks like Matt. Currently he is buying into the family tradition of promoting carbon extraction and pollution as progress: 'he wants to end all energy subsidies and fast-track exploitation of shale gas. This would shatter any ambition for the UK of keeping to targets for renewables or greenhouse gases.'[8]

The views of people like Matt Ridley and the idea that they are taken seriously by so many in positions of power, despite their practical failure through the ages, can bring others to the brink of despair. The failures on Matt's part alone in the rational optimism fable – the suggestion that greed will prevail – range from his family's private mining endeavours requiring nationalizing, if just to bring in a little humanity for the coal miners, to the collapse of the privatized building society he chaired, resulting in the first run on a British bank in living memory. However, stories about how greed is ultimately good give people with power and wealth a warm feeling that they are somehow part of the solution. This is why such stories have a lot of clout behind them, and why they spread.

Angry pessimists counter rational optimists with stories that try to expose such fanciful musing. They warn of what may happen if the rational optimists are believed. The term 'rational optimism' itself is a misnomer, labelling all others as being irrational and holding pessimistic views on human nature, to be compared with the supposedly optimistic but hard-faced corporate elite.

What we need more of are 'practical possibilists' and their stories; stories that sit between those who say that all will be fine, and those who claim that we are doomed. I believe that there is a chance we might stumble through after all, just as we have in the past. Whether you think this is possible depends on which stories you hold to and how you act on them. If greed prevails, we are probably doomed. If doom-mongers prevail, who is going to care about trying to prevent the greedy from hammering the final nails into humanity's coffin?

Right now, different people are telling very different stories of how the world works. Maybe it was always like this? However, at times of greater stability, the stories tended to become more uniform. During such times, speaking out of turn could be heresy. Galileo, for example, suggested that he had discovered that the earth orbited the sun, a crime which he almost paid for with his life. Today we have hundreds of professional and thousands of armchair astronomers gleaning knowledge, each looking through differently focused telescopes, all appearing to discover a slightly different story of the current arrangement of our galaxy, and each forecasting a very different world to come.

In summer 2012, in London's exclusive Sloane Square, a play was put on at the Royal Court Theatre. It featured a computer scientist with a background in biology named Stephen Emmott.[9] The play was a monologue of his agonizing over what is to be done (to save humankind). What was it that brought Stephen to tell his story, a story of a man who appeared to be past the brink of despair? The answer was the arguments of those self-styled rational optimists and their claims that unbridled selfishness, left unfettered, would bring all the solutions needed to safeguard the planet's future; population growth, climate change, poverty, everything could be solved by greed!

In Britain, just as Matt Ridley personifies rational optimism, Stephen Emmott is the embodiment of angry pessimism. Wherever you live, there will be the equivalent pairs of individuals. Stephen knows that people seeking only to profit financially will not come up with the solutions needed. He works through their arguments, but is so alarmed that he ends up quoting the colleague advocating teaching children how to use firearms (see below). Surely there is a middle way between the apparently opposing world views of these two forceful men? Here is an account of Stephen's position:

What's to be done? Emmott takes us through the ideas offered by 'the rational optimists' who believe that, faced with the species' near extinction, human inventiveness will engineer a solution. Desalination plants, a new green revolution, seeding the oceans with iron filings to absorb more CO_2: all of these threaten to produce as many problems as they solve. He believes the only answer is behavioural change. We need to have far fewer children and consume less. How much less? A lot less; two sheets of toilet paper rather than three, a Prius instead of a Range Rover – that kind of sacrifice won't really do it. And does he believe we're capable of making this necessarily far bigger curb on our desires? Not really. He describes himself as a rational pessimist. 'We're fucked,' he says. If a large asteroid were on course to the Earth and we knew when and where it would hit – say France in 2022 – then every government would marshal its scientific resources to find ways of altering the asteroid's path or mitigating its damage. But there is no asteroid. The problem is us. Recently he asked one of his younger academic colleagues what he thought could be done. 'Teach my son how to use a gun,' said the colleague.[10]

Just as Matt Ridley has a history, Stephen Emmott can be shown to be an interested commentator. He has a lab of scientists to fund, and needs powerful people to be concerned with these issues. Apprehension that we are facing a worrying common future is widely held; if it is not population numbers, it is often something associated with those numbers. Some people hope that their country and their family might be safe as disasters are concentrated elsewhere; others see that there are no escape pods from earth.

The world is awash with newspaper stories, TV shows, films, plays and above all books concerning the end of eras, the great crises to come, the crisis we are experiencing now, how we are living through the annihilation of many species, through climate catastrophe, impending pandemic, clashes of civilizations, economic meltdown. You name it – someone will be suggesting we fear it. There will be things we should fear, but what should we be most frightened of and what should we not worry about?

Nothing is too bizarre when it comes to fears over future human population numbers. There is even a voluntary human extinction movement that suggests that the best that can be done for the planet is 'phasing out the human race by voluntarily ceasing to breed [which] will allow Earth's biosphere to return to good health'. However, even this group may have some conflict of interests, as on their web page there is also a button labelled 'How do I order stickers, T-shirts, and stuff?'[11] It is as if the only group out there without a profit motive is the group in the middle who we have yet to meet, the boring old practical possibilists. There are no T-shirts to buy with the slogan: 'There probably is enough food for all', or: 'Worry less, humans are cooperative'. What is reassuring tends also to be bland.

It could all go wrong. We could have a global famine. We might descend into a global war, the first true world war that includes all countries. It could happen. But it might not. This book is about why and how it might not. The argument here is not that we have reached the end of history – a twenty-year-old prediction of that turned out to be remarkably premature.[12] Neither does the book imply that we can sit back and all will be OK. That has never happened before, so it is unlikely to occur now. This is also not a book suggesting that technological change will save us; such ideas have also been suggested often before as a panacea. What it does point out is that there are many hopeful signs that are often overlooked, signs which have mostly only recently become apparent and which it is worth observing if, at the very least, we are to keep our hopes up.

Reasons not to be pessimistic abound. Only very recently has it become commonplace to be able to say: 'By most estimates, the explosive population increase still under way will end near AD 2050 as global population levels out at some 9–10 billion people . . .'[13] We can now see that human population growth is not just slowing, but is set to stabilize within the current lifetimes of a majority of people on the planet; these should be the first people to see that occur without it being caused by the Black Death pandemic of 763 years ago!

The majority of the world's population is young. Most people alive today will be alive in 2050. The mid-century date is coming around when, for the first time in centuries, the sun will rise over the Pacific and cast its light on one fewer living soul than the day before. For the first time ever, that can occur without it being due to thousands more suffering from both unusual and agonizing deaths than the numbers who are born that day. The population explosion is ending peacefully.

The deceleration of the growth of our algae-bloom-like explosion of humanity is just one reason to set the worst pessimism aside for a while. A further sign of hope is that for the first time ever, the large majority of people alive today are literate. Around sixty millennia ago, a majority

10

of humans learnt to speak. Only within the last sixty years have a majority learnt to read and write. It is no coincidence that this is happening just as we can expect to see human numbers fall not due to disaster, but due to the winning of rights, principally women's rights.

There are more signs. For the first time ever, almost everywhere, women are about to live longer than men.[14] Women are fitter, but a combination of patriarchy and lack of care during childbirth has until now killed more of them earlier than men. Very soon, maybe already, a majority of people on the planet will be female, as we now live long enough for this to occur. This will be the first ever female majority of humans on the planet. It will happen any day now.

For the first time ever, majorities of people today say they would not fight for their religion, their country or creed if told to. In addition, the current generation are the first to mostly live in cities, to mostly have the vote; almost everywhere in the world there is a vote of one kind or another. The majority of those alive today have heard a radio and hence have received ideas which have leapt over great distances and old customs. Print and the moveable typeface did the same in the past, but only for the minority who could then read.

Practical possibilists rejoice in trends that suggest that a decent human future is possible. Typical of this group is Hans Rosling, the Swedish doctor now best known for his Gapminder movies and YouTube talks.[15] For practical possibilists, a term coined by Hans, it's not how many of us there are but how we live that will matter, and – as I'll show in the chapters which follow – there are many signs that we may well collectively be choosing to live more sustainably, and that this is occurring far faster than could have been expected a generation ago.

As geographer Ash Amin, another possibilist, puts it, referring in particular to those who are afraid of extra people and especially immigration: 'It is time to give a politics of reasonableness a chance, to stop the politics of purge from ushering in the calamity it purports to avoid.'[16] There are signals in the language writers are using, in the points commentators are now making, that the plots of some of our most common stories are changing, but so too are the facts we unearth about ourselves. Not least among these are signs that reasonableness and practical possibility may be flourishing anew. This is the emerging story of how we are already controlling our numbers and avoiding calamity, not through authoritarian diktat, but as we rebound from a population explosion and what was a huge historical and geographical shock – the 'discovery' of the New World. But to understand all this, we have to take it step by step, steps of one billion at a time.

Although Chapters 5 to 8 in this volume are all about the future, this is mainly a book about the present and how it concerns the future. It is also a book about new ideas about the past. These are often ideas that have only emerged within the lives of most people currently alive. Just as our population numbers have only very recently exploded, so too has our understanding of who we are and our theories about how we got here.

Principal among the new ideas that influence the story of this book is the concept of *geographic shock*. Just over 500 years ago, when my great-grandfather's great-grandmother's great-grandfather's great-grandmother's great-grandfather was alive, we encountered a new planet, a planet with a human population. It was a shock, such a shock that we called it the New World – the Americas.

At school I was taught that we in the West discovered the New World rather than encountered it. But that semantic change from 'discover' to 'encounter' itself tells you how quickly understanding is changing. We also now laugh at how it suited schoolteachers to describe the Spanish people as advanced, and the economic exploitation of the Americas as some kind of scientific discovery. We are changing our ways of thinking about the world faster now than we have ever done. Our collective human thoughts, our collections of aggregate knowledge, are rapidly evolving as we learn more about our own evolution.

Our future is not in our genes but in our minds and our collective ability to organize. *Not in our Genes* was a book written in 1984 by Steven Rose, Dick Lewontin and Leon Kamin as a response to the excesses of sociobiology, and was so good that it upset eminent biologists, who claimed it to be an 'idiotic travesty'.[17] However, if our collective future is not held in our individual genetic constructions, then that future will not depend on either some rational optimist's survival-of-the-fittest fantasizing, or some angry pessimist's despair that only those most inclined to be brutal among our offspring will make it through, those we teach to shoot the straightest but who are somehow able to not blink as they kill.

We now know that groups that are more cooperative fare better, but within each group individuals that are a little more greedy gain more. More cooperative groups curtail the greed of the few and help them to control their excesses, as well as benefiting all the rest who would otherwise suffer from such selfishness. This is a theme that will run through every chapter of this book because it becomes more important the more of us there are.

It is true that when it comes to each of us individually suffering some plight, such as heart disease, 'it is mostly genes and chance'[18] and very much more chance than genes.[19] But when it comes to what happens to groups of people, our genes are now so mixed and mutated as to elevate human traits that are beneficial to us all. It is not our personal abilities that vary much; instead it is what we do with our common natural endowments that matters and can vary most.

When the New World was first encountered, both genes and the lack of conditioned immune systems did matter. Those humans who had never before been exposed to Old World illnesses died far faster from those diseases than from any conquistador's sword. Those people who did not carry genes that protected them from malaria and yellow fever perished quickly.[20] Back across the Atlantic, the shock was so great that the economy of the Old World was transformed; riches plundered from the New World turned the social order of continents upside down.

After 1492, the western edge of the Old World, which was so often drawn at the bottom of old maps, grew to be the richest place, the east of the Old World was destabilized, and what we now call capitalism was born in response to the shock of the 1492 'encounter'. Geographically, the peninsula of Western Asia became so powerful that it could successfully apply its once minor label – Europe – as the name of an apparently entirely separate continent.

From continent to continent human populations began to multiply rapidly as the established social orders were overturned. The first, fastest and most destabilizing population explosion was within Europe itself. Africa was depopulated through the spreading of slavery and 400 years of forced migration, mostly to the New World. India was colonized (twice), Chinese empires were destroyed, partly through the British Empire-orchestrated opiate trade. A North American empire was born.

The shock of encounter still isn't over, but the fact that we are finally recognizing recent world history as being largely a reaction to the geographical shock of the New World's incorporation, rather than some natural evolution of human selfishness and self-destructive tendencies, is a further reason to be optimistic. Shocks can be overcome. And if, after the Neolithic revolution, what we have been living through since 1492 has been the second greatest perturbation in human history, no wonder it has taken us some time to grasp this enormity.

Theories of the geographical shock have not been widely reported outside of the pages of academic journals. There is no uniform opinion as to how important 1492 was to what occurred thereafter. There is a great deal of evidence to suggest that even if most of us are not that selfish or self-destructive, far too many of our leaders are, and that the way we promote such people to the top encourages them. The last five hundred years may not be a great guide to how humans in the next one hundred may fare, but looked at in a certain way, told with a certain kind of story in mind, it is possible to paint a picture which has a ros-ier, less optimistically combative and less pessimistically catastrophic ending than many presume. That is what a practical possibilist paints.

In the pages that follow, the glass is always at least half full and ever so slowly becoming fuller. It is a story of the signs of hope. It is not that we are entering some utopia; rather that all may be far from lost. The reasons for many of our current calamities might be far from any of our making. We might just rub along OK, and you never know, it is even conceivable that things could possibly get better, especially if we are more hopeful.

Start off by seeing the tales underlying much of recent human history as being those of the shock of the new, and a global reordering that moves the European peninsulas and islands from the periphery of the known planet to its centre.[21] After 1492, Europe became the trade-winds and trade-routes centre. See that change as key and you start from a very different place from the one where most of us were philosophically dropped off at the end of school history lessons.

After the Tsunami, being a 'possibilist'

> At present there are no well charted ways for 10 billion people to achieve lifestyles like those enjoyed in the Most Developed Countries, because the only known way forward is economic growth, and that will come into collision with the finite earth. Technology can help, but without socio-political change it cannot solve.
>
> Paul Nurse,
> President of the Royal Society, 2012[22]

Swedish medic turned world development specialist Hans Rosling loves statistics. His background is in public health medicine and the curing of rare tropical diseases, but he now looks at what is most common rather than most unusual. With the help of his son and wider family he popularized the animated bubble chart. How did he do this? He charted stuff of great importance, and if all that failed, he swallowed a sword live on stage to wake the audience up to what his animated graphs were showing.

Hans Rosling's graphics show that the world is rapidly changing. As he himself admits, he's not an optimist, he's not a pessimist, he's a 'possibilist'. He just happens to be the possibilist who has done more than any other living human being to show statistically that a better world is possible, not least when it comes to understanding declining fertility and rising freedom. As he says: 'so when you discuss resources and when you plan for the energy needs for the future, for the humans on this planet you have to plan for ten billion'.[23]

To plan is not to say that the future will be OK, that you can decide now what it will be and it will be that way. To plan is to prepare. To plan is to accept that it is possible to imagine a world containing ten billion people, but also to say what conditions would necessarily have to be in place for that world to be both sustainable and pleasantly habitable. It could be a world of a great many wind farms, and people wearing their shirt for three days or more, so that energy would not be spent unnecessarily washing clothes too often, most especially when wind speeds were low.

A recent report by one respected think tank found that the 'reliability and security of wind power does not depend on the variability of wind but instead on how well changes in wind power output can be predicted and managed'.[24] Wind energy is viable and is predictable enough to keep (reading) lights on, but it may not be predictable enough for some industrial processes to be kept running at any time of day or night should we wish to run them like that.

A possibilist sees what is possible. It is possible to generate enough electricity to read at night and to wash clothes as much as they need washing. It may not be possible in many places on earth to produce enough energy in future to smelt as much aluminium as some may wish to, even if this is achieved by hydro power.[25] Providing energy to keep us clean and warm is possible. Providing enough for some of our most extravagant wishes is not. Sometimes that extravagance is simply wishing to have an endless supply of cans of baked beans. What is unsustainable is the can, not the beans.

Almost every practical possibilist report that is published attracts instant detractors. A few of the readers of the newspaper in which the report on wind power reliability first appeared reacted predictably. One was particularly angry: 'Sorry DT [*Daily Telegraph*], this article is utter bullsh*t and you know it. The report is biased, was written by the wind energy company.' Both angry pessimists, who see little chance of wind power without nuclear backup providing an alternative, and rational optimists, who often think that climate change is not severe enough to stop burning coal, react with apoplexy when it is suggested that there might be solutions that already exist, that require little technological development, but which do require a change in common conceptions of how much power we really do need and what levels of reliability might be acceptable in future.

Think tanks veer between distributing optimistic and pessimistic stories. A week before that spat on windmills took place, a portent of doom was announced. On 22 August 2012 it was proclaimed around the world that 'Today is Earth Overshoot Day . . . a concept originally developed by the Global Footprint Network and the UK based think tank New Economics Foundation (NEF) which represents the annual marker of when we begin living beyond our means in a given year.'[26] Many readers might have thought, 'so what, it's just those greens moaning again', but the story came with an extra warning. Earth Overshoot Day was moving backwards in time.

Annual commemorations around the world are mostly supposed to be positive and full of hope and expectation, but Earth Overshoot Day has been designed to lack festivity. In 1992, this date was said to have fallen on 21 October, while in 2002 it was 'celebrated' on 3 October. Ten years later, in 2012, the date of 22 August was announced as the point during the year by which we had collectively consumed too much. Each year in the 1990s the date moved forward 1.8 days. Each year in the noughties it shot forward 4.2 days!

If the rate of our accelerating approach to Armageddon is to continue to speed up, then Earth Overshoot Day will begin to move forward 6.6 days a year during the next decade, to be announced at mid June in 2022. A further nine days a year in the following decade and it will be in March. Soon Earth Overshoot Day could even fall before the first signs of the northern hemisphere's spring, which are themselves moving forward in time. The underlying message of the numerical literature is that we'll never reach 2040 if the current rate of planet-burning and wasting continues to grow unabated.

The 'Overshoot Day' press release that sparked concern during 2012 continued to give further details, and in many cases these were turned straight into newspaper copy. One story read:

> Given current trends in consumption, Earth Overshoot Day tends to arrive a few days earlier each year. This day marks the approximate date our resource consumption for a given year exceeds the planet's ability to replenish. From this day on, it would mean that humanity has exhausted nature's budget for the year and we are operating in overdraft. After today, we are already in 'debt' towards nature and planet Earth and this is where the other name of the day (Ecological Debt Day) comes from.[27]

Debt is scary; debts have to be repaid if you are not to become a pariah. Stories about Earth Overshoot/Ecological Debt Day are the stick; stories about the potential reliability of wind power are the carrot, but between these buffetings of doom and optimism it is easy to lose hope and interest, or to think that this is all too much to comprehend. It has even been suggested that the planet is currently entering a new geological phase, the Anthropocene,[28] as the effects of humans are now significant enough to alter climate, the environment and hence eventually the deposits laid down in rock strata. But will our layer of rock be thick, thin, or extremely thin?

The two think tanks referred to above, IPPR and NEF, did not coordinate their reports. Faced with an onslaught of over-jingoistic suggestions that a country's economy depends on it being willing to burn more fossil fuel, or build more roads for more cars, researchers who recognize the dangers may well feel forced to produce estimates of how the end of times is approaching more rapidly than was thought a few years ago. Be afraid, be very afraid, be even more afraid than you were last year is a message that can lose its edge in the same way as does crying wolf too often. In the long run, the more pedestrian, the possibilist, the reasonableness of softer stories may gain surer ground. Being afraid only gets you so far; being determined moves you further on; being better informed can give you hope.

Ultimately no amount of new wind power or other technical changes to how we produce energy or grow food, build homes or travel, will solve our growing problems of overconsumption and greed without our changing how we behave and what we wish for. We who consume most have to consume less. However, there are many recent reports that demonstrate how it is possible to reduce consumption in rich countries. Many are used throughout this book to show what is already taking place. The least visible changes are happening in those homes where increasingly people buy a little less of what they don't need and recycle a little more of the waste from what they do need. The most visible changes occur when change is suddenly forced upon people.

The 11 March 2011 Japanese earthquake was so powerful that 'parts of eastern Japan are now 12 feet closer to North America and Japan has dropped 2 feet in height'.[29] More than 20,000 people were killed by the subsequent tsunami, or pronounced missing and presumed dead. Official life expectancy estimates for the entire country stalled as a result. The financial cost was estimated at being between US$195 billion and US$305 billion, and within the first seven days after the earthquake, 18 trillion yen had to be injected into the banking system by the Bank of Japan to prevent outright panic. The yen also rose rapidly in value as currency speculators were reluctant to sell, assuming its value would rise as the Japanese government and businesses tried to repatriate capital they held overseas to allow Japan to pay for the clear-up. For currency speculators, no event is not worthy of trying to turn a profit.

We should not forget how the speculators reacted to the news of tens of thousands of deaths in Japan by calculating how they could come out even further on top financially. They will have added to the costs of the clean-up and rebuild, and led to less being done than could have been achieved without their contribution, and we should blame them for that. A few years earlier, they speculated on world food prices and how those would influence the values of currency, and thousands are thought to have starved to death as a result of their price hikes making food unaffordable in the poorest of places. The inhumanity of a tiny minority can harm both some of the richest (Japanese) and the poorest (starving) people on earth.

21

The tsunami of March 2011 did not just reveal the worst of human behaviour. It also made far more evident some of the most laudable of human accomplishments. Japan being a very equal country meant people looked out for each other. Food was quickly sent to where it was needed. When I was there, shortly after the disaster, working on collecting statistics on its equality, the students in the university in Kyoto I was based in were collecting for skin cream to send to the north-east. Almost every other need was being catered for.

When I visited the Japanese census offices in Tokyo in early May of 2011, I was told that a very large prefabricated building in the courtyard below me was about to be dismantled and taken north for people to sleep in. It had been full of census forms. I watched people helping each other and being in no fear of each other in a way that was almost the very opposite of what the world had seen when Hurricane Katrina had hit the Gulf coast of the USA just over five years earlier.

I witnessed the most surprising aspect of the aftermath of the earthquake and tsunami while staying in a hotel practically opposite the headquarters of Tepco, the Tokyo Electric Power Company, which had been running the reactors at Fukushima Daiichi and Daini nuclear power stations. That was where reactor core cooling failed, with results viewed with horror around the world. Around the Tepco headquarters were stationed just a couple of riot police, each holding a six-foot staff. That was enough to quell any thoughts of storming the building by angry protestors. Instead, protestors used debate to attack the policy of relying so much on nuclear power. Even before that debate began, many of the 128 million people living in Japan in 2011 became the first large group on earth to be forced to rapidly reduce their electricity consumption.

The first things that changed in mainland Japan were that the neon lights started to fade along the main streets in Tokyo. It turned out that the country had an incompatible national electricity grid, and so from further to the west, nearer Kyoto, the power could not be drawn off for the east. Nevertheless, almost everywhere people began turning off the lights. At night you could see stars again instead of advertising signs. Homes no longer shone like beacons in the dark. People started taking the stairs rather than the lift. There were concerns about how air-conditioning would be powered in the summer to come, and how the elderly would cope, but in the event, much less power was used and the elderly turned out to know all about coping through difficult times.

What the reaction to the tsunami within Japan showed the world was that it was practically possible to consume less. It is easier to do that if the threat from consuming more is imminent and foremost in our minds, rather than gradual and ever-present. The main threat in many minds in Japan was not simply the potential pollution from relying too much on nuclear power, but the unpredictability of that supply in the event of natural disaster:

> Prior to the March 11 accident, Japan had plans to construct nine new nuclear power plants by 2020 and more than 14 by 2030. Nuclear power supplies about 25 percent of Japan's energy, with renewables accounting for around 10 percent. But after the disaster, Prime Minister Naoto Kan advocated phasing out nuclear energy, with an aggressive push for renewables. A poll in June 2011 by the *Asahi Newspaper* found that 74 percent of the public was in favour of abolishing nuclear power after a phase-out period . . . To meet these targets for renewable energy, however,

Japan will also need to reduce its electricity consumption by 50 percent compared to 2010 levels through energy efficiency and power-saving measures.[30]

Acceptance is spreading of the fact that there has been too much reliance on nuclear power as a supposed technical solution to our addiction to overconsuming energy. In France in late 2012 it was reported that:

the Socialists agreed last year not to field any candidates in around 60 constituencies. In exchange, the Greens accepted the Socialists' goal of reducing France's dependence on nuclear power for energy to 50 percent from 75 percent by 2025 – far short of the Greens' own goal of zero ... energy companies say they have identified significant deposits of shale gas in the south of the country, Parliament passed a law last year outlawing its extraction via hydraulic fracturing, or 'fracking', because of concerns over its potential to pollute drinking water.[31]

The times really are a-changing, but you have to look around the world to see just how quickly change is coming, and remember how just a few years ago we were so much more cavalier about pollution and our lack of planning.

Above all else we have to be prepared to confront some myths. It is common to see images of coal-powered electricity generating plants springing up across poorer countries such as China in an apparent demonstration that whatever is done in richer countries can have only an insignificant beneficial overall effect. In the UK, it is often suggested that we only contribute 2 per cent of global warming. How should we see this in the light of being home to less than 1 per cent of the world's population? This is an exercise

24

in testing just how well educated we are in understanding percentages.

China generates over twice the renewable energy of the second largest generator, the USA, despite producing similar amounts of energy overall, and far less per person. Per person neither the UK nor USA gets into the top ten nations by green energy production. If you are a possibilist, then there is so much more that can be done, so much more that is already being done elsewhere, and so much more that we are likely to do to make things better, unless we somehow become more stupid.

The most green energy–worldwide

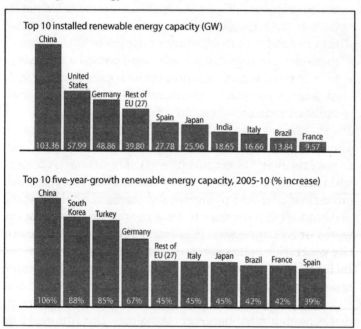

Source: http://www.pewenvironment.org/news-room/reports/whos-winning-the-clean-energy-race-2010-edition-329291.

The long-range forecast

In 1974, in the song 'Idiot Wind', Bob Dylan included a lyric that suggested it was surprising that humans were able to feed themselves given their general level of stupidity. In 1951, possibly before the 10-year-old Robert Zimmerman had even thought of changing his name to Bob Dylan, a group of distinguished scientists published the book *Four Thousand Million Mouths*. They wrote that 'if in the next century we have a population of 4,000 millions as precariously fed as the present population and still expanding [then] there is little time in which to transform an illiterate peasantry into thoughtful and far-sighted men and women, capable of taking the future of their planet into their own hands'.[32] Dylan will not have read these words, but he did grow up when the general understanding was that we could barely feed ourselves.

Bob Dylan suggested that we might soon starve in 1974. However, by the end of the twentieth century it was well recognized that we were, on average, 'better fed than in 1951'.[33] It was also becoming clear that we were not all idiots, that it was no wonder that we could feed ourselves and that the global majority of peasantry of 1951 had been transformed. None of us are ever likely to be so far-sighted that we are capable of taking the future of the planet into our own hands, but a majority of people in the world had become working class. All this occurred in just one generation, and within that one generation we, in the rich minority of the world, have also learned to become more modest about what we may be able to know.

John Wilmoth is no idiot. A professor in the Department of Demography at Berkeley, University of California, he was seconded to the Population Division of the United Nations from 2005 until 2007. Wilmoth's main interests are in longevity, and how long all of us may one day get to live. At the foot of his web page is a tribute to Christian Mortensen, 1882–1998, the Danish American who appeared to enjoy smoking (Danish) cigars almost up to the point of his death, at age 115.[34] Mortenson may have lived a long time, but Danes in western Europe generally die a little earlier than their neighbours, it is thought most probably due to their smoking a little more.

What is true for one person – that a man can smoke and live to 115 – is almost never true for the group. When John Wilmoth was asked for his comments on the 2004 UN population forecasts, the first ones to look forward not just 50 years but 300 years, he explained that:

> I should emphasize that these comments are highly speculative – they are limited by the inevitable narrowness of my knowledge and experiences, and they are based in some cases on very little empirical evidence. Of course, they are not being delivered entirely 'off the cuff', and they do reflect some months and years of thinking about such topics in the present and other contexts. Nevertheless, they are no more than the careful speculations of an informed observer.[35]

It is often only when people get to the very top of their field that they become confident enough to say that they don't really know the answers to questions that cannot easily be answered.

On 9 December 2003, the population division of the UN Department of Economic and Social Affairs released a report on the long-term prospects for humanity. It was the first ever official long-term guesstimate. Entitled *World Population to 2300*, it documented the highlights of several years of work which had been quietly undertaken to try to model a range of possible prospects for humanity.[36] As it was the first time the UN demographers had attempted such a bold extrapolation, they were understandably circumspect. As far as I know, to date it has also been the last time such an exercise has been carried out.

When new projections are announced, most attention is given to the middle or 'medium' projection, the one it is said is most likely, all else being equal (whatever that means). In 2003, the UN medium projection was that the global human population level would reach 9.1 billion by the year 2100 and then slowly fall to stabilize at 9 billion two centuries later, by 2300.[37] If that projection had not subsequently been updated, this book would be entitled *Population 9 Billion*.

To illustrate just how unsure the demographers were of their estimates, they also published a 'high' projection of people having a fraction more children per average family. This results in there being some 36.4 billion humans alive by the year 2300, four times as many as the medium projection. It received quite a lot of media attention. The UN demographers also published a 'low' projection of what would happen were fertility falls to be just a fraction below that expected at the time. This one received almost no attention, but I think it should not be ignored. The low fertility assumption suggests that there could be as few as just 2.3 billion humans on the planet by 2300!

If you find talk of rapid fertility decline unbelievable, then consider Turkey a decade ago. Turkey is a country similar in population size to Germany, with 80 million people. Its second largest city, Ankara, is the capital. Its largest city, Istanbul, is more populous than London and yet Istanbul 10 years ago had a lower fertility rate than London has today, namely 1.88 children per couple. Even at that time the Turkish national total fertility was

2.23 children per couple and falling. By 2010, the World Bank put the national Turkish fertility rate at 2.09. At this rate of decline, Turkey might soon have a lower fertility rate than the UK.

Total fertility rates by region in Turkey, 2000–2003

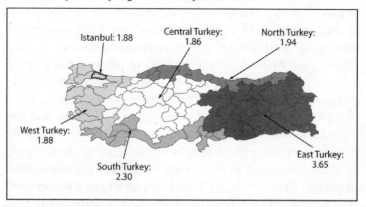

Source: Sutay Yavuz, 'Fertility Transition and The Progression to a Third Birth in Turkey' (Presentation, Institute of Population Studies, Hacettepe University), 2005. Available at http://www.demogr.mpg.de/papers/working/wp-2005-028.pdf.

John Wilmoth suggested that we should be careful about assuming that the low fertility observed quite recently in many places will necessarily continue: 'I would be cautious about assuming the continuation over many decades of a phenomenon that is only a few decades old.'[38] However, we should also be cautious about limiting our imagination to think that just because the average number of children per couple in the world has rapidly fallen, those rapid falls have come to some kind of natural end at roughly two children per couple; in other words, at stability.

In a future world where brute human labour is valued lowly, and where, if you cannot pass financial assets on to your children they may find themselves near the bottom of a very large pile, the incentives to have fewer, or no, offspring are growing. If children become labelled as a financial burden on their parents, if the media start to say that you should not have children if you cannot afford to do so, then why should we be cautious about thinking that the fertility decline has only just begun?

Personally I do not believe that we should think of people as costs that you have to decide whether you can afford, but I also believe that in some of the most inequitable of rich countries my way of thinking has become rarer. I would pay as much attention to the lower line in the first graph below as to the higher line. Note how the range for 2050 varies between 7.4 and 10.6 billion people. These were the estimates first made in 2003 and used in a second UN publication in 2004. The graph below that, from the most recent 2011 UN projection, shows how, just seven years later, the 2003/2004 figures were considered grossly out of date. John Wilmoth was sensible to call the first set of figures guesses and his comment on them 'careful speculations'. But could they have been better guesses than what came after?

By 2011, the UN were no longer projecting forward 300 years. Instead they went no further than the year 2100, and all their projections were higher. The second graph in the Figure below shows the most recent 2011 update. At first glance it is as if some pressure group had got to the demographers, a group who believed that the demographers were not sufficiently alarming people and that the numbers needed to be larger.

In this graph, the old estimates are shown in parentheses under the new. To the 'low variant' estimate were added an extra 600 million people by 2100, to the medium variant an extra billion (hence this book's title), into the high

UN Population Projections

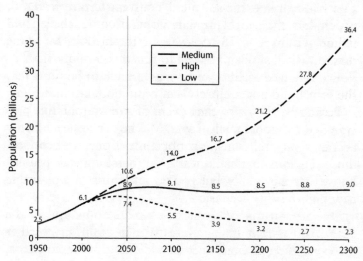

Estimated world population: 1950–2000, and projections: 2000–2300, UN revision, 2004.

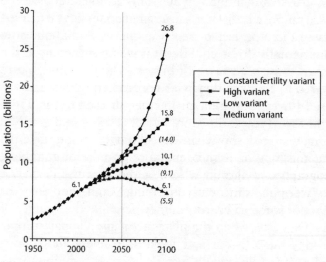

UN revision to 2000–2100 projections, 1 June 2011 (previous estimates in brackets).

variant total an extra 1.8 billion, and then they even added a new fourth line, the so-called 'constant fertility variant', which has the world human population reaching 26.8 billion within less than 90 years from now if, for some reason, we all suddenly revert to breeding rapidly again.

The renewed fertility spurt would have to be for a reason which did not itself result in rapid population decline, so it can't be following the advent of a new Stone Age precipitated by global nuclear war. Maybe everyone suddenly becomes very religious, but not abstentious, and chooses those religions that claim it is a sin to use contraception. I know that this is silly, but you try and think of a plausible new high-fertility scenario.

One reason that the official estimates now end in the year 2100 is that if you were to take them any further forward, the extremes become ridiculous. The constant-fertility assumption soon sees the planet overrun with humans breeding in the way we think rabbits do.

I'll say more a little later about what could have occurred to revise these projected trends upwards, and about how rabbits actually do breed. Here it is worth reflecting on the shock of those who saw just how rosy the possible future appeared to be when they were confronted with the above Figure's lower diagram after having got used to the upper one for seven years.

If you want to know what was behind the sudden upsurge in the gnashing of teeth over future population numbers, it was someone altering a few of the parameters on the world's population forecasting model, and they did that because of some news from somewhere like the County of Keck. That was when the machine in the Plexiglas dome (the one which listens and looks into everyone's home) found a few more (small) people.

The demographically experienced were, of course, not

shocked. One eminent commentator, Michael Teitelbaum, had counselled in 2004 against even including the figures for the so-called 'constant scenario' in the original report, let alone graphing such impossibilities: 'Another unintended effect of including the "constant" scenario in the tables is to trivialize what would otherwise be very significant differences among the other scenario outcomes.'[39] Note that the 'constant' scenarios are not included in the related figures, perhaps for this same reason. But also note that for some (other) reason, the result of that 'no-slow-down constant fertility scenario' was included by 2011.

So, something changed between 2004 and 2011 to make the UN demographers behave in a way that just seven years earlier had been described as trivializing the issues. It was partly due to the fact that a few more babies were born than had been projected worldwide, as far as we can count them. Towards the end of this book, I'll argue that it was not realized that these additional births were part of a mini global baby boom – echoing earlier larger booms. But that was not the main reason why the 2011 projections were drawn higher.

I think the UN forecasts were increased because it became more politically expedient to increase them, to appear to be warning that the numbers of people might be getting out of control. Even the numbers of population projections themselves were expanding in size over time. Would someone next project forward the projections assuming they would always underestimate and come up with an estimate of an even higher number of billions?

The main reason for the scare stories of 2011 and 2012 was that some demographers had been influenced by those with other agendas, people who were becoming interested in demography because they believed there were too many people already. Projections that indicate a 'soft landing' of human population growth do not help the agenda of those who want to cry wolf. As the world economy faltered in 2008, there were groups that wanted to put the blame for the fact that there would be too little to go round in future on there being too many people, rather than not enough sharing.

Other interpretations are rare, but some do place emphasis on the UN tendency towards overestimation. Discussing Muslim majority areas, but applicable more widely, researchers in 2011 pointed out that 'In its 2000 revisions of World Population Prospects, UNPD [UN Population Division] medium variant projections envisaged a population for Yemen of 102 million people; in its 2010 revisions, the 2050 medium variant projection for Yemen is 62 million.'[40] (United States Census Bureau projections for Yemen for 2050 as I write this are even lower: under 48 million.) Unanticipated but extremely rapid fertility declines would likewise militate for downward revisions in the trajectory of future demographic growth. So why is there not a UNPD or USCB scenario for the possibility of more rapid fertility falls?

There is no 'extremely low fertility variant' on either of the two graphs in the Figure drawn above. This would be a variant that shows what would happen if the current trends in places like Germany, Italy, Japan, Macao, Hong Kong and Singapore were to spread. No such scenario is presented because there is no global lobby worried about rapid population falls in the near future. If there were, then those lines would come to appear on the graphs. The reason we don't have such a lobby is that most people who can imagine such falls also don't imagine that they would necessarily create any great problems for humanity.

Researchers who think that the slowdown could happen faster than predicted tend not to be worriers. These are people who look at fertility rates of around only one child per couple in Hong Kong, Singapore and Macao and wonder why we don't produce a projection assuming that such behaviour could spread more quickly than is currently thought likely. However, these researchers also often don't see particularly high or particularly low population numbers as being a problem in their own right, as neither do they consider an especially young or ageing population as necessarily problematic. Nevertheless, it does help to have some idea as to how many people there will be both soon and in the distant future. That is why the 2003/2004 UN revision was so good.

The 2004 revision and its 2003 pre-release was a great improvement on earlier UN work. Its publication reduced many people's worries resulting from the earlier 1994 revision, one which had projected some 9.8 billion folk on the planet by 2050.[41] When I first saw the 2003 report, I thought someone had made a mistake with the data; that they had put the '3' in the wrong place and it was a forecast for 2030. But I was wrong. It really did include projections forward to 2300. What's more, it wasn't just a forecast for the future population of the planet. It was a forecast for the geographical area of each country of the world between now and the start of the twenty-fourth century.

Too few people realize how volatile demographic projects are over time, or just how wide are the confidence limits around the estimates for any one time even in the near future. Prior to May 2011, the top demographic experts of the United Nations had suggested that world population would peak at 9.1 billion in 2100, and then fall to 8.5 billion by 2150. In contrast, the 2011 revision suggested that 9.1 billion would be achieved much earlier, maybe by 2050 or before, and by 2100 there would be 10.1 billion of us.

The new May 2011 projections implied that the global human population count might still be slightly rising a century from now. However, a billion or so people here or there is within the bounds of even the smallest of errors in all these models. A billion sounds a lot because we have got used to the term million, but not yet to the idea of a billion. It is not hard to make a billion sound small. It is 10 per cent of the currently projected 2100 world population. It is one extra, on average a fifth, grandchild for every second couple on earth.

The world did not react in horror when 10 billion humans were first predicted. Population forecasts are incredibly fickle things, and the long-term prognosis was still for stability. When the news came in from the County of Keck (or rather from Niger, or one of the more inequitable states of India) suggesting that a few more babies were being born than had previously been thought and a few less folk were dying, the machine in the Plexiglas dome was recalibrated. The button was pressed and the number that came out had eleven digits rather than ten.

The global human forecasts were not increased because the world was becoming a worse place to live. There were fewer wars, and that saved lives. Malaria was being tackled a little more effectively, and more people were being successfully treated for HIV/AIDS than had been the case to date. Most importantly, a few (million) more children had been born recently than had been expected. As suggested at the very start of this book, just a tiny change in fertility can be magnified in a century to an extra billion human beings. A tiny change in the other direction, and there'll be fewer than eight billion of us in the near future. And that is quite possible too, if not currently thought probable.

Yet with less war, fewer deaths from HIV/AIDS and malaria and a lower death rate of children overall, people in future could have even fewer children than they are currently forecast to have. Wars tend to be followed by baby booms, and high infant deaths often result in high fertility to compensate; conversely stability breeds slowdown and yet more stability.

What difference would it make if world human population were to peak at 8 or 10 billion, or even a little lower or higher? Later on, this book suggests that what will matter most is how people behave, not their total numbers, and that many people are coming to understand that – which is why the news of an expected extra billion humans should not result in panic. But in some quarters, people think differently. They think warnings need to be issued. And indeed, some warnings do need issuing, but not about too many or too few people.

The projections to 2300 are more likely to be incorrect than shorter-term predictions simply because of the distance into the future and also for some practical reasons. Already some countries have split and others merged. In 2002, East Timor split from Indonesia. Montenegro and Serbia became separate states in 2008. Kosovo declared its independence the same year. As of 2011, there were two states in what was Sudan, one in the south and one in the north. Conveniently, both are still called Sudan. It is not inconceivable that most countries as we know them today will not exist in 300 years' time. Most did not exist 300 years ago as we know them today.

In general, the trend is for the number of states to grow over time. So the UN projections, called 'scenarios' in the 2003 report, are for areas which in many cases might be home to more than one country in future. Simultaneously, other areas will coalesce into what become, in effect, single economic or demographic blocks. The European Union, and especially the single-currency block within it, also happens to be an area of remarkably low fertility by historic standards.

If I had to put money on any one projection, I would put it on the 2003/2004 central projection of the UN. This is because I think we are currently experiencing a small global baby boom, an echo of earlier larger booms, but projecting forward as if that boom is not going to end soon, as the 2011 report does, is foolhardy.

According to the 2003/2004 report, the one I would put most faith in, world population will rise from 6.1 billion people in 2000 to a maximum of 9.2 billion by 2075, and decline thereafter, as deaths exceed births, to reach 8.3 billion a century later, in 2175. After that, increased ageing will result in the population slowly climbing to 9 billion by 2300, despite fertility being at close to replacement level. This was, and remains, a very benign scenario. It predicts widespread worldwide ageing and, implicitly, narrowing future economic inequalities. It may not be like this, but it could be.

A variation on the central projection shows fertility rates worldwide falling below replacement rates after 2175, and the population remaining at 8.3 billion despite longevity increasing. There were, of course, many other scenarios offered. But the upper extreme that was being suggested – that world human population could be as high as 36.4 billion – would require a step change in human behaviour that is unlikely, a return to very high fertility. The low projection, that the population will be 2.3 billion by 2300, is possible to imagine. People may simply continue to choose to have fewer children. That is what they have been doing for almost three generations now, worldwide.

It is time we woke up to the change that is happening. One leading demographer in Australia, John Caldwell, reached this point almost a decade ago. Among the high scenarios, the one 'showing population reaching 36 billion in 2300 is almost certainly irrelevant. The high fertility path is unlikely to be followed short of a nuclear war decimating the human race.'[42] But why do all these projections vary so much? Surely demographers can do a better job of predicting the future than this? Before we get to what else the UN reports suggest, and what others say of them, it might be a good time to introduce Mr Fibonacci and his rabbits to try to explain why we find it so hard to project with much certainty.

Fibonacci's rabbits

> The number of children is not growing any longer in the world. We are still debating peak oil, but we have definitely reached peak child.
>
> Hans Rosling, TED talk, 2012[43]

Leonardo Fibonacci was born in the twelfth century. This son of a merchant from Pisa grew up in what is now Algeria, but travelled widely, so widely in fact that he learnt about using Arabic numerals before many others in the Christian world did. He is best known because his name is given to the numbering sequence by which rabbit populations, without hindrance, might grow. Like much else that people think was discovered in Christendom, or even in the more numerically enlightened Arab world, this sequence had in fact been known since the sixth century in what today we call the Indian subcontinent. Fibonacci used the sequence to show the advantages of the Hindu-Arabic numeral system. It is not hard to see why that numbering system won out in the long term if you try to work out his series using only Roman numerals.

To understand population growth, you need a grasp of Fibonacci, and for that you need Arabic numerals; the kind almost everyone uses nowadays. You start with a male and a female baby rabbit, one pair. A month later you still have one pair, but by two months the mature rabbits breed and give birth to twins, a male and a female baby rabbit, a second pair. Every month after that, the same thing happens: they breed and have another pair, and this happens to all mature rabbits indefinitely. The monthly count of pairs of rabbits goes 1, 1, 2, 3, 5, 8, 13 . . .

What someone realized at some point in India 1,500 years ago was that you only have to add the last two numbers to get the next. It is easy: 21, 34, 55, 89, 144, 233, 377, 610, 987, 1,597, 2,584, 4,181, 6,765, 10,946, 17,711 . . . Projecting future rabbit populations is simple arithmetic; all you need to know is how to add the numbers 0 to 9 and how to carry. The problem with Roman numerals is that you cannot do the carrying bit, as it requires place value, which Roman numerals do not have.

Simple addition not only looks difficult but is difficult with Roman numerals. (By the way, Fibonacci went on to describe, in Latin, multiplication using the Indian number system.) Demography, however, is still largely pre-Fibonacci. It is mostly about adding (births) and subtraction (deaths), and much less about seeing the second derivative: how rate of change in a quantity is itself changing.

To study changes in a rate of change, consider what happens if it takes three months before a rabbit can reproduce. The sequence for female bunnies, after three months of just having one female, becomes 2, 3, 4, 6, 9, 13, 19, 28, 41, 60, 88, 129. After a year, you end up with less than half as many bunnies. Each month's total is the sum of the previous month's total and the total from three months before. (By the way, we just count the females because we know that rabbits are not that monogamous, but you get the same series with monogamous pairs.) You could substitute for rabbits and months cows and years, or even French peasants and decades. The French peasantry was one of the earliest rural groups to decline in size, and one of the first to be studied by rural sociologists trying to determine why people did not behave anything like rabbits.[44]

With people, once you have an organized religion and other customs, the control on population numbers is no longer age at physical maturity, but what is apparently allowed in the eyes of God and wider society. Often what is allowed in God's eyes means, in practice, whether the economic circumstances are good enough to enable marriage.

Sex outside of marriage that was not kept secret was forbidden almost everywhere until quite recently. In fact, organized religion and its rules on reproduction and inheritance can be thought of as a form of population control. Then, as religiosity declined, other customs and norms took its place. Today teenage pregnancy is lowest where there are most atheists, in China and in Europe.[45]

During economically bad times, the age difference between married partners tends to widen. On average, older men marry younger women, more often so when it takes longer to become financially independent enough to set up home, and when, under patriarchy, setting up home mostly depends on the man's wage and perhaps a little on the woman's dowry. Fertility also tends to fall during economic downturns as a result.

In the 1930s, fertility became so low across much of Europe that there were fears that if the decline continued, there would be almost no one left by the year 2000! Then there came great hope after the Second World War, and more babies were born across Europe during 1946 than at any time since 1919. In India, the baby boom was associated more with independence in 1947. The echoes of those booms hit again in the years around 1965, 1985 and 2005. Precisely when the new lower birth peaks were recorded differed slightly in timing around the world, coming later and later where average ages of giving birth were rising the fastest. At this point you may be wondering why death rates have not yet been included in the Fibonacci rabbit model. Population growth is not about deaths; they happen anyway – everybody dies. It is true that a particular bulge in ageing will also have a temporary effect on boosting total numbers, but it is births that matter most, and understanding that very small differences in birth rates can have very big effects on later population numbers, both up and down.

Here, for the sake of silliness, is what happens if we do breed like rabbits. The following text is taken from the 2003 UN report: 'If, for the sake of illustration, the fertility of countries is kept constant at 1995–2000 levels, the world population soars to 244 billion by 2150 and 134 trillion in 2300, a definitely impossible outcome.' In the UN's final 2004 report, the one you can now most easily find on the web, this has been rewritten to read: 'an almost unimaginable world population of 134 trillion by 2300'.[46] Note the subtle change in wording. The implication is that trillions of humans are no longer definitely impossible! So, let's try to imagine a scenario in which such a number might be possible.

Suppose, for instance, that we found a way to travel through space very quickly, and also that we found there were other habitable planets out there, some 20,000 of them. Imagine that each of these planets contained vast prairies of land to be settled, and across each one human settlers had made camp, rather like those Europeans who set forth in wagon trains westwards across North America in the nineteenth century. Let us also assume that on all these 20,000 habitable planets, also bursting with plants and animals to eat, there was no effective competitor for space. Then, if on each of these new worlds between six and seven billion people settled, some 134 trillion people could all be happily singing around camp fires.

Alternatively we can imagine the far more likely scenario of a rapid return to replacement-level fertility coupled with increasing longevity, which produces a total earth-bound human population reaching between 9 and 10 billion by 2100, mostly living in cities and only sitting around fires when on holiday, and 9 billion by 2300 for whom it might be foolish to try to guess around what they might sit. The question is not whether our population will stabilize by 2100, but at what number it will stabilize.

All the sensible UN scenarios assume fertility convergence to around two children per couple (although convergence to a lower average may soon be warranted) by 2100. They do that because the very latest data suggests that fertility rates are rapidly falling to at least that point. The Figure below shows this. The data used to draw this figure, which is described further towards the end of Chapter 7 in the section on 'The new world geography', shows the population growth rates that result when these actual and projected declines in fertility are coupled with actual and projected declines in mortality. That is all a bit technical, so it is deliberately left until later to allow a few more interesting issues to be covered first.

For now, have a look at the graph below and ask one question: why is fertility in Africa assumed to be slower to decrease in future than the fall which has already occurred across all other continents? Why is the thin solid line at the top of the graph placed so much higher than the others, still at over four children per woman by 2013? Many answers are possible, but I want to suggest one key reason for this line being so much higher than the rest. I suspect that the fertility rate in Africa not appearing to fall so quickly after 1980 was a reaction to the economic crisis there, which has partly abated since. But first, what implications does this graph have for all those concerns about population numbers?

Total Fertility 1950–2100

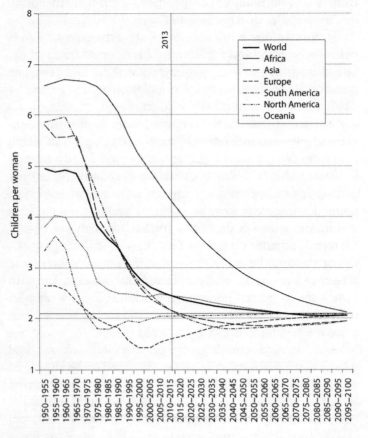

The data used to draw the graph above is taken from the same release of information as accompanied the last UN population estimates.[47] The curve for Africa is higher than all the other curves because of recent information from countries such as Niger, which suggested that the plunging levels of fertility seen across the African continent in the years up to 1980 had slowed down a little between then and 2010. Project that slight deceleration in population forward from 2010, and almost all the above replacement fertility in the world is in Africa. Look back at the graph and at the fortunes of the other continents shortly after that global baby boom of 1965, and you'll see that the initial fertility falls then accelerated rapidly downwards, to quickly reach between 2.5 and less than 2 children per couple.

The Figure shown opposite really does report an amazing picture. Today far fewer than two children are born for each woman in Europe. Fertility is very low in North America, despite the American demographic exceptionality of more births due to high economic inequality; fertility is below the 2.1 children per women steady state. One of the highest rates of teenage pregnancy in the rich world is still found in the USA, but it is still low enough not to lead to overall population growth.

The steady state is 2.1 rather than 2 because some of our offspring, even in the best-off places, still die before they can have a chance to reproduce. In a world in which every couple had exactly two children, and where everyone formed a couple, where no one did not want children or could not have children, where all gay couples gained children, and where there were exactly equal numbers of women and men, population would fall. That is because some offspring would die before having their own first or second child.

Today deaths in childhood and young adulthood are becoming rarer but infertility is growing as pregnancy is delayed, often because the couple, that stable relationship, has not yet formed. Many more people are also choosing not to become parents. If this continues, the steady-state might require those that do have children to have nearer to three than two in the medium term.

In South America and Asia taken as a whole, largely because of China, natural growth is almost at the 2.1 children steady-state point already. In fact some demographers assessing recent changes in India, Bangladesh and Pakistan believe that fertility is about to fall even faster there than the UN demographers appear to believe. This, they suggest, is because of recent improvements in allowing young women to enjoy secondary education, and falling infant mortality leading to falling birth rates.[48] Commentators on these predictions explain: 'It's the perfect chicken and egg. Education means lower fertility – and lower fertility can mean more education.'[49] So why should Africa, after 2010, not experience what was occurring in Asia when fertility across that continent was as high in 1975 as it is in Africa today? And could parts of Asia experience less of a fall in fertility than is expected?

More education means, among much else, both a better grasp of the need for good and varied nutrition, and increased political, social and economic scope to secure it. You might argue that it is wrong to extrapolate from one time to another, from 1975 to 2010, or from one continent to another, from Asia to Africa, but greater historical and geographical leaps of comparison have been made successfully before. Put in careful academic prose, researchers have shown that it is 'certainly legitimate to use standards derived from contemporary industrialised populations to investigate aspects of the health and mortality of people in the past, and among people living in less industrialised countries today'.[50] In other words, we can, if we are careful, generalize and extrapolate both forwards and backwards with some confidence. We can learn lessons from a particular time and place and apply them elsewhere.

We might even note that what is often despairingly referred to as the current Chinese economic invasion of Africa might do far more to help in lowering fertility, raising the position of women in those parts of the continent where it was lowest and equalizing incomes a little further there. At least far more than did centuries of European colonialism.

In 2011, British prime minister David Cameron 'warned African states over China's "authoritarian capitalism" ... claiming that it is unsustainable in the long term'.[51] By unsustainable, he meant it would not make as much money as he thought British capitalism would; he was not referring to its environmental record. However, African integration with China may well be more sustainable and sensible than the alternative Western psychological imperialism he might have had in mind. Given all the Chinese investment in Africa and all the knowledge in China about the actual benefits of fertility decline, I suspect that contraceptives will flow from Chinese factories to African villages in some quantity.

Lessons from 'Coconut Land'

> All we know about the future is that it will be different. But perhaps what we fear is that it will be the same. So we must celebrate the changes. Because, as someone once said, everything will be alright in the end. And if it is not alright, then trust me, it is not the end.
>
> Sonny Kapoor, manager of the
> Best Exotic Marigold Hotel, 2012[52]

When it comes to sustainability, nominally communist countries and states have some of the best records, albeit far too often achieved by being almost as authoritarian as British, French and Belgian colonial officers once were. Communist and former communist countries within Eastern Europe had and still have some of the lowest fertility rates, and had those earliest worldwide. The position and power of women in these countries often rose faster than elsewhere. This is more an indictment of how women were held back in supposedly freer countries than a celebration of communism. Abortion was legal across most of the Soviet countries from at least 1955 onwards. Women in the 'free world' were often not allowed to have a mortgage in their name, or carry on working after getting married, well into the 1960s. In many of the more affluent Western countries, it was not until the late 1960s or even the 1970s that abortion was legalized. In a few rich countries, and many poorer ones, it is still illegal.

Communism is no panacea, and the more democracy involved in its implementation the better the effect; but it would be misleading not to point out how the communist movement has been connected to rapid fertility decline, mostly notably in China, where fertility rates fell from six to two children per couple even before the one-child policy.

Fertility falls worldwide began with left-wing birth-control advocates and early on were most pronounced under communist governments. Often this involved coercion, though in the case of India, the least coercion was that found in the most left-wing state. In India, improvements in education for women occurred first and were most widespread in the state of Kerala. The communist government there was first democratically elected in 1957.

Just as David Cameron is frightened now by China, half

a century ago the Kerala communists frightened many people in the West. One, John Robbins, wrote a book two years after the communist election victory titled, without subtlety, *Too Many Asians*. Early Western commentators, including environmentalists like Robbins, tended to denigrate Kerala. One way in which he did this was to poke fun at the origins of the name of the state, suggesting that when it came to population growth:

> the immediate reasons for the continuing crisis are much the same as those which have turned Kerala – 'Coconut Land' – into a Communist state. They consist of a complex welter of economic, political, psychological and sociological factors. And . . . if two reasons can be picked out as the prime causes of the difficulty, they are that vicious pair – the overcrowding of the land and the hopelessness of the future. There are already too many Asians. There are more appearing on the scene every hour.[53]

Under democratic communist rule, fertility in Kerala fell, as far as we know without much coercion, from 5.6 births per woman in 1957 to 1.7 in 1993. Elsewhere in India, forced and strongly incentivized sterilization was far more common.[54] Western insults about 'Coconut Land' did not help in uncovering the not too complex reasons why the hope and equality that the communists brought to Kerala had such a positive effect.[55]

Fertility changes are often not noticed for decades because they tend to be slow changes year on year. Across Europe, below-replacement fertility has been the norm now for over three decades. The spread of what many in the USA may think of as near-communist-style welfare states has almost certainly helped. In contrast, in the USA fertility rates remain very high, given the mean average affluence there. However, having at least the per capita per annum income of the USA is an arithmetic average only a minority even in the USA enjoy. Within the rich world, US fertility rates are among the highest, because the majority of citizens of the United States are much poorer than most people in the rich world, and the poorer you are, and the less power and education you have, the more children you tend to think you may need and subsequently have.

In contrast to the United States, which has polarized economically since the late 1970s, across most of Europe the average amount spent on the median child's education has risen faster, more so for young women than for young men as more young women now go to university. In the USA, the average debt young adults amass to attend university has risen (because university tuition fees rose quickly there first). Many Americans are put off going to university and start families early instead. Student debts in the USA cannot be discarded if you become bankrupt; they stay with you for life. That is a great disincentive to carry on studying and an incentive to start a family young.

The average family in the USA has 2.1 children. In contrast, the average European family has 1.4. In other words, for every two couples in Europe, slightly more have one child as compared to those who have two children. The number who have three is similar to those having none. Very few now have four or more.

In Europe, it has been determined as almost certainly causal that the principal driver of the most recent change to very low fertility and delayed first pregnancy has been the increased participation of young women in university education. Even in Britain and other English-speaking countries where there have been recent increases in fertility rates, these increases can be attributed to the particular timings of large numbers of young women entering university, and the longer time lag before first births. Thus, 'enrolment patterns may explain the emergence in recent decades of a "hump" in the fertility schedules of English-speaking countries'.[56] Across both the poor world and in some of the richest countries on earth, the increasing education enrolment rate of women, either at age 8 or age 18, continues to play a leading role in bringing birth rates down.

European governments have been almost silent about this shift to lower fertility. While promoting population control elsewhere in the world, they appear not to want to point out that the apparent need for wider control has been abated slightly by the greater than expected fertility decline in Europe. It is as if they don't see Europeans as being the same as people outside of Europe, as potentially interchangeable; in short, many European views on population control may be a little racist.

If immigration to Europe were to increase, world population would decline even faster than the slowdown already forecast. The reason for this is that people tend to rapidly adopt the fertility rates of the places they move to. If this does not apply so much to those who move there, then their children almost always assimilate when it comes to their own fertility. If we Europeans want to be well cared for in our old age, and we also want fewer future people in the world, the last thing we should be doing is trying to reduce migration to Europe. That is something we do partly out of fear. The next Figure below shows why that fear has been growing, but also why we can have some hope that it may begin to abate, and that fertility rates in Africa may fall faster than currently projected.

Real growth per decade in GDP (% over 10 years) 1955–2001, worldwide

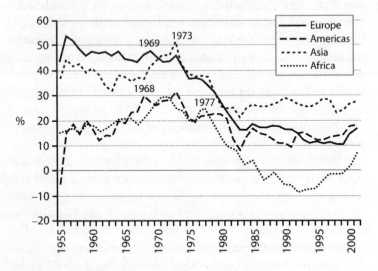

Source: Dorling, D. (2010, p.135), *Injustice*, Bristol: Polity Press.

The Figure shows average decadal GDP growth rates in the 10 years prior to each date shown; this smoothes out annual fluctuations, recessions and booms. It shows that from 1955 until 1973 there was global convergence, but that European economic growth rates peaked in 1969. I believe they peaked because such growth was unsustainable, with economies of whole continents growing at up to 50 per cent a decade. This was not green growth, it was not intellectual growth, thinking growth; it was physical material growth.

Imagine a human growing from four feet, to six, to nine feet in height in 20 years. That is 50 per cent growth per decade. If that were to continue, then within 80 years they would be 102 feet high! Just like people, economies can grow in height quickly, but only as they change from one state, like childhood, to another state, like adulthood. Green growth can continue for longer, just as you can learn more as an adult as you age. However, the growth the world saw in the 1950s and 1960s was far from green; it was fuelled by oil, and when the price of that quadrupled in the 1970s, fear set in.

The economic downturn of the 1970s and 1980s was accompanied by an increased fear of other people in other places. During the 1930s, the scapegoats had tended to be people within national borders: Jews and gypsies. By the 1970s, there were people from elsewhere. This is part of the reason why books such as *The Population Bomb* of 1968 became so popular. We began to fear each other's existence.

The economic downturn in Africa was so severe that for almost a decade and a half from the mid 1980s, the continent on average experienced economic decline in real terms. This coincided almost perfectly with the slower fall in fertility reported above for that continent from 1980 onwards. It also coincided with Fortress Europe building up its walls, visible (barbed wire) and invisible (visas), as the economic gap across the Mediterranean Sea became a gulf. In the light of the economic and fertility trends shown above, all this is understandable, but Europeans should also remember what occurred in an earlier period of economic decline, and beware.

It was at a time when racism was last at its height, in Europe in the 1930s, that many European governments brought in explicit policies to coerce or cajole women to have more children. The men in charge required armies to fight their wars. Today there are fewer such natality policies, because increasingly wars are fought, on one side, by drones and bombs, while on the other, large numbers of the casualties are unarmed civilian families, including many children.

Today, civilian war casualties occur mostly in Afghanistan and Pakistan. Tomorrow it will be some other very poor country. But there is no reason why this kind of killing could not end, just as we no longer march troops to war alongside men on horseback playing bugles. What has to end, though, is the racism that is required to kill large numbers of others; to see them as subhuman.

Thirties-style racism is rearing its ugly head again in a far more muted way. During 2012, some 300 attacks, mostly on south Asian immigrants, were reported in Athens as hate crimes. In one incident, 20 masked men attacked recently arrived immigrants in their homes.[57] Today, large numbers of poorer people are labelled as unwanted by European governments for no reason other than that they may be of use to those governments in diverting blame.

Many of the poor in Europe, often including large numbers of the children or grandchildren of poorer immigrants, are seen as an 'unemployment problem', good for nothing but absorbing welfare payments. This is another reason why European governments are so quiet about Europe's current remarkably low rates of fertility. Those in power often no longer value having so many people, even people born in Europe. They are now seen as consumers rather than potential producers. The economist's favourite measure, GDP, only puts a value on production.

However, opposing views are rising too. In 2012, the *New Yorker* magazine celebrated the arrival on 5th Avenue of a new Japanese chain store that was seeking to maximize its employment rather than minimize it: 'there's a strong case to be made that corporate America's fetish for cost-cutting has gone too far. Some of the highest-profile retailers to flop in recent years were companies that made a big deal of slashing payroll costs.'[58] This move may simply have been driven by a wish to raise further the consumption habits of shoppers impressed by how many staff were around to help them, or it may have been just one of thousands of signs of a slow change in our attitudes to each other.

What I argue later in this book is that the period 1851–1971 was an aberration in the long-term human demographic and economic record. We need to stop seeing our recent past, and the downturn and polarization that followed it, as normal. We need to regard economic growth as evidence of moving from one form of society to another, not as a never-ending process. Look at things this way, and the future is far less frightening. But to get to that point requires a few more chapters first, as those rationalizing pessimism and optimism currently hold sway and there is quite a lot of accepted wisdom to debunk if we are to counter the extreme views that either all is lost, or there is little to worry about other than big government. Thankfully, increasing numbers of people are joining in the debunking. Others, though, tend to steal the headlines when they tell us we are all doomed.

In that play put on at the Royal Court Theatre in London during the summer of 2012, the scientist explained to his affluent audience: 'We are facing a crisis, with ecosystems being destroyed, the atmosphere polluted, temperatures rising and a billion people facing water shortage.' Things, Emmott sombrely reminds us, 'will only get worse' as the demand for food doubles by 2050, climate change intensifies and the transport system that sustains our needs grows. Describing himself as 'a rational pessimist', Emmott says there are two solutions. We can 'technologize' our way out of trouble, through building solar shields, or we can change our behaviour – by consuming 'less food, less energy, less stuff'. He sees little chance of this happening. He tells us he's fed up with reading about celebrities giving up 4x4s in favour of energy-saving cars, and says it's not going to affect the world's water supply if we wee in the shower rather than the loo. But at least every little helps.[59]

Wee in the shower rather than the loo by all means, but also understand that scientists don't have all the answers; none of us do. Scientists know about science and often like to technologize, but when it comes to history, geography, economics, politics and sociology, their attention span wanes. If your view of the world is that progress is made from standing on the shoulders of giants, then you tend to imagine that you have a very privileged and high-up vantage point. It is time to get down and start again from the beginning, from 64 millennia ago. It is time to understand that ecologically, the situation has never only ever got worse and it need not only get worse this time.

CHAPTER 2

THE FIRST HALF OF HUMAN HISTORY

> When you are old, you become impatient with the way in which the young applaud the most insignificant improvements – the invention of some new valve or sprocket – while remaining heedless of the world's barbarism. I don't say things *have* got worse; I merely say the young wouldn't notice if they had. The old times were good because then we were young, and ignorant of how ignorant the young can be.
>
> Julian Barnes, *Flaubert's Parrot*, 1984[1]

The first half of human history lasted from around 62,000 BCE to roughly 1988 CE. It is the first half because it was during 1988 that we became five billion, half of the most people we will ever possibly see alive at one time. The second half need not be long. It could be very short. As I write in 2012, the Doomsday Clock of the Bulletin of the Atomic Scientists stands at five minutes to midnight. In 1990, shortly after the first half of human history ended, and as one Eastern European country after another freed itself from Russian diktat, the minute hand on the clock had been moved back to ten minutes to midnight.

It was in 1984 that Julian Barnes's melancholy words were published, shortly before that halfway point. They rang true. Famine had gripped East Africa. By October, news cameras had panned across thousands of starving bodies laid out across the plains of Korem, an image of hell forming east of Ethiopia's highlands. Occasionally the cameras would zoom in to focus on the flies buzzing around the face of a dying child.

At home in the rich world, people raised money through Band Aid's 'Do They Know It's Christmas?' but many had Christmas worries of their own. Unemployment was soaring again around the planet to new highs of millions of wasted years of life. In Britain, it was the Christmas of the miners' strike. Worldwide, the AIDS pandemic was just beginning. That four-letter acronym for a disease, an acronym that conjures up images of giving, was then only two years old. And the world was on the brink of a possible third and final global war.

During 1984, the world's atomic scientists set their Doomsday Clock to three minutes to midnight. In their bulletin they reported that 'Every channel of communications has been constricted or shut down; every form of contact has been attenuated or cut off. And arms control negotiations have been reduced to a species of propaganda.'[2] Barring the Cuban/Turkish missile crisis, this is the closest the world would come to outright nuclear war at any point since that day in 1953 when hydrogen bombs were first tested and the scientists pronounced: 'Only a few more swings of the pendulum and, from Moscow to Chicago, atomic explosions will strike midnight for Western civilization.'

It need not have been the halfway point of human history. It could easily have been the end.

In this chapter, the stories told range from the Neolithic revolution to nuclear Armageddon and through much else that touches on our population numbers and how they came to rise to five billion. Theories of hereditary intelligence and superiority raise their ugly heads as well here, because it was during the very end of this extremely long period that they rose to the fore, and they matter crucially for population levels too. The plot jumps about rapidly, and speeds us on quickly.

We could easily not have made it this far. The closest the human world is thought to have come to ending was during 1962, when the Cuban missile crisis arose but receded again so quickly that there was no time to reset the Doomsday Clock. The crisis could equally be known as the Turkish missile crisis, as it was begun by the USA wishing to site nuclear missiles in Turkey. The USSR responded by threatening to site some of theirs in Cuba. It could all have been over so quickly. A committee had to meet to reset the clock. But before they could gather, humanity stepped back from the gates of Armageddon. Twenty-two years later, when that committee met in 1984, was the last time they had to set the minute hand so near to midnight. Things are getting better.

Since 1984, there has been no famine to match the one which began in 1983 in Ethiopia, no disease (yet) to match the now subsiding AIDS pandemic. The atomic Doomsday Clock has moved a few more minutes away from midnight and currently stands at least twice as far away from the final hour as it did in 1984. Julian Barnes might have thought the young wouldn't notice, but we did. He had his sixteenth birthday in 1960. I had mine in 1984. I was not optimistic.

The world is no longer on the brink of Armageddon. Things have improved, though many older people have not yet noticed that they have. Today, for most people worldwide, life is better. A large part of the reason for this is that we are beginning to slow down. We are also becoming more watchful of wider threats. In 2007, the remit of the Doomsday Clock of the Bulletin of the Atomic Scientists was widened to include 'destruction of human habitats from climate change'.[3] But 2007 is outside the scope of this chapter. This part of our demographic fortunes ends in 1988.

The end of the first half of human history was hectic and erratic. Economic growth was slowing but also polarizing. The variation between growth rates in different parts of the world was widening. The same was true for the global growth in human numbers.[4] Global population acceleration had, we now know with hindsight, ended in 1971, just after annual global growth had peaked at 2.1 per cent; it fell to 1.6 per cent growth worldwide in 1982 but then jumped and peaked again in 1983 at 1.9 per cent before slowly descending continuously thereafter.

The last 'twitch', in 1983, was a twitch that saw a net gain of 88 million people on the planet in a year; it was the end of a very long era. I think it is optimistic to call the period the first half of human history; the half which is best summarized by slow, then medium, then fast, then almost exponential population growth, cumulating in five billion people being recorded as alive in 1988.

We may actually have numbered five billion a few years earlier or later. Most babies then were not issued with a birth certificate, and of all the people who died worldwide, the majority of whom were still children, most did not have their deaths certified or well recorded. But even despite our inability still to record all deaths, there has been great and rapid progress in the few years since we numbered five billion.[5] It is as if the rate of progress is proportional to the passing of all human lives lived worldwide, and is hardly related at all to how many times the earth has completed an orbit of the sun.

Suggesting that the last 64,000 years is the first half of human history does not mean that we should expect a similar length of time to come; it all depends on how we behave and how you measure time, in years or in people. The vast majority of people who have ever lived have lived in a time of history, during a time of written and recorded texts. Measured in human lives, only a tiny fraction of all the people who have ever lived on the planet have lived through those eras that can only be studied through archaeology. If human history were measured in human lives, then the second half could be over in a matter of a few generations, and still as many new humans be born as have ever lived.

Human history, including the history of the present, is an evolving process. Currently we tell too many stories about this process soon being over. Perhaps we do so because a great change is occurring and change is unsettling?

Stepping on the gas

> China, home to a fifth of the world's people, is already below replacement fertility and has been for nearly 20 years, thanks in part to the coercive one-child policy implemented in 1979; Chinese women, who were bearing an average of six children each as recently as 1965, are now having around 1.5.
>
> Hania Zlotnik, director of the
> UN Population Division, 2011[6]

In the first millennium of the current era, world human population grew very slowly, usually at a rate of increase of under 0.1 per cent a year, often under 0.01 per cent a year on average. In a cold winter, or when volcanic ash ruined a harvest, or when plague hit, or when widespread war occurred, across the planet human numbers could fall. It was not until 1492 that a change took place that would later result in equilibrium being punctured, caused by just 88 people. That was when the *Niña*, *Pinta* and *Santa Maria*, the smaller two crewed by only 18 men and the largest by just 52, crossed the Atlantic and returned with news of gold.[7]

At the time, it was on the very opposite side of the planet that population growth was greatest, averaging 0.4 per cent a year in China between 1500 and 1600. However, that spurt of growth was partly reversed in the subsequent century, with an average annual decline of 0.15 per cent across all of East Asia's population (see Figure below). Equilibrium was maintained as it had been for centuries, because customs only changed slowly and ways of living had developed whereby for 35 centuries roughly the same numbers of people could live at relatively high density on the same pieces of land and not deplete it of nutrients.[8]

During most of the first half of human history there were long periods of stability. It was really only after a few million people had lived that there was first great change, in the Neolithic revolution. Then not until around 1820, when approaching our first billion, did it become apparent that a second great demographic change was under way, a change that had been quietly stirring for a few centuries, ever since that 1492 puncturing of the human equilibrium.

In 1501, within just nine years of Columbus's encounter with 'Indians', the first enslaved Africans had arrived in what was then Hispaniola. In 1520, the first large groups were deposited in what is now Cuba.[9] To reap the tiny numbers of slaves that were at first deposited, entire African civilizations had to be destroyed. Later, due largely to the huge numbers transported, population growth across large regions of the African continent stalled and at times fell (it later rose rapidly as colonization destroyed customs of sustainability).

Plundering of the Americas indirectly provided China with the silver it needed for its sixteenth-century stability. The silver flowed through Europe and across Asia to China as mercantile trade relied on it; as it ran out in the seventeenth century, Africa was stripped of people to repopulate the Americas. When societies are greatly disrupted, people often have more children. So of all the continents and great regions of the world in the period 1600–1700, it was central Africa which experienced the greatest population growth, 0.6 per cent additional people on average a year, an extra one for every 182.

In the eighteenth century, the fastest population growth of all the world's regions was recorded to be occurring in North America, 0.9 per cent growth per year on average. A small part of that growth was due to the importation of slaves, but so many slaves died without having children and so many of the children that they did have died before becoming adult slaves that transportation would contribute no more than a very small fraction of the human lives lost in Africa. The majority of North America's population growth was from the high birth rates of recent immigrants from Europe.

Slaves were purchased from Africa to, among much else, pick cotton in the Americas. The growing wealth of the Americas provided an emigration destination and usually a social hike up for Europeans, and with fewer hikes, for a good number of Chinese too. Industrialization boomed as Europe spun American cotton. This was why that 1492 encounter of the Spanish with the people of

Hispaniola led to great demographic change. The Old World changed economic, political and social course when that smaller and highly exploitable planet of the Americas was 'discovered'.

Within 300 years of 1492, in 1783, Manchester's first cotton mill was built, on Miller Street in cold damp north-west England.[10] By 1841, almost a quarter of a million people were living in Manchester, this despite the fact that from 1801 to 1850 the city suffered an average life expectancy of only 25.3 years.[11] What later became the slave-like conditions of the mill workers prevented life expectancy from rising, but the famine in Ireland kept a steady supply of migrant workers travelling to labour in the mills of northern England. All this relied on the triangular trade between Europe, America and Africa, and the 400 years of tyranny following 1492.[12]

During the nineteenth century, the population of central Africa fell, the only large region to experience a decline worldwide after the one billion threshold had been passed in 1820. At the same time, the population of North America was now rising rapidly, by 2.2 per cent annually, with the next highest increase being in South America, averaging around 1.5 per cent a year. The 1 per cent annual population growth barrier had been breached, not only in the Americas but across all of south-eastern Africa and the Middle East. This was very unusual. In particular territories it had occurred before, but such growth had never taken place across whole regions. The table in the Figure below tries to make the story clearer by shading darker those decades and continents when population growth rates exceeded both 1 per cent and 2 per cent per year.

By the end of the twentieth century, only Europe and Japan enjoyed population growth rates of below 1 per cent. Japan is separated out in the regional divisions used here because demographically it is such an interesting set of islands.[13] It is the first very large area where population is, in 2012, declining due to a drop in fertility, not because of net out-migration or high mortality rates. What has occurred in Japan is very recent. As the table below shows, from 1971–2001 the country had higher average population growth rates than Western Europe, as high even as Western Europe had experienced some 30 years earlier.

World Population Growth year 1 to 2000 by Worldmapper Regions

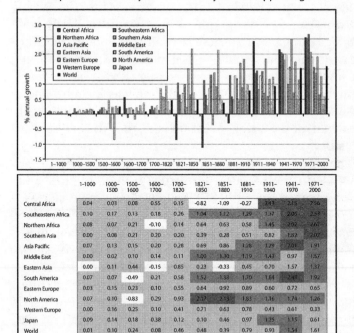

	1–1000	1000–1500	1500–1600	1600–1700	1700–1820	1821–1850	1851–1880	1881–1910	1911–1940	1941–1970	1971–2000
Central Africa	0.04	0.03	0.08	0.55	0.15	-0.82	-1.09	-0.27	2.43	2.15	2.56
Southeastern Africa	0.10	0.17	0.13	0.18	0.26	1.04	1.12	1.29	1.37	2.06	2.53
Northern Africa	0.08	0.07	0.21	-0.10	0.14	0.64	0.63	0.58	1.45	2.02	2.60
Southern Asia	0.00	0.08	0.21	0.20	0.20	0.39	0.28	0.51	0.82	1.82	2.07
Asia Pacific	0.07	0.13	0.15	0.20	0.28	0.69	0.86	1.28	1.29	2.01	1.91
Middle East	0.00	0.02	0.10	0.14	0.11	1.00	1.30	1.19	1.43	0.97	1.57
Eastern Asia	0.00	0.11	0.44	-0.15	0.85	0.23	-0.33	0.45	0.70	1.57	1.37
South America	0.07	0.07	-0.49	0.21	0.58	1.52	1.38	1.70	1.84	2.48	1.92
Eastern Europe	0.03	0.15	0.23	0.10	0.55	0.64	0.92	0.89	0.60	0.72	0.65
North America	0.07	0.10	-0.83	0.29	0.93	2.17	2.13	1.83	1.16	1.74	1.26
Western Europe	0.00	0.16	0.25	0.10	0.41	0.71	0.63	0.78	0.43	0.61	0.33
Japan	0.09	0.14	0.18	0.38	0.12	0.10	0.46	0.97	1.25	1.15	0.61
World	0.01	0.10	0.24	0.08	0.46	0.48	0.39	0.79	0.93	1.54	1.61

Note: Growth rates of above 0 shaded light grey, above 1 per cent grey, above 2 per cent dark grey
Source: www.worldmapper.org in turn based on the work of Angus Maddison.

Examination of the table above shows how easy it is, when decades are averaged, not to see the turning points. Population growth worldwide in the 30 years prior to 1851 was, on average, higher than in the 30 years after that date. It is only by looking at annual data that it is possible to pinpoint 1851 as the date at which the current population explosion began. The Figure below illustrates how it was then that the acceleration we currently worry so much about began. It also shows how this is an acceleration that we mostly don't realize has already ended.

You can see so much more when you look at the detail, rather than when you just consider the average. As the political scientist Edward Tufte tries to explain to researchers who like to draw graphs, if you want 'to clarify add detail'.[14] Similarly, I suggest later in this volume that the great population slowdown began in 1971, even though the table above shows that average global population growth in the 30 years after that date was higher than in the 30 years before it! Again, it is only through looking at the detail, at the changes year on year, that you can see the full story.

The stories you tell depend on how you look at all the evidence in the round. The picture I see is of slow and steady changes prior to 1851, followed by a rapid increase in growth until 1971, and then the beginnings of a return towards what had been normal before. The next Figure summarizes it all. But you only see this pattern if you show the change within every year, not across every decade.

The point at which you touch the accelerator on a car is often the point at which you have just slowed down and feel the need to go faster. Your speed will be at a low, the number of metres you are passing per second might be the least on your journey, and yet this is the moment at which you begin to speed up. That was 1851.

World Annual Human Population Growth 1821–2001

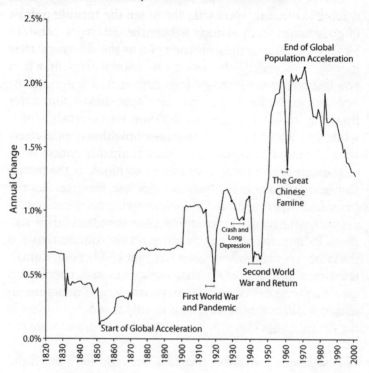

Source: Angus Maddison's historical datasets.

Precisely what happened around 1851 is much less important than the fact that it did happen. To continue the above analogy, this is the same with you driving a car. Quite why you might have accelerated – boredom, impatience, you noticed the time – is of much less importance than the fact that it was at that moment that you did accelerate, and the subsequent impact that had on your entire journey time, your safety and the safety of others, and the amount of ground that you covered.

The point at which you apply the brakes hardest when driving is often the point at which you are travelling most quickly, when most ground is being passed per second. In terms of population, this is the point at which the greatest growth is recorded. However, it is still the point at which you begin to slow down. Before this point, it was not possible to know precisely when you might slow down. After this, it is clear that you are slowing down, though for a while you might still be going faster than you were a few seconds earlier. Braking takes time. There is a certain stopping distance involved, from when you begin to decelerate, to when you are going slower than you were some time before, to when you actually stop moving forward.

In driving manuals, stopping time is measured in seconds. In demography, it is measured in decades. In terms of the effect on your journey, the fact that you began to brake is much more important than why you began to brake. You might have needed a pee, or have been avoiding an accident. Whatever it was, you slowed down.

How many of us were there?

> Now that it is possible to travel right round the globe, the real challenge lies in staying at home and discovering the world from there.
>
> Judith Schalansky,
> *Pocket Atlas of Remote Islands*, 2012[15]

One good way of discovering the world from the comfort of our homes is through examining our origins. Not long ago, global tourism would have appeared to be as fanciful as time travel, if not quite as potentially damaging to the fabric of spacetime. A temporal tourist accidentally dislodging some artefact a few millennia ago could transform subsequent world history.[16] Today a single geographic tourist emitting just a little extra carbon could theoretically contribute the final straw's worth that comes too quickly and breaks the North Atlantic climatic oscillator, transforming the future. It is hard to be greener than an armchair tourist, historian, geographer or demographer.

The reasons why we want to know more about our demographic past are many, from wanting to discover, in the broadest terms, where we have come from, to trying to gain a sense that even if we are not in full control of our destiny, we at least have a grasp of what the range of our possible destinies might be.

All population predictions begin with a census. Without a census you do not know where to start. A wide variety of places have been suggested as being the site of the first census. Early censuses were taken so that kings, pharaohs and emperors could estimate their tax base, but there were other reasons for holding such a count. Invading armies needed to know the size of the population they had to keep suppressed and the number of soldiers they could raise. The most widely referred to ancient contemporary reporting of a census is Job's summing-up of the potential numbers of fighting men in Israel and Judah.[17]

Modern-day repeated census-taking began once it became apparent that the population was growing. New states often needed a census to establish their extent and to appear to legitimize authority, as happened in Prussia in 1719 and the USA in 1790. Once the first census had been taken, it was found to be useful and the imperative to take more grew. Censuses were also taken for the first time in some countries to allay fears that there were too many mouths to feed and simultaneously too few well-nourished men to fight to secure the colonies from which to collect tribute in order to pay for all the extra food that was needed. This occurred in Britain when its first census was held in 1801.

Once a census is taken, it next dawns on some bright spark that it is possible to calculate birth and death rates. Having calculated such rates, it next becomes possible to project population numbers both backwards and forwards in time. Such projections could include estimates of future and past migration flows. Regularities in migration are harder to include, but possible. Ernst Georg Ravenstein laid out some laws for migration a century before we numbered five billion in 1988. Had he been around today, he might have added that people still tend to live in much the same river valleys they lived in millennia ago, just in far greater numbers. Project far enough back in time and you can estimate how many people have ever lived, almost all of them along the banks of the same rivers that they first settled by in each continent they reached.[18]

Demographers enjoy tormenting their students by asking them how many humans have ever lived. Today the most oft-quoted answer stands at about 100 billion, although some put it at as low as 60 billion.[19] It is not just the future that is uncertain; most of our history is veiled in mystery. Most people who have ever lived have done so in a time of tablets of clay, runes or parchment, but the fate of the vast majority was almost never carefully recorded. Give or take 40 billion humans, we are as unsure of our middle-distance past as we are of our near future.

What we do know is that it took until the year 1988 for the human population to reach five billion, or what is now assumed to be the probable halfway point in the eventual maximum size of the species. At first, at least, we got there very slowly. In 1988, by the way, the Doomsday Clock stood at just six minutes to midnight, a minute further away than it stands today, despite the Cold War still then being very warm. And around that time, just as we were working out how to potentially annihilate most human life, we were also just beginning to nail down a possible accurate start date for our species. So, let's start at the beginning.

It is a moot point as to when we really became modern humans. We are still only just starting to discover that Neanderthals also produced cave art and sang.[20] And we are becoming a little less sure of our unique human heritage.[21] Nevertheless, at some point in our distant past we evolved to become us, mammals that experience the menopause, use language, and have developed to work well in tight-knit social groups, but also mammals that routinely use weapons and other tools. Look through human waste dumps from the past and you often find weapons.

For most of human history we have been used to seeing very few other people who were not our near relations. Often when we saw others we fought them. Later we developed greeting rituals to avoid violence, and later still we saw others as having the potential to trade. We have learnt to view strangers with wary mistrust while simultaneously developing survival customs of hospitality.

As hunter-gatherers we travelled in small groups and we spaced out our children with an average age gap of at least four years between siblings. Quite how we did this is far from certain, but that we did it is well known.[22] Population growth was almost always extremely slow, as much due to low fertility as to high mortality. These people were as human as you or me, but they did not have children as frequently as most of our very recent ancestors did. They were biologically the same but fundamentally socially different, just as we have become fundamentally socially distinct from the customs and practices of our grandparents.

Today we are almost all educated well beyond the level to which our very recent ancestors were, and we almost all have far fewer children than they did. We are returning to very old levels of population growth and decline, but not because we need to carry only one breast-feeding infant at a time as we follow herds of reindeer.

Breast-feeding for several years spaced out conceptions but it is hardly a safe form of contraception. In our distant past we may have simply had to abandon surplus new-borns that we could not carry. The piercing cry of a very young baby is designed to be heard at a distance, to force the mother to turn back. Infants with slightly weaker vocal cords were left behind, for ever, a little more often than were louder babies.

Socially we live in an almost completely different time compared with the past; physically we are nearly identical. Take infants from around 60 millennia ago, or even a bit earlier, and transport them in time to today: other than some possible lethal difficulties with the new diseases that have evolved in the meantime, those transplanted infants would grow up to be just like us, because they effectively were us. Biologically we have not changed very much; it is only socially that everything is different.

The genetic differences between modern humans and those humans living 60 millennia ago are almost all associated with diseases. Of 42 genetic mutations found to have occurred since those times, 34 appear to have developed in response to new disease threats; only a few of the remaining eight may be associated with the last few changes to our brain structure, and even that may be wishful thinking.[23] Ancient humans, older than 50 or 60 millennia, might not survive in our current world because a virus or bacterium now harmless to us could kill them. Their problems would not be a failure to fit in socially.

We create religions, we make and adapt our social worlds and we change and develop new technologies in response to our growing needs. Long before all this, we had evolved to fit neatly into whichever world we found ourselves born into. The few misfits who were unable to fit in tended not to be selected to produce children. For humans, survival of the adaptable produced flexibility.

Human beings spread over such a range of territories that they developed the ability to cope with both good and bad circumstances; circumstances not of their own making. They became their own worst enemies, as well as being highly cooperative, adding to that diversity of situations they could find themselves in. Born into a settled tribe, you had to quickly learn to fit in and be peaceful. Born into violent anarchy, you had to adapt to fight your corner. Born into live-and-let-live anarchy you had to be self-reliant but not a troublemaker. Hence we evolved to be socially malleable, to be neurologically pliant.[24]

Technology changes what it means to be human. Bronze, an alloy of tin and copper, was first created around 6,000 years ago in what is now northern China. The wheel dates back a little earlier, and to south-eastern Europe. The Iron Age began about 3,000 years ago in an area which was then described in writing, albeit not in English,[25] as southern China. Irrigation of large areas in China and wider South East Asia altered how many humans could be fed, and simultaneously began to increase the amount of methane in the atmosphere, released from the anaerobic decomposition in flooded areas of all the extra weeds that grew alongside the newly irrigated rice. Enhanced human-made global warming began early and slowly.

The argument that human-made global warming may have older origins than we commonly think remains to be proven. As early as 1,000 years ago, in the most peripheral north-western edge of the then known world, a conqueror called William conducted a census and found that over four fifths of the lands he had won in the land of the Angles (England) had already been deforested.[26] Much use had already been made of all those trees to heat homes, to cook and to smelt a great deal of iron.

It has recently been suggested that Victorian demographers massively underestimated the numbers of people living at the time of the 1086 Domesday Book, the census that recorded all the estates and acres of land under plough in that survey of the far north-western tip of Europe. This is one of the reasons why we cannot be sure, give or take 40 billion, how many of us there have ever been. Our earliest accounts often missed out many people. Some may have been trying to evade tax even back then.[27]

The transition from foraging to farming did not just result in more methane being released and many trees being felled. It also resulted in a great increase in human fertility. Instead of there being roughly a four-year spacing between the births of siblings, the fact that parents no longer needed to carry newborns and toddlers as travel ceased meant that they could have more surviving babies.

Worldwide where farming prevailed women had, on average, two extra babies each. These extra babies added up to so many that they were called 'demographic masses' by people living through a much later but equally dramatic transition (our current demographic transition). Here is how one of those people, Jean-Pierre Bocquet-Appel, the director of Centre National de la Recherche Scientifique (CNRS), the largest research centre in Europe,[28] recently explained it:

> The unprecedented demographic masses that the Neolithic Demographic Transition rapidly brought into play make this one of the fundamental structural

processes of human history . . . [which] triggered a major geographical redistribution of the population, with colonization or invasion by early farmers with their technologies, lifestyles, and languages that in some cases reached the continental scale . . .[29]

Part of the answer to the question of how many of us there have ever been is that the numbers before the Neolithic transition were so low that knowing them would make no discernible difference to the total. It is from when we farmed that we multiplied, and changed much else about how we lived and who we were.

There is now new evidence from the island of Cyprus that shortly after the Neolithic transition, people were able to use their stored foods to travel across the seas. Cultivation occurred on Cyprus well over 10,000 years ago, and there were even domestic dogs for use in hunting boars, and cats for keeping down the rats that would eat their stored grain. These were our middle-distance relatives, living just 400–500 generations ago. It was they who were the first to construct huge 10-metre-diameter 'multifunctional communal buildings for collective storage, meetings, and ritual use'.[30]

What it meant to be human changed when communal buildings were first raised, when meetings were first held and ritual established. As two men distinguished by their distinct initials, David Sloan Wilson and Edward Osborne Wilson, like to put it: 'Evolution proceeds not only by small mutational change, but also by groups and symbiotic communities becoming so integrated that they become higher-level organisms in their own right.'[31] It isn't that people ceased to be people, or that what it meant to be human changed; it is that what it meant to be in a human *group* changed.

Farmers could and sometimes did revert (or depending on your view, re-ascend) to hunter-gathering; it was often an easier life, but it needed more space. What was new was that something larger than immediate family and other close kin, an institution bigger and more complex than the hunting and gathering group, emerged – a different kind of society. Institutions evolved as human numbers increased. More people meant more possibilities, specialization and coordination.

The higher-level organism, the institution of the Neolithic transition, was the village. Villages are now seen as the antithesis of progress and of the city, as a model of society that the geographer Ash Amin likes to summarize as 'regressive and unrealistic: regressive for its veiled xenophobia and exclusionary nostalgia, and unrealistic for its denial of the plural constituency of modern being and belonging'.[32] However, if you take the really long view, this complaint will have once been made of hunter-gathering by the new villagers, although perhaps a little more concisely. Ten thousand years ago, the new plural constituency of modern being and belonging was the village.

Villages sprang up around the planet, not just in one place. They formed in the Americas in isolation from the Old World. Farming had multiple geographic origins. For most of human history measured in years, we have been nomadic. For most of human history measured in lives, we have been settled. Villages were how people everywhere came to live, and most people who have ever lived have lived in villages. If you want to know how many people there have ever been, then you need to estimate villagers. Unfortunately for demographers, villages tend to leave little trace. Fortunately for us, they have been remarkably self-sufficient and biodegradable forms of settlement.

It was when people travelled between villages to trade, and especially where such travellers bunched up, that larger settlements formed, from where more relics of buildings survive. Because of this, we tend to think of cities as old. A few are very old, but most people who have ever lived in cities may well be alive today. This is not because there are too many of us; it is because what it means to be a human group is again changing. A revolution as great as the Neolithic is taking place, and this time the higher-level organisms are changing from villages to cities; not cities as existed in antiquity, but something quite new.

Doom-mongering through the ages

> Overpopulation has power as a folk myth ... It is a myth in that one has to appeal to extremes of ever-increasing numbers to make a convincing point that there is a definite limit to the human population. Overpopulation chimes with a certain sense that we all have, that our local world would be a more comfortable place without a few (often particular!) people.
>
> Radstats Population Studies Group,
> 'Moral Panic and Overpopulation', 2011[33]

It was overpopulation, some archaeologists suggest, that led to humans settling to farming. Farming is a precarious life. If the harvests are bad, you starve. Moving to better farmland involves a huge loss of sunken capital. Social hierarchies become established with settlements and freedoms are lost. Human beings shrank in physical stature, and drastically reduced the range of nutrients they could rely on when they settled and cultivated grains. And yet many greens now look back on early village settlement as some kind of utopian achievement.[34]

It was in that short neck of land where Africa, Asia and Europe meet that the first demographic revolution, the

Neolithic revolution, occurred. It is not absolute geograph-ical determinism that places it there – a little like locating the first Garden of Eden according to the soil – but simply high statistical likelihood: it was the land between the riv-ers, in Mesopotamia, and later along the Nile, where one locus of the revolution was found.

Where three continents join

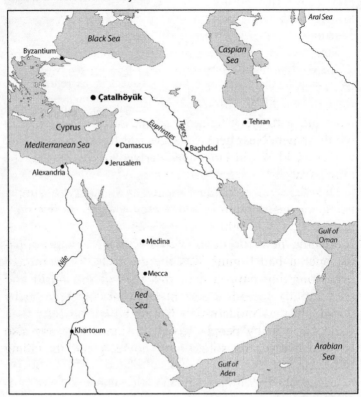

Note: Selected cities that were founded and seas and rivers that were named after Çatalhöyük in lighter type

Source: Re-drawn from author's map.

Other points where the revolution first sparked off can be found in other continents. The best soils for cultivation would be found further east in Asia, on the banks of much wider rivers in China and India, and later cities would spring up at bridging points. Earliest of all, and thanks most probably to proximity to Africa and the largest initial abundance of people, it was at the near intersection of three continents, within the area encompassed in the map above, that both village and early urban life are now known with some certainty to have begun a very long time ago.

The current top contender for the place with the first 10-metre-diameter multifunctional communal buildings is Cyprus. An island like Cyprus was quieter and safer than the mainland isthmus to its south-east where, much later and with much fighting, all the Abrahamic religions would spawn. Near here too in Anatolia is the place where modern Old World languages derived from, west of the Himalayas and north of the Sahara.

Did the first settlement occur due to there simply being too many hunter-gatherers as a result of overpopulation 8,000–11,000 years ago, or was it the start of something new for other reasons or simply unstoppable once it had begun? Was the great change in human behaviour that happened in this part of the world and then rapidly spread a portent of what appeared to be doom? Just as modern-day Istanbul may be seen as a sign of too many people, given its slums, but may also be evidence of the solution to come, given its falling birth rate.[35]

One problem with settlements is that they require people to settle, but we also have an apparently innate wish to wander. However, we mostly do not wander on a flat plain that to outsiders can appear largely featureless, learning how to live in some kind of dreamtime. Our wanderings are usually funnelled between mountains and through the narrow isthmuses of land, around lakes and along the edges of seas.

The geographical origins of Indo-European languages

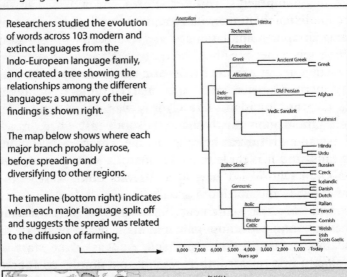

Researchers studied the evolution of words across 103 modern and extinct languages from the Indo-European language family, and created a tree showing the relationships among the different languages; a summary of their findings is shown right.

The map below shows where each major branch probably arose, before spreading and diversifying to other regions.

The timeline (bottom right) indicates when each major language split off and suggests the spread was related to the diffusion of farming.

Source: http://www.nytimes.com/2012/08/24/science/indo-european-languages-originated-in-anatolia-analysis-suggests.html. Redrawn and simplified.

In 2012, a computer simulation was published in the journal *Science* identifying Anatolia as the likely source of all Indo-European languages.[36] The simulation helped to explain the geography of those languages that remain today and also calibrated the average degree of wanderlust among humans. Because the paper was published in a scientific journal, human wanderlust was measured and given a number.

The extent of human wanderlust was determined by running computer simulations to see what level was required to produce the spread of language. The simulations tested whether there appeared to be a preference for 'a smaller wanderlust over higher . . . The optimal value for [wanderlust] w thus found was 0.0002.'[37] Squeeze humans through the narrow gaps between the Red, Mediterranean, Black, Caspian and Arabian seas, at whatever the rate of 0.0002 means, and it is there that new ideas were most likely to mix first with other new ideas. It was there that people who believed that voices were telling them to lead other people to promised lands would most likely find themselves, along with those they had managed to convince to accompany them.

When first released, there was heated debate over these computer models of archaeological migrations and their associated language claims. The *New York Times* recorded Dr David Anthony (of Hartwick College) claiming that the theory was 'a one-legged stool, so it's not surprising that the tree it produces contains language groupings that would not survive if you included morphology and sound changes' (such as root words and nuances of intonation).[38] As you can see, there is much disagreement as to how we got to be the five billion we were by 1988. You may also be surprised to find that there is dispute over whether the city came before the village and forced hunters to form villages,[39] and as to quite how villages spread. East of the Himalayas, archaeologists still argue over which were the first 'large fortified settlements with princely burials [which] can be regarded as towns',[40] and whether these began along the Yangtze Valley or on the Central Plain.

What became half of our modern-day languages appear to have spread east and west from Anatolia 8,000 years ago. These did not reach the Americas until only just over 500 years ago. Less than 50 years ago, words were first spoken in one of these languages on the moon. The European encounter with the Americas brought doom to many of the first Americans. Those who introduced the diseases, and then slavery, were not just on a fact-finding mission; they were seeking spice and found gold. By 'discovering' the Americas, they moved Europe centre stage for 400 years, before the focus moved across to North America itself with US hegemony. We have just jumped forward eight millennia in one paragraph.

The moon landing of manned rockets sent from the US in 1969 was as much an expression of military might, and the ability to send missiles to annihilate whole nations, as an exploration driven by scientific curiosity which happened to then change humanity's collective and literal view of the planet. The rate of change in how we currently see ourselves is faster today than it has ever been. No generation living has ever known so much more than the generation that died just a century before it. Take, for instance, what we now know of the first cities.

The Neolithic site of Çatalhöyük was first discovered and excavated in the late 1950s. The archive report of the 2011 excavation suggested that the archaeologists had found a 9,000-year-old painting on a plaster wall: 'the new painting helps us to understand the social geography of

Çatalhöyük, reinforcing the impression gained from other data that there were widespread social and ritual networks across the community, binding it tightly together'.[41] The introduction of agriculture might have allowed new forms of art to develop, but it also led to, and may well have been driven by, the exploitation of farmers by warrior aristocracies supported by priesthoods. Mortality rates among young children rose as the land was settled. Farmers could not escape climatic vagaries, despotic leadership or weird cults, at least not as easily as hunter-gatherers could.

One reason to look back nine millennia when seeking to try to peer forward less than 90 years (to 2100 at the end of this book) is that there are similarities between that long-ago transition and what we may be experiencing in our current era. During the Neolithic revolution there was 'an abrupt 20 to 30 percent increase, over 500 to 700 years, in the proportion of immature skeletons'.[42] Jump forward again nine millennia, and mortality rates in the Industrial Revolution in the first modern city, Manchester, rose quickly during the period 1800–50 as its children could not escape the open sewers and cesspits, the increasingly despotic mill owners, and weird but supposedly Christian beliefs that their short lives were somehow expendable for the greater economic good.

Because of incredibly high infant and child mortality in Manchester, life expectancy was only 25 years across that 1800–50 half-century, yet despite this, and because of a rushing flood of immigrants, the city grew in size to number more than a quarter of a million souls by the end of the period.[43]

What Manchester lacked more than anything else was a sewage system, something that was quite new at the time and something that was only installed after the third great bout of cholera hit the city, when the authorities came to realize that they needed to act to ward off further doom. Stretched out on a flat plain, jerry-built homes had been constructed upon jerry-built homes. The worst of these were dug out from beneath the cellars of existing buildings to provide accommodation for ever more desperate and hence not discerning incomers. Jump back in time again.

Çatalhöyük, with a population that rarely exceeded 10,000 souls, lacked something even more obvious today than a sewer system. It had no roads, no streets or even alleyways between buildings. Why would it? Why waste space leaving gaps between buildings when you can walk across your neighbours' roofs to get to where you wish to be? By the time it became apparent that streets might have been a good idea, it was almost certainly too late to try to incorporate them. Humans live and learn, and are most disconcerted, yet learn fastest, when almost everything changes.

The world's first town plans are often dated back to Çatalhöyük. Fields were the first spatial objects to be mapped. My favourite maps are the ones showing people apparently dancing in fields, evoking a multimillennia-old rave. The most popular redrawing of a mural depicting part of the layout of Çatalhöyük, the world's first city, shows a town lying beneath what appears to be a portent of doom, a somewhat distant volcano. Other observers think the volcano may actually be a man or woman wearing a leopard-skin print.[44] As we still worry about volcanoes, and as we still suffer from people wearing leopard-skin prints, it can be tempting to think that nothing much changes, but that would be wrong. Nothing much changes between demographic transitions. During demographic transitions, almost everything changes.

Çatalhöyük, the world's first city (without streets)

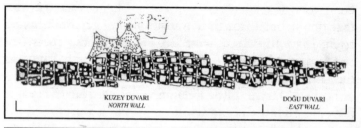

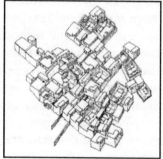 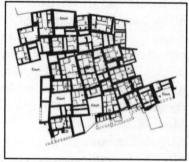

Source: Redrawn from many reconstructed images that now appear on the web.

Çatalhöyük was populated for almost two millennia. Manchester may have been a village named by the Romans two millennia ago, but it remained barely a village up until a few hundred years ago.[45] It then became one of the first partly planned grid cities in the world. Manchester didn't just have streets; it had streets in parallel lines. But they initially forgot the sewers. Today it is the fibre optics, the light rail system, the rooftop water collectors and the urban vertical gardens that are more often being retro-fitted to our cities. And today we still worry that we have forgotten something, that volcano (or leopard skin) smoking away in the distance, our own effluent or other more invisible and less initially noxious pollutants.

It is easy to see portents of doom in what is new. It is far harder to realize that you are not living through normal times, but through a transition. In the two decades from 1840 to 1860, some 13 priests of the parish of St Mary in Manchester died of typhus while working in the Little Ireland area of the city.[46] Frederick Engels dated a girl called Mary in Little Ireland; vomiting from the stench there, in 1844 he began work on his book warning of the industrial end of times, *Die Lage der arbeitenden Klasse in England* (four years later, together with Karl Marx, he penned *The Communist Manifesto*). In 1860, the Bishop of Salford invited the Jesuits to take over the dead priests' work at St Mary's. The opiate of belief they offered, that all would be all right after death, held greater sway than the lure of revolution, and their church still stands on Manchester's Oxford Road.

A modern-day Jesuit might say: 'Give me a child from fifty or nine millennia ago, and I will give you today's men and women.' Humans were just as daft then as they are now, and just as clever. We are presiding over a period of the mass extinction of species, but we have done so before and survived. Jump back in time much further for a moment.

It was around fifty millennia ago that the first modern-day people arrived in Australia (before they arrived in cold Europe). Within a very short period of their arrival occurred the extinction of 'a marsupial lion, three kinds of wombat, nine genera of kangaroo, and a range of nonmarsupials including a giant tortoise the size of a Volkswagen "bug" and several kinds of lizards and flightless birds. Every vertebrate species larger than humans disappeared. Nothing even close to this concentrated pulse of extinction had occurred for millions of years on Australia.'[47] For the next 52,000 years, these new Australians would live in the most stable, sustainable and long-lasting human civilization the world has ever known, until new human invaders arrived on 22 April 1770.[48] But jump forward not as far as then, to the Year of the Pig in the Christian year one, when Pingdi, the Han dynasty emperor of China, was 10 years old, and look north of Australia.[49]

Two thousand years ago, the population of what is now China, Mongolia and Korea combined was the same as the population of the United Kingdom today, around 62 million souls.[50] The population of what is now India, then at the centre of the (known) world, was, at 78 million, less than that of Germany today. Across all of the rest of the planet the remaining 90 million humans were unevenly spread out. There were then fewer people across the whole planet than the current population of Indonesia. From nine millennia ago to two millennia ago human numbers increased slowly and steadily. Villages spread down the archipelago towards Australia, across the seas, though nomadic life in colder parts of North America and the far north of Europe and Russia didn't succumb to settlement until much later imposition.

For the next thousand years, little changed demographically. The population of what had become China, though it may actually have dipped slightly, was stable, as was that of India, itself centred on two rivers, the Indus and Ganges. Human populations can be stable for millennia. The population of the rest of the world grew by only 38 million in a hundred years! That was a net growth averaging only 102 additional people a day, every day, for a thousand years. People were still moving into uncharted areas, still settling on the best land, still fanning out over the planet. By the Christian year one, only a few people had reached Madagascar. Even by the year 1000 CE, no humans had yet arrived in what they came to call Aotearoa, and what most people now call New Zealand.

For the 500 years from 1000 CE to 1500 CE, the rate at which worldwide human population growth was increasing, the change in the usual annual change, rose tenfold in magnitude, but was still hardly noticeable. Decade on decade, from annual population growth of 0.01 per cent a year, mean rates of global population increase rose to 0.1 per cent a year.

For many, the ultimate doom arrived when the Black Death came; few today realize that this, and other more minor plagues, arrived during a long period of more quickly growing population. The Black Death may even have happened partly because human population was becoming a little more crowded in towns. People and animals were living in closer proximity, human waste was less well disposed of, food stores were a little more abundant, and fewer cats were being kept to kill rats. Why keep cats when grain was becoming so plentiful you could afford to lose some to rats?

All the time exploring, conquering and then trading further and further away was increasing, eventually to include the Americas in the last eight years of these five hundred and to visit upon them the worst of all plagues. Global population may have last dipped in the years immediately after 1492.

The value of labour

A Scotch physician of long experience in Shantung, who took the steamer at Tsingtao, replied to my question as to the usual size of families in his circuit, 'I do not know. It depends on the crops. In good years the number is large; in times of famine the girls especially are disposed of, often permitted to die when very young for lack of care. Many are sold at such times to go into other provinces.'

Franklin Hiram King,
Farmers of Forty Centuries, 1911[51]

It is well known that the value of human labour rose as the population fell following the Black Death. It is also well known that for centuries humans have practised infanticide when they have believed potential human labour to have fallen so greatly in value that an extra newborn puts those already living at risk. Population did not fall only with disease; it fell when rates of slavery and famine rose too.

Over the course of the century directly after the 1492 encounter, from 1500 to 1600, human population fell in many parts of the world: in the Americas, in Africa, but most importantly in China. Bubonic plague, many natural disasters and repeated Mongol invasion only came to an end during the Ming dynasty when the Great Wall was strengthened to provide an effective barrier against barbarians, a barrier never bettered before or since. The reduced pool of human labour inside China became more highly valued and the Ming dynasty is now remembered as a golden age. China was then the richest place on earth.

China may no longer be the richest place on earth, but it is now the engine of the world economy, and within it there will soon again be a labour shortage. In the not too distant future, the population of China is again expected to fall. This is hardly surprising. In 1979, having seen the fortunes of other once great nations crushed by imperialism, the Chinese took a gamble that within a generation they could switch from being a third-world country to having near first-world status through, above all else, one simple policy. They would have many fewer children and they would become so much better-off so quickly that they would not have to rely on their children in old age. Now old age is here, and their children want something better than their parents had, not a life of such toil.

Between the great demographic transitions are demographic shifts. All demographic shifts have economic and psychological effects. The last time we are sure that there was a very large fall in population worldwide was when the Black Death struck in the middle of the fourteenth century. In Europe, wages had to rise in consequence. Economic inequalities fell. But then, in places, land was enclosed as many smallholdings were abandoned or requisitioned, and that eventually led to great rises in economic inequalities.

The Renaissance, which began in Florence, took on full form only after the Black Death struck and the influence of the Church fell. God appeared not to care. The Black Death was not a geographic shock akin to the discovery of the New World, but it did result in changes to economic systems which provided the mechanism a little later for how New World wealth could be distributed around the Old World. Europe sent gold and silver from the Americas to China and India in exchange for crockery, spices, gunpowder, steel, silk and all else that was then seen as sophisticated and secret.

As wealth flowed to the Old World from the Americas, death came to the New World. A mid-Americas population of up to 100 million people in 1492 was possibly reduced to fewer than 10 million shortly after the encounter, by disease, murder and societal collapse. Plague alone killed off up to a quarter of the first Americans and as many as a third of the population in places. This was not the worst of plagues – worse cases included the Plague of Justinian in the sixth century CE, and the Black Death eight centuries later – but coupled with the equivalent of aliens arriving from outer space (conquistadors), it decimated more than ten times over.

If you decimate a population ten times over, killing a tenth, then a tenth of those who are left, and so on ten times, more than a third still survive (38.7 per cent). The early Americans were not so lucky. It is possible that at least 50 million Americans died, 'just from having come into contact with Europeans'.[52] This was about a tenth of world population at the time. Population falls are not alien to human history.

Our populations have not been rising inexorably, bar the odd drop, for millennia. Because of falls such as that following the Black Death, we know that sudden changes in human numbers can alter how each individual human is valued. It took the spanning of continents for the modern-day rise in population numbers to begin. Initially in both the Americas and Africa populations fell. Suddenly, as the value of human labour rose, it was economic to expend vast sums of money buying people from Africa and shipping the minority who survived capture and transport across the Atlantic to the new plantations. Often banks lent money to promote these endeavours.

In the fifteenth century, the Renaissance was partly financed by the Medici family, whose bank became the largest in Europe. The family became rich as the usury laws of the Catholic Church were relaxed. Those laws promoted stability during the time before gold and silver flooded in across the Atlantic. Once the wealth began to flow, those laws could no longer be maintained.

Modern-day European capitalism was born when the demographic shift that followed the geographic shock made feudal societies unstable. The New World gold and silver which flowed back in return made men blind to previous morals, and also actually turned a few blind as an epidemic of syphilis spread with the silver. Colonial Spanish silver underpinned European economies.

Travelling in the opposite direction to Columbus, in his 1497–9 Portuguese expedition to India, Vasco da Gama had determined that 'the only way for trade with the East to grow and prosper was for Europeans to find large and reliable sources of gold and silver, and to acquire the precious metals as cheaply as possible'.[53] Discovery altered geography, so, now placed at the centre between India, China and the Americas, Europe shifted to become the demographic centre of the world.

The centre of Europe was moving too. It rotated from Venice to Lisbon to Amsterdam to London, each place having a minor advantage over its forebear at a particular time. The United Provinces had become the first world economic superpower in the seventeenth century when trade and profit centred on Amsterdam. With hindsight, it is perhaps unsurprising and a little reassuring that the ways in which human beings came to organize themselves tended to be quite stable and self-replicating, until some outside and unforeseen force intervened.

Being fixated on exactly where in Europe prospered most is rather like worrying about where in the Americas the death rate elevated by Old World disease became highest. All of Western Europe grew rich, Russia most slowly, as it was furthest from the Atlantic. That it was eventually London and not Lisbon where most riches were amassed is as unimportant as whether it was Mesoamericans or the Maya who suffered most, or why.

Jump forward a few centuries from the 1492 encounter. In the middle of the eighteenth century, the disaster of the Lisbon earthquake crushed Portugal's colonial ambitions and spurred on enlightenment thinking and a growing distrust in God. By the end of that century, the world's first salaried economist, the Reverend Thomas Malthus, had published his *Essay on the Principle of Population*, forecasting never-ending population growth, war and famine. Within two centuries it became clear how wrong he had been, at least about future population growth.

Global economic power shifted next to the most rapidly populating countries: the United Kingdom, and then a further anticlockwise turn to New York and the United States. Within the United States, people, money, power and newspaper titles[54] moved forwards and anticlockwise again during the twentieth century, down towards the Pacific coast and to California. People migrate to where the new opportunities to work are, and they have far more children than usual when social norms are overturned. This occurred when land enclosure, fuelled itself by Spanish (American) silver, disturbed British feudal society. The extra English, Welsh, Scottish and Irish babies were later, as adults, exported in great numbers to the Americas, Australia and lastly New Zealand. A few also found themselves in Africa.

That overseas territory was usually appropriated through carnage has still not been widely accepted. Along the banks of the Congo river, the statue of Henry Morton Stanley, the man immortalized for saying 'Dr Livingstone, I presume?',[55] was torn down in the 1970s. Forty years later, councillors in Stanley's home town of Denbigh raised money to erect a new one to place at the intersection of two of the local streets. There was only a small amount of protest.

Henry Morton Stanley told his men that when encountering Africans in one small village they should 'fire on them as if they were killing birds'. His men shot dead 33 people and wounded a further hundred. On this particular expedition Stanley himself reported having attacked and destroyed almost 30 large towns and 60 to 80 villages. A contemporary, Richard Burton, 'charged that Stanley [would] shoot negroes as if they were monkeys'. In December 1878, Stanley 'signed a five-year contract with King Léopold [of Belgium] to establish their enterprises in the Congo'.[56] The result was the first modern well-planned genocide.

In summer 2009, on a tour of the Royal Geographical Society in London, I was shown Stanley's pith helmet, a prized relic of the Society. Then they gave me a medal for the things I had learnt. To understand why we should stop fearing future population numbers, we have to learn from colonial mistakes and not celebrate the European past as if it were spreading a particularly enlightened civilization. Much evil is done in the name of royalty, for king, empress or just country.

Mass killing required new inventions. In 1901, just before her death, the Empress Queen Victoria bestowed a knighthood on Hiram Stevens Maxim for inventing the machine gun. From killing in faraway places, to shooting people as if they were birds or monkeys, to now killing at a distance with flying robots (drones), people are often driven to see others as not human. From 'Negroes' to 'the Hun' and today 'Muslims' in faraway lands – some people can be portrayed as being more expendable than others. These strangers are also often presented as if there is a never-ending supply of them; the implicit suggestion is that there are already too many of them. In reality, 'they' are just like 'us': 'in the foreseeable future an increasing number of Muslim-majority countries may face the prospect of coping with manpower declines. If current USCB [United States Census Bureau] projections prove accurate, Lebanon's 15–64 cohort would peak in the year 2023 – twelve years from this writing – and would shrink more or less indefinitely thereafter.'[57]

The last century has been the century of greatest turmoil, of the most war, the most widespread famines in human history. People react to both war and famine by having more children, perhaps as an insurance against raised uncertainty. Nevertheless, population growth has slowed and is about to go into decline. We should expect the economic impact to be just as great as the impact that followed all previous large demographic shifts, if not quite as great as those that are assumed to have accompanied the last major demographic transition. Furthermore, great shifts in our thinking also tend to accompany demographic transition.

Huge numbers of statues of what is assumed to be a goddess were found in Çatalhöyük. Our current long population explosion and subsequent demographic transition is synchronous with moving from a largely religiously ordered world to one in which the quasi-religion of a particular scientific way of thinking becomes pre-eminent. The majority of the world's atheists and agnostics are found in China.[58] If the near future is more Chinese, it will also place even less trust in invisible deities.

The slowing down of population growth and the first few decades of renewed stability may similarly be accompanied by a shift in thinking, a new take on science rising against some of the old scientific certainties, and a less frantic accumulation of new ideas than that associated with both exploding population numbers and our current fundamental reordering of social systems. Within my parents' lifetime, traditional science, after all, has given us the ability to annihilate ourselves. Science is no panacea. Shortly before her third birthday, when she heard on the radio the announcement of the Hiroshima bombing, my mother asked her mother what the atomic bomb was. My grandmother told the truth: she did not know.

Apocalypse then

> ... nothing remains. No houses, no installation,
> no trees, nothing.
>
> Judith Schalansky,
> *Pocket Atlas of Remote Islands*, 2012[59]

Somewhere between the announcements of the third and fourth billion living human, we became gods, or at least a few of us did. For the French few the moment came on 24 August 1968. On that day, just 500 metres above sea level, a helium balloon floated gently upwards. A second later, as it rose a further 20 metres, it, the three-tonne hydrogen bomb it was carrying, and much of what was once recognizable on the surface of the coral reef isle of Fangataufa in the Tuamotu archipelago was gone for ever. From the edge to the centre of the atoll, even two decades later, radiation levels exceed 50 to 10,000 Becquerels per kilogram of water. This figure compares to 3.4 to 4,400 Bq/kg in dry soil found kilometres away from the Fukushima Daiichi nuclear reactor just a few weeks after the explosions there.[60]

The island of Fangataufa, often referred to as an atoll, is on the opposite side of the planet to Europe. It is where one of the largest man-made explosions of all time was created. It appeared to many people that the final 20 years of the first half of human history would be the last ever. The radiation levels remaining over time confirm how deadly nuclear war would be, not just in the short term.

The Cold War was still warm, if no longer so hot, as the population of the planet speeded up towards five billion and the end of the first half of human history. The hot wars had been in Vietnam, in Fangataufa, in Angola, Mozambique, Chile, Afghanistan, from where the Russians were only just then retreating, and in hundreds of other places.

Fangataufa Atoll, location and radiation levels

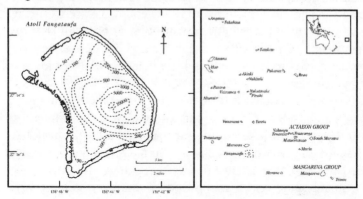

Note: Radiation levels, French measurements 1987, $^{239+240}$Pu (Bq/kg).

Source: Povineca, P. P., et al. (1999, pp.249–67), 'Marine radioactivity assessment of Muroroa and Fangataufa atolls', *Science of the Total Environment* 237–8.

Often these were places as remote from the rich world, from the United States, Europe, and Japan, as it was possible to be. The great powers mostly played out their proxy wars in Africa, Asia and Latin America, but also near to the borders of the Soviet Union. They still fight abroad, often with money as much as if not more than with troops, now in Syria, Libya, Iraq, Somalia and, again, Afghanistan.

Behind these wars were ideas of superiority and of the right of one group of people to subordinate others who were often seen as being backwards or even not quite human. It is far easier for nominally Christian countries to wage war in places where fewer Christians live. So-called 'scientific thinking' was used to bolster the racism that made all this possible. And all this matters intensely for our future prospects of demographic survival.

One form of racism that grew strong in the final century of the first half of human history was the idea that

97

some groups of people were somehow naturally cleverer and hence more valuable than others. If we are to survive the current demographic transition and come out of it in a more sustainable and less divisive and disruptive way, one necessity is to learn to be a little less stupid about ideas of inheritance.

Many scientists find it very hard to talk about intelligence sensibly because a particular way of thinking about it is part of the justification for being a scientist. The debate on intelligence in science is similar to clerics finding it hard to discuss the existence of God. Religions and universities can still serve very useful purposes whatever your view on, say, the existence of God, or variations in intelligence.

In 1892, the second edition of Francis Galton's *Hereditary Genius: An inquiry into its laws and consequences* was published. It claimed that the greatest mental superiority was to be found in the 'modern European' and the lowest in 'the lowest of the Negro races'.[61] Twenty years later, in 1912, at the height of inequality in Britain, Galton's protégé, Karl Pearson, published *The Intensity of natural selection in man*.[62]

It had been common from mid Victorian times up until the late 1930s to unthinkingly accept that some people were born with inherent strengths and weaknesses and that the weak should die in childhood. However, in 1934, a landmark paper was published in which 'Kermack and colleagues counter the eugenic argument',[63] showing that it was more important, for instance, when considering health and possible natural selection to 'direct attention to the importance of good environmental conditions during childhood'.[64] William Ogilvy Kermack's comments have had to be reiterated continuously as ideas of apparent superiority appear to be very attractive to a small minority.

In 2012, two researchers explained further that:

Many of the statistical methods that are widely used today were invented in the late 19th century and the first half of the 20th century by a group of accomplished British statisticians. Francis Galton invented regression, Karl Pearson consolidated Galton's work into a general theory of correlation and regression, Charles Spearman and Cyril Burt made significant contributions to both correlation and factor analysis, and Ronald Fisher pioneered analysis of variance . . . All of these statisticians believed in eugenics, a term invented by Francis Galton – literally meaning 'well-born' – to characterise his 'moral philosophy' belief that the human species could be improved by encouraging society's brightest and best to have more children and by reducing the number of children produced by people who were physically or mentally 'deficient' . . . These white male statisticians were from the upper middle class in England and firmly believed they owed their place close to the top of the class, 'race' and gender structure of the British Empire to their own innate superiority to virtually everyone else on the planet.[65]

When it comes to looking for genes for genius, there is as yet no compelling evidence for there being 'alpha' children, the all-round winners so chillingly described in Aldous Huxley's 1932 novel *Brave New World*. Huxley's older brother, Julian, was a leading eugenist of the time, becoming vice president of the British Eugenics Society in 1937. In 1926, he had written: 'unless [civilized societies] invent and enforce adequate measures for regulating human reproduction, for controlling the quantity of population, and at least preventing the deterioration of quality of racial stock, they are doomed to decay'.[66] Aldous had poor eyesight; perhaps he believed that his older brother was suggesting him personally as a flaw in the quality?

In 1949, a view of the world in which a 2 per cent/ 13 per cent/85 per cent split of society becomes normal was described by George Orwell in the novel *1984*.

> Below Big Brother comes the Inner Party, its numbers limited to six millions, or something less than 2 per cent of the population of Oceania. Below the Inner Party comes the Outer Party, which, if the Inner Party is described as the brain of the State, may be justly likened to the hands. Below that come the dumb masses whom we habitually refer to as 'the proles', numbering perhaps 85 per cent of the population. In the terms of our earlier classification, the proles are the Low: for the slave population of the equatorial lands who pass constantly from conqueror to conqueror, are not a permanent or necessary part of the structure.[67]

Within 60 years of the *1984* prediction being made, the OECD (Organization for Economic Cooperation and Development) think tank, mostly a group of economists, was releasing figures suggesting that only 2 per cent of children were being educated in affluent countries to an advanced level and only 13 per cent were at all well developed educationally. However, when it was pointed out that the OECD's categorization of children into the same-sized bands as Orwell predicted was due to their assuming that distribution before testing, it was simply suggested 'that all the methodology appears to be standard. In particular the use of latent variable modelling with a normal prior is widely used in educational testing.'[68]

The use of latent variable modelling with a normal prior, more commonly called 'the bell curve', should only be used by those who still think like Francis Galton, who states: 'I have been surprised at finding how often insanity or idiocy has appeared among the near relatives of exceptionally able men.'[69] He was a cousin of Charles Darwin.

Heritability is a concept that grew up as largely accepted in the first half of human history, but its fallibility was being exposed by one group of scientists just as another group was helping to arm the five major (and then secretly a few very minor) world powers with the means of apocalypse. In 1974, the evolutionary biologist Richard Charles Lewontin explained that in animals a 'trait can have a heritability of 1.0 in a population at some time, yet could be completely altered in the future by a simple environmental change'.[70]

One example that Lewontin gives to explain that even high rates of hereditability do not necessary imply a definite fate is the medical condition known as phenylketonuria, a genetic disorder that can only be inherited from parents, and which affects metabolism and causes mental retardation. However, if infants with this condition are given a particular set of foods to eat at the right time, then the metabolism is not affected and the retardation does not occur, although a special diet has to be followed for life.

In 1974, researchers pointed out that even if a trait was found to be 100 per cent 'heritable', that did not mean it was 'inevitable', nor that a child should suffer the repercussions of that inheritance. This was part of a much wider debate taking place in the early 1970s as eugenic thinking was again on the rise. A 1968 study had been designed to find genetic factors behind human mental traits. In the 40 years that followed its publication, it was found to have been fabricated. It had not even discovered heritable factors that could be environmentally influenced, but was part of a wider movement, 'an attempt to reproduce an existing set of ranks (social class) in another, the test scores, and pretend that the latter is a measure of something else. This is, and remains, the fundamental strategy of the intelligence-testing movement.'[71]

In 1969, the psychologist Arthur Jensen published a paper in the *Harvard Education Review* claiming that black people were less intelligent than whites. Between then and 1974, there was a concerted attempt at reviving the reputation of the eugenists:[72] 'The underlying assumption of the hereditarians . . . is a simple one, echoing one of Jensen's key contentions. In the course of history, the mass of people have lost all their "intelligent" individuals to the upper classes as a consequence of social mobility, leaving a *muddy sediment* at the base amidst which only the occasional pearl is still found by careful probing.'[73]

Ten years later, by 1984, the fact that science is not necessarily value-free was revealed when it was argued that nothing 'demonstrates more clearly how scientific methodology and conclusions are shaped to fit ideological ends than the sorry story of the heritability of IQ'.[74] A quarter of a century on again, and by December 2010, heritable genes for specific diseases had only been identified for cystic fibrosis, sickle cell anaemia, Huntington's disease and an increased susceptibility to Alzheimer's, breast cancer and the degenerative eye disease age-related macular degeneration.[75]

If we are to survive the rest of the current demographic transition and come out of it better people, then we are going to have to very quickly learn to accept that almost all of us are pretty much equal in ability and potential, as well as consistently capable of stupidity and other fallibilities. How else do you explain why we continue to wage so many wars and still stand so near to the edge of potential nuclear and other apocalypses, other than by understanding that everybody, especially those at the top, has a great capacity to be stupid?

One of my favourite, if fabricated, urban myths is one which suggests that there is an Assyrian clay tablet dating from around 2800 BC (800 years before any Assyrians existed!) bearing the inscription:

> Our Earth is degenerate in these later days; there are signs that the world is speedily coming to an end; bribery and corruption are common; children no longer obey their parents; every man wants to write a book and the end of the world is evidently approaching.[76]

The tablet does not exist, but it is a story well worth preserving. It is the first urban myth, set where the move to cities began. An urbanization that might help us most now, as we have fewer children and consume less in cities. Also helpful might be our rising concerns about degeneracy, about bribery and corruption, about the young being greedy and the old no longer being listened to. Or should that be concern that the old have become greedy and the young have had their future stolen? We have arrived at 1988. There are five billion of us; many people think that is already too many.

CHAPTER 3

6 BILLION FOR THE MILLENNIUM

Sometime in the next year, a woman will give birth in the Lagos slum of Ajegunle, a young man will flee his village in west Java for the bright lights of Jakarta, or a farmer will move his impoverished family into one of Lima's innumerable pueblos jovenes. The exact event is unimportant and it will pass entirely unnoticed. Nonetheless it will constitute a watershed in human history. For the first time the urban population of the earth will outnumber the rural. Indeed, given the imprecisions of Third World censuses, this epochal transition may already have occurred.

Mike Davis, 'Planet of Slums', 2004[1]

It took us roughly 64,000 years to reach our first billion. We hit it in the year 1820. In fact, just after the summer solstice of that year, it is estimated that the number of live humans on the planet reached 1,041,834,000 people. These first 64 millennia contain the entirety of our collective experiences of overall population decline, of the most terrible of plagues, the most devastating wars and famines. It is also the only period we can look to for understanding about what population stability is like. But we have to rattle on. Time is pressing. More and more people are being born.

Since 1820, there have been pandemics, the most deadly being the pandemic of influenza in 1918 and 1919, but the world population carried on growing, even during these years. The nineteenth century was a century of European warfare and colonial invasion, followed, in the twentieth, by two world wars. Still, world population rose every year, even including the years of most war deaths.

Famines increased in frequency and intensity as parts of the world became more badly governed under the antagonism of colonial rule. Famine struck for the Irish towards the start of this period. For Chinese and Indian families it was a regular feature of life during the later nineteenth century, reaching well into the twentieth, while for East Africans, the worst famine was to strike towards the end of the period, just as world population had almost reached six billion. The death tolls were in millions, but still overall global population growth was barely dented.

Something began shortly after 1820 which by 1851 meant that worldwide population acceleration had taken off and would continue rising for another 120 years. That something was so powerful that it resulted in millions of people becoming parents to greater than normal numbers of babies, and in far more than enough of them surviving globally to replace their parents. The effect was to mitigate any disaster that occurred in the years that followed. That something had many triggers, from the first American encounter to the rise of mercantilism and perhaps also the fortunate beginnings of the imposition of new public health measures around 1848. But it resulted in six billion humans being alive by the year 2000 and a very turbulent 180 years between the billionth and sixth billionth living humans.[2]

For the first century of those 180 years, as the second billion was being amassed, it felt as if everything was changing too rapidly, but there was far more rapid change to come. Taking the millennial perspective, and imagining a kind of temporal 'god view' of a century, this was just a blink of human history. From mills in Derbyshire to factories in Detroit, all that was solid quickly became uncertain. The most advanced manufacturing plants and production lines of one era became the museums of the next, often within workers' lifetimes.

Sometime after the start of the twentieth century, half the people of the globe were experiencing at least some industrialization. Henry T. Ford would pronounce: 'The time will not be far when our very own workers will buy automobiles from us . . . I'm not saying our workers will sing Caruso or govern the state. No, we can leave such ravings to the European socialists. But the workers *will* buy automobiles.'[3] Ford was correct about the car workers of the United States; they were soon able to buy automobiles. Unions striking to secure fairer wages saw to that. In Europe, workers ascended to even greater achievements than buying a car: they got to govern whole states, usually through their victorious socialist parties, and they did so long before many car workers could afford to buy the machines they made.

In the 1970s, I used to wait for a break in the lines of car-plant workers cycling to work on their bikes so that I could cross a road to get to school. Today, there are almost no workers employed by that factory any more; much of the work is done by robots. Today in Henry Ford's Detroit there is little work even for the robots. So much has changed so quickly.

Our second billion was achieved 600 times more quickly than our first, in just 106 years. The population reached two billion by 1926.[4] It might have come a little earlier but for the influenza pandemic that swept around the world towards the end of the First World War, a war that only involved a very small proportion of the world but the proportion with enough power and imagination to call it global. Worldwide, though, these were quite stable demographic times.

Perhaps because of this stability, it was in the 50 years up to 1926 that fertility was first seen to fall in the richest of countries. Towards the end of the nineteenth century, condoms became popular, which also contributed to the fall. However, for people in much of the rest of the world, condoms remained expensive and were of little use in those places where you needed to have more children to ensure your own survival into old age. Over time, though, as spreading knowledge and lower subjugation meant that survival, literacy and emancipation rates rose, contraception increasingly grew in acceptance and importance.

Our third billion was achieved in just 34 years. We hit three billion in 1960, fittingly the year of the contraceptive pill. The pill became available in the USA just as the population numbered roughly 3,038,795,000 people. Our fourth billion came very shortly after, in just 15 years. Those of us who were alive added up to 4,076,419,000 people. This was in 1975. For the first time my beating heart meant that I added one to the count. But there is almost no time to stop and celebrate. Our fifth billion came even faster; we were estimated to be a total of 5,084,974,000 people by 1988, just 13 years later. No wonder we were worried.

A billion in 34 years, another in 15 years, then another in just 13 years, and the next would come even faster again. Where would all these people fit in? How would they be fed? Wouldn't they all fight? Would they want what we had? Would they start off in slums and then spill out into the suburbs? Scientists began to take note. In 1968, a husband and wife wrote a book called *The Population Bomb*, forecasting mass starvation in the 1970s and 1980s. I take the book personally, as I was born in 1968 and don't think that I, or anyone else, was one human too many. Their predictions were wrong but their spirit lived on. 'If not now, then soon' became their mantra.[5]

The science of slums

> One of the most fascinating yet elusive aspects of cultural change is the way certain ideals and arguments acquire an almost self-evident power at particular times, just as others come to seem irrelevant or antiquated and largely disappear from public debate . . . As with changes in the use of language generally, readers and listeners become inured to what were once jarring neologisms or solecisms, while phrases that were once so common as to escape notice become in time unusable.
>
> Stephan Collini, Professor of English,
> Cambridge, 2011[6]

The 'population bomb' is a solecism, a grammatical mistake, an absurdity. In 1968 it was a neologism, a newly coined phrase or doctrine; today it appears antiquated as a term. Now simply 'population' without the suffix 'bomb' has a self-evident power. We should be 'concerned about population', we are told. No longer scared out of our wits, as any sane person would be about a bomb, but concerned.

We became scared. We hit six billion in just 12 years, during the year 2000. To be a little more precise, it was announced (by the statisticians relied upon for the figures used here) that there were 6,071,144,000 of us at that point. Later, their revised estimates suggested that we had actually hit that magic number earlier and that by 2000 we numbered 6,122,770,000 people; we just had not known it. Was this due to cataclysmic growth? One sign that it might be was that by then around one in six of us, some 927 million souls, were living in slums.[7]

A simple observer who just looked at the totals would conclude that if human population growth were to continue at the pre-millennial rate of acceleration, then by 2050 there would be 13 billion of us; by 2100, 44 billion; by 2200, some 1,775 billion and by 2300, some 133,592 billion. As you know by now (especially if you've been looking at the endnotes), I haven't been making these numbers up; they are the 'constant projection' of the United Nations.

The UN produce their multibillion ridiculous figures partly to illustrate that what humans have just experienced is the equivalent to what happens when sewage floods a sea and there is an algal bloom, a rapid growth in algae. The 133 billion is what would happen if we were algae floating on an almost endless newly nutrient-rich ocean, but humans are not algae, and our growth in numbers is slowing down.

We are slowing because we have to; it is simply that we are only just starting to see it and are surprised to find this slowdown happening without a grand plan. Those of us who think we are particularly clever and needed, those of us who understand ideas such as parabolas and derivatives, ask ourselves conceitedly: how did this happen without our help?

In the decade to the year 2000 there was a significant change in what's called the second derivative of population. Imagine you throw a cricket ball straight up into the air. Before it begins to fall back to earth, it has to slow down, and before it can begin to slow down, it has to decelerate.

When it comes to a cricket ball, it is from the point that it leaves your hand that it starts to decelerate. When it comes to human beings, that point, the time at which the speeding up stopped, even though the total population continued to rise, was 1971, though that only started to become clear in the dozen years up to 1989. And so it was not until the 1990s that the first reports of optimism were released to an unbelieving world.

Before the 1990s, doom-mongering was normal. The world had good reason not to believe that a positive turning point was being reached. When you have just added a billion people in a dozen years or less, on top of another billion added in the 13 years before that, you get slums, you get fears of pandemic, you get films like *Silent Running* (1972), and you get a great many reports of the growth of shanty towns spreading out of control, and of dystopian *Blade Runner* (1982) scenarios.

My favourite dystopian movie is *Mad Max Beyond Thunderdome* (1985); this was followed by films such as *They Live* (1988), which 'echoed contemporary fears of a declining economy, within a culture of greed and conspicuous consumption common among Americans'.[8] Soon after 1988, I stopped going to the cinema so much – I had a PhD to write – but hopefully you get the idea from this little list. Towards the end of the twentieth century, the end of times was a recurring theme.

To counter a childhood when we were dosed with a diet of doom, it is worth beginning with the strongest evidence first. Evidence, that is, that all is not lost. This evidence concerns how poor is the record of those who forecast doom. The greatest failure came when the Reverend Thomas Robert Malthus wrote that essay claiming that the end was nigh when it came to the ultimate results of human population growth.

Malthus had little chance of realizing the significance, but he was writing 300 years after the demographic shock of the discovery of the Americas, and the data he was looking at reflected a great deal of the influence of that event.[9] He had studied the population record of the larger part of just one small island (England), and determined that people would carry on multiplying like flies until they starved to death or killed each other in search of food. He was writing only as recently as when my great-grandfather's great-grandmother was alive, and he was proved wrong not long after I was born. He was not just wrong because he lacked imagination; he also cheated. It is now known that he even made up the correlation he used to try to suggest causation.[10]

Even writers who have some sympathy for Malthus, the ones who have read all the various revisions he made to his original essay, are prone to believe that there was something within the man that led him to pessimism: Lloyd T. Evans, one of the world's best-known plant physiologists, suggested in 1998 that 'Many projections of future world food supplies tell us more about the innate optimism or pessimism of the projectors, as expressed in the critical assumptions, than about what will actually happen. Moreover, the uncertainty principle may operate in that what eventually does happen may be influenced by policies adopted on the basis of economic projections.'[11]

Other commentators have been less kind. Malthus's intervention has been described as akin to something like a '200-year war against welfare'.[12] He wrote six versions of his essay, the first in 1798 and the last in 1826, substantially changing its message as he revised it.[13] Sadly, the damage, huge damage, was done by the first draft. If it had not been Malthus, it would have been some other fool, but throughout this period he remained wedded to

111

the idea that population could only be checked by famine, disease or war; that European society was not improving; that most people were not of great value, and that without strict oversight from members of the clergy such as himself, others were unable to control their sexual urges. He had issues.

It was the sexual hang-ups of an economist of the cloth that resulted in ideas of population control making their political debut in early-nineteenth-century Britain. The Malthusian theory of population growth gave Britain's rising middle class exactly the moral insulation it needed to defend its selfishness. Terrible poverty was just about to tear through the country during the economic slump and the restructuring that followed the Napoleonic Wars of 1803–15. Two decades further on, and 'Malthus's arguments were used to drive through the New Poor Law of 1834, which attempted to imprison in the workhouse anyone improvident enough to claim welfare. The workhouse system took decades to dismantle, and it presaged in some detail today's anti-immigrant system: notably its distinction between "deserving and undeserving", and its parallel, unaccountable, cut-price policing and judicial system.'[14]

In the country of Malthus's birth and work, England, there is currently an attempt to reintroduce the old Poor Law, with local worthies deciding what assistance the poor are entitled to. There is also widespread antipathy towards immigrants; it is common to hear that England, in particular of all of the countries of the UK, is 'full up'. All this dates back to ideas first promulgated by the Reverend Malthus.

Could we – and were we foolish enough to – resurrect him, Thomas Malthus might be less shocked at finding himself alive than at finding himself alongside so many other living people and so many living so well. He would be most shocked to know that we are currently having so few children. He would be stunned to hear that if this fall in fertility carries on much longer, there is no reason to believe that the human population won't soon fall, and that this is, in fact, what many United Nations demographers believe. He might also be a little taken aback about there being a United Nations, based in New York!

That the first population fall without a disaster is coming is as near to a demographic certainty as it is possible to get. Across the globe today the average family consists of two parents and three children. Global average family size has never been so small and is falling rapidly. Already, across over half the peoples of the planet, it is now normal to have fewer than two children per woman. People can and do control their urges to have children.

Malthus lacked the imagination to see it, and even had he been endowed with such powers, he was in no position to know how widespread and advanced contraception would become. He also had a problem with thinking about sex. He believed that too much of it resulted in revolution. After all, what else could have led (in his mind) to the turmoil in France and the revolution there, the one that was taking place just as he was drafting the first version of the first edition of his now far too famous essay? It was as much an essay on his fantasies about French men and women as about anything to do with most people, or science, or population.[15]

What Malthus could also not easily have foreseen was the ascendancy of women. His puritanical views labelled women simply as temptresses, the first being Eve with her apple. It is largely because women have become more powerful and better educated, and have stood up to men like Malthus, that the central projections of United

Nations demographers are for the average future family unit of today's children to be made up of two adults and two children. This is how the fall in fertility will result in slowdown in the affluent world and how the fall will continue, through women gaining greater equality with men.

More women in future will have no children than will have four or more. Fewer will have three children than have one. But we don't have to wait long to see that fall; it is already here in the richest countries of the world and has been with us for some time. Most of our thinking lags behind our recent sex lives.

Malthusian thinking is the science of slums. It sees in the rise of poverty and squalor evidence for Armageddon. This is evidence not just that poverty will always be with us, but that it will always grow as people breed. Such thinking includes no space to understand that there will come a day soon, maybe just within our lifetimes, when the first minute will pass in which more people die than are born that day, the first minute ever when this was not due to catastrophic disaster, mass famine or global epidemic, population falls not attributable to a Malthusian logic.

It is because of the novelty of the coming population stability that up to now in this book the story has repeatedly travelled back in time to consider the last few falls, or other omens, in order to try to appreciate just how different this time could be. The point that needs to be made most clear is that when the first non-Malthusian population fall occurs, everything changes. A new demographic transition will have taken place. Much of how we now live is a feature of the transition, including our slums, which are halfway houses for migrants travelling from the countryside to the city.

If you see aspects of a transition as normal, then the poor will always be with us and demographic growth will only be checked by disaster. If you see change as business as usual, then the slums will continue to grow. Science works by observing that certain regularities are reoccurring. Science works better when it determines within what range those regularities are normal. A narrow science of the human condition is a science of slums. A wider science sees that the mechanical laws of our current times need not apply to the new epoch that is just beginning.

Migration and consumption

> Virtually all this growth will go into metropolitan areas. Much of the increase, of course, will come directly from big cities themselves, because big cities are no longer eaters of people as they were not so long ago.
>
> Jane Jacobs, writer and activist, 1962[16]

Industrial revolution led to precariousness. Cities sucked in labour and spilled out death. All cities at this time were cities of slums. They relied on the countryside and continued in-migration for their stock of human labour. As cities grew during industrialization, infant and child mortality rates reached heights that had not previously been measured, partly due to overcrowding and disease, but also due to measurement initially being an urban phenomenon. The concentration of plague deaths within cities led to bills (paper records) of mortality being first collected.

To understand the era we are living through, and why people move where they do, we need to better understand consumerism. It is sometimes claimed that the basis of the Industrial Revolution was a new consumerism. However, the existence of novelties to consume required migration to the new tea and sugar plantations of people both to run them and to work in them. It is worth bearing in mind this migration, much of it forced, when reading accounts of an apparently virtuous feedback loop coming into effect. Historians trying to produce a credible argument for why England became the richest part of Europe have suggested that it was 'English manufactures like books and clocks and imports like sugar and tea [which] gave people the desire to earn income',[17] but this is an odd argument.

The argument continues by suggesting that to buy the new goods, people in England decided that they would work longer hours to secure more income; that it was only in the ancient world that men were 'forced to labour because they were slaves to others; [in England] men are now forced to labour because they are slaves to their own wants'. But of course the English used indentured labour and slaves to produce the tea and sugar, and many child labourers to make manufactured goods more cheaply.

Although the new consumerism of the seventeenth century was not sufficient to explain economic progress, according to this school of history, which often lauds the Protestant religion as part of the explanation, it was apparently necessary. This was because consumerism led to a frenetic pursuit of income to buy those novel consumer goods. Many of the goods were imported from abroad. Luxury goods then became global goods, and this is claimed to be the cultural basis of the Industrial Revolution, and the start of widening globalization. An alternative view sees it as partly the rise of waste that always results when imbalances in power emerge and the victors become greedier. And while that new greed might have been necessary to raise wealth in Europe, so was slave migration to the Americas.

Growing population numbers made consumerism possible, as there were always more younger labourers than older savers, and a surfeit of youngsters also promotes migration. Demographers especially enjoy suggesting that there are mechanical laws to patterns of migration, and it does often look as if particular laws, or some kind of social physics, are at work when you study migration flows. However, what appear to be laws are often just the averaging of trends; millions of people each making partly constrained choices and millions of others being forced to move between places.

The number of freely choosing migrants that arrive in a country depends partly on the conditions they start from and whether those where they end up are more or less hospitable. More push factors cause more to leave, greater distance and difficulty will cause fewer to travel, and more pull factors and enough space to stay will cause more to come and more to stay.[18] Thus people spread out.

Global population reached six billion by the millennium largely because Europe's excess population did not die of famine or disease but were exported as overseas migrants and multiplied there. They also took with them the knowledge of what was needed to result in such rapid human increase. This included the spreading of public health measures to reduce mortality, but also the reduction of precariousness, the enclosure of land and the overturning of established social conventions around the world.

Colonization destroyed old mechanisms and conventions whereby population control had become established, often through late marriage or as a result of many men, and a few women, never marrying, but living in monasteries and convents. The second great demographic transition spread out from Europe, along with people, their ideas, and the overturning of thousands of ancient civilizations.

When it comes to migration, Europe is now best known for trying to stop migrants coming in. Passports are just a hundred years old. Only a few odd places like Russia had them over a century ago, and then only for internal security, to control movement within the country. Already passports are being rolled back. Across most of Europe, once you are within Europe, they are not required. Europe is a space of free movement of labour.

To get into the UK, a few favoured nations – Australia, Canada, New Zealand, the US and Japan – are being given special fast lanes at Heathrow.[19] Of course this is racism thinly disguised by allowing the Japanese in fast too, but it is also a relaxing of controls. The population movement control explosion, from 1914 through to the present day, is a result of the population explosion and should be assumed to be a temporary feature of global population control, one which will ebb as our numbers ebb.

There are very strong incentives within many affluent nations to relax population controls, as the Figure below shows, redrawn from a graph produced by the UK's Office for Budgetary Responsibility (OBR). Increased migration into countries like the UK would help reduce current debts, and also help in caring for a growing elderly population. It would also reduce global population growth faster than even the current very fast rate of growth slowdown. That is because young migrants from poorer countries who move to countries like the UK tend to have fewer children than they would have had had they not migrated.

Although many other factors will influence the future level of public sector debt in the UK, increased immigration reduces debt, while emigration of younger adults from Britain will increase it. One school of thought promoted to try to explain why the USA charges its young people so highly to attend university, to be later paid back as a debt, is that those debts can be collected even if the young Americans subsequently leave the USA, should they ever wish to return. Student debt cannot even be cancelled by declaring bankruptcy. The same is true in the UK, although it is a smaller place and so the student loan body projects a higher rate of default, as it is likely that fewer of those who leave will come back.[20]

Public sector debt (% of GDP)
Variant population projections

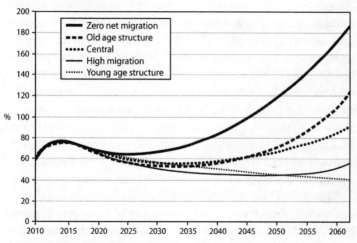

Source: OBR Fiscal Sustainability Report 2012.

Put in economist speak:

> Figures from the Office for Budget Responsibility illustrate that zero net migration would itself (independent of the policies needed to achieve it) have negative fiscal consequences in the short and long

term. Under a zero net migration scenario it estimates that within the next five decades public debt would double to nearly 200 per cent of GDP compared to the expected level of debt under current policy. By contrast, in a high migration scenario the OBR predicts that the long-term health of the public finances would dramatically improve, without the need for reforms to either taxation or public spending.[21]

Demographers have been suggesting that we should continue to expect migration to partly balance out fertility and mortality disparities for some years to come. In effect, just as migration helped stoke up the population explosion, it could also come to help dampen it down far faster than would otherwise occur. This is because 'demographic and economic differentials will continue to operate far beyond the year 2050 to promote, for example, migration from regions like West Asia and North Africa to regions like Europe and North America'.[22] And as those migratory moves happen, the fertility rates of those who migrate will fall faster than they otherwise would be expected to.

When world population hit six billion, there was large-scale migration from poorer and younger regions to richer and older ones. Such migration evens out age structures a little and further dampens fertility, both within and between countries. It also provides work for some of the current bulge of young people in North Africa and parts of Asia. But how great might migration in the future be? Well, how great was it by 2000?

Migration has tended to be at the whim of those with the most power, either to expel excess population, as Europe did for many centuries, or to coerce additional slave labour to the Americas, or to bring in people to Europe when they are needed and to try to slam the door shut when they are said to be no longer required. As geographical balances of power alter, so too the direction of these pushes and pulls will alter.

We find it very hard to imagine today, but in the not too distant future people may be trying to leave Europe again. As François Héran, who became president of the European Association for Population Studies in 1998, put it in 2004:

> In three centuries, anything can happen in the area of migration, including (as incongruous as it may appear today) major migratory movements from North to South, the reverse of current flows, linked to new forms of development cooperation. If the South develops around a few countries or a few major population areas, it may well polarize an immigration originating from the North, bringing transfers of technology and training. This assumption is consistent with the fact that migration continues to be controlled by countries in a dominant position, regardless of the direction of the flow.[23]

Whether particular countries will have such dominant economic positions as they do today depends on whether the world in future becomes more economically equal or unequal. Inequality tends to breed fear and mistrust. It separates peoples, and when inequalities are high, racism, mixed with a fear of other religions, tends to grow. For example, currently there is a fear in some quarters of Europe that a Muslim influx is under way. In fact only 3 per cent of Muslims live in richer regions of the world, 'that is to say, around 40 million out of its total of 1.2 billion people'.[24] However, a fifth of all people in the world are Muslim, and 97 per cent of them live among the poor majority of the world. So, is the rich world about to see an influx of Muslims from the poor world?

Understanding current demographic trends helps mitigate some of the fear which is currently so widespread and which in particular places is spreading. When you study the facts, you find that in almost all 'of the Muslim-majority countries and territories, however, significant or dramatic reductions in fertility have been registered – and in many of these places, the drops in question have been truly extraordinary'.[25] In other words the demographic slowdown is even faster among Muslims than among almost any other religious group. Muslims may also be making the transition towards cities fastest as a result.

Demography and deniers

> Despite alarmist predictions, historical increases in population have not been economically catastrophic. Moreover, changes in population age structure have opened the door to increased prosperity.
>
> David Bloom, Professor of Economics
> and Demography, Harvard, July 2011[26]

Used vindictively, 'denier' can be a nasty label. It implies that whoever has been accused of being a denier not only does not understand the truth but is actively seeking to subvert it. 'Demography denier' would be an easy alliterative label to apply to a person like David E. Bloom, the chair of Harvard University's Department of Global Health and Population, when he explains that many population predictions have been alarmist. But it would be an unfair assertion.

When David explains that changes to age structure have opened the door to increases in productivity, he is implicitly referring to modern-day China and how, by the millennium, the number of adults needed to care for young children was so low because so few children had been born in the previous decades. One result of this has been a rapid increase in both the proportion and the number of adults who can work; a one-shot economic acceleration. China could subsequently sustain low fertility at a much higher level of both national wealth and economic security.

Such talk of pragmatic progress can lead those who fear our current population growth to propose that the advocates of arguments suggesting we are not doomed are part of some conspiracy of silence, contributing to imminent catastrophe through not realizing the enormity of the true crisis ahead. This suggestion is repeated endlessly in various subtle and less subtle ways. One of the conclusions of a symposium held in London in March 2010 was that 'We won't find the answers . . . if we remain complicit in the silence about population.'

It was at this symposium that the Ugandan Minister of Finance and Planning, the Honourable Professor Ephraim Kamuntu, felt he needed to point out to the audience that '. . . the developing world contributes the least greenhouse gas emissions, that they will be most affected by climate change, and that they are least able to deal with the negative effects'. He was then, in effect, rebuked by the keynote speaker, Jonathan Porritt, son of the former colonial governor of New Zealand, who '. . . reminded the audience that we need to get beyond the "crass" consumption versus population debate'.[27] But Kamuntu was right and Porritt was wrong. What is crass about explaining that it is consumption, not population, that matters, and why does Porritt either not appear to understand that, or not want us to understand it? Does he want a world with fewer people but where a minority can still consume very highly, in place of the thousands who don't exist?

Suggesting that consumption and population both matter is identical to suggesting that when it comes to murder, both violence and population matter. The higher a level of violence you have, the more murders you get, and simultaneously, the more people you have, the more murders you get, as there are more people available to murder. This is simply stupid. Murder rates fall in countries where levels of violence fall, even as population rises. Our rate of murder, if the number of holes in ancient human skulls is any indication, was highest in our distant past. Most of us have never been as peaceful as we are today. Anything can be suggested to be linked to population numbers simply by producing the following form of equation:

$$\text{Murder} = \text{violence\_rate} \times \text{population}$$

Where:

$$\text{Violence\_rate} = \text{murder} \div \text{population}$$

Which is the murder rate, so:

$$\text{Murder} = (\text{murder} \div \text{population}) \times \text{population}$$

And thus the more people you have, the more are murdered.

But that is not true, and it is similarly not true that the human environmental impact on the planet is a product of the number of humans. Proponents of population scare stories say that as every extra human must consume something, this argument does not apply to consumption. You cannot have a negative consumption rate for a person. However, the same is true of murder. You cannot have a negative murder rate for a group, but some extra people can help others to murder less, just as some extra people can teach others to consume less and hence reduce consumption overall, even as population rises.

It is not easy to teach others and yourself to consume less, just as it is not easy to preach non-violence. However, as human societies have grown and become more complex, they have also become less violent internally even while sometimes becoming more violent abroad.[28] It may be partly because of our increased density within cities that we have learned to live together better. We had to. Similarly we have to learn to consume less. Our greater density is helping make this more apparent. It is harder to use landfill to dispose of waste when you have less empty land.

You do not need extra people to do the teaching, but without that teaching, you may be doomed. However, teaching is not that easy and learning can be even harder. We have finite supplies of many of the resources we need. Even substitution and technology may struggle to plug the gaps. In fact it may be something as simple as soil erosion that causes the greatest future headaches, but without teaching and learning we know none of this. We have no chance.

As world population hurtled towards six billion, those who did the simplest of mathematics panicked that the train appeared unstoppable; if not the population train, then the ever-accelerating consumption train. Surely reducing our numbers faster would help alleviate this growth in our consumption of food, soil, fossil fuels, rare materials, and everything else that might soon be in short supply?

It is often suggested that only 'climate change deniers' cannot see that we have too many people. At the turn of the millennium, it was predicted that by 2011 there would be 135 million human births in the world and only 57 million deaths. This figure of some 78 million more souls in just 12 months was frequently converted into a list of countries it was equivalent to. However, during 2011, a leading article in *Science* magazine would repeat these figures but also point out that it was by then obvious that deceleration was rapid, and that the brakes had been put on some time ago. More importantly, that article implied, there was some evidence that much of the recent rampant overproduction and consumption was also linked to the demographic transition, and hence might itself be transitory.[29]

Demographic optimists and those who doubt the importance of recent climate change are not groups that overlap much. Climate change doubters, a far better term than deniers, tend to be led by right-wing politicians and people with financial interests in the oil industry, backed up by what have been described as

scientists whose reputations in the scientific mainstream never amounted to much, or whose early career successes faded away. Disappointed by the lack of recognition, they may have chosen to make a new 'mark' by taking a different, far more publicly visible, path. Resentment over lack of mainstream success may also help to explain why these commentaries so often have a strident tone that mocks those with different views in a way that has no resemblance to the style of legitimate science.[30]

In contrast, pragmatic possibilists, who do not see current population growth as a great problem, tend to be quiet, not mocking, and to write very long and interesting books that patiently explain what is going on.[31]

One problem with criticizing the opposition through mockery is that they tend to throw your insults back at you. An argument about being properly scientific runs through this debate. However, often participants in the debate reveal their true natures by asides they cannot help making. Recently a British report by those on the rational optimist side began in one of the most partisan ways possible, taking a sideswipe at the whole of the welfare state in its argument on the need to reduce pollution: 'Government plans to combat man-made global warming are perhaps the most costly programme since the introduction of the Welfare State – over £17,000 per household.'

Nick Stern's review of the economics of climate change was widely praised when it was published in 2006. It claimed that climate change is the worst-case market failure ever recorded, and it was this casting doubt on the efficiency of markets that most annoyed Stern's critics. The rational optimists' report goes on to suggest that farmers in places like India will adapt rapidly to global warming, so that 'Stern's approach has been called "the dumb farmer hypothesis"'. On future water stress, these particular climate change doubters suggest that what they term 'Stern's selective quotation of the results might be called "the gullible reader assumption" . . . his analysis is largely based on the work of Professor Arnell, whose study does . . . not include adaptation'.[32]

The more mocking critics of climate change become, the more I am tempted to believe people like Sir Nicholas Stern, who was the head of the UK Government Economic Service. This is despite my having little time for knighthoods or economists. Stern's critics complain too much and so make this reader, at least, suspect their motives. The foreword to the critical report these examples are drawn from claims that the 'Stern Review was a tactical masterstroke, but it will likely prove to be a strategic blunder. Its academic value is zero.'[33] I've rarely seen economists suggest something has a value of zero: very small, yes, but zero? Stern got the rational optimists worried, perhaps because he was pointing out fundamental flaws in their models, the models that suggest that never-ending growth is our only escape route.

Increased economic growth may partly be a result of what occurs during great demographic transitions to lower fertility. Adults, especially women, can work more at toil that is given an economic value when they have fewer children. From the origins of Ireland's rapid economic growth and then economic burnout being traceable to the legalization of birth control in that country in the early 1980s, through to a massive one third of economic growth in all of Asia being linked to the demographic transition in the east of that continent between 1965 and 1990, it is not just that people become far more economically productive when they have fewer children, but that they can produce far too much. All this overproduction is unlikely to be a prolonged situation.

The speed of current change is hard to grasp because things are now changing so quickly. Ireland's economic growth, as fertility declined, culminated in by far the largest financial crash of any Western European country. According to 2007–10 IMF (International Monetary Fund) figures, the rise in public spending required to bail out Ireland's banks was greater than that measured anywhere else by that institution.[34] The population began to emigrate again. Ireland is thought to be the only island in the world to be home to fewer people in the twenty-first century (6.5 million in 2011) than during the middle of the nineteenth century (8 million in 1841). The reason is famine.

Famine still scares. But even the climate-change-doubting

128

son of a former Conservative chancellor is wary of those who tell us to fear future famines:

> There is an increasingly noisy claque of Malthusians who insist that an 'exploding' global population (as they put it) is going to lead to disaster – from Boris Johnson to Joanna Lumley, not to mention Jeremy Irons and Prince Charles. For example, last weekend *The Independent* published a lengthy interview with the Bermuda-based philanthropist James Martin, who has given Oxford University $125m to set up a forecasting institute in his name. Mr Martin's own forecast is that 'by mid-century we're going to be using the term "giga-famine", meaning a famine where more than a billion people will die, a catastrophe on a scale that's never been known before on Earth'.[35]

The great Irish famine was really the British famine. Ireland was part of Britain at the time, a colony but with MPs, although no Catholics could sit in the House of Commons. It was the British who prevented the famine from being alleviated and the British who allowed grain to be shipped out of Ireland even when the potato harvest repeatedly failed.

If there is a giga-famine in the middle of this century, it will only be because those with power act in the same way. To act in the same way, they will have to see others as less human than themselves. It is hard to think how this will happen unless hedge-fund morality becomes the norm and betting on future food prices is not curtailed. Most Protestants in Britain no longer view Catholics in the way their great-great-grandparents did. Hopefully we have learnt a little since 1841, not least from the famine in Ireland. However, British diplomats are still accused of mocking the victims by not attending annual memorials to the famine, unlike American and Australian ambassadors to Ireland.[36]

It is not just the English who need a better understanding of their colonial pasts. In many parts of the world today a kind of colonization of the poor is taking place. Researchers who want to deny that social inequality is a great and growing global issue like to suggest that growing economic inequalities will somehow soon naturally result in a trickle-down of riches from above. The nastiest Conservatives still imply that the poorest simply don't deserve to exist, just as their predecessors regarded most of the Irish in the 1840s as expendable, and just as they are not concerned about future potential victims of the human-created and unalleviated environmental disasters that could result from climate change. Underlying all of this is a problematic acceptance of social inequality and a denial (a doubt if we are being kinder) that inequality between humans is quite as toxic as it is.[37]

People who doubt that social inequality is a great problem can become exasperated when they cannot convince others of their views. When they find that their opinions are generally regarded as abhorrent and they cannot publish them in refereed journals, some turn to writing for right-wing think tanks and discover that they could in just a few weeks 'knock out reports that would be presented at high-level meetings . . . and earnestly discussed in the press and in radio interviews. [They say] It was exhilarating to find an audience.'[38] Although it might be exhilarating for the former academic involved, it can be highly confusing for those who have to listen to half-formed ideas knocked out in a couple of weeks by someone who does not understand when their peers repeatedly tell them that there is a problem with what they are proposing.

Social inequality creates problems. One that is least recognized is that the persistence of inequality requires a reliance on future economic growth to give those at the bottom something to hope for. Living standards at the bottom will never be seen as adequate while great inequalities prevail. Growth is offered as a panacea, but how much growth is possible?

Carrying capacity

> This market society seems to have obliterated from most people's memory another world that once placed limits on growth, stressed cooperation over competition, and valued the gift as a bond of human solidarity.
>
> Murray Bookchin,
'Death of a Small Planet', 1989[39]

Carrying capacity is an old concept and usually a highly objectionable one when it comes to talking about humans in small spaces. It makes much more sense when it comes to talking about how much energy we each might consume and have access to. Related to space, or the Nazi *Lebensraum*, it equates people to animals farmed under intensive conditions at levels at which introducing an extra animal into the cage results in less meat being produced. This is no way to treat animals, including people. Even our most numerous mammalian cousins, bats, have their numbers limited by energy supply (food), not space (roost).[40] All mammals are animals which fill niches, but rarely are those niches overfilled, because there is a sustainable level of energy intake for any species.

During the 1950s, the obsession that people were

multiplying too fast began to take spectral form again. It had been dampened by the low fertility of the 1930s and then by the global war of the 1940s. In 1958, the Disney Corporation released a film, *White Wilderness*, which purported to show thousands of lemmings, small rodents, hurling themselves off cliffs. The word lemming has come to mean 'a person who unthinkingly joins a mass movement, especially a headlong rush to destruction', or a member of a crowd with no originality or voice of his own; 'one who speaks or repeats only what he has been told'.

Today it is not hard to see how, during the 1950s, as they were trying to understand why communism was spreading, and to warn against what they believed were its dangers, American media corporations such as Disney might produce films purporting to portray nature but which were really more of a hidden warning about possible mass human behaviour.

It is depressing, but it may be useful to consider who behaves in the most lemming-like way today. Here, as examples, are some extracts from the stories written by three sports clothes shop (Adidas) employees to gain themselves a chance to carry the Olympic torch around Britain. The first said they deserved to carry the torch because they had 'made a fantastic contribution to the Adidas group business'. Apparently the second 'breathes Adidas . . . Her positive attitude and "money in [the] till" approach is legendary', while a third was a worthy Olympic torch bearer because of 'achieving my sales targets in every market I have worked in'.[41] Trying to sell people as much clothing as you can, clothing that they almost always do not need, but which they can be trained to want because of the label, is one way of contributing, in a lemming-like manner, to exceeding our energy-carrying capacity. But this is unfair to lemmings.

132

Lemmings don't throw themselves off cliffs or reproduce to such levels that the carrying capacity of their area is exceeded and they find themselves squeezed over the edges of the abyss. To be able to film the most famous sequence in *White Wilderness*, the camera crew purchased some baby lemmings from Inuit children, placed them on a snow-covered turntable and then filmed them as if they were herding together. Next they took the baby lemmings to a cliff and forced them to jump into the water below it as they filmed.

A report by an Australian broadcaster found the lemming fabrication explicable in that it was more dramatic than the truth: 'The cliff-death-plunge sequence was done by herding the lemmings over a small cliff into a river. It's easy to understand why the filmmakers did this – wild animals are notoriously uncooperative, and a migration-of-doom followed by a cliff-of-death sequence is far more dramatic to show than the lemmings' self-implemented population-density management plan.'[42] Just like James Martin's predictions of the mid-century giga-famine to come, migration-of-doom is so much more interesting than the far more probable truth. But the probable truth matters most. Let's go back to Australia again, not because it was there that the lemming libel was exposed, but because it has a lot of space.

Australia is an interesting place to study to observe human fears of overpopulation. It is odd to hear of fears of crowding on such a very large and sparsely populated island. However, as always, it is not how many people there are but what those people do that matters. In Australia, a tiny number of people extracting huge amounts of coal from under the ground can be far more environmentally harmful than a million living more carefully. But millions living carefully cannot make a few people rich.

I've visited Australia only once, in 1995, for a conference on 'Computers in Urban Planning and Urban Management', back when some of us thought we only had to program our way out of trouble. I was driven around Melbourne, out past what appeared to be never-ending rows of detached homes each sitting in their own unsustainable garden, each requiring so much driving time into the city that I could stop feeling guilty over having flown almost halfway round the world just to go to a conference of fellow nerds. We finally reached the city limits, where they were still building new very low-density, very water-needy housing. It was as if everyone wanted their own swimming pool.

Fifteen years on, and even further out from the centre of Melbourne urban sprawl has continued almost unabated. The billboards for property developments such as 'Renaissance Rise' and 'Woodland Waters' have beneath them, as one contemporary commentator on the ground put it,

> luxuriant fronds of fake green grass. Irony is not a characteristic of real estate promotion, but I had to wonder if a tongue was firmly in a cheek when the copywriter came up with the line on the next billboard: 'Kiss the urban sprawl goodbye' . . . A friendly salesman extolled the virtues of country life – though he admitted to living further west, in Sunbury, along another of Melbourne's stretching suburban fingers. 'It's much safer than the inner-city,' he said. 'There is no crime, no theft, no need to lock your door.' (I refrained from asking him why all the display homes were equipped with burglar alarms.)[43]

Maybe the alarms are there in anticipation that these areas will become more 'inner-city' as the sprawl goes on and on?

In some ways, standards of living in Melbourne have deteriorated in the last two years. On 3 October 2012, the city's entire road system appeared to shut down due to too much traffic and computer software crashing on the control systems of some road tunnels. The government's response was to say that they needed to build another road across the city. A caller to the local radio station explained, instead: 'Each time we look for the basic cause of these problems, and the basic cause is the suburban sprawl.'[44] What is changing in places like Melbourne is that today, it is callers to radio shows who can explain the problem. Seventeen years earlier, it was a few town planners with early computer models who were suggesting that all might not be well.

As Peter Mares, the contemporary commentator from 2010, put it when talking about Mernda, the most recently built outlying Melbourne suburb:

> The problem is not so much the escalation of our numbers but the escalation of our wants. Growing up in a house with only one bathroom did not mean my childhood was deprived. My parents were not unhappy because they lacked an ensuite and a walk-in robe. The average floor area of new homes increased by 40 per cent between the mid-1980s and the early 2000s, even though the average number of people per household fell sharply during the same period. Our homes are now the largest in the world, though the blocks they cover are no larger. Mernda, in the aptly named Plenty Valley, is just one of many sites of collision between our growing numbers and our ever-inflating aspirations for 'lifestyle without compromise'.[45]

Just two years later, the citizens of Mernda found that the roads to downtown Melbourne were blocked with all the other commuters' cars. Australia shows how, even in the most spacious of lands, it is possible to quickly exhaust carrying capacity by asking the land to carry us, our cars, gardens, en suites, walk-in wardrobes and idylls of living far apart from each other in a way that cannot work. What went wrong in Australia was too little value given to time, and an overconsumption of energy.

We work out ways of living sustainably over time. We almost always have. If we don't, we don't survive. We think we know this from Easter Island[46] stories of the few places where we were too negligent and there was no turning back, but mostly there is still time to turn back, still time to change. Too many people came too quickly to the urban fringe of Australia with too many ideas of each satisfying their own individual wishes and wants. A minority preyed on that majority, bought up land on the outskirts, planted the fake grass and printed the brochures with the swimming pools on the front. Now the majority have to work out how to fix their cities.

Australia is far from being the island that causes most concern when it comes to issues of possible overpopulation, although it is often islands which are the cause célèbre of the carrying capacity crowd. One writer who also observed how this began in earnest as a Cold War Disney-fuelled obsession recently tried to explain what he was up against: 'Someone who Googles overpopulation in 2011 will find near 2.5 million sites to visit, about 750,000 images to see, close to 325,000 blogs in which to participate, near 55,000 articles to read, around 5,000 youtube.com style videos to watch, and almost 400 books to buy. Far from being a unique 20th-century obsession spurred by Cold War imperatives, concerns of overpopulation still inspire many contemporary political and scientific debates.'[47]

Issues of the earth's potential human carrying capacity came to the fore during the Cold War, culminating in 1968 in the forming of the Club of Rome, 'a global networking of independent . . . and renowned thinkers', which by 2012 wishes to encourage debate that will result in '. . . actions that by the middle of the century will ensure a more secure, equitable and prosperous world'.[48] The Club of Rome, perhaps staffed these days by more students of 1968, has grown up and now puts the need for greater equality between issues of security and prosperity.

To say that old-fashioned carrying capacity was a Cold War fear of apparently 'swarming' and rapidly multiplying 'Asians' does not mean that we do not have to be concerned about how much material and energy we use, just not by how much we use from a particular territory. The key point is that we should not be too obsessed about where the material we use comes from, but more concerned about how little we can use with the least energy being expelled in using it. It is fortunate that the majority of humans are now crowded into cities into which their food is sent. We should be obsessed with whether our per capita use is falling and whether our crowding may even be helping those falls in consumption. Above all else, when people crowd into cities, they tend to give birth to fewer new people.

It does not matter if the coal we burn was originally deposited directly under our feet, or a very long way under our feet, in what is now Australia. What matters is that some of us have been burning too much of it. Coal is a global resource. It does not stop being coal when you ship it from one place to another. What matters is global carrying energy, material and pollution capacity, not the land areas of Australia, Asia, the Americas, Africa or Europe.

We have what we now think of as an instinct, a feeling in our guts that what is on our continent is somehow ours, but there is nothing at all instinctive about this. It is learnt and taught. Put a map of your country up on classroom walls and children will, over time, come to subconsciously see that map as part of their identity. This happens in the USA. Fly the European Union flag over public buildings in Europe, outside of the UK, and more people come to see themselves as European, and others as being from outside.

The promotion of feelings of nationalism and common ownership of a nation state is not in the interests of most people within any territory, but always helps strengthen the position of a few. However, not since nation states were formed have we had so many people unwilling to fight and die for their country as we have today. We have never had so many who see themselves as citizens of a wider world. Many of us are learning and teaching differently to much of what we were once taught ourselves.

There is new scope for hope; many consumption peaks may be being scaled. For instance, in the first depths of the current financial crisis, and for the first time measured globally, remittances declined by $20 billion between 2008 and 2009. Less money being transferred from rich nations to poor nations has an immediate harmful effect on those poorer nations. Only some of those remittances came from servants, but having fewer people slaving to clean and cook for others, and fewer who pay for the privilege of having servants, is what will occur in a world that becomes more economically equal. The Club of Rome cannot have a more equal world if it is a world of more servants.

You'll know when greater equality has been won in the world when there are fewer private servants. That does not mean that more of us will do everything for ourselves.

It makes more sense for a supermarket to send a van round with food to our homes, after we have ordered online, rather than for us each to drive to buy it. That van can visit several homes, just like the milk float still does where I live. Far less gas is used, less energy. You might pay someone to tidy your garden, but they would be choosing to do it in a more equal world, and they would be doing it for many other people too, so that they had that choice.

Simultaneously with the decline in remittances, within the United States one million fewer illegal immigrants (net) arrived in 2009 as compared to 2007, which, as the Department of Homeland Security said, was 'coincident with the US economic downturn'.[49] Less luxury home building means fewer illegally employed and very poorly paid Mexican labourers in the USA.

The economic downturn in Europe means fewer flowers being grown in Africa instead of food, to be air-freighted to Schiphol Airport for continental redistribution. Continued low growth in Japan means fewer Japanese tourists and far fewer identical videos of the world's major landmarks being taken. And as the United States becomes economically weaker following the crash, perhaps there will be fewer wars in faraway places in future and more understanding of the alternatives to war. All this has to continue if sustainability is to increase.

A century ago, it was found that in rural China, for at least 40 generations, people had been living sustainably at very high densities, in great contrast to what was then usual in the USA. One very well-travelled writer, who died just before his last chapter on advice for the West could be written, described sustainability in China coinciding with very high population levels: 'Here is a density of population equal to 3,072 people, 256 donkeys, 256 cattle and 512 swine per square mile . . . The rural population of the

United States in 1900 was placed at the rate of 61 per square mile of improved farm land and there were 30 horses and mules.'[50]

The parts of Asia with the best sustainability records do tend to have some hard-to-reproduce advantages: soil depths are considerable in these parts and people have been improving the soils for millennia. It is also true that most of the cultivable land is at a kinder lower latitude than that in Europe or the USA – kinder for those times when people did not live in well-insulated flats and mostly farmed; but the main point seems to be that area of land was almost of irrelevance even in 1900 as to how many people it could carry. The really important thing is how much work you put into it. We don't have too many people but we may have too many people who too badly want the next new phone, car or other toy.

Carrying capacity should be far greater in well-ordered cities today than it was on the north China plain a century ago, and life far less arduous. Less energy per person should be required if we are efficient. But good order and avoiding wasted labour requires organizing. However, some evidence has just emerged that suggests that even without concerted international organization, even in a place as wasteful of resources as the UK, people have already begun to consume less.

Peak everything

> . . . total activity growth has halted relative to GDP in recent years in the eight countries examined. If these trends continue, it is possible that accelerated decline in the energy intensity of car travel; stagnation in total travel per capita; some shifts back to rail and bus modes; and at least somewhat less

140

carbon per unit of energy could leave the absolute levels of emissions in 2020 or 2030 lower than today.

Adam Millard-Ball and Lee Schipper,
Stanford, USA, 2011[51]

Many consumption peaks had already passed around the time of the millennial end date of this chapter. For others we had started on the downward slope before the 2008 global economic crash began for real. That crash has now accelerated the rate at which we are consuming less in rich countries. This may be temporary, or it may be part of a more gradual slowdown, but it is necessary and it gives pragmatists reason to hope.

The most obvious peaks are in oil. Consumption has to peak as production slows. The best data to show production decline concerns areas outside of the OPEC countries, where depletion is currently very rapid, and outside the former Soviet Union, where resources are not well known. North Sea oil production in British waters peaked in 1999 and in Norwegian waters in 2001. Land-based production peaked earlier in many countries.[52] There is wide-ranging debate about sources not yet discovered under the Arctic, or unconventional sources such as shale oil, but little dissent on our basic understanding that the easy oil has already been taken. Similarly, it is widely recognized that burning oil in car engines is not only one of the quickest ways to pollute the atmosphere, but one of the least sustainable uses of a substance which can be used to make plastics and many other objects that are hard to otherwise replicate.

The UK saw oil production peak in 1999. In the 12 months following January 1999, the price of a barrel of oil rose from just over $10 to over $30. At the time it was reported that 'US President Bill Clinton said the rise was "deeply troubling" and refused to rule out any US action to deal with the situation. "The market is sceptical of words. It needs action in the form of physical oil," said Peter Gignoux, head of the energy desk at Salomon Smith Barney in London.'[53] Ten years later, the price of Brent crude was over $100 a barrel, despite world economic recession, but the price was falling, even with the supply becoming scarcer. Consumption was also slowing, not just because there was a recession, but partly because the slow-down had already begun. Some affluent families had given up their second car in the good times. They then found it easier to save in the harder times.

Oil production of countries outside of OPEC and the former Soviet Union 1900–2013

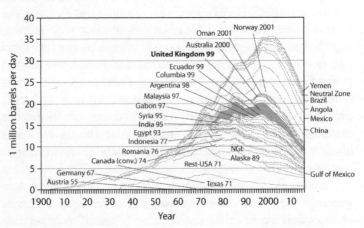

Note: peak year of oil production shown when known. NGL = Natural Gas Liquids.

Source: Zittel, W., Schindler, J., and L-B-Systemtechn (2004), 'The countdown for the peak of oil production has begun – but what are the Views of the Most Important International Energy Agency?', *Energy Bulletin*, 14 October (using LBST estimate on January–August data 2004, IHS 2003, and BP Statistical Review 2004).

The United Kingdom provides a useful example of how it is possible for a country to grow in terms of population, or, to be more precise, to see its population growth accelerate slightly and yet see its consumption fall. This consolidation was even occurring at a time when the economy was growing. Between 2001 and 2007, the total material consumption index of the UK fell by 4 per cent. That index is the government's measure of all material extracted from the ground in the UK, less that exported abroad, adding in that which is imported, and including the contribution held within 'goods imported into the UK [that] are made using resources of biomass, minerals and fossil fuels in their country of origin'.[54]

The UK total material consumption peaked at 2,174 million tonnes in 2001. By 2007, it had reduced to 2,091 million tonnes. The absolute amount of material being consumed by the peoples of the British Isles fell despite population numbers growing and mean wealth increasing faster than population. It was not that people were consuming less. They were consuming more that was light and less that was heavy. People were buying more e-books and fewer paper books, more downloads and fewer CDs, less newsprint, more experiences and fewer mementos. After 2007, our consumption patterns became much lighter again, as the economic crash hit. However, the point being made here is that environmentally damaging consumption had begun to fall long before that crash.

The drop in consumption that came with the crash was so great that we now often do not see the changes that were occurring before it, shortly after there were six billion of us in the year 2000 and long before the population hit seven billion in 2011. In the UK after the crash the quality of air in most of the country rapidly improved as fewer people drove. Power stations reported annual drops in demand for electricity of over 10 per cent.[55] Nationally, emissions of polluting gases fell rapidly, but it was beginning before then, just so quietly and slowly that the British did not notice, while events since the crash have been so dramatic that many now do not accurately remember the world shortly before 2008, let alone how even earlier there were great changes afoot.

In the UK, direct material extraction from the ground of minerals by weight, including exports, but subtracting imports, peaked in 1973. As the British began manufacturing less, they needed fewer raw materials from abroad. Fifteen years later, in 1988, total domestic extraction of biomass, minerals and fossil fuels peaked as most of the coal pits were closed, but also as the need for such weight of material fell, not just because of less manufacturing, but because people were beginning to have enough. That is, enough on average, if not for everyone.

In the UK in 1988, some had too much, others had too little, and the divide was growing. Thirteen years later, a new 2001 peak of consumption was reached. From 2001 onwards, consumption of material in the UK began to fall, even including the implicit weight of resources used in constructing everything the British imported. Consumption by weight had peaked. Less coming in then means less waste, less landfill, less incineration and less harmful economic activity mostly carried out to enable us to consume more and more.

Eleven years later, in 2012, all began to become clearer. Before then, the trend was far harder to see. The economic slowdown accelerated the shift towards being more green, to more make-do-and-mend, to a more sustainable economy that will in some ways resemble a 'less developed' economy where people have less but value what they have more, rather than valuing the next item to be bought the most. The British are becoming greener, and they are some of the least green consumers of Western Europe. To understand why requires examining trends in different commodities in turn.

Domestic water use peaked in 2003, at just under 15,700 million tonnes of water being used annually. It was down to under 14,600 million by 2010, despite the population rising. Taking out industrial consumption, Ofwat, the industry regulator, found that 'The average consumption in a typical household peaked in 2003/4 and fell to 96 per cent by 2007/8 and decreased a further 1 per cent by 2009/10.'[56] They reported this as a peak because it was a reversal of the rising trend in water consumption between the financial years 1998/9 and 2003/4, when UK domestic consumption of water was reported to have risen by 7 per cent.

People were having more showers; more were sharing a bath. Some put bricks in the cistern, or when it came to replacing their old toilet they bought one that used water more efficiently. Fewer outdoor swimming pools were built; more water meters were installed. Because of the weather, there really is little point in having an outdoor swimming pool in almost all of the UK, and people began to wake up to that. It became fashionable to install rainfall-collecting butts and numerous more ingenious devices, to begin to turn your home eco-friendly. All the innovation was by a minority, but it had enough impact to begin the great slowdown in water consumption.

Next came food; the British began to eat less. In the UK, calorie intake of food has been dropping from a peak of about 2,500 calories a day in 1974 to as low as around 2,300 calories per person by 2012. It may have reached a previous minimum around 1990 and then rose to just over 2,400 calories by 2002. People have been getting fatter because they take less exercise than they did in the 1970s – they now drive far more than they walk – and they also do not use up so many calories shivering in winter, as their homes are better heated and are becoming progressively far better insulated. So the British can eat less and feel better.

Even as they eat less, they still, on average, get a little fatter each year that passes. This is partly good news. Consumption of food should fall further – of what we put in our mouths as well as what we waste. Between 2001 and 2007, average per person calorie consumption fell by 4 per cent. Then, as food prices rose after 2007 and average income in the UK fell, food came to make up over 11 per cent of household expenditure and calorie intake is now falling again, but the fall in consumption had started long before the economic crash.[57] Meat consumption has been falling since 2004.

A few people in the UK are now going seriously hungry and have to get food from food banks. Far more actually need to eat a little less. Some are now doing so, though the overall amount the British eat is still far more than they need. With a little more financial equality, no one in Britain need be hungry. With a little more overall restraint, all could be a little less fat. And restraint is on the rise. It is not just food and water and petrol; it is in almost everything, at least everything that has weight.

Take wood, a carbon store that we overconsume. Around 5 per cent of electricity in the UK is used to make paper. Consumption of paper and wood peaked at just below 13 million tonnes in 2001, fell during the economic boom to just over 12 million tonnes by 2007 and then plummeted to well under 11 million tonnes in 2010 with the fall accelerated by the economic crash. But consumption was falling before the crash, so we can assume that we have passed peak levels. Decreases in book and newspaper sales coupled with increases in digital reading are part of the reason. The falls are even greater if the rise in the recycling of paper is also considered. The annual reports of the paper industry's trade body, from which these statistics come, are now available in digital form.[58]

It is good news that wood consumption is falling, but wood is easily renewable, as is food and water. The land that is forested is on the rise, but more of our forests need to be made up of very large, very slow-growing trees, and more of the wood that is used needs to be used for more worthwhile purposes than becoming yesterday's fish and chip paper. We need to start using wood again in place of less easily replaceable materials, for building, for heating using the waste, and for what we really need, not just what we think we really want.

What of the consumption of less easily sourced minerals? We rely on oil to help make nitrogen fertilizers, for example. In the UK, nitrogen fertilizer use peaked in 1987; some 40 per cent less was used by 2007, and its use is still falling. Less nitrogen is wasted in run-off that pollutes rivers and streams and which, at the worst extremes, is associated with blue baby syndrome, leading to infant death. But nitrates are not the only fertilizing mineral being consumed in smaller quantities even in a not especially environmentally minded place such as the UK.

Both phosphate- and potassium-based fertilizers peaked in use in 1984 and both were down to under half their peak level by 2007. Consumption of both is still falling. This is despite the fact that 'the country is still broadly self-sufficient in cereals, for example, which are the crops receiving most fertiliser'.[59] It is not that less food is being grown; just that fewer fertilizers are being used to grow it, so it may not end up as bulky. A little more is also organic.

This is good news and fits with lower calorie consumption, but there is other great news, at least from affluent countries like the UK, and it concerns cement.

'Cement plants account for 5 per cent of global emissions of carbon dioxide, the main cause of global warming. Cement has no viable recycling potential; each new road, each new building, needs new cement.'[60] Some 45 per cent of all cement production is in China, and that is rising, but in the UK production is falling. There does come a point where there is enough cement, when you don't have to add many more roads. There does come a point where you have so many buildings that what matters most is how well you use and renovate what you have.

Cement use in the UK fell in two rapid drops. It first fell by a quarter, from 16 million metric tonnes a year in 1989 to 12 million by 1993, as the housing market declined and building slowed. It then fell by a third, from 12 million metric tonnes a year in 2007 to under 8 million by 2010, as the housing market outside London crashed. It did not rise during the housing boom from 1993 to 2007. The British are learning to use less cement even when they build more homes. When they slow down on building homes and roads and schools, they use far less than they used before. They could maybe do with a few better-built schools, but they have more roads than most European countries already. Part of the reduction in cement use is due to the incredible rates of wastefulness in the recent past. Part is more deliberate. The fastest way to save is not to spend.

A colleague who works on climate science suggested to me in an email that 'I did wonder whether this was a real effect, or related to something else. Despite the economic crash happening in 2008 I've always felt that in many ways the consumer society entered its debt crisis around the top of the housing boom in 2003 and that it just took a few years to become critical. I also wonder whether continuous warfare in Iraq and Afghanistan since 2003 has diverted resources out of the country.'[61] The same processes may be even truer of the USA, while in mainland Europe and in Japan, green movements and environmental thinking have been stronger for longer.

The slowing of our consumption is not due to the great foresight of a few leaders and our ability to plan collectively. Instead it is the beginning of what appears to be a global economic realignment as destructive economic growth in the richest countries falters. Perhaps it is the very start of a return to much lower economic disparities between continents, countries and peoples. It is also partly due to the positive actions of millions of people who care. This includes less long-distance tourism, with millions of people from outside the UK becoming a little greener too and not coming to the UK as much.

In 2012, tourism receipts in the UK passed a peak, despite the fall in the pound making travel to Britain cheap. Tourist sites in the capital, London, recorded a 15 per cent fall in visits during May–August as compared to 2011. The Olympics were only held towards the end of that period, and it was not clear at the beginning that the summer would be wet. The Games and the rain were of course blamed, but maybe more potential tourists chose to save money and carbon by watching London on the TV?

There were falls of over 20 per cent in the numbers of people from overseas visiting London's parks, gardens and other such attractions. London Zoo and the Royal Botanic Gardens in Kew saw catering and toy-shop spending fall by about 10 per cent during the year. 'But heritage sites and cathedrals – including the Tower of London, St Paul's Cathedral and the Houses of Parliament – were also casualties, with visitor numbers slumping by 20.3 per cent and retail and catering spending by 20.2 per cent and 8.6 per cent. Visitor numbers to museums and galleries in London fell by 13.1 per cent.'[62] Chinese tourist numbers may be up; others are down by more.

Visiting your local museum and gallery more often turns the tide, as does visiting faraway places less often. A park is a park whether called royal or not. When you travel, take the train; fly as little as you can. Explore places, see art, read books, meet people, but more often in cyberspace if they are any distance away. Enjoy life where you live more. If the British can begin to do this, with their consumption culture, it is possible in all rich nations. But what of the rest of the world; what of the parts that are just trying to catch up, the people who don't ask for much, though if they all got half of what we have, the planet would burn up? That was the key question being asked as the population moved past seven billion in December 2011.

We may, in both the UK and other rich countries, finally have passed peaks in consumption of most physical resources by weight. This possibly also includes the weight of the resources involved in most of the production of what we consume. But we still consume too much, enjoy what we have too little, throw away too often and buy again too frequently. However, we may have turned the corner towards a lower consumption economy. This would further facilitate population slowdown, engender optimism and lead to less need for greed if people learnt to want less. But can we learn to be less impressed by advertisements and to wear clothes until they are worn out, not only while they are in fashion?

At Christmas 2011, there was as yet little sign on the high streets and malls across the rich world that an epiphany of understanding had been reached. Across the middle-income world, shoppers were also buying as instructed by the TV adverts and frequently a little more than they could afford, in emulation of those with more than they had. But there was also a general refrain mounting to the effect that the inequality that fuelled such overconsumption was wrong. The 'Occupy' movement was spreading to some of the smallest of towns and cities and reaching its greatest extent before the winter weather and police violence finally took 'their toll on the public encampments'; the tent cities.[63] The camps were mostly dismantled in 2012. But the ideas were spreading. People were forecast to have spent much less during Christmas 2012.

CHAPTER 4

7 BILLION IN DECEMBER 2011

> Humans have now become the major environmental force on Earth.
>
> William Ruddiman, palaeoclimatologist, 2005[1]

We are moving into an era of far greater uncertainty in respect of human impact on the environment. Whilst it is true that a narrative of great optimism can be constructed, at the same time some severe challenges await. Fundamentally the force of money, neo-liberal capital, has undermined both the power and influence of both nation states and supranational bodies such as the UN, OPEC and the IMF. This often leads to despair, as it is thought that it will be through unprecedented levels of global cooperation that the market interventionist policies that have to be enacted will need to operate. However, if population growth rates ease as they are projected to, the power of money may also ease and the value of each new human may rise rather than fall.

If during the last dozen years you had felt that things were changing faster than ever before, you would have been correct. In just the 11 years prior to Christmas 2011 we gained (net of deaths) an extra billion people worldwide and hit seven billion. The period 2000–11 really was the period of fastest ever human population growth. It was the age of excess. Some of the panic that some people appear to feel is understandable.

What had happened was that the deceleration had briefly been reversed. It is as if the cricket ball had taken on a life of its own. Powered up by hidden rocket boosters it had set off again, soaring up into space. There had been a mini baby boom. That wasn't in the plan. That was why during the 11 years 2001–11 the official UN predictions for the end of the century had to be increased by a further billion. Suddenly there were going to be ten billion of us rather than nine. We learnt that just as we were told that our collective count had hit seven billion.[2]

In the short time (132 months) it took to go from there being six billion to seven billion of us, a global war of terror had begun, there were two economic crashes, the banking system almost collapsed from the latter; world food prices soared, hundreds of millions more people went hungry; the poor became absolutely poorer, there was again absolute immiseration; and the world's super-rich continued their advancement up the upper slopes of Mount Olympus to take on what initially appeared to be a god-like status. It wasn't hard to start believing that the end of an era was almost upon us.

Absolute immiseration was a notion defined by the economist David Ricardo in the 1810s. Ricardo suggested that as more and more people were born, the median wage would fall to the subsistence level or slightly below it. Karl Marx adapted the idea in the 1860s and talked of there being a reserve army of chronically unemployed labour. These were people who were then forced to work, if they could find work at all, for less than they needed simply to live. Leon Trotsky raised the issue again in the 1930s. It comes to the fore during economic depressions.

Apparently a rising level of absolute immiseration almost always occurs hand in hand with a few people becoming extremely rich. One substantial group becomes poorer partly because the share of the economic pie they could claim is contracting, despite the overall pie growing in size in most years. The rich tend to suggest that all will be well if only the pie grows even larger. Groups of them meet to announce this towards the end of January each year.

Mount Olympus is too difficult a place to protect and it doesn't have good skiing. Instead, Davos, a Swiss municipality that boasts good access to the mountain resort of Klosters, is where the world's chief executive officers and other members of the super-rich meet annually to discuss global events and, no doubt, their growing absolute wealth, but also increasingly issues of wider concern: food security, carbon pollution and climate change, energy, urban sustainability and water feature high on their list of discussion topics.[3]

Often the messages from the annual World Economic Forum meetings in Davos can be condensed down to 'trust us and all will be OK in the end'. However, with each year that passed in the turbulent noughties, this message appeared less and less reassuring. Journalists began to mock the 'Masters of the Universe' who met at the resort and tried to be reassuring, especially as economies crumbled while they partied.[4] Davos became the favoured location after 1999 when the Battle in Seattle meant that no large city was safe for the world's richest to meet in public and en masse.

As the world economic recession deepened during 2009, 2010 and 2011, the message from up high began to change from 'follow us and we will bring you to prosperity' to 'do what we say and we will protect you from Armageddon'. It became much harder not to fear immigrants, climate refugees, all manner of people coming to destroy society. Uncertainty about the future was used to fuel discrimination.

It was an unfortunate world, the Masters of the Universe explained, but better to live in the shadows of the castles of financiers than outside the city walls. In Europe, in North America, in Japan you were safe; outside you were not: be fearful. People in the rich world needed defensible space, to guard the resources they had, and to compete ever harder with each other and with emerging China, Brazil and India. And yet all around, if only you looked, there were reasons to look on the bright side.

This is the last chapter of this book which is not mostly speculation. It lists the knowledge we have which we did not have a generation ago when, as a reaction to all those 1960s babies, *The Population Bomb* was published. That book followed on shortly after Rachel Carson's exposure of so many pollutants in *Silent Spring*, which energized environmentalists. *The Population Bomb*'s neo-Malthusian narrative was a driver of the green movement. Much of that movement now realizes that population never was the problem; pollution is. Everything after this is mostly speculation. This chapter is still, but only just, history.

Forecast and project

> In Iran, with the support of the Islamic regime, fertility has fallen more than 70 percent since the early '80s. In Catholic and democratic Brazil, women have reduced their fertility rate by half over the same quarter century. 'We still don't understand why fertility has gone down so fast in so many societies, so many cultures and religions. It's just mind-boggling,' says Hania Zlotnik, director of the UN Population Division.

Robert Kunzig, *National Geographic Magazine*, 2011[5]

To forecast and to project both mean the same thing: to throw forward. The two words differ only in that one has Latin and the other Greek origins. Demographers (Greek origin *demos*) sometimes try to claim there is a distinction between the two, but in doing this they simply spread confusion. The one forecast and projection they make that receives almost all the attention is their central guess, the median variant, the middle one of many.

The median variant projection is not a best guess but simply the middle of a large number of possible variants. However, 'even the most sophisticated consumers of such information do not see demographic projections and forecasts as mere illustrations of possible future paths for the world's population – in other words, at best they view them as predictions with a degree of uncertainty'.[6] The reason there is such scepticism is that the range of forecasts made is so incredibly wide. For just 90 years ahead they are often, at the low side, just a couple of billion above human species eradication, and at the high side so many tens of billions that the increases could mark a shift to numbers that might require humans to develop insect-like social organization!

The more statistically minded of demographers sometimes don't see the gravity of what they are considering. Statisticians (Latin origin *statisticus*) can also become embroiled in the trivia. I saw this recently when talking about the income of the top and bottom fifths of society and what have become known as 'the 1 per cent' compared to 'the 99 per cent'. I made the mistake of using the words 'quintile' and 'percentile' when talking about just how wide the gaps had become, and was told that I was using the wrong words. But rather like statisticians trying to claim there are only four quintiles and ninety-nine percentiles (they do, and strictly speaking they are right!), demographers asking for their forecasts not to be taken seriously but to be seen as merely estimates are misguided as to what will occur.

Words change their meaning over time depending on how they are used. In late 2012, the Macquarie Dictionary, Australia's premier definer of words, altered the meaning of the word 'misogyny' following Julia Gillard's great oration on the multiple failings of the leader of the opposition, Tony Abbott. Tony will now go down in history as the man who made 'misogyny' a meaningful word to millions of people who had not really known what it meant before, as well as epitomizing what the redefined word now means.[7] Unfortunately, 'forecasting' and 'projecting' do not stir up quite such strong emotions as to result in a public debate about the meaning of these words and calls for a clarification of their modern definitions.

Forecasting is an uncertain game, but a fun one. It happens most often in sport, where numerous theories are put forward as to why one side should do well and another not so well. Around the time that the seven billionth human being was born, we were learning about new ways of forecasting the results of soccer games (European football). Forecasting is almost always based on the changing frequency of past events. What was found for soccer is illustrative of how changing techniques for forecasting can change the forecasts that are made.

You might think that the probability that a team will win at soccer is mostly influenced by how good the players are, and that can be indicated by how much they are paid. The better players are, the more money they receive. A forecast based on this theory would suggest that the team with the highest wage bill will score the most goals, but it turns out that this is not the case.

An academic paper published in 2012 and written by

authors who worked in one of the world's most prestigious business schools, at Harvard, compared the fortunes of teams in the Italian football league as recorded between 2009 and 2011. It found that teams that didn't pay their star players too much did better as compared to teams within which the pay distribution was more unequal. That finding was historical, albeit very recent history. The forecast from it would be to suggest that a similar trend would apply in future: that the best-performing team would not necessarily be the one with the highest overall wage bill.

The effect of spending the same amount of money on hiring a set of over-average players rather than a superstar and 10 average players was very marked. It was the difference between probably winning the next game and winning just over a third of games: 'Our estimates suggest that, everything else being equal, the differentiated pay distribution will make the probability of winning a match fall on average by 20 per cent, from 0.56 to 0.36.'[8] (A probability of 1.00 means a team wins every game, and a probability of 0.00 means it always loses.)

In that 2012 paper it was argued that working together was important because soccer was a team sport. It was also a good sport to study, as all players were aware of all other players' salaries because they were reported by the press. If paying some more than others had an adverse effect on the lower paid, an effect strong enough to offset any incentive to work harder by the better paid, then this should show up in the team's results.

Why should inequality matter so much? Is it jealousy? Are the less well-rewarded players passing the ball a little less often to the superstars? The paper's authors tested this theory: they knew how many minutes each player had the ball, and found that lack of cooperation was not the problem. Instead it would appear that being looked down on, through receiving less pay than others, had a demotivating effect on the majority of players.

These soccer findings on how small groups of men behave matter for population forecasts because they show how it may be factors you have not considered before that can strongly influence what you are studying, and hence why your forecasts and projections can be so wrong. They also show that human behaviour is very much influenced by how other humans behave.

At a major conference on demography in London, held just a year before the Harvard research was released, it had been suggested that wealth inequalities could also influence population growth. Research results had been mounting up which in aggregate suggested that the number of children a couple had was partly influenced by the amount of wealth they had compared to other couples in their society and other families in the world, and that great wealth inequalities led to further population growth. This was because 'Social inequalities, including wealth, consumption, gender and health inequities, are significant as both drivers and consequences of unsustainable consumption and population growth, and present a major social and moral issue. Vast and highly unjust levels of wealth in a small minority of the population correlate with high rates of consumption and contribute to environmental degradation and poverty.'[9] Economic inequalities can be very harmful.

If income inequalities fall within a football team, most of the players, on average, play better. If wealth inequalities fall in a society, it becomes better organized, gender equalities tend to improve more quickly, and families have fewer children. People nearer the bottom of society work better when they are better rewarded. People at the top are less likely to behave in stupid ways when they are not so financially separate. Due to a reinforcing combination of reasons life expectancies rise quicker under more equitable circumstances, and when they rise, fertility among women of childbearing age usually falls very quickly.[10] This is, perhaps, a little surprising given that it is much older women who are mostly living longer.

Over time, the relationship between life expectancy and fertility has become more linear. By 2010 across the world, for every 6 extra years people lived beyond 50, they had one fewer child per couple, falling to around 1 child where people were usually living for more than 80 years. Once life expectancy exceeds age 55, births start to fall. This was true in the 1960s and it remains true today; it is just that today there are very few places where life expectancy is below 55 years. The Figure below illustrates these trends.

Niger and South Africa are two places with low life expectancy. The first graph below shows that in 1960 they had very similar fertility rates. By 2010, the fertility rate in South Africa was just over two children per couple. The widespread prevalence of HIV/AIDS means people are more careful now, but it also shows how hard it is to forecast changes in future behaviour, and that fertility can fall even when material conditions do not improve much and even, in the case of South Africa, when great economic inequalities prevail.

It is partly because the declining fertility trend has been so fast, and partly because only the populations of a few countries in the 1960s exhibited the behaviour that almost all do today that some people still think that population growth will not continue to fall as fast as it appears to be falling now. But look again at the two graphs below, look at where most of the population of the world now falls in terms of the average number of children people have and consider how quickly this came about.

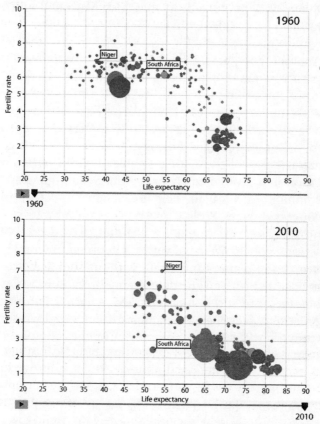

Global trends in life expectancy and fertility, 1960–2010

Source: Google public graphs based on World Bank data.

The seven billionth person may have been born as the second of two twins, taking their first breath just after the second-billionth-alive human died (the one born in 1926), especially if there were a particularly neat mathematical symmetry to these trends. Demographers like such neatness, but it is also part of why we still think there is a problem, and it takes a dead anarchist, Murray Bookchin, to most clearly explain why:

> Another popular explanation of the environmental crisis is population increase. This argument would be more compelling if it could be shown that countries with the largest rates of population increase are the largest consumers of energy, raw material, or even food. But such correlations are notoriously false. Often mere density of population is equated with overpopulation in a given country or region. Such arguments, commonly cynical in their use of graphic-scenes of congested New York City streets and subway stations during rush hours, for example, hardly deserve serious notice. We have yet to determine how many people the planet can sustain without complete ecological disruption. The data are far from conclusive, but they are surely highly biased – generally along economic, racial, and social lines. Demography is far from a science, but it is a notorious political weapon whose abuse has disastrously claimed the lives of millions over the course of the century.[11]

The century he refers to is the twentieth, and among the many abuses then was the Nazis' claim that they had both to expand Germany and to kill within it to find living space, or *Lebensraum*, for the German folk.

Simple demographics can have disastrous outcomes, not just at the extremes during the fog of war, or for some of the poorest people in the world, forced into mass sterilization programmes. Simple demographics can also lead to great stupidity and even neurosis among affluent folk. This can occur when people take seriously the claim that, for an affluent couple in a rich country, 'having a child leaves a carbon footprint as big as flying back and forth to New York [presumably from London] every day for seven years'.[12] In fact it is only the people who frequently fly back and forth to New York in this way who add so much carbon pollution, not any one additional child. Since Concorde was grounded, slightly fewer have behaved as badly individually. But as we put more 747s up over the Atlantic, and as London and New York banks merge their workforces, more wasteful people in aggregate add to the pollution. The vast majority of those business trips do not add to the sum of human happiness. The birth of a child does.

Any couple considering not having a child to save the planet could well be said to be suffering from neuroticism, defined by one commentator as 'a good word to describe a couple overly worried about climate change and their baby's carbon footprint'.[13] When people respond poorly to stresses, including to environmental stress, they can be 'more likely to interpret ordinary situations as threatening, and minor frustrations as hopelessly difficult . . . Pretty well bang on a description of alarmists,' this insightful observer concluded. So let's take a look at the alarm that is being spread more generally and about how extra people are thought by some to add to the threat of riot and disorder.

Riot and disorder

> Privatize everything. Abolish help for the weak . . . the sick and the unemployed. Abolish all aid for everyone except the banks. Don't look after the poor; let the elderly die. Reduce the wages of the poor, but reduce the taxes of the rich. Make everyone work until they are ninety.
>
> Alain Badiou, 'A Recipe for Riot', 2012[14]

Speaking of the August 2011 London riots, and why they did not spread to the northern English city of Leeds, one youth worker explained: 'If we'd had a JD Sports on Chapeltown Road, if we'd had a Nokia shop, if we'd had a Vodafone, they would have been hit. Because young people feel that these shops take all their money.'[15] But take a step forward, many more logical steps forward: why do these shops take all their money, and why are they encouraged to do so? And, as population growth rates hit their maxima, why should we be surprised that a few try to profit so hard in such exceptional circumstances where markets appear to be growing year on year as the population swells, and as there are ever more young people to make and buy what sells?

JD Sports does not sell people clothes to wear to undertake sport. It sells clothes labelled as sportswear that are tailored to be fashionable. Nokia and Vodafone make a large part of their profits selling young people expensive high-tech phones that do far more than make calls and send texts. Again, this is more about fashion than function. People are not sold phones to use until they wear out. Why is waste encouraged, why such profligacy? One reason is that up until now, the growth in population and the growth in capitalism have gone hand in hand. Markets could make much more than was needed, still giving choice to everyone, because more consumers were arriving each year.

Demographic transition always results in economic transition. Our current demographic transition to a steady-state population is almost certainly not possible without a transformation of capitalism. When capitalism was beginning, it was those parts of the world that had not yet been incorporated into global markets that most often enjoyed a stable population. The population boom began in Europe as capitalism spread from there; in 1631, mathematician René Descartes noted on the dockside in Amsterdam that 'everyone is so intent on his profits'.[16] He noticed this behaviour as strange because he was not a merchant. It helps to be disconnected from the mêlée to see it as a selfish scrum.

European capitalism spread as population numbers grew. That was what made growing profits every year possible. Demand expanded due to there being ever more humans. Capitalism helped to construct its own growth by so disrupting the societies infected by profit-taking that whatever traditions had emerged to limit population were eventually everywhere broken. Some 381 years after Descartes first saw this at work, another scientist came to a similar conclusion, but at the point at which the process was slowing down, rather than when it was just starting.

Paul Nurse won the Nobel Prize in Physiology for discovering part of the process of how cells divide. A little later, with a group of colleagues, he came to realize that:

> Not only is a nation's status in the world perceived to rise if it enjoys GDP growth, high GDP enables a nation to tilt the terms of trade with the rest of the world to its advantage. The benefits associated with GDP growth lead to nations vying with one another for competitive advantage by bolstering GDP. No single nation can step aside from this competitive game without jeopardising the jobs, financial security and self esteem of its citizens. International recognition of the wasteful nature of such a form of competition is a needed first step.[17]

Three hundred and eighty-one years is a very long time to wait before taking a first step, but that step is now being taken, partly because global demand is declining as the number of new young consumers rapidly falls. Once that first step is taken, many other arguments begin to change. For example, if GDP growth of itself is not good, then not all new jobs are good simply because they make money.

One respondent to a report that suggested that the supermarket chain Tesco was creating 20,000 jobs explained in an open letter that this would 'actually destroy a further 100,000 jobs. And since local shops employ an average of one person for every £50,000 of annual turnover, while for supermarkets the figure is £250,000 per job, this will also represent millions of pounds a year being taken out of (already struggling) local economies.'[18] Less money being made, but spread between more people, more locally, is much better for all than a fast growth in profits for a few.

When any kind of economic profit is seen and presented as being good, people begin to be valued more and more in monetary terms and cultures of resistance to the dominance of a few wealthy individuals become portrayed as nihilistic. Immediately following the 2011 London riots:

> Controversial medievalist historian David Starkey made reference to a 'nihilistic but fashionable' gangster culture that had drawn inspiration from black culture ... Arguments like these form part of a much longer lineage of social commentators whose focus on criminality and moral decline distract from more serious analyses of causation and add little to our understanding. Such explanations link in to Conservative arguments around the 'problem of youth' as recalcitrant, anarchic and amoral, the result of 'poor parenting'.[19]

Profiteers like to present themselves as moral.

Often when riot and disorder is discussed, it is in the language of class war, a language not of Karl Marx but of 'French historians. But it is the masses, much more indistinct, who are feared.'[20] And it is not classes, but the unclassified, the almost uncountable and numerous who can appear on the streets in a matter of hours and disappear in minutes.

Especially feared are the masses of younger people with little to lose who are still living with hope. Fear of the young is part of a growing concern of the affluent with an unruly underclass emerging beneath a larger working class. Even some members of the lower middle class are starting to become unruly and insubordinate. Further up, parts of the upper middle class are beginning to realize that their interests are not allied with the 1 per cent who live just above them. It is these higher-up people who more often go on protest marches across Europe and North America; those lower down and young are more likely to riot.

The class system that we talk about today was defined by historians and is still widely thought to operate. Old French terms like 'proletariat' and 'bourgeoisie' are employed, but these words are of distant times and places. The bourgeoisie were those placed economically just below the king, the clergy and the aristocrats. They were wealthy but they were commoners. Following the French Revolution, they rose to the top.

Proletariat is a Latin word and a Roman class, rekindled as a term by a set of French historians who were describing what came after the French Revolution. Today the proletariat has a Facebook page, where it is defined as 'those people who had no wealth other than their children'.[21] By this definition, most of the world remains in the proletariat. Most people's wealth is too meagre to be counted, or to last for more than a few weeks should they need to rely on it.

Even the middle classes of rich countries can count only a few months after redundancy until the wolf comes to their door (on average it is about 13 weeks).

World GDP hit $70 trillion by the end of 2011. Divide that by seven billion souls, and the mean average share would be $10,000 each, every year, leaving everyone with enough to live a basic life and save a little. A family of two parents and two children would enjoy $40,000 annual income. Most of the parents of the proletariat were peasants; most of their children will be working-class labourers, builders, factory workers, cleaners, cooks and security guards.

The United Nations University was the first to follow the money globally and determine how much wealth a tiny minority now hold and where inequalities in wealth have grown to be the greatest. The university researchers calculated what are called the Gini coefficients of inequality, which range from 0.00 where there is perfect equality to almost 1.00 when just one person holds all the wealth.

The wealth share estimates reveal that the richest 2 per cent of adult individuals own more than half of all global wealth, with the richest 1 per cent alone accounting for 40 per cent of global assets . . . in all countries which have the requisite data, wealth distribution is more unequal than income . . . wealth Gini estimates range from 0.547 for Japan to 0.801 for the USA and 0.803 for Switzerland. The global wealth Gini is estimated to be even greater at 0.892. This is equivalent to the Gini value that would be registered for a 100-person population in which one person receives $900 and the remaining 99 people each receive $1.[22]

If people thought of themselves as citizens of the world, rather than comparing their lot with others within each country, there would be revolution.

As a household (say of four people), measured in US dollars, or the equivalent where you live, you need to hold assets worth at least $61,000 to be in the global top 10 per cent and/or have an annual household income of $32,000. Below this and you are in the proletariat. Within the proletariat there is stratification upon stratification, no class with common cause. At the bottom are untouchables. Near the top are people who might even think of themselves as middle class, but their position does not guarantee safety. However, it gives their offspring a chance out and up. These are what 1980s French sociologists called the 'precariat', the precarious hovering between the proletariat and their 'betters'. But above them precariousness is spreading as, locally, income inequality grows within most countries.

Worldwide, above the precariat are those who often appear to be a disillusioned middle; this is despite them being above 90 per cent of the rest of humanity. Almost always their position is not self-realized and they feel poor living in their usually affluent country, especially within the neighbourhoods they tend to inhabit, ones they can only just afford to rent or buy in. They have household incomes under $66,000[23] a year and wealth, including all future pension costs and housing equity, of less than $510,000. Often these are members of the precariat who took a chance and it turned out OK – not a runaway success, but OK. These are the 9 per cent of the world, above the 90 per cent but below the 1 per cent. However, above them there is no harmony either. There is more inequality in the top 1 per cent of the world's most affluent than in all the rest of humanity combined.

Those at the bottom of the top 1 per cent could be called the 'pompositat', derived from 'pomposity', the collective noun for a group of professors. These people are very well off. To those beneath them they may appear unduly grand, but they don't think of themselves like that. The top 1 per cent of the world's population in 2013 is made up of just over 70 million people; by wealth, only a seventh of them, 11 million people, are dollar millionaires.[24] But even among these, the large majority – maybe 10 of those 11 million – are only 'just' millionaires, and the majority of their money is mostly tied up in a home (or two) and investments that they see as pensions. They are not the jet set.

The jet set are the million or so multimillionaires in the world with disposable wealth of over $7 million apiece. They can fly (mostly) where they want, and need no longer work. Within them are an even more exclusive group of roughly a tenth of them, some 100,000 people, who each have assets worth over around $50 million to play with. These are the 'special people', very high net worth individuals (HNWI). But even they compare themselves to each other, and those above, and often want more. Among their number a majority own a ski chalet or beachfront property and around two thirds of the rest are thinking about buying one. Presumably a sixth of them enjoys neither skiing nor the sea.

Most of the richest 100,000 people on earth, a seventh of the 1 per cent of the 1 per cent, invest in wine or are about to, in artworks or jewellery; a fifth in sports teams. For them, the 'US and UK are the most popular locations for a second home. Singapore is the fifth most popular. Asians favour the UK. London and New York are the most important cities to the HNWI. 27 per cent believe "availability of luxury housing" is an attribute for a city to be "considered globally important" ... 91 per cent think global economic factors are the biggest threat to future wealth creation, 6 per cent think terrorism.'[25]

In Singapore, the fifth most popular second-home destination of the richest of all of earth's human inhabitants, 'the state has attempted to actively court the global super-rich through specific place-based strategies including customized urban policies such as creating a favourable tax (-free) environment and "fast-track" permanent residency status coupled with the deployment of dazzling real estate products and super-rich enclaves such as Sentosa Cove'.[26] Singapore is also attractive partly for its rigid law and order. There is little chance of riot there.

Singapore has many fans. Among them is James Lovelock, who believes that it is one possible future model:

> You don't even have to do the experiment. You only have to go to Singapore. You could not have chosen a worse climate in which to build a city. It's a swamp with temperatures in the 90s every day, and very humid. But it is one of the most successful cities in the world. It seems to me that they are treading the path that we are all going to go. It's so much cheaper to air-condition the cities and let Gaia take care of the world. It's a much better route to go than so-called 'sustainable development', which is meaningless drivel.[27]

Could he be correct? After all, he is the man who made up the idea of Gaia. Or has he not looked behind what it is that allows Singapore to function as it does?

Take a look at Singapore. Zoom in on Sentosa Cove and its 'Paradise Island' and 'Treasure Island' enclaves to view the results of an extremely concentrated collection of money and the human attachments that travel with such capital. Have a look at the Figure below and the satellite photo of where the yachts are moored. Think of the air miles needed to fly the residents in and out, the electricity to air-condition so many cubic feet of real estate, the servants required to manicure the gardens, and then think what kind of attitudes might be festering in such places.

Is this really the future, while sustainable development is 'meaningless drivel'? Or it is a billionaires' playground where multimillionaires can attend social functions only feeling a little inferior as they bid, literally, for the best parking bay for their boat?

One of the few academic studies of the extremely rich found that 'The protection and enforcement of private property is key and it is easier to accumulate great wealth in richer than in poorer countries.'[28] The multimillionaires' biggest fear is not a slowdown in economic growth or a rise in terrorism, other than the personal risk of kidnap. As inequalities within certain countries grow, it is threats to their private property claims that keep the rich awake at night.

The rich, who know what is possible, fear a land-value wealth tax. They fear what occurred to the Japanese aristocracy after 1945, when almost all their lands were confiscated by the Americans and redistributed. Perhaps that fear is part of the reason why more affluent countries tend to be a little more equal. By allowing more equality in their affluent homelands, the elite reduce the risk of insurrection at home, but they do find it very hard to share. Singapore, the USA and the UK, favourite destinations of the world's super-rich, are also three of the four most inequitable of the 25 richest countries on earth. Are the rich there taking too much of a chance?

Sentosa Cove, super-rich enclave, Singapore

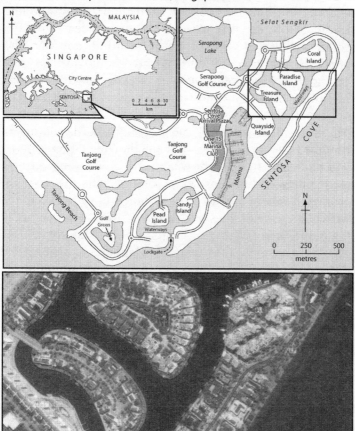

Sources: Pow, C.-P. (2011), 'Living it up: super-rich enclave and transnational elite urbanism in Singapore', *Geoforum* 42,382–93; Google Maps.

At the very top of the grossly elongated global wealth pyramid is a praetorian guard of billionaires, numbering 1,226 in 2012 according to *Forbes Magazine*.[29] Through their existence they are, in effect, surrounding the richest

1 per cent of all, the 1 per cent of billionaires who are among the dozen wealthiest individuals on the planet. Those at the very top have a combined wealth of around US$400 billion, a tenth of all the wealth of the 1,226 billionaires, a wealth that does not fall far short of that held by the 1,000 richest people in the UK, but assetts held worldwide by just 12 individuals.

Global wealth inequality is fractal. Take a group of people in most places in the world, be it Manhattan or Madras (Chennai), and within any block in either city you will find a distribution of wealth that looks similar to the inequalities within most other blocks. It is just that the average levels of wealth vary so much both between and within these two cities and between most other parts of the globe. It is because of inequality that those with less, even in a very wealthy part of Manhattan, believe that they need to get more, and feel that it is legitimate to do almost whatever it takes to make more money. This results in behaviour that appears to others like the enactment of violence with money. Factories are closed down in faraway places at the whim of a New York banker; money is made selling goods abroad that are harmful because making money becomes the most important thing.

When money becomes the most important thing, it is paraded as a sign of success: 'the global super-rich remain as much defined by their consumption patterns and cultural habits as their wealth per se, with the acquisition of a number of icons of global *savoir faire* (e.g. British motor cars, French wine, USA art, Italian clothing) marking off the super-rich as truly transnational'.[30] In the face of such inequalities, when times become hard, what might be construed as envy is more clearly transformed into disgust. It is then that it is said that riot is 'an expression of the general will',[31] in contrast to voting, which is largely ritual. Voting usually changes almost nothing, even when a political party falls. Your own vote almost never alters the result. Take part in a riot and you see the effect of all your actions, including on you if you are caught. Riot is a world apart from marking an X on paper. And riots almost always only occur where there are great and growing inequalities, and no other way out appears possible. But there are other ways out, and they are being taken now. Look to places like Norway, where it is often too cold to riot, to see the alternative.

Energy and equality

> By raising the tax rate from 210 Norwegian Krone to 410 Krone (or €28 to more than €55 [or $72]) per ton of CO_2, the Norwegian government is setting one of the highest carbon tax rates in the world. 'The commitment to the environment must be followed up on in the budget and resolutions,' said Bård Vegar Solhjell, minister of the environment. Much of the newly generated tax revenue will go into a governmental fund devoted to investing in clean energy, the environment and public transportation.
>
> *International Herald Tribune*,
> reporting on Bård Vegar Solhjell, 2012[32]

Some of our greatest costs are now energy. Just two generations ago, we spent more on food than anything else. Now many of us in rich countries spend more on gasoline for our cars, fuel to heat our homes and electricity to run our gadgets, as compared to how much we spend on food to fuel our bodies.

The Norwegians are leading the world in energy taxation, but they are also one of the major world polluters as they extract all that oil from their half of the North Sea. However, they are a model nation compared to the UK, which has squandered its share more readily to get a faster buck. The UK also failed to invest its oil profits in the kind of sovereign wealth fund that Norway has established to help future generations and to reduce global harm in other ways. Instead, the money was used between 1979 and 2012 to cut top income tax rates for the rich, mostly just a few people living in south-east England. It is no wonder so many Scottish people want independence when they look at what Norway has done so much better, although even in the UK, overall energy use and especially petrol use has been falling both recently and from before the 2008 financial crash.

Energy use peaked in the UK in 2001 and had fallen by 3 per cent by 2007. It fell even during the noughties economic boom, despite more people driving, as cars became more fuel-efficient, as more homes were insulated and as energy prices rose. It matters that consumption was falling in the good times. The foundations established then are now being transformed into a thrift that is becoming essential. Between 2009 and 2010, in the depth of economic gloom but environmental benefit, coal imports to the UK fell by a further 31 per cent; this was by almost a third in just one year![33]

In Norway, price rises for fuel reduce consumption but do so in a way that does not cause great hardship to huge numbers of Norwegian people. Norway is the most equitable country in Europe. The poorest fifth of its people receive more than twice as much income as do the poorest fifth of people in the UK. Once a little greater equality is won in Portugal, where the rich are being taxed most to pay for austerity, the UK will become the most economically unequal country in Western Europe.

The poorest fifth of households in the UK have to get by on less than one seventh of the income of the richest fifth, even after receiving benefits and paying taxes. They receive less in a week than the richest fifth get in a day. When fuel prices in Britain rise, the poorest have to turn off the heating and freeze. The richest are still so rich that some can leave the windows open and the heating on. Economic inequality is not energy-efficient. Because of all this, the reduction in consumption in the UK has resulted in far more hardship than any reduction in energy consumption in Norway ever does. And Norway is a far colder country.

Domestic energy use in the UK peaked in 2004 and fell by 3.5 per cent by 2007 despite overall rising living standards in those years. Average per person ground-travel kilometres, mostly by road and a little by rail, peaked in 2005. The most efficient travellers walked, cycled, or – like most of the poorest fifth – used the bus as they had no car. The volume of aviation fuel burnt by UK fliers peaked in 2006 and has fallen each year since then.

Although people in Britain and across much of the rest of the world are flying slightly longer distances each year, on average, this form of transport is becoming a little more fuel-efficient and hence slightly less polluting. But many flights could be avoided. Three quarters of UK air passengers are middle class, and that proportion is rising. Fewer working-class people flew in 2004 as compared to the year 2000.[34] More frivolous flights are taken in a more unequal society, fewer flights to the deathbed of a relative, or to help a friend who has just become a parent or who is ill. We need to fly less but we also need to fly more fairly.

Since 2002, the greatest rise in any form of transport in the UK has been in cycling and walking. Similar trends have been reported for eight other countries. On this subject, see the remarks attributed to Adam Millard-Ball and Lee

Schipper at the start of the last section of Chapter 3 ('Peak everything') and the evidence presented in their paper.[35] Imagine what would happen if the UK became a slightly more economically equal nation, if it moved towards the average level of inequality for the EU. Imagine how those at the top would be much less frivolous and wasteful in their use of energy if they had a little less money to burn, and how those at the bottom would use the extra money they had more wisely, buying a bike rather than catching the bus, for example. In the long term, it is cheaper to buy a bike than bus tickets, but you need more money in the short term to do so.

Some of our greatest polluters are our cars, our general rubbish and our addiction to buying so many new clothes (and the waste created in manufacturing and disposing of them), but in all these areas, and despite the best efforts of advertisers, we are becoming ever so slightly wiser. This all began to occur just before our global population hit seven billion. It happened partly because people were being more careful. But it is not hard to do this. In the USA, the 'average woman has worn just 20 per cent of her wardrobe in the last year, but continues to spend upwards of $6,000 a year on new clothing and accessories'.[36]

As yet we have no supranational body working to wean us off so much use of fabric. In other areas of consumption, consideration is now being bolstered by others tilting the playing field to encourage less waste: 'By 2013, 33 countries and 18 so-called sub-national jurisdictions will have some sort of levy associated with the emission of CO_2 . . . The EU prefers a system that taxes more of what we burn and less of what we earn. If we want to consume less energy, we need a smarter way of taxing,' said Isaac Valero-Ladron, EU spokesman for climate action in response to Norway's new tax. Mr Valero-Ladron points to the successes of environmentally progressive tax schemes put in place in northern European countries during the nineties. According to his data, these tax policies have already led to significantly lower levels of CO_2 emissions without impacting economic growth.[37] In fact they reduced harmful economic growth and encouraged good economic growth.

Even in the UK, which has been slower than many countries in the rest of Europe to tax some forms of CO_2 waste, new car registrations peaked in 2003 and fell during the economic boom, a total fall of 10 per cent by 2007. This was long before people started to queue to take their savings out of Northern Rock. New models of automobile were developed which emitted far less pollutants but which tended to weigh a little more, so there was no great reduction in vehicle weight and hence no fall in our measures of overall vehicle consumption and the consumption of the materials used to make cars, vans and lorries.

The fashion for larger cars in the more unequal of the richest nations has prevented there being a more impressive reduction in consumption. In the USA, a big car is still thought to imply a big man, not a fat man with a small penis (as it is understood in most of Europe). In Japan, they simply don't have large cars. Fashion and those who try to promote it often appear to be a final barrier preventing our progress to a successful second demographic transition.

Only when it becomes fashionable to consume less will success become obtainable. But imagine what could happen if advertisers started to explain that it was only people who felt inadequate about themselves who needed large or expensive vehicles to drive? Or wardrobes full of clothes of which they only ever wore 20 per cent? Even better, imagine such ideas spreading without the need to pay advertisers to spread them?

Since the economic crash in the UK, many households have downsized to one car and got their first or an extra bike. We worry that others, in China and India especially, are abandoning their bikes for cars, and we are right to worry, but the long-term trend is normally set by the most affluent, and the most affluent are increasingly using pedal power. Business people in Germany travel long distance by train, not air, and more and more people (who can) are valuing their time more highly and Skyping rather than travelling to meetings. The first public use of Skype (internet telephone) was in 2003, less than a decade ago!

What of the energy involved in dealing with waste and producing huge quantities of clothes? There is, as yet, no digital substitute for clothing. Well, in the UK people are now consuming a little less in general, consequently requiring less energy to be expended to meet their wants, and so throwing less away and needing less energy to be used by garbage lorries and other waste facilities. The waste of the British peaked in 2003 and fell by 5 per cent between then and 2008;[38] it is falling faster now, and a far higher proportion of that smaller amount of waste is being recycled, although recycling, especially of glass, can consume a lot of energy. But it is worth ending on stories that are not so good, and the one big area where consumption is not falling is in clothes.

In many rich countries, but especially in the UK, we still buy so many clothes that most are only worn a dozen times and hardly any are worn out by their wearers. Fashion is still dangerous. Far better to have fewer clothes made, exported and bought than to more carefully recycle all those millions of almost immediately regretted purchases. But even in the years building up to seven billion people being alive all at once, all needing feeding and clothing, the people of the UK managed to reduce consumption in most areas where what they were buying had weight. Just not in one key area – what they wore.

It was not that people were wearing more clothes because the weather had become colder. It was that they had been persuaded to buy more because it would apparently make them look good. Consumption – the novelty of newly filled shopping bags – is partly a way of drowning your sorrows and insecurity.

There is something harder about giving up buying so many new clothes as compared to buying less food (which can make you look thinner), fewer plane tickets (which saves a huge amount of money) or using less cement (which you often don't realize you are doing). This is especially true in more economically inequitable affluent nations where how you look appears to matter much more than how you really are, something you may have to try to hide by what you wear. More people are poor in more unequal affluent nations. Overall people in such places spend more to try to look better. The poor go into greater debt to do this. If we wish to see ourselves travel more surely over the peaks of consumption trends, then we urgently need to become more equal. Of any large nation, it is the Japanese who consume and hence throw away the least, just over 400 kg of waste per person per year; Japan is the country in which income inequalities are the lowest of all.[39]

Commodity peaks are part of the story of future fear, including even fearing that there will be no future because there will not be a peak for many years to come, as in the case of peak oil. The fear that oil will not peak is the fear that we will continue to find new reserves and burn so much more that climate change will be further accelerated and for a time that acceleration itself will become irreversible. But along with encouraging further extraction, higher prices for oil in future should, as campaigner

Lucy Care suggests, 'also support renewable technologies, speed energy-saving investment and the development of new low-energy technologies. Let's try to see the upside sometimes.'[40]

Care is right. It can be hard to see the up side when so many are concentrating on the down side: 'As coal begins to replace oil and gas as an energy source, both CO_2 and sulphur emissions will go up for each unit of energy used. Technological innovations may mitigate sulphur emissions from coal burning, but affordable ways to reduce CO_2 emissions are nowhere in sight. Based on what we know now, global CO_2 emissions will rise markedly as the world turns to coal for energy.'[41] There is more coal than oil and gas combined. Others complain that as soon as it is mentioned that gas emits less carbon than coal, gas-producing companies try to get gas labelled as green energy. Low carbon is like low-nicotine cigarettes: still bad for you.

One great failure is carbon trading. To understand the problem you don't need to know the details. What you do need to know is that former top UK civil servants, such as Joan MacNaughton, don't believe that what they were involved in devising is working: 'The carbon market is profoundly weak, and the CDM [Clean Development Mechanism] has essentially collapsed. It's extremely worrying that governments are not taking this seriously.'[42] CDM also stands for Carbon Derivatives Market.[43] Any large-scale market will tend to operate to maximize the profits of a few. It is local markets that are most efficient in satisfying people's actual needs and minimizing transaction costs.

The government action which does work is carbon taxing rather than trying to create a global market in carbon and then expressing surprise when a very small number of financiers profit from it while carbon pollution continues to rise. Can you imagine the government in the 1970s establishing a tobacco trading treaty to allow firms to buy and sell the right to produce cigarettes? Instead governments taxed cigarettes and put their efforts into explaining to people how they would die earlier and often painfully if they continued to smoke as much. It would help if we learnt from that and listened to financiers less. It might also help if we were more doubtful over the wisdom of the anecdotes of celebrities.

Future fear

There's lots to worry about these days but you know what worries me most: the news I read day before yesterday that by something like 2045 there will be 10 billion people on the planet – or more! This is profoundly bad news. There are already millions and millions of people that are starving in the world and even more without drinkable water. There simply won't be enough of the things that human beings need to survive – much less thrive – not enough food, water, jobs, space. Then there's the issue of our souls – what will the world be like when there's no more wilderness, or wild animals or marine life because one species of animal – homo sapiens – has taken up all the space and resources? What happens when everything is even more crowded, crammed, angry? Where will we go to find peace and calm? What about empty lots? As a child, much of who I am was formed by exploring in nature and playing in overgrown empty lots. Where will discovery come from in 2045?

I am in New York City as I write this. I lived here in the 1950s when there were a little over 2 billion people in the world. My children (never mind my grandchildren) will never know what a city

183

like New York was like with 5 billion fewer people in the world. Even now, with 7 billion people, it is hard to walk down Broadway or Fifth Avenue because of the almost solid mass of bodies jostling to find a space to walk through. Forget about walking a small dog down those streets. Forget about meditating in the courtyard of the Frick Museum which used to be a place of calm refuge for me.

I'm scared. I'll be gone but I am scared for my grandchildren and for the wild animals and for the whole human race.

Jane Fonda, American actress, 2011[44]

When I was at school, I feared winter. What I actually feared was nuclear winter, the conditions I would have to survive if I was one of those unlucky enough not to die during the first few weeks of the then frequently forecast nuclear war to come. This fear helped. It stopped me worrying about the other winter to come, the one that I learnt of in geography lessons. The next glaciation was, apparently, imminent.

Glaciation was thought imminent in the 1970s and early 1980s because some scientists at the time jumped 'to an erroneous short-term conclusion: they inferred that the brief levelling out and slight downturn in global temperature under way during the 1960s and 1970s might be the onset of a new ice age'.[45] The immediate descent into ice age did not worry me, because I had the greater fear of nuclear war to occupy me. Then, just as I encountered puberty, the government began to play advertisements on TV where certain people had a little red dot following them about, explaining that if you had sex, you might die (HIV/AIDS had just been discovered). Suddenly nuclear war didn't seem so bad.

Fear of the future waxes and wanes. Sometimes there is great optimism. The millennium was one of those times, although largely stage-managed optimism that was short-lived. The ending of the Second World War was a far more solid period of looking forward to a better world. Pessimism ranks highly when it is generally understood that conditions are deteriorating and there is good reason to be gloomy. There was much pessimism in the 1930s and towards the end of the 1970s. In the 1930s, it turned out, this was not justified for the medium term. A child born in the 1930s would live through some of the best of times despite WWII, enter the labour market with full employment and retire on a good pension. In the case of the 1970s, much of the pessimism was warranted, not because of where we were, but because of where we were heading.

The prevailing mood of the times can be found in all kinds of signs. Children's fiction is one source. Melissa Wilson, an authority on books for children, has recently explained how 'modern children's literature revealed a deep anxiety about childhood on the part of authors who wrote the books and parents who buy them. The children in these novels have become the hope that will lead us, the readers and adults, to a better place. The child is the modern figure in the post-modern mess, the scientific, rational and reactionary figure.'[46] The kind of stories that are celebrated now include Steven Butler's *The Wrong Pong*, which is all about a boy who leaves his selfish parents and chooses to live instead with a family of trolls. I have not read it so do not know if he moved to Norway at the same time to find these less selfish creatures.

If the glass is half full rather than half empty, the optimist sees dirty coal use declining, or at the very least a little more of the carbon being captured and stored. The possibilist sees increased reliance on wind, marine, hydro and solar power, and all the much disputed major sources of sustainable energy. Debate has moved on from seeing whether these are essential, to asking whether nuclear power should be considered as sustainable. With nuclear power, the main threats are long-term pollution and cost, medium-term risk from climate change and flooding, tsunamis and earthquakes, and the immediate risk from terrorism or simply a Chernobyl or Three Mile Island type accident.

Blowing up a wind turbine has little effect; plunging a fully fuelled light aircraft into a nuclear reactor is, as yet, untested in impact. Simple natural earthquakes and tsunamis are enough to cause widespread panic when nuclear power is involved, but none of this debate may be necessary. There is a far greater source of power than nuclear energy, and that is simply not using the energy in the first place. Many argue that this is what we should do, because nuclear power is not safe, and there are green alternatives that would achieve much more than make vast profits for a few, as nuclear power tends to. In contrast, there are only a few 'players' in the nuclear industry, which, with governments underwriting most of the risks, can expect to become very rich indeed. Ironically, one of the key risks involved in nuclear power is climate change.

In August 1666, the City of London burnt in a great fire. It burnt partly because it had become so dry. The River Thames had been reduced to a trickle upstream in Oxford. In 2007, a nuclear power plant was proposed nearby at Didcot on that river. Even when not generating power, the kind of nuclear plant proposed requires three megawatts of power to cool the fuelling rods. The French, who rely the most on nuclear power, know a great deal about these problems.

In a short letter written to a national newspaper in

2012, Susan Roaf, Professor of Architectural Engineering at Heriot-Watt University in Edinburgh, explained that:

> In August 2011 Dominique Bestion, research director of the French Atomic Energy and Alternative Energies Commission, said he foresaw no new inland nuclear power stations being built because of climate change. He cited the experience of France, where they increasingly have to put their nuclear plants into sleep mode on rivers such as the Loire. In the summer of 2003, when 15,000 people died in the heat wave in France, three of the Loire plants were shut down and blackouts ensued. In response France installed over 200MW of distributed photovoltaics to meet summer peak demands, when such inland nuclear plants fail to generate. Nuclear energy in a rapidly warming climate, with more extreme weather, is unsafe, whether inland or by the sea. We already have the technology to build a safe and sufficient renewable energy future at much lower costs. The question is, who is actually stopping us doing it?[47]

And the answer is, as almost always, the people who will lose profits if we do.

In March 2010, a UK government report was leaked which revealed that:

> As many as 12 of Britain's 19 civil nuclear sites are at risk of flooding and coastal erosion because of climate change ... Nine of the sites have been assessed by the Department for Environment, Food and Rural Affairs (DEFRA) as being vulnerable now, while others are in danger from rising sea levels and storms in the future. The sites include all of the eight

proposed for new nuclear power stations around the coast, as well as numerous radioactive waste stores, operating reactors and defunct nuclear facilities. Two of the sites for the new stations – Sizewell in Suffolk and Hartlepool in County Durham, where there are also operating reactors – are said to have a current high risk of flooding.[48]

None of this is surprising, as reactors tend to be sited on very low-lying land, usually by an estuary, sea or ocean, but the fact that it was felt necessary to keep secret something so obvious is surprising.

There is a powerful pro-nuclear lobby that is part of the industry wishing to see people use more energy. It swung into action after the Fukushima Daiichi plants were brought down by the March 2011 tsunami, making claims that the fact that there was not an even bigger explosion meant that nuclear power was safe! The private nuclear industry exists to make profit, not to make sense. The state nuclear industry has in the past existed to provide the raw material for nuclear weapons, and it has been very secret.

In public, a few greens rally against the anti-nuclear bandwagon. When it was announced in 2012 that Japan planned to phase out nuclear power entirely by 2030, and that the French president had revealed a plan to dramatically reduce his country's reliance on nuclear energy, renowned environmentalist Mark Lynas made the following statement: 'Let me be very clear. Without nuclear, the battle against global warming is as good as lost. Even many greens now admit this in private moments.'[49] He continued:

But in response to the nuclear shutdown, oil and gas imports to Japan have doubled, and carbon dioxide emissions soared by more than 60m tonnes. Any environmentalist who celebrates this outcome is not worthy of the name. Japan is already backing away from its own climate change targets. As a participant in the UN climate negotiations last year, I watched this happen. Under the 2009 Copenhagen accord, Japan pledged to reduce CO_2 emissions by 25 per cent by 2020. The plan was to increase nuclear to half of national electricity in order to facilitate the carbon cuts, supported by an increase in renewables to 20 per cent by 2030. To reach the same targets without nuclear is impossible; wind and solar combined meet barely 1 per cent of electricity production today in Japan, and there is no way they can be deployed at sufficient scale to meet the gap. So the climate targets will be dropped, as Japan re-carbonises its economy.

As should be clear, nuclear power is currently at the heart of a great debate over how best to provide energy to some eight, nine or even ten billion people in future, without releasing more carbon into the atmosphere.

Most energy is not used to keep people warm or to keep the lights on. It is used to manufacture goods and to transport them to us. Do goods that require large amounts of electricity in their construction need to be produced where there is less scope for renewable energy to work? Do we need as many goods as we currently consume? If more that we consumed was not physical, but digital, would the slight increase in energy required to power headphones or light up a screen be greatly outweighed by the gain made by not spending the money on something more tangible that required more carbon emissions to produce?

Anti-nuclear greens explain how it is not just that they fear nuclear waste, but also that the nuclear industry creates only a few jobs for a few Homer Simpsons, while non-nuclear renewable energy, partly because it is initially not so efficiently garnered from a reactor, generates many more opportunities for useful work without potentially dire long-, medium- and even short-term consequences: 'Over the last ten years, Germany has seen a boom in green jobs. More than 340,000 new jobs have been created in the renewable energy sector. By contrast, Germany's only domestic fossil energy source, lignite coal, employs only 50,000 people along its entire supply chain, from mining to the power plants. Unemployment is a big challenge in Germany, too, but the renewable industry is providing many new jobs.'[50] If Germany closes as many nuclear power stations as it currently promises to do, even more such green jobs will have to be created.

In 2011, German chancellor Angela Merkel announced plans to shut all 17 nuclear power plants in the country and ensure that by 2050 four fifths of all energy was provided by more renewable sources, especially wind and solar power. On 16 October 2012, it was announced that:

A year and a half later, the costs of that plan, known here as the *Energiewende*, or energy transformation, are becoming painfully clear, and they threaten to present one of the steepest popular challenges to Ms Merkel as she prepares to face a general election next year. The country's four main grid operators released estimates this week showing that households will see a nearly 50 percent increase in the tax needed to fund the transformation, meaning that an average three-person household could be expected to see an additional €60 or $78 on their annual electricity bill.[51]

Four days earlier, in the UK, it was announced that energy

consumers would pay on average £80 more (€98 or $128) in the coming winter, which many believed was purely to grow the privatized electricity and gas companies' profits.[52] And four days before that, it was explained that: 'Hundreds of wind farms could be built on the great bog of Ireland to generate electricity exclusively for the UK's national grid under plans being considered by ministers.'[53] Wind energy is coming, even to the belligerent Englanders and even if they first have to pay the Irish for the privilege. England is downwind of Ireland. I suspect many in England are glad that the Irish have no nuclear power plants.

Fears of nuclear power are continually sparked by reports of possible cancers,[54] although it is fear of a larger accident that worries me more. Nuclear power provides just a small fraction, below 6 per cent, of the world's energy. Fossil fuels provide 87 per cent of our energy and other more renewable sources contribute the remaining 7 per cent. Nuclear power plants simply create electricity – which is quite easy to do in many other ways. Fuelling aeroplanes, which cannot run on electricity, is harder. With solar power the prices are falling very quickly and are as cheap as nuclear, though you have, additionally, to take into account the costs of looking after the nuclear waste for thousands of years.

Photovoltaic prices have a long way to go before they stop falling. Put solar panels in the deserts of the world, connect them up with high-voltage power lines and many claim that we'll have safe and cheap electricity for as long as humans exist. Further away from the equator there tends to be more wind, although wind can have some advantages where it is arid.

In contrast to nuclear power's great need for huge amounts of water and its potential to pollute with radioactive waste, wind power has now been adapted to allow turbines to produce at least 1,000 litres of drinking water a day for a minimum of 20 years by condensing the water out of the air using the power they generate. This has been shown to work in the most arid and inaccessible areas and is designed to require almost no maintenance. As the US's ABC News explained to viewers watching its reports, simply using the 'mechanics of a dripping air conditioner, French inventor Marc Parent was inspired to create a solution that could bring fresh water to the most remote, driest parts of the world'.[55] It is hard to think of a greater contrast to nuclear power.

Waste from energy production is a huge problem and is predictable. It is not an unexpected environmental catastrophe. These are insured against and so their likelihood and frequency are known, and have been known from at least as long ago as 1989, when one of Exxon's ships spilled hundreds of thousands of barrels of crude oil into the bay of Alaska, almost as much as was released in the Gulf of Mexico by the Deepwater Horizon spill of 2010, a disaster, like its predecessors, waiting to happen. 'The *Exxon Valdez* spill was, therefore, not an unforeseen accident but a dead certainty – and one that may yet be beggared by others to come. It was as predictable as Three Mile Island and Chernobyl.'[56]

There is, of course, far more to being green and fearing an unsustainable future than simply worrying about nuclear waste and carbon emissions. Trees are not just sticks of carbon; they are essential habitats. We even find we are healthier when we see more green out of our windows. Good-quality unpolluted local food matters for us, as does clean air and water, maintaining biodiversity and more quickly bringing to an end the high extinction period we are currently creating. But too much fear can paralyse.

Scaremongering is a trade. A 2009 student dissertation based on a study sponsored by the Optimum Population Trust was widely quoted during 2012 and found that 'Based on various scenarios and depending on the level of precautions taken to preserve the environment and ecosphere, calculations show that by 2100 the world will only be able to sustain between 2.7 billion and 3.2 billion people. The corresponding figures for the UK for 2100 vary between 7 million to 9 million people.'[57] This conclusion was reached by listing a series of things that could go wrong, such as dead zones being created in lakes and the sea through fertilizer pollution resulting in eutrophication, and then assuming that many of them would go wrong all at once.

When they lack good sources, grand organizations rely on student dissertations to back up their dodgy dossiers. This particular dissertation continued: 'According to the Earth Policy Institute, on a worldwide basis, annual fertiliser use has increased 10-fold since 1960 and is now 145 million tonnes. Correspondingly, the number of dead zones has also doubled and at present there are some 146 dead zones worldwide';[58] it went on to claim that the fossil fuels used in fertilizing and transporting food, falling food yields as global temperatures rise, more desertification, more cyclones, rising sea levels, biodiversity loss due to pesticides, and increasingly energy-intensive agriculture can all add weight to the claim that up to 90 per cent of the population of the UK and more than half of the current, let alone future, population of the planet has to go.

This widely quoted student wrapped up his argument by suggesting that our only sustainable future is through organic farming. Ending by raising the spectre of when one baby too many is born, the baby that could break the planet's back, he concluded: 'We should aim at achieving the optimum population level rather than the maximum sustainable population. If the population is at the maximum sustainable level, a birth without a corresponding death will make the population unsustainable. Thus, no margin of fluctuation is provided in the case of the maximum sustainable population. In addition to this, there is a high possibility that the biocapacity of the Earth might be affected due to unpredictable floods, droughts and forest fires.'[59] If it were just a student dissertation it would not matter, but, rather like the dissertation relied upon in the dodgy dossier presented to the UK House of Commons to justify the start of the US–Iraq war, this one is being used by others with a desire to spread fear for their own ends.

There is an alternative to fear. The fastest way to make money is to stop buying things you don't need. It is also the fastest way to become more sustainable. And it is happening. By 2012, after 'three decades of torrid growth, China is encountering an unfamiliar problem with its recently struggling economy: a huge build-up of unsold goods that is cluttering shop floors, clogging car dealerships and filling factory warehouses . . . At the same time, the municipal government in Guangzhou, one of China's largest cities, has sharply reduced this summer the number of new car registrations it allows so as to reduce traffic congestion and air pollution.'[60] It is not just that markets had overheated by 2008. It is that there is currently a planned scaling-back taking place too: planning by the Chinese government to cut back, and planning by individual families in richer countries to consume less. The vast majority of families in poorer countries do not need to plan to consume less.

Just a few years ago, in 2005, it was possible to see almost no hope and write that: 'Investments in alternative energy sources also make good sense, but such sources seem likely only to delay the burning of our fossil fuels by a few decades, rather than replace them entirely.'[61] Now, thanks partly to an economic crash which proved that there was an alternative, albeit a painful one, to growth, the idea that we will not simply burn up all the fossil fuels a little slower than was otherwise planned can gain strength. For one thing, much is now held under the Arctic and in other disputed zones. For another thing, the reserves may soon become worth so much for other purposes, such as making plastics, that the burning of fossil fuels is reduced. For a third thing, we are beginning to realize that we might need to even better temper our energy markets, just as the Norwegians announced they were doing in autumn 2012 in the quotation that began this section. But for now, we have to begin to think whether we are up to any of these challenges, or are we just simple village people?

Village people

> The amygdala, sometimes called the lizard brain, is the fear centre of the brain. It is on high alert during moments of stress. It is afraid of snakes. It causes our heart to race during a scary movie and our eyes to avoid direct contact with someone in authority. The shortcut to compliance, then, isn't to reason with someone, to outline the options, and to sell a solution. No, the shortcut is to induce fear, to activate the amygdala. Do this or we'll laugh at you, expel you, tell your parents, make you sit in the corner. Do this or you will get a bad grade, be suspended, never amount to anything. Do this or you are in trouble.
>
> Seth Godin, American business guru, 2012[62]

We are village people. We have inherited customs, deference and fear of authority that maximizes our chances of survival in both a small tribe of related nomads and a slightly larger village. When it comes to larger settlements, these are social inheritances as much as genetic bequests. In situations where authority is not well established, we do not avoid eye contact. The writer George Orwell wrote about his shock in 1936, when visiting Barcelona during the Spanish civil war, of finding that waiters looked him in the eye.

Snakes we fear for old reasons, possibly now embedded in our psyche. Snakes in suits are a new learnt fear. You know not to trust a person in a suit just because they are wearing a suit. However, most of the parents of most people on earth may never have seen a man in a suit. Even fewer have seen a woman wearing one. The first time I ever shook another person's hand I was aged 18 and it was a shock that the suited individual put their hand out. It took me a little time to work out that they wanted me to shake it. Where and when I grew up in Britain, people did not shake hands. The ways people behave in the city, how they act when they are innovative, even what they choose to wear, is a shock to most village people.

Mass consumption and the crucial importance of fashion for the majority of humankind is very recent. Fashion has always been with us, ever since we strung seashells into necklaces, but that was not an early version of fashion in its current form. In France, the wearing of jackets became standard in the countryside only around 1895. In 1885, most men had worn smocks. Now what was observed in France in the late 1880s has spread to every poor-world small town, where there is 'a real clash of civilizations . . . the whole urban world . . . [versus] peasant culture'.[63] Peasants today mostly do not want to look like peasants. In the rich world, the poor, understandably, do not want to look poor.

The fact that industrialization came quickly in France meant that peasants began to perceive themselves as peasants in the presence of better-dressed people from the cities. As most of the world has seen industrialization very recently, as compared to market towns, the perception that 'urban is advanced' has only just spread globally, and peasants almost everywhere have rapidly begun to abandon their normal demeanour, the clothes, the look of peasants. This is part of the transfer from village to city. At first it resulted in the widespread growth of anomie, of a heightened sense of not belonging and of urban isolation, but that too may be abating.

Other far less tangible peaks than our material consumption, as measured by the weight of goods, may also be being passed right now. In most affluent countries, especially the more unequal ones, there has been an extraordinary rise in the rate at which young people have been reporting frequent feelings of depression or anxiety and the rate at which those rises have been assessed as independently verifiable. Generally, rates have been roughly doubling between the 1980s and the middle of the last decade.[64]

In the England where I went to school 30 years ago, in a class of 30 boys one child, on average, suffered from mental illness; a decade ago, two were suffering by age 15 or 16. For a class of 30 girls, the rise has been from three to six. However, since the middle of the noughties, the rise in severe teenage angst appears to have reached a plateau and may be beginning to fall. As yet it is too early to tell. The current economic crisis may increase the anxiety of the young to another even higher level of depressive thoughts, but there is the possibility that we are just over peak anxiety too, and that our children, including my children, may grow up a little less at risk of poor mental health than my own generation was.[65]

197

Between 2003 and 2007, the first large drop in the proportion of children regularly using alcohol by age 13 and in the proportion being drunk by the age of 15 had been recorded across the majority of the regions of Europe and in East Asia. These measures had been recorded as mostly rising from at least 1995 through to 2003.[66] Could drug use in general be peaking? We hide drug use well, from President George Washington's grimace on the one-dollar note, attributed to dental work aided by laudanum (an opiate), through to Florence Nightingale's possible addiction to laudanum while confined to bed for years. Grimaces appeared to be in style among some men in the past. Matthew Boulton, the businessman often most associated with British industrialization (whose face appears on £50 notes), appears to be grimacing a little in his banknote portrait too, but we have no record of his mental health or addictions.

Anxiety and general poor mental health is indicated when people give a series of positive answers to generally negative questions. These are negative in that most of us would not wish to be saying yes to them. The things that are asked tend to concern sleep, strain, concentration and your feelings about your contribution. Here are what are called the General Health Questions (GHQ-12): Lost much sleep over worry? Felt constantly under strain? Not been able to concentrate on what you are doing? Felt that you are not playing a useful part in things? Not been able to face up to your problem? Not felt capable of making decisions about things? Felt you could not overcome your difficulties? Not been feeling reasonably happy, all things considered? Not been able to enjoy your normal day-to-day activities? Been feeling unhappy or depressed? Been losing confidence in yourself?Been thinking of yourself as a worthless person?[67] Try answering the questions yourself and count up how many you would concur with.

Then compare yourself to what is probably a very different group of people.

In 2003 in Iran, youngsters aged 18 to 24 tended, on average, to answer yes to 3.7 of those 12 questions (when carefully translated into Farsi).[68] Dutch studies of people of all ages reported rises from 3.1 to 4.6 average positive answers between 1983 and 1997, attributed to the fact that 'the increasing complexity of life apparently takes its toll, even of the socially best-equipped'.[69] Rates in Britain appear to rise from 3.7 in 1991–4 to 3.8 by 2000–4,[70] but 'a fourth wave of data collection from 2004 suggested that by this time the trends may have been levelling off, providing cause for guarded optimism . . . this still, however, leaves young people today with a general level of emotional and behavioural problems that is significantly higher than it was for 16-year-olds living through the 1970s and 1980s'.[71] If we have passed the peak in Britain, then we have only just passed it.

Some people are concerned that individuals with the same problems might answer yes to more questions over time as society becomes more open. However, a study that looked in detail at whether the GHQ-12 measure could be used to track trends over time found that 'Overall, these results indicate that the GHQ-12 is a consistent instrument over multiple applications with relatively long time periods between applications in general population samples. These properties make it particularly suited for long-term studies that require an indicator of minor psychiatric morbidity.'[72] That particular study reported average rates that rose in men aged under 65, up until 1996, and then fell across Britain for that group, but which continued to rise to 1997 for women (although even for women the proportion suffering poor mental health then fell using the Health Survey for England sample).

Why might we be seeing the beginning of a slowdown in anxiety? It may be partly because we are beginning to better understand many people's problems with modernity, especially when dealing with the problem of no longer knowing our place as we move from the village to the city, and then subsequently coping with how we appear to be ranked. The extent to which there is a causal mechanism between knowing how we are being ranked and judged and whether that appears to be biologically harmful is still much debated. Geneticists who have been looking for the causes of apparently very high correlations have recently come to realize that there must be a psychological component to the harmful 'effects of social stress and SES [Social Economic Status] in humans, in which observed "social gradients" in disease risk remain in large part unexplained by resource access alone'.[73] It is as much knowing that others have more (than simply not having enough) that hurts, especially as more and more of our basic needs are met.

Two years before the geneticists began reporting on how we appear programmed for cooperation, a social mechanism was being outlined by Richard Wilkinson, an epidemiologist and researcher in social inequalities, in this case in a journal of business management. He suggested that:

At the bottom of all this is the potential (which Hobbes made the basis of his political philosophy) that because human beings, like the members of any other species, have the same needs as each other for food and shelter, there is always the potential for terrible conflict between us for scarce resources. That is why Hobbes said that in a state of nature, without a sovereign government to keep the peace, the 'competition of each against all' would lead to life being 'nasty, brutish, and short'. But what he missed is surely that we also have the opposite potential – that of being each other's best source of assistance, learning, cooperation and love, so other people can be the best or the worst.[74]

Others are your worst enemy when it becomes clear that they disrespect you, that they rank you low.

In 2008, two years before that work, and Richard's publication, in collaboration with Kate Pickett, of the book *The Spirit Level*, the importance of rank became so evident in neurological brain scanning that it was found that 'social hierarchical consequences of performance were neurally dissociable and of comparable salience to monetary reward, providing a neural basis for the high motivational value of status. Our results identify neural mechanisms that may mediate the enormous influence of social status on human behavior and health.'[75] It really does hurt us village people to think we are being looked down on, and this can be a great problem in the city, where it appears that strangers would more happily trample over you than assist you, were you to fall. In urban areas the mental consequences of not feeling you are supported can be made worse again. However, you can also escape the stultifying effect of rural hierarchies by being a stranger in the city.

Four years prior to those 2008 brain scans, an anthropologist had come to the conclusion that:

The most striking quality of the human SES/health gradient is its imperviousness. Do socially subordinate animals suffer a disproportionate share of poor health? The answer can only be, 'Often, but certainly not as a rule.' Do poor humans suffer a disproportionate share of poor health? The answer must be a robust, Yes — regardless of gender, age, or race; with or without universal healthcare, in culturally homogeneous societies or ones rife with ethnic tensions, and under governments with socialist or capitalist credos. The developments of class, stratification, and poverty are fairly recent in hominid history. What these findings suggest is that nothing in the world of nonhuman sociality involves such an utterly, psychologically permeating sense of subordination as does the human invention of poverty.[76]

And the worst of poverty is now found in cities, places where people can have literally nothing, not even a scrap of land. It is, perhaps, surprising we do not fear the city and our current demographic transition more.

This account of anxiety and depression can itself read as depressing, and it should, because it is an account that has been travelling back in time. Now work forwards towards the future. From the 2004 findings in anthropology of how debilitating poverty is, to the 2008 results of neurological brain scans identifying how it is that we react negatively to being looked down on, we are learning. From the 2010 findings of epidemiologists that we are each other's best source of assistance, of learning and cooperation, we learn more. Then in 2012 come the findings of geneticists studying other apes and suggesting that our poor health outcomes from living under great inequality are unexplained by resource access alone, but could be partly locked up in our genes; that we have evolved to be cooperative.

As we are moving forward in time, we are making progress. Look back further in this section and see those apparent slight improvements in some of our mental health test scores. Do all this, and like me, you may not be so fearful that we are about to urbanize even more, that our numbers may reach eight billion by 2025, and will do so with such apparent, albeit decreasing, speed.

We are beginning to learn much more about ourselves. Things we will need to know to survive better collectively. The evidence that great proximity leads to greater societal stress is far from overwhelming. So let's turn back a little to basics and ask some questions which are more fundamental than whether we are psychologically and organizationally up to the task of living with more humans. The next chapter begins by asking: will there be enough food and water for eight billion of us, and will we learn to stop being as stupid as we have been at a fast enough rate to secure what we need?

CHAPTER 5

8 BILLION BY THE QUARTER CENTURY (2025)

> [C]apital has one single life impulse, the tendency to create value and surplus-value, to make its constant factor, the means of production, absorb the greatest possible amount of surplus-labour. Capital is dead labour, which, vampire-like, lives only by sucking living labour, and lives the more, the more labour it sucks.
>
> Karl Marx *Capital*, Volume One, 'The limits of the working day', 1867

Capital is about to experience the start of a shortage of young blood. The quarter century is almost upon us. The year 2025 is the date when the current UN median projection suggests that there will first be eight billion humans on earth, but a lower proportion than ever will be children. I'll be 57 years old, if I am still alive. I don't think any of us are going to get to leave earth to set up elsewhere anytime soon. But I had better be careful about any predictions. I'll still hopefully be around to be proved wrong. Such caution is rare in futurology, where for a commentator to be taken notice of it helps if their predictions are not dull.

One commentator, Decca Aitkenhead, quotes from an economist, Dambisa Moyo, who had 'stepped off a transatlantic flight only hours before we meet, but arrives looking like a supermodel',[1] and who suggests that

> in less than 20 years we will witness the creation of a middle class of roughly the same size as the current total population of Africa, North America and Europe. Naturally, they will want mobile phones, fridges, cars and washing machines; 2,000 new cars already join Beijing's streets every day. In 2010 China had 40 cities with populations of more than a million; by 2020 it plans to have added another 225. The implications for the world's commodity resources are stark and sobering: global demand for food and water is expected to increase by 50 per cent and 30 per cent respectively by 2030, the pressure on copper, lead, zinc and corn is already becoming unsustainable, and no one has a clue where the energy we'll need is going to come from.[2]

This is the case according to Dambisa, who completed her PhD thesis recently and has been working at Goldman Sachs. She describes herself as an 'international economist who writes on the macro-economy and global affairs'.[3] She doesn't have much faith in people being able to settle their differences outside of markets. Instead she is reported to think that 'the world will be drawn into a war for resources . . . I think we'll see more wars'.[4]

For now let us accept the latest UN population forecasts and not assume more wars than normal. Wars result in more deaths, but are also often followed by a baby boom. The latest UN projections suggest that in the 14 years following 2011, we will increase in number from seven to eight billion humans. What kind of a world can we expect to live in by 2025? Will even more people be hungry? Will the rich be even richer and the poor poorer? Will we really have begun to curtail our consumption? How will the United States have coped as it becomes ever more obvious that the top slot is slipping from its grasp?

Well – how bad will it actually be? Look at the graphs in this book of where population growth is forecast to occur – almost all the extra people are to be born where pollution by humans is least. And notice the deceleration. It is going to take longer, another 14 years, to add this extra billion as compared to the billion that came before. This is the first time we have ever seen an increase in the number of years it has taken to hit the next billion. These should be the years in which it finally becomes clear that we are not facing a future of greater human numbers, a period in which the slowdown and its implications begin to become apparent. If we are hopeful, then these should be the years in which we begin to fear less, and plan more, or at least the years in which more of us become angrier and force such positive action. We can compel that which is already taking place to accelerate, partly by decrying what is already being done as, possibly, too little too late.

Food and farming

The primacy of the population–environment link is not substantiated by empirical evidence. Environmental damage may be the result of a small number of individuals exploiting resources without regard to the social consequences of their actions. Or it may be the result of a large number of farmers who lack the resources to properly manage the land.

Radical Statistics Population Studies
group report, 2012[5]

In very recent times, even the Optimum Population Trust has started to sing to a different tune. Today one of its patrons, Sir David of Attenborough, extols the virtues of places like Kerala, states lampooned half a century ago for having 'too many Asians'.[6] In a video narrated by Sir David entitled 'How Many People Can Live on Planet Earth', now uploaded on to YouTube and originally broadcast by the BBC in late 2011,[7] this celebrated knight of the English realm explains how left-wing governments and access to contraception are bringing down population. Sir David can't avoid the odd reference to the older, more elitist tune that the Trust once used, at one point saying: 'Often it takes individuals of vision to lead the change.' But the transformation from the past rhetoric of the Optimum Population Trust, now recast as the group Population Matters, is astounding. And very similar changes can be found elsewhere in the wider debate.

Unsurprisingly, the Stockholm International Water Institute, a think tank set up to address water needs, produces reports that worry about our access to water. Water matters more than many people think, and the next section of this chapter is dedicated to it. In a statement released by the Institute towards the end of the year 2012, their members remind us that 'each person requires 50 to 100 times more water to produce the food they eat than they use in their home'.[8] This is the figure for people without personal swimming pools, but it is an astounding figure nevertheless.

The Stockholm Institute's report doesn't mention private swimming pools and other excesses, but concludes that: 'There will, however, be just enough water, if the proportion of animal based foods is limited to 5 per cent of total calories and considerable regional water deficits can be met by a well organised and reliable system of food trade.' That conclusion is based on the extent of existing cropland and does not allow for the great savings that could be made through lowering food waste and reducing overeating. There is enough water, but they are right: we do need to eat less meat. Luckily eating a lot of meat is not good for us, and increasing numbers of people are choosing to eat no meat at all.

Consider a third sector, not a charity like the Optimum Population Trust, or an NGO (non-governmental organization) like the Stockholm Institute, but a private consultancy firm and its global map of food security risk. This map has been produced by yet another interested 'player', Maplecroft, a 'global risk and strategic consulting firm based in Bath, UK'.[9] Maplecroft draws a great many maps. The food risk map they have produced shows that, according to their analysis (precise details of which you would have to purchase should you want to know more), extreme food risk is now confined to only a few very poor countries. Their main problem would appear to be poverty, not land or water or too many people.

Too little food is not our problem, globally. We have enough. In many places we have too much. Obesity reduces life expectancy for men by almost six years and for women by almost seven. The effects may be far greater once you take into account that serious illness is often associated with losing weight, so some obese people become much less fat shortly before death. It is not that being slim is ideal, just that being overweight has much less effect than being obese; being overweight may even have almost no

Food Security Risk Index with ranking of countries at extreme risk of hunger or unrest

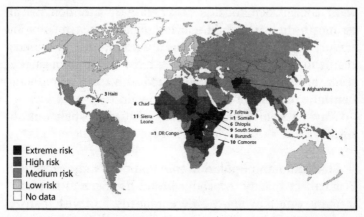

Source: http://maplecroft.com/2012.

effect depending on where the fat is on the body. But if we have enough food for so many people to be fat, then we also have enough to share better.

Becoming obese late in life is less problematic to health than earlier in life. If you don't worry about taking more than your fair share, but do worry about your health, you can look forward to overeating in old age. However, most people in richer nations need to eat less, often much less.[10] What they don't eat could provide enough for all those who go hungry, both now and in the future.

In total, all human beings in the world alive today weigh 287 million tonnes, of which 15 million tonnes, or 5 per cent, is due to some of us being overweight and a further 3.5 million tonnes, or 1 per cent, is due to obesity. Just over a third of that percentage is accounted for by North Americans. If all countries moved towards being as fat as the average citizen of the USA, then the increasing 'population fatness could have the same implications for world food energy demands as an extra half a billion people living on the earth'.[11] However, unlike the citizens of the USA, the rest of the world has a warning. It can see how big those Americans became. We have also known since at least the 1960s that we could feed us all were we able to continue to fertilize land as we now do.

Way back in 1992, *Discover Magazine* spelt out the history:

> [The] human population that could be supported by Earth's capacity to produce food has been estimated many times, by many different means, and with many different results. In outline, if food is the limiting factor, the potentially supportable population equals the potentially arable land area times the yield per unit of area divided by the consumption per person; easy enough. But of course, there is much uncertainty about the numerical values of arable area, yield, and consumption per capita. Estimates of agricultural carrying capacity have ranged from a low of 902 million [people] in 1945 to a high of 147 billion [people] in 1967. In 1965 Walter Schmitt of the University of California estimated that 30 billion people ultimately may lead fairly free and enriched lives on this planet.[12]

Despite food for humans being one of the least of our potential problems, there are constant worries because it is easy to envisage it running out. Pollinators (which include bees and bats) are declining, very probably because of the indirect effects of our greed and stupidity. Global fish stocks are falling, and yet aquaculture is increasing. Fish farming can be better than fish hunting, although as we first try it, we encounter issues of disease.

A Neolithic revolution in the water is taking place right now. It is urgently needed, according to Professor Callum Roberts, a marine conservation biologist, oceanographer and author at the University of York, whose 'team examined the effect of rising ocean temperatures on the growth and distribution of more than 600 fish species around the world and found that they are likely to shrink in size by 14–24 per cent by 2050, most notably in tropical regions'.[13] Callum goes on to describe his research as 'the most comprehensive to date', which always makes me a little cautious when there is so much research now out there.[14]

Moving from the oceans to land, hydroponics is used to grow more and more crops under glass with almost no polluting run-off. Estimates of food being wasted in affluent countries between basket and mouth (food bought but not eaten, past its sell-by date and so on) vary between a quarter up to as much as half in poorer countries due to it perishing because storage conditions are still so poor. There would be fewer rats if we were less profligate with the food we grew and stored, and if we transported it better. The amount of food we waste worldwide is enough to feed billions more.

Even if we were just to get waste rates down to the current high amounts of the affluent world, where most food waste is created by consumers, not producers, the 'majority of studies show that as the proportion of income spent on food declines, food waste increases'.[15] There are many calls today to make food a little more expensive so that we value it better and can afford to increase its quality. In a more equitable world, the disadvantages of rising food prices might well become advantages. We pay more, eat less and eat better. However, it will only be when those wider advantages of greater equality are both realized and won that we can hope for that. Today, even the *Economist*, a stalwart of the right, is advocating some of the advantages of greater equality. That magazine has yet to print the green gospel on its front cover, but any comparison of its content today, compared to a decade ago, reveals how much progress is possible.

Take again the issue of sustainable fishing. The *Economist*'s writers, quoting in their defence from a 'new statistical study', came in 2012 to realize that:

> In most fisheries, the fishermen would make more money by husbanding their resource, and it should be possible to incentivise them to do so. The best way is to give them a defined, long-term right to a share of the fish. In regulated industrial fisheries, as in Iceland, New Zealand and America, this has taken the form of a tradable, individual share of a fishing quota. Developing countries, where law enforcement is weak, seem to do better when a group right over an expanse of water is given to a co-operative or village fleet. The principle is the same: fishermen who feel like owners are more likely to behave as responsible stewards. The new statistical study confirms that rights-based fisheries are generally healthier.[16]

That was in February 2012. By October of that year, newspapers from around the world were reporting that: 'After defending capitalism stoutly for 169 years, the British weekly, *The Economist*, made a reluctant admission this week. "Inequality has reached a stage where it can be inefficient and bad for growth."'[17]

When faced with ever greater numbers of people, it can be hard to be optimistic that we will all be adequately fed in future, but the failures of what was once accepted wisdom also become more evident. People may tell you how much food is wasted, how much more we could have to eat if we fed cattle less grain, but always some are thinking, 'What happens after that efficiency gain? What next?' Under current population slowdown, there is an end in sight. There is suddenly a very obvious solution to a rich world plagued with greed and obesity and a poor world suffering oppression and starvation, a solution that is only possible because we are not going to have additional billions to be fed decade after decade after decade, and our numbers are not being reduced by famine or war but by the personal choices we are making over how many children to have, how to eat and where to live.

So, how will we farm and where will we all live when there are eight billion of us? Well, mostly where we have lived for the last few millennia. Humans have a penchant for wide river valleys and particularly favour the last bridging points on the broadest of rivers for their greatest cities. What is remarkable about where we live is how little it has altered as our numbers have soared. In many ways, as the great cities of India and China grow in size today, human population distribution is returning a little towards its original centres of gravity. And as we crowd together into those cities, delivering food to the people becomes much less of a logistical problem than it was when we were more sparsely spread out. Within many of the largest cities on earth are also found patches of urban farmland; green lungs within concrete jungles. What is a more difficult issue is how we will continue to draw all the water we require.

Water, water everywhere

Water, water, every where,
And all the boards did shrink;
Water, water, every where,
Nor any drop to drink.

Samuel Taylor Coleridge,
The Ancient Mariner, 1798

The Ancient Mariner is the best-remembered text of 1798. It was written in a time of ferment, and published in the same year as the originally anonymous *Essay on the Principle of Population*, later attributed to Thomas Malthus. Today we have water everywhere but an average child in an average affluent nation will consume 30 to 50 times more water in their lifetime compared with an average child in the majority world of poor nations.[18] Even the smallest of redistributions would provide enough for all our needs, while taking away from the most affluent only that excess water use which they would hardly notice. But water is remarkably heavy. It is not easily redistributed geographically.

It may well be water scarcity, not food, not minerals, not oil, that is our undoing. It could be something as simple as this that does for us in the end, something basic, but something we could not make more of without using huge amounts of energy through desalination. Whether civilizations end through water wars or just from the effects of prolonged drought (made more likely by human-induced climate change), water could be the key. Humanity begins to unravel as we individually simply consume too much. It has been estimated that, on average, we humans each have the environmental impact equivalent to a 30-metre-tall mountain gorilla. The thing we consume most of all is water. It is with water that we are the greediest. But too many don't care. We don't measure how many litres are required to grow a single Brussels sprout, let alone are involved in creating the polythene bag (from crude oil – and refineries that need a great deal of water) in which it and a few of its compatriots sit on the supermarket shelf.

Simultaneously sea levels rise, glaciers melt, fresh water is diminished. But see the glass of liquid as half full rather than half empty. All of this is likely to happen, and yet we could still survive on what water is left. This would not be by high-tech solutions. Not by making water in the desert; not even through nuclear-powered desalination plants. Just simple human adaptation – as has always occurred before. You can adapt as population slows down. You can't easily effectively adapt when you are experiencing a population bloom. We have been using too much water because we have been using it like we used to, when there were so many fewer of us.

As a species, we have harnessed the elements in ways that have then changed us. We first harnessed fire many millennia ago to cook food. That is now said to have saved us from having to spend seven or eight hours a day chewing and digesting raw food as other great apes do. There is evidence in the archaeological records of old cooking sites, hearths, dating back to 800,000 years ago. Our brains then grew again in size about 600,000 years ago, it is now claimed as a result of cooking that allowed us to get the extra energy we needed to fuel a larger brain: 'our brains consume 20 per cent of our body's energy when resting, compared with 9 per cent in other primates'.[19] We harnessed water when we began to irrigate. Irrigation was the technology that made much farming possible in the Neolithic revolution. We harnessed earth when we discovered the energy locked up in fossil fuels, the energy that fuelled our current demographic transition and which we also used to make fertilizer. And then we polluted the air.

Fire, water, earth, air: such a different view of human history than was held when I was at school, and one which could change as much again, perhaps faster still, before I die. We now know so much that we did not know, of what we were so ignorant just two or three generations ago. For instance: 'Irrigation began in the Tigris–Euphrates region, and, when it failed, it also led to the first regional-scale abandonment of farming. In AD 900–1200, the Maya abandoned farmland in the Yucatan Peninsula because of a combination of droughts and cumulative nutrient depletion of the soils.'[20] Repeating our mistakes millennium after millennium is far from inevitable, but only if we unearth them, record them, teach from them and learn from them.

Only a century ago, half of the original topsoil layer of the American Midwest was lost due to farming practices, with the soil 'flowing down the Mississippi River to the Gulf of Mexico'.[21] But none of those farmers knew of the Maya disaster 10 centuries earlier, or why much of the land of Mesopotamia had to be abandoned so early on in human history. Now we know. It is hard to believe that we will carry on repeating tragedy and farce. Just as we have now learnt that preventing natural forest fires only results in a greater fire eventually occurring, so too are we learning about water, and especially about great stores of fresh water and how precious they are.

In the United States, the Ogallala Aquifer, which is used to supply water to a huge area of the Great Plains for irrigation and direct human use, is said to be falling at rates of between one and three feet annually. However, the research that is often used to make this claim is also indicative of work that has been carried out since 2003 to attempt to alleviate the problem, and which finds that a particular

kind of farming is needed: 'no-till dry-land farming promotes rainfall infiltration to greater depths in the soil,
thus possibly encouraging an increase in recharge to the
aquifer. Studying the effects of climate change on irrigation demands indicates that a drought of the magnitude
experienced in the early 1950s in the Texas Panhandle may
increase the demand for irrigation beyond what the aquifer and wells can deliver.'[22] People are planning to change
crop practices to make their agriculture sustainable; this
is occurring now even in the United States, where climate
change scepticism is so very common.[23] The severity of the
2012 US drought makes comparisons with the failures of
1950s even more urgent.

Water conservation is also both planned and happening
over the North China Plain aquifer. Swedish researchers
talking of the Chinese government suggest that: 'In the
North China plain, they will have to decrease its irrigated
area to stabilise the water table, but while doing so they will
need to find ways to maintain social stability by continuing
agricultural production by synchronising crop production
with rainfall.'[24] Water flow within the Yellow River is now
so low that there are plans to divert Himalayan river water
eastwards. This could cause great suffering in India, but
water conservation often comes second to other political
issues there.

The third most vital aquifer for human food production, under Gujarat in north-west India, has a less effective
government above it compared to those found in either the
USA or China. Often the Gujarat state government appears
more concerned with oppressing Muslims than promoting sustainability.[25] Perhaps as a result of this, fewer plans
are either being made or put in place there to conserve
underground water stores. A 2011 study found that, of all
the rivers of Asia, the Ganges and Indus have the highest

vulnerability to overuse.[26] However, even in Gujarat, politicians have introduced schemes separating domestic and agricultural electricity use which reduce pumping and which have 'indirectly raised the price of groundwater supplied by tubewell owners in the informal market by 30–50 per cent, thus providing a signal of scarcity, and reducing groundwater overdraft'.[27]

The extremes are usually what are highlighted in debate. The Aral Sea is just a tenth of its original size, due to the diversion of entire rivers. Advocates for pessimism shout out that 40 per cent of our oceans have been heavily affected by human activities, that ocean chemistry is being acidified by pollution, that our current loss of species to extinction is occurring at hundreds to thousands of times 'higher than "background" rates in the fossil record'.[28] And if they had not warned before of other environmental dangers, or had done so in a far more muted way in our recent past, then no rivers in industrialized nations would contain drinkable water, ozone-depleting chemicals would never have been banned and those changes currently under way would not be there to be lamented as too little too late.

It may be too little too late, but as a species we only very recently grasped the idea that there *are* species, and what their origins might be. Alfred Wallace first pointed this out in 1858. Charles Darwin published his book in 1859, just six generations ago. Consequently we have grown to understand that environmental pressures on species, as environments change, force them to adapt to their shifting local environment or die out. This thinking followed that realization, first explained in 1858 by Wallace, that 'no unbalanced deficiency in the animal kingdom can ever reach any conspicuous magnitude, because it would make itself felt at the very first step, by rendering existence difficult and extinction almost sure soon to follow'.[29]

Just 150 years after Wallace suggested that all needs to be in balance or else there is extinction, the question that lurks behind every debate on human population growth today is whether the unbalanced deficiency is the number of humans. In an incredibly short length of time, in the space of barely more than five human generations, we have moved from just beginning to understand that there are species and that thus extinction is a possibility for any species, to concentrating on trying to prevent the possibility of our own collective demise. It is because of the explosion in our knowledge, far greater even than the rise in our numbers, that we should believe we can survive.

In 2012, the Royal Society of London, a society similar to the Linnean Society, to which Wallace and Darwin first presented their findings, announced that 'major improvements in food production are possible not only through varietal improvement but also through the wider application of known crop management practices'.[30] What they meant was that the old knowledge might be enough.

The Royal Society came to its 2012 conclusion that we could manage water well enough to grow the food we need, without needing to rely on as yet unrealized scientific discoveries, not because they are especially clever in London, but because they were picking up reports from all over the world suggesting that adaptation was not just possible, but was occurring. A year earlier, in 2011, adopting a similar global focus, the UK's Institute of Mechanical Engineers had suggested that existing technology could meet the food needs of a growing population, but only if international regulation could provide for shared technology and funding across national borders.

The conclusions of the Institute of Mechanical Engineers were brief, blunt and practical: '[1] Use existing sustainable energy technologies and reduce energy waste. Don't wait for new technologies to be developed . . .[2] Replenish groundwater sources, improve storage of excess water and increase energy efficiencies of desalination . . . [3] Reduce food waste and resolve the politics of hunger . . . [4] Meet the challenge of slums and defending against sea-level rises . . . [5] Finance: Empower communities and enable implementation.' But they concluded with a warning, and the warning was about issues outside of their mechanical competencies: 'Even though the Institution of Mechanical Engineers believes there are no insurmountable technical issues in sourcing enough energy for an increasingly affluent larger global population, and providing it to where it is needed, the solutions that will deliver a successful outcome are by no means simple. The difficulties lie in the areas of regulation, financing, politics, social ethics and international relations.'[31]

Two years earlier again, in 2009, French agricultural scientists had shown that it was possible to find water for crops to feed nine billion people in a sustainable way across the planet by 2050, but only if markets were controlled. They suggested there would need to be United Nations regulation of international food distribution if agriculture were to develop in a sustainable way, not to intensify too much but also to feed everyone well: 'Faced with this new situation, the regulation of markets has therefore also [to aim] to avoid price volatility which was very strong at the beginning of the century and largely responsible for food crises.'[32] Volatility was seen once more in late 2012 as bad weather harmed many harvests and a tiny number of speculators again saw a way they could profit out of the necessity of food.

In contrast to the French and other international scientists' approach, and jumping two years forward again, to 2011, a group of researchers working directly for the

British government produced a 'Foresight' report on food and farming which did not emphasize such a sustainable route as others had been advocating. It also sought to have wider influence than the UK engineers' or French agricultural scientists' reports. The Foresight report was made available in more languages than just French and English. It was also heavily influenced by economists of the old school of market primacy, the school that had held sway before the 2008 crash, and who still believed in the supposed logic of what they call 'international comparative advantage'. This was a theory dating from 1817 and relating not to necessities, but to wine and fine cloth, and which took no account of what was most environmentally sustainable to produce in each place, but simply what was most profitable.

David Ricardo's infamous example of how it would be better if Portugal concentrated on wine production while Britain wove wool from sheep is often repeated.[33] It sounds ever so simple, but taken to our current extremes, it results in wine being shipped today from the furthest corners of the earth to maximize profits, while more clothes than humans could ever get to wear (for more than a few weeks per garment) are manufactured in China, again maximizing profits and also environmental damage. Wine is extremely heavy. It can be turned into a powder and rehydrated halfway around the planet. It is better to source it more locally and drink alcohol, essentially a poison, less frequently.

Available also in Chinese, Russian, Spanish and Arabic, the British government's Foresight report included an extra section for readers in China in which it suggested that: 'China's over-riding priority is to maintain 95 per cent national self-sufficiency in food grains in the long-term, and the 12th [Chinese state] plan is consistent with this objective. This is contrary to the position of the Foresight

221

Report, which in general argues against self-sufficiency policies and in favour of accepting international comparative advantage.'[34] Given that the most recent human-induced global pandemic of starvation to be seen to alter global population growth rates was in China (1958–62), caution on the part of the Chinese government appears highly warranted, while the ignorance of this recent history by the Foresight staff is lamentable.[35]

Although the 2011 Foresight report ended positively, what is seen as equitable by the British researchers may also be what they see as in their economic interest. The Foresight team conclude by saying that they can see a reason for optimism, but when they refer to 'very difficult decisions ahead', they imply that these are decisions to allow the free market to rule and that it is unfortunately necessary to let the devil take the hindmost.

[T]here are real grounds for optimism. It is now possible to anticipate a time when global population numbers cease to rise; the natural and social sciences continue to provide new knowledge and understanding; and there is growing consensus that global poverty is unacceptable and has to be ended. However, very difficult decisions lie ahead and bold actions by politicians, business leaders, researchers and other key decision makers will be required, as well as engagement and support by individual citizens everywhere, to achieve the sustainable and equitable food system that the world so desperately needs.[36]

The report this quotation is drawn from is subtitled 'Choices for Global Sustainability', as if there were some kind of menu to choose from. The preface is authored by Caroline Spelman, then the British Secretary of State for

Environment, Food and Rural Affairs, but more importantly closely connected to the firm 'Spelman, Cormack &
Associates, a lobbying firm for the food and biotechnology
industry, [where she recently worked] with her husband'.[37]
Here, biotechnology means genetically modified (GM).

Often right-wing economists in Britain mean GM when
they say 'sustainable' and they mean free-market when they
say 'equitable'. GM foods are backed up by a well-financed
lobby who are often disingenuous in their advancement of
the supposed benefits of modifying the genes in food far
faster than can be done purely by selective breeding, and
also in ways that selective breeding could never achieve,
even given millennia. It is claimed that GM strains can
be produced that become more tolerant to drought and
which require less water, but if we begin to become reliant
on such plants for food and clothing, what happens when
those crops fail?

One advocacy report claimed that pesticide use in both
treated and surrounding fields in China has halved since the
introduction of a particular strain of GM cotton in 1997,
a strain that produces a poison that kills some pests but is
thought not to be harmful to people. The study claimed
also to demonstrate that this led to a doubling of the
numbers of natural insect predators found. That predator
group included ladybirds, lacewings and spiders, insects
and arthropods which apparently kill pests not targeted
by the genetically modified (Bt) cotton (Bt is shorthand
for the soil bacterium and pesticide *Bacillus thuringien-
sis*). Next the study suggested that these predators moved
on to eat pests in conventional corn, soybean and peanut
fields. In 2012, the head of policy at the Soil Association
responded to these claims by pointing out that: 'What
it doesn't cover is other recent research in China that
has discovered increased insect resistance and increased

numbers of pests developing in and around these GM cotton crops.'[38]

The greatest problem with GM technologies is that the companies that promote them are driven almost entirely to maximize their profits. Safety comes second and justice is not on their agenda. It is not just problems in China that have hit the news. Recently in India (Bt) GM cotton was banned because it was found that traditional 'Indian cotton seeds greatly reduces the demand and need for additional inputs like water, fertilizers, pesticides and other nutrients'.[39] GM crops may well not be the solution to having too little water in particular places.

The readers of the British newspaper in which the pro-GM report originally appeared also took it to task. One stated: 'Given the countless billions that have been spent on GM it's about time that a vaguely positive story came about, shame that the caveats could fill another five articles.' Another pointed out that the use of the phrase 'traditional GM' made a mockery of the term 'traditional', while a third explained: 'I've always understood the objections to GM crops to be less to do with how effective they are, but more about not allowing control of our food production to be exclusively in the hands of a very small number of already dangerously powerful people.'[40] Some aspects of GM may be positive, but there is a consensus growing that if we manage the old technology of irrigation better, then we do not have to rely so heavily on such new and potentially unreliable innovations.

Even more important than working out how best to marshal water to grow crops is working out how not to marshal water to grow food that we then don't even think of eating. The argument regarding this is so obvious and overwhelming that all I can do is simply lay out how well campaigner George Monbiot has already stated the case:

Already, 40 per cent of US corn (maize) production is used to feed cars. The proportion will rise this year as a result of the smaller harvest. Though the market for bio diesel is largely confined to the European Union, it has already captured 7 per cent of the world's output of vegetable oil. The European Commission admits that its target (10 per cent of transport fuels by 2020) will raise world cereal prices by between 3 per cent and 6 per cent. Oxfam estimates that with every 1 per cent increase in the price of food, another 16 million people go hungry. By 2021, the Organisation for Economic Co-operation and Development says that 14 per cent of the world's maize and other coarse grains, 16 per cent of its vegetable oil and 34 per cent of its sugar-cane will be used to make people in the gas-guzzling nations feel better about themselves. The demand for biofuel will be met, it reports, partly through an increase in production; partly through a 'reduction in human consumption'. The poor will starve so that the rich can drive.[41]

We, the rich, on average already drive too often and too far. Cars are the most common killers of people aged between 5 and 25 in some affluent countries where other causes of death are now so much less common,[42] while mostly outside of rich countries, worldwide, the number of deaths on the road is rapidly rising and is expected to soon overtake deaths from HIV/AIDS.[43]

There is nothing 'bio' about growing food to turn it into supposed biofuel. While people are starving, it is simply wrong. We are already creating traffic jams that can appear never-ending. In Los Angeles, drivers spend 72 hours a year just sitting in jams burning fuel partly created by growing crops using water that in California is

225

especially precious; Americans spend an average of nine years of their lives in cars.[44] Imagine growing food to fuel all that! You don't need to imagine it; it is happening now and campaigners are working hard to stop it.[45]

It is not at all hard to see that there is a better way, although it is especially hard for some of those in the USA to alter their views. It is always hard for people in the country that is currently economically dominant in the world to imagine that one day soon their way of thinking might not prevail. As Murray Bookchin, the American labelled the main 'theorist of the anti-globalisation movement before its time', put it in 1989: 'Unless growth is traced to its basic source-competition in a grow-or-die market society – the demand for controlling growth is meaningless as well as unattainable. We can no more arrest growth while leaving the market intact than we can arrest egoism while leaving rivalry intact.'[46] More people will have read Murray's books and papers since he died in 2006 than while he was alive and making this case for change, because change is coming.

Many writers suggest that fundamental changes to the organization of society hardly ever occur, but in fact they are occurring all the time during an era of demographic transition. Imagine how impossible it may have appeared a century ago to suggest that across most of the rich world the majority of adults in many of our largest cities would not be married. Today the institution of marriage is no longer an institution. As the world sees human numbers approach eight billion around the year 2025, more and more cities will see a majority of their working-age population being single. This was the case in Greater London way back in 1991.[47] If we can change the fundamental rules of our society, of how we live together in pairs under a particular contract, wasting less water in future should be far from impossible.

No *marriage city*

> Pessimism wins the headlines and book contracts, but has often been shown to be mistaken . . . or luddite . . . Since authors owe it to their readers to declare their dispositions, I am like René Dubos, a 'despairing optimist'.
>
> L. T. Evans, plant physiologist, CSIRO, 1998[48]

The writer of these words was referring to food and the despair that there might not be enough, but his words could as easily be applied to many other aspects of human life. He was despairing because other people may not be optimistic enough to do what they need to do to ensure enough food for all, and because he knows that if they become too optimistic, they may then become complacent. He remains an optimist because he sees no fundamental impediment to feeding us all.

A pessimistic view of the rise of city living might see its implication being increased loneliness and singlehood, the subject of this section. Should you wish, you could see the decline of marriage, that traditional village social structure, as spreading like a curse across the planet. An optimist might see great hope in humans no longer being forced to form identical pair-bond contracts that controlled the behaviour of so many of their ancestors. A despairing optimist might say that we need to consider the down side to greater freedom too, but that all might turn out OK in the end.

From 153 million in 1996 to 277 million in 2011, the number of people living alone globally has increased by 81 per cent in just 15 years. At the same time, the total world population grew by 'just' 20 per cent and the world urban population by 39 per cent. By 2011, in the United States alone, there were some 33 million lone adult households, making up a quarter of all households and a seventh of all people.[49] More and more people are living in cities; more and more of them are staying single, or at least childless.

Interestingly, despite women being more likely to end up with the children after divorce or separation, these solo dwellers are slightly more likely to be women than men. There are now nine women living alone in the United States for every seven men living on their own. This is not because demographic growth in the USA has been mostly about more people being elderly, and the sex disparity is only slightly about so many men in the USA now living communally in the armed forces and/or prison.

Of those now living alone in the US, the 'majority, more than 16 million, are middle-aged adults between the ages of 35 and 64. The elderly account for about 11 million of the total. Young adults between 18 and 34 number more than 5 million, compared with 500,000 in 1950, making them the fastest-growing segment of the solo-dwelling population. Unlike their predecessors, people who live alone today cluster together in metropolitan areas.'[50] All these are further signs that future population slowdown might take place a little quicker than current predictions suggest, predictions simply based on the past record rather than taking into account the social trends towards greater singlehood and what that implies for even further reduced fertility.

Modern-day apartments in some key ways resemble the caves our distant ancestors lived in. We still decorate our homes with art of one kind or another, even if it is just painting the walls, but once you start to build apartments and condominiums, eyries of hundreds of thousands of caves in the sky, you create the possibility for new kinds of society to emerge. As our new caves become clustered closer (so making new types of cities), and we have fewer children, the need to share the same cave diminishes. But these can be in small old cities as well as the new megalopolis. Sweden has the most solo dwellers of anywhere in the world. Single adults almost occupy a majority (47 per cent) of all Swedish dwellings, but they are still far from being a majority of all Swedish people.

In Norway, 40 per cent of households have just one resident; greater economic equality between the sexes makes solo living more financially practicable. At the opposite edge of Eurasia, in Japan, in a similarly economically equitable but far more space-strapped land, today 'about 30 per cent of all households have a single dweller ... Living alone and being alone are hardly the same, yet the two are routinely conflated. In fact, there's little evidence that the rise of living alone is responsible for making us lonely. Research shows that it's the quality, not the quantity of social interactions that best predicts loneliness. What matters is not whether we live alone, but whether we feel alone. There's ample support for this conclusion outside the laboratory. As divorced or separated people often say, there's nothing lonelier than living with the wrong person.'[51] Perhaps we marry less because we fear future loneliness in an unhappy relationship more?

Living each in our own little cave, but socializing between caves, might not make us lonely but it can come with high environmental costs. Unless we are exceedingly careful with wasted food when cooking for one, with the insulation of our properties and with how many material goods we each really need when we do not share them within a larger household, we can easily consume more when living alone. You can't easily share the light from a lamp or the bathwater when you live alone, unless you have a friend round most nights, and then you are not really living alone any more.

The primary reason that living alone is becoming more popular is that marriage, and especially early marriage, is becoming less popular. Many of the world's leading demographers recognize that traditional marriage is part of the old order of things. Alaka Malwade Basu of Cornell University makes this clear: 'If there is one institution that will continue to change radically in the coming centuries, it must be marriage.'[52] Marriage in the future will increasingly occur on different terms, including same-sex, but there will also a different kind of love in future, not one where roles are so prescribed.

Marriage traditionally has been an economic relationship. Economic hardship curtailed marriage rates among peasant families in areas as diverse as rural Japan and France as a means of trying to preserve what little capital a family had accumulated. Controlling fertility is how village life operates and is sustained, but it caused continual resentment during bad times when, purely because some had a little more wealth, 'idiots from good families marry easily'.[53] These words were spoken by a French peasant who accepted that older siblings inherited more as some kind of a given truth, but who was annoyed because, no matter where they came in birth order, for those from richer families their overall amount of inheritance, and hence marriage prospects, was always higher.

There is today a city where most people never marry, where a Pied Piper took the children away before they were even born, as if those potential lives have to be imagined occurring in some hidden underground cavern until a ransom is paid. That city is not Hamelin in Lower Saxony, the city from where the legend of the Pied Piper comes;[54] it is a city not too far from where you most probably live, a city which only maintains its population levels due to in-migration greatly exceeding out-migration. It is a city where already more people die than are born within its boundaries every year. And where is that city? It is now most of the large cities in Europe (including Istanbul); it is those across most of Asia to Japan, including China and Korea, but not yet many in the Indian subcontinent; it is also the vast majority of the urban areas of the United States, where the 'average number of births per woman . . . is likely to plunge to a 25-year low in 2012 and 2013'.[55] These lows are between 1.8 and 1.9 children now being born per couple due to the slowdown accelerating during the 2008–12 recession, and that figure is the national rate; in the cities of the US it is even lower now, and the US is behind the slowdown of almost every other affluent nation. The future is already here, in the city.

The current slowdown in world population growth has an extremely uneven global geography and also an extremely uneven geography within most countries. At times and for a few years the slowdown can appear to have reversed, as has occurred in the United Kingdom recently when women who had delayed childbirth had their children (see Figure below). That coincided with the arrival in the country during economic recession of many people for whom English was their second tongue, and some more babies, but even in that 2010 UK baby boom, fertility was below two children per potential couple.

Where there is still the most turmoil, war and distress, in the Congo and the Niger basin in Africa, and in Afghanistan in Asia, women still give birth to an average of just over six children each over the course of their lifetimes. But these are almost the only places where fertility remains so high. When life expectancy rises, fertility almost always falls. A century and a half ago, fertility was as high across all of Europe as it is now only similarly high in a few of the poorest places on the surface of the planet.

231

Selected trends in fertility and life expectancy 1980–2009

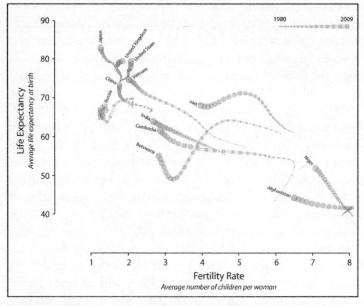

Source: Redrawn from Stefaner Moritz's work: http://moritz.stefaner.eu/projects/remixing-rosling/.

In Japan, it has become normal to have just one child or none. A few couples have two and even fewer have three children. By 2012, the average was 1.39 children per Japanese couple.[56] Across Italy, Greece, Russia, Korea, Hong Kong, Singapore and much of Eastern Europe, fertility is similar, at 1.4 or lower. In Hong Kong it is 1.1; in Macao it is 0.9; and a new low rate of 0.8 children per couple was recorded for the first time in Singapore in 2012.[57] Across Western Europe, fertility is not much higher; nowhere there does it exceed 1.9 children per couple.

A few years ago, European fertility rates were highest in Sweden, where there are pro-natality policies and a significant number of recent immigrants from areas where people tend to have slightly higher than average numbers of babies. However, recent immigrants soon reduce their fertility rates to those of the area they join, and pro-natality policies possibly encourage earlier childbirth rather than more children overall. It is intriguing that Sweden also has the highest rate of people living alone. Sometimes the explanations are complex but not incomprehensible.

Since 2010, European fertility rates have been highest in the United Kingdom, where they are currently around 1.9, but as explained earlier, this is associated with a burst of older-age delayed fertility and the recent arrival of more than usual numbers of young people from abroad. The 2011 UK census found far more extra young women than it did extra young men, but more people had arrived in very recent years than were thought to have arrived, so no wonder there were a few more babies born too.[58] In the UK, adults are only counted accurately in censuses, but every baby gets a birth certificate, so the authorities tend to overestimate fertility rates when they underestimate the adult population.

Among rich-world countries fertility is highest in the United States, despite the recent falls, because immigration rates remain high and recent immigrants, almost everywhere, tend to have slightly more children than the population they join, but slightly fewer than the one they left behind. But even in the United States, where so many religious groups recommend abstinence, rather than the more reliable condom, much more reliable condom and pill (or IUD) combined, or ever-so-reliable vasectomy, fertility has been falling rapidly since 2008. Before then, births had been slowly rising since the turn of the millennium. In the US, marriage rates hit a record low during 2010 when results from the census revealed that: 'The most dramatic decline in marriage has occurred among adults ages 18 to 29. Just 20 percent of them were married last year, compared with 59 percent in 1960.'[59]

All round the world fertility is falling, and it usually continues to fall fastest when and where it is highest. In China, fertility fell from just below six children per woman to just over two children in the decade *before* the urban one-child policy was introduced. By 2011, the *Economist* magazine was reporting that across Eurasia in general, 'Asians are marrying later, and less, than in the past. This has profound implications for women, traditional family life and Asian politics.'[60]

In Iran, couples also now have far fewer than two children each and have done since around 2001. In 2000, when the total fertility rate of Iran as a whole was 2.2 children per couple, it was clear that in the majority of the country rates were already below replacement level.

Almost nowhere in the world is fertility now rising; almost everywhere it is falling, and it is falling fastest mostly where it needs to fall in order for global population to decrease earlier than the UN currently predicts. In those odd cases where it does rise, it tends not to rise for long and there is usually an obvious and short-term explanation. All the time and almost everywhere marriage rates are falling. And the reasons are now generally well known and understood because the process began a long time ago.

Ten years ago this was written:

> Fertility decline so liberates women from the domestic domain that in many ways the lives women lead become increasingly like those lived by men. And men don't have children, and they spend little time in childcare activities if their partners do. Consequently marriage, in the sense of a life-long commitment for

Total fertility rates by province in Iran, 2000

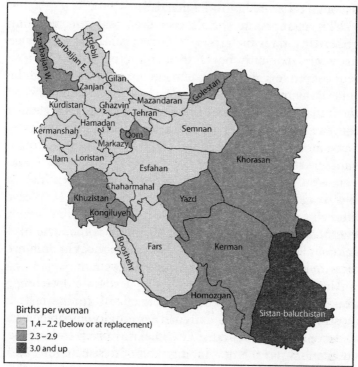

Source: Iranian Ministry of Health and Medical Education et al., Demographic and Health Survey, Iran 2000, Preliminary Draft Report (2002). Reproduced in Eberstadt, N., and Shah, A. (2011, p.5) *Fertility Decline in the Muslim World: A Veritable Sea-Change, Still Curiously Unnoticed*, The American Enterprise Institute Working Paper Series on Development Policy, Number 7.

the having and rearing of children, becomes increasingly unattractive – especially for women, who can lead lives that are quite independent of those of men. These developments are not only happening in places like Europe and Japan; spurred by declining fertility they are unfolding in many other regions of the world too – and usually far quicker than anyone expects.[61]

235

Today urban society is increasingly a place where it is becoming normal not to be married.

It is changes in social structures that are affecting underlying rates of fertility. Contraception may often be necessary, but it is not sufficient to reduce fertility. To understand this, it is worth remembering, when reading the otherwise unobjectionable and very sensible quotation by the current president of Britain's Royal Society, that when 'developing' countries are mentioned, this is the majority of countries and most people. The reason I mention this is simple. If all countries were to 'develop' to the level and behaviour of so called 'developed' countries, then human life would be blighted by war and pestilence. So please read this statement in that light. It is not just the cost of contraception that limits its wider use, it is the logic of it in areas where so many are still so poor that children are their only possession: 'The cost of making family planning universally accessible in developing and least developing countries and delaying the age of the first birth in the least developed settings are extremely modest compared with the cost of inaction in these two fields. Implementing family planning in the developing world is estimated to cost between $6.7 billion and $7.7 billion per year.'[62] The cost to the rich world of not constantly impoverishing the poor world is a little higher than that, but there are many ways in which the rich world could make savings.

The United States spends more on its military than most of the rest of the world put together. The rich countries have polluted, in absolute amounts, far more, despite their minority population status. Calling them developed is rather like calling the aristocracy developed (or 'noble') in pre French Revolution Europe. It is much clearer to call the rich countries of the world the 'minority' and the rest the 'majority', but also to recognize that we are stretched out along a continuum. It is not that those people in the poorer parts of the world are having too many children; it is that wherever life expectancy is low, people have more children. As life expectancy rises, as female emancipation increases, as marriage rates reduce, as the expectation to have children young falls – and as contraception is made more easily available and its use is more attractive than becoming a parent more early and often – then we all have fewer children. Ultimately it is when we learn to be a little less stupid than we might have been before, to share more and to see that others are not beneath or above us, that fertility falls both fastest and furthest.

Learning not to be stupid

> . . . future ages will certainly look back upon us as a people so immersed in the pursuit of wealth as to be blind to higher considerations. They will charge us with having culpably allowed the destruction of some of those records of Creation which we had it in our power to preserve; and while professing to regard every living thing as the direct handiwork and best evidence of a Creator, yet, with a strange inconsistency, seeing many of them perish irrecoverably from the face of the earth, uncared for and unknown.
>
> Alfred Russel Wallace,
> geographer and natural historian, 1863[63]

Alfred Russel Wallace was the propagator of great ideas: 'activist, land reformer, early opposer of social Darwinism and eugenics, supporter of women's suffrage and opponent of militarism';[64] less attention was paid to him in his day simply because he was not born into the upper classes.

Controlling our population numbers is partly about controlling those forces among us that try to propagate stupid ideas.

One particularly stupid set of ideas became popular just under a century ago. These ideas, labelled 'eugenics', claimed that particular families had a pedigree that resulted in them passing on superior genes to their offspring. Often rich families intermarried to keep their wealth in the family. That intermarrying then became falsely linked with keeping some assumed great mental wealth locked up in those same families. These ideas were known to be false even when they were most popular, when they became common knowledge. In the 1920s, a psychiatrist explained: 'We often hear of hereditary talents, hereditary vices, and hereditary virtues, but whoever will critically examine the evidence will find that we have no proof of their existence.'[65]

In 2012, a landmark paper was published that used high-quality large-scale survey data from both the UK and the USA. Part of the work involved people born in 1958 who were enrolled in the National Child Development Study (NCDS) and a group born in 1970 who are now part of the British Cohort Study (BCS). These people were assessed for cognitive ability, how well they performed at simple tests at ages 11 (or 12) and 10, around 1970 and 1980 respectively; later their attitudes on racism and other prejudices were elicited in their early thirties, this being around the years 1990 and 2000 respectively.

Study members were deemed more socially conservative if they agreed more often with statements such as 'Give law breakers stiffer sentences', 'Schools should teach children to obey authority', 'Family life suffers if mum is working full time'. Members were deemed less racist if they agreed more often with statements such as 'I wouldn't mind working with people from other races' and 'I wouldn't mind if a family of a different race moved next door'.

Study members who were behind in their cognitive abilities at age 10 and 11 (or 12) were found to be much more likely to express racist attitudes in their early thirties, even after controlling for co-variates such as the final level of education they achieved, their job and socioeconomic status. However, in forming those racist attitudes, 'the total predictive effect of childhood cognitive ability on adult racism, [of] between 92 per cent and 100 per cent was indirect, mediated via conservative ideology'.[66] In other words, people first had to be more likely to agree about being stricter with criminals, authority and school, and with beliefs favourable to women not working, to on average later be more likely to express racist attitudes. All of these prejudices were, on average, much more pronounced in those who fell behind in learning earlier in life.

What is being suggested by the study authors and many of the researchers they cite is bolstering the idea that the ability to imagine well, to think in the abstract, allows you to better comprehend the position of other people.[67] This requires quite different mental processing to that needed for being a conservative. You are dealing with what is often novel information when you are trying to think about an issue from the point of view of someone who is not in your group. A propensity for extrapolation, abstraction and interpretation is required that is hard to achieve if you find basic things difficult at age 10 or 11 (or 12), or if you are told at those ages that you are not good enough.

Being behind is relative to the group you are put in competition with. This can include young people from privileged backgrounds who found cognitive tests harder at these ages than their peers. They could be especially sensitized to feelings of failure as they were more often tested.

Thus, when forming life views as a teenager and young adult, even if coached to do well in your exams at 16 and perhaps again at 18, you are likely to remain more insular for life (or at least up to ages 30 and 33). Similar results were found in a laboratory setting in the USA. To see others as below you is easier if you once felt disrespected.

It is not being suggested that some people are stupid and that it is their stupidity that leads to them holding prejudiced views. The word used up to now has been *behind*. That word is important because it implies that in any particular school class a group of students are likely to feel they are not doing as well as others. It is not that they may find school work harder. They are likely to feel inferior, and that felt inferiority can result in stoking up future prejudice. Intelligence tests do that to people: they harm many, as well as make a few others feel and then behave as superior. Such harm is amplified when a further suggestion is made: that the results of your intelligence test are partly a product of your genes.

It has turned out that those in the past who suggested that our personalities are fixed by, or even much influenced by, our genes have been way off-beam, yet often they are still revered as great thinkers. This is because they tell the ruling elite, and those who have more luck as entrepreneurs, that they are intrinsically gifted and so deserve more wealth than anyone else, and even more importantly (to them), that so are most of their offspring, who (they believe) receive more of their genes than those of their wife or girlfriend. Most of the super-rich are male and married; many marry more than once.

The most famous of the so-called great thinkers on genes and intelligence, Hans Eysenck, who died of a brain tumour in 1997, 'argued that smoking did not necessarily cause lung cancer by itself but interacted with other factors such as personality. He championed Arthur Jensen's belief in inherited IQ racial differences. He supported [Michel] Gauquelin's conclusion that planetary positions correlate with the personality of eminent professionals. In each of these cases (many more could be cited) he adopted a position that his opponents found outrageous.'[68] So why, if he was so silly, did so many choose to believe him? It was not just that his ideas could be attractive to some. It is also that people find it hard to distinguish between tiny genetic influences on most aspects of our physiology, and genes being the determining influence on a notion as abstract as intelligence. To understand this, it can help to think about how genes might influence a less abstract condition, one which Eysenck pondered: lung cancer.

Even if there are tiny genetic influences, they can be a great distraction from what matters most. To understand that smoking is an environmental cause of lung cancer required variation in the rate at which people smoked. In a population where everyone smoked, lung cancer could easily come to be seen as a genetic disease, as the variations between different groups dying could be influenced by how the linings of their lungs differed, something that could be explained by genetic difference. However, in virtually all the cases risk could be removed by stopping smoking. Thus what appears to be high heritability adds nothing to our potential to alleviate this particular disease. To know this you have to be told it; you are very unlikely to think it up yourself, no matter how intelligent you may think you are. If you are very intelligent, then you will know that you are not necessarily that clever.

Intelligence tests are not very intelligent. They are designed to reproduce predictable results. When a new test is introduced, it is validated by checking that its results correlate with older test results: 'Moreover, it is not just the existence of a high correlation but also that particular group differences are maintained, for example between males and females for spatial ability tests. It is not difficult to see that such requirements will tend to impose a kind of historical determinism.'[69] At least, it is not difficult unless you want to defend intelligence tests, which tend to be the preserve of a small minority of people who have been told that they have scored highly on them. These are people who usually belong to the social groups to whom the tests were originally designed to give the highest scores.

It is easy to be pessimistic that humans will remain stupid and carry on conducting and believing in intelligence tests as so many do today. The last section of Chapter 2 of this book, 'Apocalypse then', explained how Francis Galton, an early statistician who died over a century ago, created many of the present-day myths.

People can carry on believing Galton's folly even when some of our most eminent living educational statisticians try to explain otherwise. Indeed one, Harvey Goldstein, speculating in 2012 on the future, said that in 'some ways there are good grounds for pessimism. Much of the development of mental testing since Galton's time has become fixed, either through the educational tests that are current or, perhaps more importantly, through the very large commercial interests associated with the testing industry, who, by and large, do not seek innovation unless it is likely to bring financial reward'.[70] Educational testing is not backed up by theory, by objective twin studies, by double-blind trials, but by an industry that seeks to make a profit out of giving children grades.

'Twin studies' formed part of the basis of the ill-informed pseudo-science of eugenics. Today they are no longer seen as confirming that some of us carry genes for great ability that outweigh other influences enough to suggest 'pedigree'. Researchers are moving forward in those parts of the psychology business that are less obsessed with making money through justifying examination and testing. It is now regularly reported in leading social science journals that 'There is little reason to accept that studies of twins, whether reared together or reared apart, measure anything more than environmental influences, error and bias.'[71]

Twin studies not only have little future and a much-criticized present, but also a terrible past. Since the 1990s, it has been widely taught that it is 'certainly true that the history of twin research is one of the most appalling chapters in science, having been born in Galton's aristocratic notions of the natural worthiness of the English upper class, taken to its evil extreme by eugenicists, and too readily used by American scientists to rationalize racial injustice'.[72] Despite this, preaching the allure of the idea of a few exceptional people with exceptional genes remains common. Such beliefs, based on the falsehood that just a few are truly able, provide a terrible recipe for how best to organize ourselves in future.

As inequalities in income and wealth within the USA and the UK increase, it is hardly surprising that those currently at the top would like to avoid having to realize that they are creating an even more unequal world in which many of their own grandchildren and great-grandchildren are likely to flounder. It is far more comforting for many at the top to believe that they are specially able, and that if they find thinking hard, then the common people below them must find it all the more difficult. It is also comforting for them to believe they are doing good for all when they channel their genetically well-endowed offspring into a few select educational institutions. The problem is that the best education we have tells us that they are wrong.

In 2011, the popular scientific press reported studies which, if naively interpreted, appeared to suggest that 'about half of intelligence differences between individuals can be attributed to genetics – specifically, the sum of many small effects from hundreds or even thousands of genes'.[73] These results, however, say something very different when properly interpreted, even when interpreted by those who view intelligence to be a little heritable rather than being, say, the product of living in a time after Gregor Mendel had made discoveries about the sex lives of peas. So even if a little mental ability is inherited, 'molecular genetics suggests that a myriad of Mendelian influences of individually tiny effect contribute to the heritability of intelligence . . . shuffling of such tiny Mendelian effects could, [American biologist Raymond] Pearl said, "be relied on, I think, to produce in the future, as it has in the past, Shakespeares, Lincolns, and Pasteurs, from socially and economically humble origins" . . . the eugenicist inability to see that "the economic element is perhaps the most significant biologically" was "stupid"'.[74]

What Shakespeare wrote, what Lincoln did, what Pasteur invented would have been written, done, or made by someone else had they not done it; most likely by someone living near where they lived at around the time they were living. The same can be said of Mendel himself. All that would differ is that the effects would not be called 'Mendelian'. Indeed, it could be argued that if we had only become a little less stupid a little earlier, more of us would know this to be the case by now, but we humans are limited by our brains. They evolved to handle far simpler problems than those that perplex us today.

The great argument over our relative mental merits matters deeply for the question of our common human survival because it has always been during times when a few of us have seen most of the rest of us as inferior that past civilizations have crumbled. We need now to more widely accept what so many today understand: that 'a genetic notion of socially and historically varying racial categories must lie well outside the scope of "what the best contemporary science tells us about human genetic variation"'.[75] When it comes to our mental abilities, we are not made up of races that vary in their genetic endowment. We are not made up of groups that are clever and groups that are slow and we do not need some kind of continual survival-of-the-fittest contest to ensure our future adaptability, as if species evolved within a matter of years rather than aeons. We will not evolve to become less racist; we have to learn to.

Widespread belief in the inherent inferiority of particular racial groups still leads to the legitimization of racism. In the 1990s, among the Los Angeles Police Department (LAPD), racism resulted in the code 'NHI' being invented, a code that is still in use, if more covertly, today: 'Some LAPD officers reporting on disturbances in the black communities of South Los Angeles in 1992 used code to describe disturbances in their areas: NHI – "No Humans Involved". Members of the predominantly white, male police force said it was "gallows humour" and regularly described the African-Americans they were meant to protect and serve as "monkeys" and "gorillas".'[76] In countries where the police behave better, there is greater equality and people have fewer children than in the United States. As the geographer Waldo Tobler said, without realizing just how far the implications of his statement went: 'Everything is related to everything else, but near things are more related than distant things.'

Why have we not learnt to be less stupid already? We currently receive our views of the world through an incredibly warped lens. It is not just that many of the main TV channels are owned by somewhat sinister corporate interests, or that the newspapers with the widest of circulations in many countries are often peddling arguments designed to increase mass stupidity. Educational knowledge itself is controlled and disseminated through a very small set of places.

Globally there is a 'staggering amount of inequality in the geography of the production of academic knowledge. The United States and the United Kingdom publish more indexed journals than the rest of the world combined. Western Europe, in particular Germany and the Netherlands, also scores relatively well. Most of the rest of the world then scarcely shows up in these rankings. One of the starkest contrasts is that Switzerland is represented as more than three times the size of the entire continent of Africa.'[77] Is it any wonder that so many people look down on Africans as slow when just a few of the eight million inhabitants of Switzerland are given three times as many opportunities to publish their ideas as compared to all the peoples of a continent of over one billion souls, a continent predicted to number 1.42 billion people by 2025?

In June 2012, Andrew Haldane, executive director with responsibility for financial stability at the Bank of England, and his colleague Benjamin Nelson, a bank economist, explained: 'Like de Mover in the 18th century and Galton in the 19th, the economics profession has for much of the 20th century been bewitched by normality. Over the past five years, the real world has behaved in ways which make a monkey of these theories.'[78] Some economists have come to realize the error of their ways, even though they may not know enough of Galton to be careful when using the phrase 'make a monkey'.[79] Similarly, more demographers may be coming to realize that what a few of their

246

number suggested was the case in 2004, rapid population slowdown, now looks more likely to come about than the slower progress envisaged in the subsequent UN Population Division revisions of 2011.

It is events from now on much more than the circumstances we find ourselves in which will determine what does happen, not least whether we more quickly learn to be less stupid, racist and ignorant. If we do that, then 'The world population will probably reach close to its maximum within the lifetime of many people now living. The low and medium scenarios show all-time maximum populations being reached in 2040 and 2075 respectively, the latter being less than one per cent above the 2050 population. Those maxima are 9.0 billion for the medium scenario and 7.5 billion for the low scenario.'[80] But if a few of us continue to consider ourselves superior and enough of the rest of us are duped into believing that, then economic inequalities will prevail for longer and the population slowdown is unlikely to be as rapid as it currently could be.

Inequality increases stupidity at every point on the income and wealth scales. It is not just some of the wealthiest people in the world who can be so stupid. Growing up as a poor child can damage your thinking. Above all else, exposure to poverty can damage the growth of the brain. Not getting enough food or sleep and especially not getting enough attention and stimulus has now been shown to physically alter the brain and hence influence thinking, although thankfully even this can be at least partly ameliorated.

Among the hundreds of thousands of scientific studies released in 2012 was one which found that: 'These results suggest that the effects of lower childhood SES [socioeconomic status] on the development of multiple cognitive

247

systems extends into adulthood, but also that such effects may be ameliorated by training in adulthood.'[81] However, it is better not to have to train later. It is better to be less stupid and not allow so many children to be brought up in poverty. Reduce poverty, you reduce fertility, you reduce extreme wealth, we all become less stupid. Above all else we require more equality, even more than meritocracy, as poverty is reduced best by sharing better.

Meritocracy for the masses?

> Even the sort of inequality produced by meritocracy can hurt growth. If income gaps get wide enough, they can lead to less equality of opportunity, especially in education. Social mobility in America, contrary to conventional wisdom, is lower than in most European countries. The gap in test scores between rich and poor American children is roughly 30–40 per cent wider than it was 25 years ago. And by some measures class mobility is even stickier in China than in America.
>
> *The Economist*, leader comment,
> 13 October 2012[82]

We really are still at an early stage in our thinking about what it is that makes people clever and capable. Referring to sociologist Peter Townsend and the economist Amartya Sen's research on poverty and human capability, one commentator helpfully explained a few years ago that if 'Townsend is correct, then Sen's claim that poverty is absolute in the "space of the capabilities" is understandable in the same way that the concept of unicorns, fairies and a loving god are understandable. However, there is no more real world meaning to the claim that poverty is absolute

248

in capability space than the claim that poverty is absolute in fairy space.'[83] I happen to agree with this commentator that Peter Townsend, since deceased, was correct and that some of the work of Nobel laureate Amartya Sen is bunkum, because we all have off days and none of us are that clever.

The commentators with whom I agree, Professor Dave Gordon and his colleague Dr Shailen Nandy, explain how Peter helped us all become less stupid:

> [T]he research of Peter Townsend resulted in a paradigm shift in poverty measurement methodology. The first paragraph in his seminal work *Poverty in the United Kingdom* is arguably the most important text ever written about poverty. It is now so well known that many researchers and students of social policy can recite it from memory: Poverty can be defined objectively and applied consistently only in terms of the concept of relative deprivation ... The term is understood objectively rather than subjectively. Individuals, families and groups in the population can be said to be in poverty when they lack the resources to obtain the types of diet, participate in the activities and have the living conditions and amenities which are customary, or at least widely encouraged or approved, in the society to which they belong.[84]

What the poor need are resources. The most flexible resource is money.

Having a well-defined theory of poverty matters, Gordon and Nandy later explain, because it 'is not possible to produce valid and reliable measures of anything (for example, speed, mass, evolution or poverty) without a theory and a definition. Validity can only be assessed

One depiction of global financial crises, 1955–2010

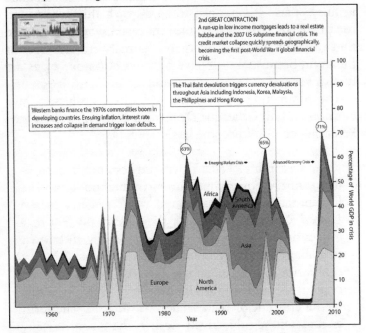

Source: Redrawn from 'History of Financial Crisis Infographic, February 2, 2012', which in turn is based on the *New York Times* and *Wall Street Journal* best-seller *This Time Is Different: Eight Centuries of Financial Folly* by Carmen M. Reinhart and Kenneth S. Rogoff. Using data developed by Reinhart and Rogoff, it maps the cyclical history of financial crisis from 1810 to 2010 for 66 countries representing 90 per cent of world GDP. See: http://www.myplaniq.com/articles/20120202-history-of-financial-crisis-infographic/".

in relation to a theoretical framework and, without such a framework, all measures of poverty remain merely the opinions of their advocates.' We need a valid theory of poverty now more than ever, because during 2008, over 70 per cent of the countries of the world (as measured by GDP) were plunged into economic crisis. That crisis came shortly after a period of remarkable tranquillity; the calm before the economic storm.

Since 2010, the number of economies in crisis has risen again. By 2013, several European nation states appeared to be approaching bankruptcy, this despite the overall debt of Europe being much lower than that of North America or Japan. Initially the living standards of people in the middle were hit hard, and those at the bottom hardest. Inequality rose and poverty soared. Three questions we need to ask now are: (1) What we are learning today that we did not learn before? (2) As more people get to learn, how will that help us to not be quite so stupid[85] in future? And (3) To what extent is the current economic crisis a product of population growth, and hence demand, slowing first in the richest countries of the world?

CHAPTER 6

9 BILLION BY 2045

During the night Pharoah summoned Moses and Aaron and said,

'Up! Leave my people, you and Israelites! Go, worship the Lord as you have requested.

Take your flocks and herds, as you have said, and go. And also bless me.'

(Exodus, 12: 31–32)

OK, so we make it to eight billion by 2025, but another billion? Just another two decades on? Will we then be satisfied with the lives we are living, and will we by then know where we are going, as the lyrics of 'Exodus', the story of the great movement, ask? Again, for now let's accept the UN Population Department's 2011 projections. They say that in 20 years, from 2025 to 2045, world population will rise to 9,106,022,000 people, of whom almost six billion, more than 65 per cent, will live in cities.

One way to look at these population projections is to say that if the projected slowdown were to occur, it would be wonderful. Worldwide, for the first time in a very long while, we would be living through a period of rapid population deceleration. A whole 20 years to add a billion. Far easier than adding a billion in 14 years and twice as much time as we had to go from six to seven billion. An extra billion from 2025 to 2045 is a 12.5 per cent increase in people in 20 years. Compare that with a 16.7 per cent increase in 11 years. It is 2.4 times slower growth than what is occurring as you read these words. But are enough people doing the maths?

Why keep going on about these numbers and the slowing rate of change? Don't I realize that we are talking about nine billion people, nine billion mouths to feed each day, nine billion warm bodies contributing to sewage, breathing in oxygen and expelling carbon dioxide? These could be nine billion hopes and dreams and aspirations that will result in ever greater competition and consumption. That's a lot of angry young men and no doubt far more angry women than were allowed to express their anger in the past. Almost all of them will be living in poorer countries. What happens if they gang up and come after what the affluent have?

Before you panic about nine billion, if you live in northern Europe, the northern half of the United States, Canada, or the north of Japan, ask first what you will have by 2045. What will be worth coming for? Will it be the snow, the cold, the wet, the huge numbers of elderly people, the tourist sites or the myths that the streets are still paved with gold in these lands of opportunity? Climate change is likely to make weather more unpredictable rather than turn such places into balmy Mediterranean climes.

Let's worry about possible limits to growth a little later in the book – of copper, oil, fish, rare minerals that make mobile phones work, and other non-renewables. For now, let's think about what it is most people are actually concerned about when population growth is discussed: immigration and mass urbanization; the new exodus, the great movement of the people.

Exodus has always been the solution to a problem, not the problem itself. The vast majority of the forecast movement of people, both now and to come, is between poor rural hinterlands and their nearest large cities. By 2045, the richer countries are almost all set to be rapidly shrinking, but will they be helping or hindering the overall slowdown? This chapter ends where the real problems are, with the super-rich and the super-poor, and how those two groups contain within themselves their own potential panacea, not just for reducing inequality but also for hastening the onset of human population stability.

Passports and pass-books

> There's an old saying among migration scholars who studied the Soviet bloc: 'When the Soviets finally lowered the iron curtain, the West responded not with open arms but by quickly constructing a steel ring around their countries.'
>
> Ted Henken, Professor of Latin American Studies, Baruch College, 2012[1]

Without continued strong in-migration, the population of the USA would fall by 2035. That in-migration is strong because the USA is the richest large country in the world: 'The absence of negative growth also distinguishes Northern America as compared to other developed regions, which can be ascribed to net migration and relatively higher fertility levels in the case of the United States of America. The projections to 2050 allow international migration to continue largely at current levels . . . Otherwise, Canada would slip into negative growth by 2015 and the United

States of America by 2035.'[2] The rich world would decline in population far faster were it not for immigration, but that immigration means the world as a whole declines in population more quickly. This is because, on average, people who migrate to rich countries have fewer children than those who don't.

We currently behave – we in rich countries, that is – very like white South Africans did in the 1950s. We have passports rather than the pass-books they distributed, which allowed some to travel while preventing others. And now there are all kinds of signs that just as they changed and were forced to change, we are both partly choosing to and being forced to change as well. Just as you could parody someone in the 1950s for suggesting that apartheid had a shelf life, so too this book could be ridiculed for apparently being over-optimistic. While apartheid did end, that closing did not end gross inequality. Population growth is expected to stop, but that will not be a cure to all our problems, just one more obstacle removed. However, population growth will in all likelihood slow down more rapidly if we were to better tackle gross economic inequalities, and those inequalities in turn are more easily addressed under population slowdown.

This book could have been titled *The Fall of Prejudice*. We are beginning to build better skills of diplomacy, not just in our diplomats, but in all of us. We now better value what philosopher Peter Sloterdijk calls 'learning to see oneself always through the eyes of others'. We are developing an 'anti-authoritarian morality',[3] improving at what geographer Ash Amin describes, in a kind of academic shorthand, as 'intercultural engagement',[4] getting on with each other better despite – or sometimes because of – our differences. Londoners may be more tolerant of outsiders than are people in Tokyo, because a higher proportion of people in London are immigrants to the UK than cross-border immigrants are as a share of the population of Tokyo.[5]

A world in which fertility plays less of a part in population growth will see future population change being attributed far more often to migration. Both in the poorer countries of the globe and within the richer world people need to better understand that when migrants come, times are generally good. The large majority of migration in the world occurs where the large majority of people are, in the poorer areas of the world. Often called south–south migration, this is when people leave one country within a continent such as Africa to move to another usually neighbouring country. Such moves are often viewed as problematic: 'The assessment of development progress is based on measurements within national boundaries. The emigration of people is still seen as a symptom of development failure.'[6] Similarly, emigration to the rich world is often seen as a failure of immigration control, rather than a success story of mass human endeavour.

Within Europe, up to 14 per cent of migrants from outside the continent are now from Africa.[7] There needs to be a change of thinking towards understanding that just as gaining migrants is usually positive, for the migrant leaving a country is often a positive move too. As leading scientists are now coming to suggest: 'Changing attitudes towards migration from [it] being a burden to a benefit of the European territory is a necessary part of the approach.'[8] People move about. As the world urbanizes, more will move, and far more often than before those moves will be over international borders, simply because it has become easier to move slightly longer distances (and to video-call back home), while the number of borders tends to remain fixed.

It is more sustainable to build up population where there is already infrastructure, an abundant water supply, flat land and a demand for new labour, as compared to where many of these things are lacking. For existing cities often the only way is up, and more apartments are the future. It makes little sense for Europe and Japan to depopulate. If migration to them from poorer areas were to *increase*, their population growth would help slow down total world population growth even faster. Almost universally, when people move countries they, or their children, quickly adopt the fertility rates of the places they are moving to.

Everywhere immigration is blamed for troubles while almost always heralding success. If there is not success the migrants stop coming. However, overall, 'Unless severe checks are imposed, both volume and rate of migration tend to increase with time.'[9] In many countries there are groups who, like the courtiers of King Canute, think that they can hold back the human tide.

Just as at present it is very common for people from all over a country to live in any one particular city, by 2045 it should have become far more common to have crossed national borders. Canute was an immigrant himself, and even a millennium ago many people moved great distances. A distant relative of Canute, the British prime minister David Cameron (fifth cousin, twice removed, of Queen Elizabeth II), recently called for the demands of the 'anti-immigration pressure group Migration Watch' to be met by reducing immigration to the UK by 75 per cent. His aim is to stop three out of every four potential immigrants to Britain arriving so as to cap UK population at 70 million. The latest UN forecast is for it only to reach 72.3 million by 2045. Cameron is playing to the gallery and ignoring the real numbers.

David Cameron announced his intended cap following the former Archbishop of Canterbury, George Carey, advocating an 'immigration policy that might produce a higher proportion of Christian immigrants'.[10] Successors of the National Front, the fascist British National Party, go even further while calling themselves the true green party in what is now known as 'the greening of hate – blaming environmental degradation on poor populations of colour',[11] as professor of development studies Betsy Hartmann describes it.

The greening of hate can be found in many guises. It leads some Australians to suggest that immigration to that country needs to be curtailed because the average Australian pollutes so much. However, the majority of that consumption and pollution is not carried out by the average Australian, European or North American, but by the few. David Cameron cannot make his party the 'greenest ever' by pandering to prejudice and building up resentment of immigrants, although he might win a few more votes in the short term from those attracted to nasty political parties.

It appears that bigoted views will always be with us; their advocates continue to propose them, apparently unabashed, even when establishment bodies investigate their claims and find them wanting. Anti-immigration views may not necessarily be the views of the elite, but it is usually the elite who stoke them up. However, the elite can have their views tempered and bigotry can be reduced in time.

In 2011 in the UK a Royal Commission reported on the impact of recent rises in population, on trends in consumption and on how changes in technology might affect the environment. The commission concluded that population change had a relatively minor impact, and that immigration is not an environmental issue. Their main finding was that 'we do not consider that there is a case for further controls to regulate non-EU migration on environmental grounds'.[12] If it is possible for a British Royal Commission, hardly a progressive body, to come to such an understanding in 2011, try to imagine just what might be understood by 2045 when the slowdown in population growth has been more prolonged and when it begins to become clearer just how much more valuable the smaller numbers of young people living will be, not least to the old and to those with power.

It is possible to imagine a world without the economic need for passports and pass-books by the end of the century. People may need to be able to prove their identity for all kinds of reasons, but not to pass over borders. However, it is harder to imagine how the apparent political and ideological need will have abated enough. Humans can be at their most inhumane when they use geographical borders to define how other humans can be treated. At the extreme are the Diego Garcias of this world: torture islands, leased by the British to the US navy and air force, containing a restricted zone named 'Camp Justice', outside of any jurisdiction, any justice.[13]

In 2045, when people look back on how we restricted movement and freedom at the start of the twenty-first century, from the extremes of our torture camps to the mundane refusal to stamp a visa, I hope they realize that it was partly because we did not understand the times we were living through, and only partly because of evil. I hope that things will have changed enough by 2045 for what appears to some as defensible today to be seen by most as abhorrent, in the way that informed people today see the British torture camps in 1950s Kenya as a cause of great shame.[14]

DANNY DORLING

An urban world

> ... an atomised, accidental antheap. Libertarian
> bores uncritically hail sprawl, the megaslum or the
> megacity depending on the occasion, and an envi-
> ronmentalist left seems terrified of the city and all
> it implies.
>
> Owen Hatherley, writer and journalist, 2012[15]

There is a part of the left that loves cities, that see them as
places where strangers converse: 'The company of strangers
is natural to economic creativity, a bedrock of knowledge
capitalism. It is salutary to remember this at a time of
suspicion or circumspection regarding the economic desir-
ability of the stranger.'[16] This is Ash Amin's defence of the
city. It became necessary to make it as xenophobia began
again to spread across Europe during the great recession
following the 2008 crash.

For the urban middle class, the strangest of strangers
are slum dwellers. What we can expect to change most
in the years to 2045 are the slums. Whenever there has
been rapid population growth in the past few centuries,
almost always accompanied by urbanization, it has been
the slums that grew first and fastest. It is only because we
don't tend to preserve slum dwellings that we don't have a
good sense of their history, but we have always had slums.
Whenever population growth has slowed in the past, the
slums have abated, slum landlords have been driven out,
and buildings have been replaced by more solid structures. Slums almost always only exist where, and for those
decades when, new people flow in.

Most shacks in early villages were slums. Most of the
older properties remaining in affluent rural areas were previously owned by the best-off, not by peasants. The rural

260

idyll of stone country cottages does not reflect the shanty constructions that a majority of our ancestors lived in at one time or another. Similarly, the great cities of industrialization were initially, essentially, enormous slums. All of that passes. Slums are the housing of population growth, not of stability.

As countries industrialized, the mass housing which was first privately jerry-built was often replaced by state-built dwellings. This was 'a means which was useful when large numbers of people had to be housed in a short space of time . . . and as an emergency measure has contributed to the fact that our civilization has survived the industrial revolution'.[17] The jerry-built constructions could coalesce into rookeries, seen as dens of vice. In places they were replaced by back-to-back dwellings, which were themselves pulled down to be replaced by state housing, which has itself often been demolished and rebuilt on since. Today, around the world, you can now see cities that look as if they were built at various times, even though the majority of buildings were mostly constructed within the last century. They look like this because some were built in places typifying the start of population slowdown, and others in places of rapid population expansion.

It is worth typing a few city names into Google and clicking 'map'. Try Lagos, Delhi, Tehran, Tokyo. When viewing only the cartographic summary of the roads and buildings, they all look neat. Turn on the satellite view to see the less organized human anthills sprawling out towards the far distance. Try to determine which appear better planned, better run, better arranged. You can only guess from the images, but some cities, just like some societies, are better planned than others, while in others there is more sprawl. Zoom down and around within Athens, Mexico City, Guangzhou, Jakarta, Seoul, Manila and New York.

We have to learn to love the megacity. By 2045, there is no other future for nine billion humans, certainly no other future that leaves space between the cities. However, within many new megacities there can be open space too. One that causes confusion as to whether it is a city or a collection of cities is Chongqing. The confusion is caused because so many paddy fields can be seen within its extended boundary. Despite the fields, among urban planners such spaces are now heralded as a new kind of megacity: 'Suddenly all the talk is about Chongqing, a city on the Yangtze which has reportedly reached a population of 32 million.'[18] When you zoom in on these cities, the centres are often near the point of confluence of two great rivers.

The reasons why the cities are precisely where they are are almost always old. India and China are about to have many more megacities, for the ancient reason that it is here that most humans have lived. It was only during Europe's rapid population growth, and the great human exodus from there to the Americas, that this temporarily ceased to be the case. Two millennia ago, the territories encompassed today by India and China were home to 121 million people, more than half the world total then of around 231 million. Most people who have ever lived have lived in much the same places and near to much the same cities as there are today.[19] It is just that the old cities are now growing again.

How many cities like Chongqing will there be by 2045? This is, in fact, an extraordinarily easy question to answer, as long as you include their rural hinterlands and everyone is included in a hinterland. There will be around 280 of them. The reason we know that is because Chongqing isn't really a city. It's a city and its hinterland. There are fields and pasture within it. So, if everyone on earth is parcelled up into groups of 32 million people, 32 such groups will number just over 1 billion people, and as world population is forecast to reach 9 billion by the year 2045, we should expect roughly 280 such areas. Many are likely to be loose cities like Chongqing, collections of cities and some countryside, so a number of these 280 areas will not be seen as cities, but it is likely that most of them will. So where will they be, and could they function well?

We already have one working example of a megacity that functions very well. It is called Tokyo, and it is increasingly held up in awe: 'Tokyo's railways are the standard by which all others must be judged.'[20] Greater Tokyo has a population of around 32 million people. That population is stable, and thus by 2045 it should look quite similar. Japan leads the world in building giant skyscrapers that sway with earthquakes, and so it is even possible that those disasters that once transformed cities, from Lisbon in 1755 to San Francisco in 1906, will not alter Tokyo as drastically and disastrously when the next big one occurs. Japan's population is predicted to have shrunk to 111 million by the 2045 date of this chapter, or to then be 'only' three and a third megacities' worth of people.

By 2045 the UK is projected by the UNPD (2011 revision) to have a population of 72 million; that's two and a bit megacities. Think of them as Manchester and London. London is already undisputed as a megacity; it only takes a little imagination to see the future London of 32 million people spilling all the way down to the surfing beaches in Cornwall and up the old Roman roads to Lincoln; a lot of green space in between, but all roads leading to the capital. In contrast, with Manchester it is unlikely that even nearby Liverpool will acquiesce to calling the great many-hubbed metropolis of the north 'Greater Greater Manchester', titled by its most vibrant and most central city. But already

North Wales looks to Manchester and South Wales to London. And what of the 10 million people in Northern Ireland, Scotland and north-east England?

If you let your imagination run wild, then by 2045 perhaps Ireland and Scotland might look more to some Scandinavian hub for solidarity, centred around Stockholm's 10 million Swedes (the number predicted by 2045) and stretching from Iceland in the west to Finland in the east and Denmark in the south, centred around the still valuable, if incredibly hard to extract, oil in the North Sea. If you think such a conception fanciful, then why is there a vote on Scottish independence scheduled for autumn 2014? We know what many Scots are trying to choose to leave. Much less is said about what they might, in effect, be joining – Greater Scandinavia.

By 2045, France, Germany, Italy and Spain will only have enough population for two megacities each. The Benelux countries will have one, Poland one; Russia's European megacity (Moscow) adds another, Greece and the rest of south-eastern Europe another, and Turkey's Istanbul one more. That's just 16 megacities' worth of people in those parts of Europe and another 7 to be squeezed out of the remainder of the continent's projected population, 23 in all. Today we talk of the North Rhine–Westphalia–Belgium–Netherlands region as an urban agglomeration equivalent to a megacity. Imagine that spread across Europe as the rest of the continent catches up with the agglomeration's transport infrastructure, which in 2045 will appear dated because parts of Europe already had it in 2012.

If the current UNPD 2045 projections come true and urbanization continues apace, then, in contrast to Europe's 23 urban agglomerations, India will have 52, China 42, the USA 12, Nigeria 11, Indonesia 9, Pakistan 8, Brazil 7, Bangladesh 6, the Philippines 5 and Mexico 4 (Mexico

City, also known as Ciudad de Mexico and three others). Together with Europe, those 10 countries alone are home to 180 of the 280 future global megacities. Remember, in many cases these are collections of large cities with even larger hinterlands. However, even Bangladesh is predicted, by the UNPD, to have 48.9 per cent of its population in urban areas by 2045 and 52.2 per cent by 2050, up from 4.3 per cent a century earlier and 30.4 per cent today! Not all these countries may have the same borders by 2045, but it is likely that wherever is already most urban in them today will be the central hubs of the future. The world will not reorientate around out-of-town airports for the same reasons that cities did not move away from rivers when the railways came.

So where will the remaining 100 sets of 32 million people be? Well, Ethiopia, the Congo, Tanzania and Egypt are projected to have four each; Kenya, Uganda and Sudan three each. That alone is 25, a quarter of the rest we have to locate. Japan still has three, as do Vietnam and Iraq. There are another 25 not yet mentioned to be spread across Asia; some will be stretched over more than one nation state. That leaves 41 to account for. Latin America (excluding Brazil) and the Caribbean are predicted to be home to 16, while those parts of Africa not so far mentioned will be home to 25 such agglomerations; these will probably still be the less urban, but still increasingly urban, ones. Oceania is almost lost in the rounding, but would qualify for one.[21]

Back in 2012, the 52 largest cities in the world were home to just over a tenth of our global population. If you were using them to assign playing cards, and you were being fair, all the aces would be in Asia: Tokyo, Guangzhou, Shanghai and Jakarta are the largest megalopoli.[22] Only one of the kings would be in the Americas (Mexico City), as would only one of the queens (New York), while Los Angeles would be a jack. London and Paris would both be eights, on a par with Lagos and Rio de Janeiro, and that is as things stand now! These are their placings among the 52 largest cities of the world today. In the very near future, most megacities in the rich world will be demoted out of the top 52.

Today if you take the top 52 cities and begin with Tokyo, you can use a pair of compasses to determine the position of every other city using flight times between the major airports. The earth appears flat if the land between these 52 megacities is not considered. I have had a go at drawing this map in the Figure below and have shaded the coastline on it, but in reality, these 52 cities are the peaks of human mountaintops connected by the fastest of modern rope bridges (Boeing 737s, soon 787s, and Airbus A380s). Currently London and New York sit at the top of the world economic hierarchy, with Tokyo, Hong Kong, Singapore and Paris another step down.[23] In the near future, we should expect the economic ordering to alter more quickly than even the population ranks. Spanning the Atlantic is no longer the main thoroughfare.

The urban world will also be a mostly Asian world. Outside Asia, such a statement can induce much fear: 'Economic success means considering what we seek to achieve over decades not years . . . From this perspective, our proposals do not constitute a significant expense: they represent a crucial investment that will enable the UK to survive the Asian century.'[24] 'Survive' is the strangest of words to use in this context. If there is a threat to human survival, it is not from any 'Asian century' to come; it is what a few people in the coming century might be allowed to get away with if we are unable to organize ourselves more fairly. The future will be of cities of more slums if it still includes as many enclaves of the super-rich as today. In the past, the slums were only finally cleared when and where wealth was more fairly shared out.

The top 52 world cities by population
(Shading is rank in world city hierarchy)

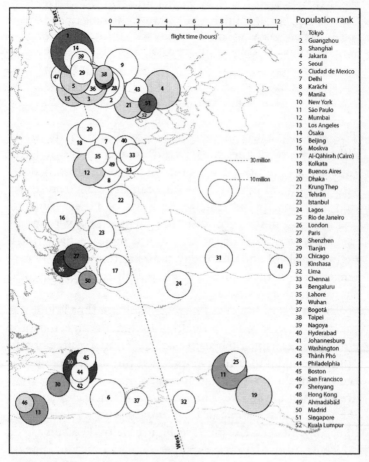

Source: Redrawn from the author's rough drafts.

An unequal world

> Before we can ask government to move on behalf of society, it seems to me there is another battle to be fought, and it might take a generation to fight it, which is to establish that society is actually worth preserving and working for. If we can get most members of our nation, of whatever social strata, to agree that the good of our society and nation has a call on all of us, we can move more effectively against those who do not recognise that call . . .

> Kevin Albertson,
> Manchester Metropolitan University, 2012[25]

The greatest levels of inequality are found in the more affluent parts of the poor world, across much of Latin America and South Africa. Sometimes these are called the semi-peripheral countries to distinguish them from those that are most peripheral to the hubs of power. Once it was in those hubs of power that inequalities were greatest. However, most of the rich world tends to have much higher levels of equality today than are found almost anywhere else. It was first (and is still mainly) in the rich world that welfare states exist.

Within the rich world I have a suspicion that London is the most unequal city by wealth and that Tokyo is the most equal. It is a suspicion because I cannot find a source of reliable wealth data for many cities, but the suggestion is that the rich in the US are geographically more spread out than are the rich in the UK. The locations of choice of some of the very richest people in the United States include places like Palm Beach, Florida (see Figure below), whereas the concentration of Europe's super-rich in London appears to be becoming tighter and tighter over time. The richest in the USA are not so concentrated as to mostly be living in and around New York with a similar exclusivity. The richest in Japan already have far less wealth and may be declining in number, so Japan boasts far fewer marinas and gated estates than less equitable nations.[26]

Palm Beach, super-rich enclave, Florida

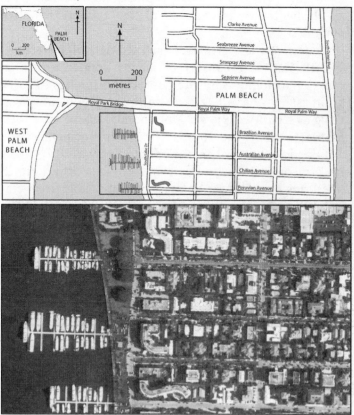

Source: Google Maps, 'Palm Beach, Florida, wealth map', September 2012.

269

It is the rich that matter when it comes to leverage on wealth inequality statistics. The poor are always with us, but in much greater numbers where there are more rich people. Poorer people are attracted by job prospects created by the requirements of the rich. For instance, we know that a tenth of Londoners each has wealth of at least £1 million ($1.6 million, €1.2 million). For the 'poorest' of that tenth it is held in property and pension rights. This is, at a minimum, some 270 times the wealth held by the best-off of the poorest tenth of Londoners.[27]

London has the greatest concentration of poverty in Western Europe because the rich in London create so many 'opportunities' for the poor. Opportunities to work in coffee shops, in hotels, in casinos, cleaning their offices, acting as security, taxiing them around, looking after their children, cleaning their homes. By income inequality New York is more unequal than London, but wealth is different to income; it is a stock of money, not a flow.[28] North Americans have not yet quite re-created the old aristocracies of Europe.

As Mahatma Gandhi said, there is enough on this planet for everybody's needs but not for their greed. However, his was an unfair statement. Most people are not very greedy. What we do not have is enough for the greed of a few. While it is true that we do not yet know if the few who are excessively greedy can be curtailed in their aspirations for more and more, we *do* now know that recently, for the second time in four years, their greed has been curtailed.

It was in June 2012 that the world found that that curtailment of the greed of the richest might be happening again, after the initial hit that their assets took in 2008. This was announced by the company Capgemini.

Capgemini is one of the world's largest management consulting and outsourcing firms. The tax authorities in the United Kingdom recently paid it to help them understand how to better maximize tax collection.[29] Another part of Capgemini advises 'High Net Worth Individuals' (HNWI, the very rich) about how to manage their wealth. This will include minimizing their tax obligations.[30]

Capgemini has the rather scary motto 'People matter, results count'. I guess if they came to the conclusion that many people did not matter they would not put that at the top of every one of their web pages. Some of their employees know an awful lot about the wealthy. On 19 June 2012, simultaneously in Toronto and Paris, Capgemini released the news that according to their calculations, the overall wealth of the very richest people in the world had, on average, declined in every region except the Middle East. They reported a 1.7 per cent overall decline during 2011 and the first decline in the value of the assets of the very rich since 2008.[31]

According to the Capgemini figures, by the end of 2011 there were some 11 million people on the planet who were estimated to hold liquid assets of US$1 million or more, excluding primary residences, collectables, consumables and consumer durables. These numbered 0.16 per cent of world population, or one person in every 636. They held a total of $42 trillion, or an arithmetical average of just under $4 million each (£2.5 million, €3 million), two thirds of world GDP. This leaves the other 99.84 per cent of us having to share out $21 trillion between us. GDP is not wealth, but as most people on the planet have zero or negative wealth, it is not a bad proxy for calculations such as this. The one very richest person in every 636 holds twice as much 'liquid' wealth as the other 635 earn in a year combined. That is not sustainable.

The super-rich

> I've known rich people, and why not, since I'm one
> of them? The majority would rather douse their
> dicks with lighter fluid, strike a match, and dance
> around singing 'Disco Inferno' than pay one more
> cent in taxes to Uncle Sugar.
>
> Stephen King, American author, 2012[32]

Today the super-rich are becoming ever so slightly poorer.
Could we have passed peak greed? During the economic
crisis of 2008, their collective assets fell in value by almost
a fifth, but that ground was largely made up in 2009.
However, their collective worldwide wealth is now beginning to fall again, though much more slowly. None of this
was predicted just five years before it all became apparent
in 2012.

When long-term trends change, it can take some time to
adjust. To understand the adjustment process it helps to
take a quick tour of the super-rich statistics and statements
made about them, all the way through from 2007 to 2012.

In 2007, the World Wealth Report was jointly published
by Capgemini and Merrill Lynch. Merrill Lynch was one
of the victims of the crash of the following year. The 2007
report was oblivious to any economic risks, suggesting
that, for the very rich their 'financial wealth is expected to
reach US$51.6 trillion by 2011, growing at an annual rate
of 6.8 per cent'. The report highlighted the fact that the
greatest consolidation in wealth during the year to 2007
was among people with liquid assets each in excess of
$30 million, who were then numbering 94,970 individuals
worldwide. These people were in the market for vintage
yachts and privately owned jets, including 10,000 such
aeroplanes in the United States alone. During that year

the report suggested that Boeing 'took orders for 11 wide-body private jets that are being customized and outfitted as "mobile mansions". The price tag: about $150 million each.' Google's management have one which they use to fly to 'places like Africa'[33] to do 'good', undertaking long-distance philanthropic trips that give them the opportunity to do charitable work.

The 2008 World Wealth Report still carried the logo of Merrill Lynch. It was published shortly before the firm ceased to exist as an independent company. The report, looking back on the 12 months prior to its publication, suggested that this had been 'a very eventful year – for the wealth management industry ... [but as] investor confidence rebounds, our expectation is that HNWIs will gravitate once again to less conservative investments'.

In 2008, the arithmetic average liquid (spare) wealth of each of the world's 10.1 million High Net Worth Individuals (HNWIs) was reported to have passed $4 million for the first time. But by page nine of the World Wealth Report of that year, the risks associated with real estate were being highlighted. No connection was made between the effect of a few people spending $150 million each on flying in mansions in the air, and the millions of people being unable to afford basic home loans on land. It would have perhaps been asking too much of the young bankers who wrote these reports to both work out the links and be brave enough to mention them, even as a footnote to their report.

Despite all the signs, the 2008 World Wealth Report raised its predictions for the total assets of the very rich to reach $59 trillion by 2012, advancing at 7.7 per cent a year into the near future, some $17 trillion higher than was actually realized. No mention of flying mansions was included in the 2008 report. Instead, some of the very rich now wanted alternative vacations, 'seeking out philanthropic trips that give them the opportunity to do charitable work, while still enjoying luxurious accommodations'. The report was written partly to advertise its authors' work in offering advice on 'generational wealth transfer'. In other words, how to ensure that your children receive almost all your wealth after you have finished flying around the world and staying in luxurious accommodation on your philanthropic trips. Perhaps some of the young bankers who wrote these words did understand a little of the irony they were providing as they chose how to juxtapose the facts being presented.

Philanthropy tends to be patronizing. Many of its proponents excel in the art. Tony Blair, for instance, the former British prime minister, wrote in 2012 that 'The best philanthropy is not just about giving money but giving leadership.'[34] The comments immediately following the original posting of this particular gem showed just how aware people still are of what Mr Blair has done: 'If your government had shown more respect for the party's traditions then perhaps philanthropy would not be so necessary . . . Tony, you fail to mention how much of your money you have donated to the cause . . . Certainly learned nothing about humility . . . Roughly where would we put depleted uranium tank shells on the philanthropic scale?'[35] The on-line comments continued in this vein and, I think, show how we are quickly learning to be less deferential than we were before the great crash. But whereas on-line commentators can be direct and get straight to the point, the authors of corporate wealth reports have to choose their words far more carefully.

On the cover of the 2009 World Wealth Report, the logo of the co-sponsor had changed to 'Merrill Lynch Wealth Management', now a subsidiary of Bank of America. The report began by admitting a grievous fault: the very rich had 'begun to lose trust in the markets, regulators, and, in some cases, their financial advisory firms'. The total wealth of the very richest HNWIs was reported to have dropped by almost a fifth, to $33 trillion. Despite this, it was still predicted to grow to $48.5 trillion by 2013, advancing at an even faster annualized rate than before, 8.1 per cent.

In the 2009 World Wealth Report, not only were flying mansions no longer mentioned, but philanthropy vacations were absent, as the very rich 'looked to secure their wealth in assets with long-term tangible value . . . [and] Private jet owners sold their planes in increasing numbers . . .' Attendance at yacht shows was reported to be rapidly falling, luxury car sales declined, art prices dropped and charitable giving decreased. Over a quarter of the very rich withdrew their assets or left their 'wealth management firm' in 2008! Only tucked away in an appendix at the end of the document was it reported that 'Merrill Lynch Global Wealth Management is part of Bank of America Corporation'.[36] Nothing about the frantic turmoil that led to this takeover was mentioned.

Transitions are rarely smooth. The 2010 report suggested that within just 12 months the wealth of the world's richest had bounced back, increasing in just one year by a huge 18.9 per cent, rising rapidly to levels last realized at the end of 2007.[37] This had partly, if not largely, been achieved by the very richest profiting from lending some of their huge wealth to stricken governments and from the bail-out of many of their financial businesses by those same governments. The very wealthy are rarely taxed on the income they gain from lending to governments. However, for the first time in the modern era there were now more very wealthy individuals in Asia than in Europe. At the same time world GDP fell by 2 per cent. The very rich were now not just taking an ever greater slice of the pie, but an ever greater slice of a shrinking pie.

In 2010, of their liquid (spare) monies, the richest on earth were reported to be using more to buy gold, and were forcing gold prices up. At the same time more jewellery, rare coins, gems and expensive watches were being bought, again forcing the prices up in all these niche areas. Unlike yachts and aeroplanes, these are items which are assumed to rise in value as time passes. The very rich were still scared and they were hoarding. Despite the apparent bounce-back in the value of their assets, caused partly by the bail-out rally in their stocks and shares, many of the super-rich knew that the good times were beginning to end. Numerous comments in the 2010 World Wealth Report attest to that, as do new absences of confidence, though you have to know what was not in the report of 2010 compared to earlier years.

On jewellery, the 2010 World Wealth Report revealed that 'many consumers bought less showy pieces and switched to silver from gold'. The very rich spent more on their health, including 'preventative medical procedures'. They were living less for today and more in fear of tomorrow. For the first time in 2010 the World Wealth Report included no forecasts for the future. In fact no dates from 2012 onwards were included at all. It was as if the authors had learnt not to lay down hostages to fortune; as if they knew that their very wealthy clients, the people the reports are aimed at, did not want to be reminded of what was probably coming.

The 2011 World Wealth Report continued cautiously; not a word of how the world might look in just twelve months was written in it. As I read through the 2011 report, I began to wonder whether those members of the very rich who had relied on the advice of its authors in the recent past might not be tempted to refer to its predictions as evidence of poor financial advice. Was this why the report's authors were now being so cautious?

The wealth of the world's very richest individuals was said to have reached $42.7 trillion by 2010. How did they achieve such a rebound in their wealth? The answer is that they did it again by seeing the value of their stocks and shares rise, and those assets rose in value because of continued government bail-outs, while other parts of their portfolios benefited from quantitative easing, from lending to states at very high interest rates, and also from preventing any state from finding a way of declaring bankruptcy. If a state becomes bankrupt, it would then have to refuse to pay back these extortionate loans that so disproportionately come from the most wealthy, those with most to lend.

The 2011 report explained: 'Equity market prices remained underpinned by ongoing government stimulus measures. The US, for instance, implemented a Treasury-purchase program in order to keep interest rates from rising, which made equities relatively attractive as an investment.'[38] The other ways in which the world's super-rich had recovered their asset values, apart from investing in the international debt markets, including lending to countries in return for very high interest payments, was currency speculation; speculating in the prices of oil, corn and wheat, and generally behaving in what appear to be many different parasitic ways. The 2011 report included a little more, thankfully temporary, bravado: 'Demand for luxury cars rebounded broadly . . . [while] a Picasso sold for US$106.5 million . . . Sales of fine wine also surged . . .' For a brief moment for some of the very rich it might have looked as if they had got away with it. Perhaps they had not passed peak wealth as they might have thought.

Perhaps everything was not beginning to change. And then came 2012.

During 2012, all around the planet the rich were being questioned and vilified more and more openly. Alan Badiou, professor at the European Graduate School, spoke for many when he asked: 'Cannot those whose only norm is profit reasonably be called "gangsters"? Individuals who are ready, in the service of this norm, to trample over millions of people if necessary?'[39] The Occupy movement had seized the agenda during the autumn of 2011. Much more importantly, the language, thinking and actions of far more middle-of-the-road organizations were changing to laud 'wealth creators' much less and to worry about the 'millions' a little more. But the authors of world wealth reports still often try to pretend that there is more stability and security than actually exists, because they need their clients to read their bumf and advertising rather than reject it as too worrisome.

The 2012 World Wealth Report featured a new logo in place of Merrill Lynch, 'RBC Wealth Management'. RBC Wealth Management is part of the Royal Bank of Canada. That bank's website runs the byline: 'Expect something remarkably different'. However, no mention of the old sponsorship is made in the report. Instead the 2012 report begins: 'In 2011, our analysis shows . . .' But who was now the 'our'?

How quickly former corporate partners can be airbrushed out of history. RBC did announce their arrival as co-author later, but only by implication: 'as our clients' trusted advisors and guardians of their wealth'. A few sentences further on in that same report, the 1.7 per cent slide in the global wealth of the very rich was made clear, followed itself by the news that these new losses were concentrated among the wealthiest. Instead of calling them 'losses', it is better to think of the wealth of the very richest falling as a form of slight global asset 'redistribution'.

According to the 2012 report, during 2011 even inequalities within the very wealthiest on earth fell, just as their share of global wealth dropped slightly. Global inequalities in wealth between the richest and poorest were also reduced by the tiniest of fractions. But there were exceptions: the number of very rich people in Ireland reportedly increased by 16.8 per cent, while most people there became poorer. Towards the end of 2011, a number of Irish businessmen were jailed for refusing to reveal where their assets were, including 'Sean Quinn, once the country's richest man'.[40] It is possible for the assets of the very richest to rise in value even while they are held in prison for refusing to say where those assets are.

In general, most of the rich did not get richer in 2011. In many parts of the world they saw the value of their assets decline faster even than the rates at which the wages of most workers fell. The assets of the rich also fell where the wages of the majority were still rising, in China. During 2011 in China, the equity market declined by 19.7 per cent.

At the same time, Capgemini (and RBC) suggested that those lending monies to the US government saw a 29.9 per cent return on long-term US Treasury investments when price gains and untaxed interest payments were combined. The very rich were putting their money in as safe a place as they could find – banking on Uncle Sam – and so the dollar rose in value. They also capitalized on their investments in crops, as people will pay almost anything to eat. Corn prices soared during the year, partly due to bad weather, partly due to their speculation, and partly due to increased ethanol production. However, despite such desperate attempts to continue to profit during others' misery, overall the assets of the richest fell and their monies were increasingly redirected, again, to the old havens of precious metals and gems. Gold rose in price by 10.1 per cent in 2011 and diamonds by 20.0 per cent, but the values of these repositories rely on other very rich, and not so rich, people continuing to see them as safe investments.

The words 'philanthropy' and 'charity' don't appear in the latest World Wealth Report. The very rich are scared. Some have stopped giving, even stopped giving in a condescending way. As a group, the fall in their wealth of 1.7 per cent in the latest year, from $42.7 to $42.0 trillion, may not look large, but it is a fall not in a year of economic crash. It is what is needed if a redistribution of assets around the planet is to begin.[41]

Relying so much on the latest years' data can appear a little like clutching at straws of good news, but there are other reasons to begin to believe that the ever-increasing excesses of the world's wealthiest may not be with us for ever. Many of the super-rich are very unhappy. Take John Hancock,[42] son of Gina Rinehart, one of the world's richest women, with an estimated fortune of £19bn (US$30.4bn, although mostly held as A$29bn). John has quite a lot of money but is not happy that Gina is denying him access to more of her father's wealth, so he inadvertently advertises the availability of his children (her grandchildren) for kidnapping, while trying to deter the threat:

> I can support my wife and children in a modest manner from the work I do but I can't provide the level of funds required to deal with security issues – real or imagined – associated with being the son of a woman worth more than A$20bn . . . When my mother buys a few hundred million dollars' worth of Fairfax, it's going to draw some attention . . . But she won't share

The changing fortunes of the richest people on earth 2004–2011

Total wealth (US$trillions) of everyone with liquid assets worth over US$1 million

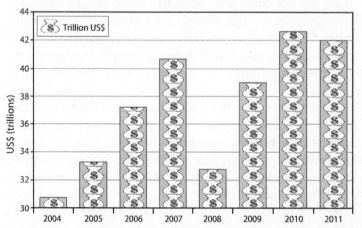

Average wealth (US$millions) of everyone with liquid assets worth over US$1 million

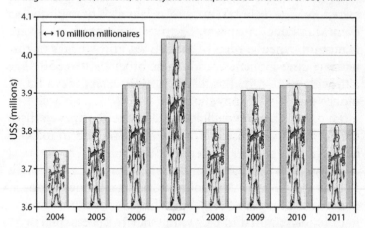

Source: http://www.capgemini.com/services-and-solutions/by-industry/financial-services/
solutions/wealth/worldwealthreport/wwr_archive/.

a penny to help protect the grandchildren from the risks she – the trustee of our family trust – is creating by her own actions. What more can I do than communicate to any kidnappers out there – over my dead body and you will be wasting your time anyway. If you think you are going to get anything from my mother, good luck.[43]

There are hundreds if not thousands of similar examples. There are not tens of thousands so disgruntled, because the world's super-rich are not that numerous. However, despite their low numbers, there is no easy place for them to hide. A few buy remote islands to try to get away from it all, including perhaps potential kidnappers. Richard Branson has Necker; one of the Barclay brothers owns Brecqhou. Of those who dwell on remote islands, 'it is far more common to find a dictator exercising a rule of terror than an egalitarian utopia. Islands are regarded as natural colonies, just waiting to be conquered . . . There is no untouched garden of Eden lying at the edges of this never-ending globe. Instead, human beings travelling far and wide have turned into the very monsters they chased off the maps.'[44]

The Aga Khan owns Bell Island in the Bahamas, where he recently annoyed locals by dredging the sea to make it deep enough to park his enormous yacht.[45] The Onassis dynasty have Skorpios island in the Ionian Sea, although Bill Gates, Giorgio Armani and Madonna have all been mentioned as possible recent purchasers, at price tags varying between €100 and €150 million.[46] In contrast to these five, most of the super-rich have surnames that almost no one recognizes. Many crave anonymity, although they may want to be seen to give to charity, to be regarded as respectable within their small group.

Kensington and Knightsbridge, super-rich enclave, London

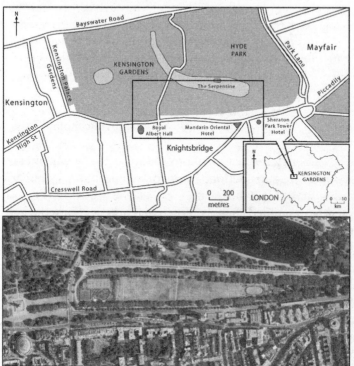

Source: Google Maps, 'One Hyde Park', September 2012.

Not all of the islands of the rich are surrounded by water. In the heart of London, centred around the Serpentine (see Figure above), is an island of the wealthy surrounded in turn, perhaps because they are thought to give some protection or anonymity, by those who are just a little less wealthy. It may only be once wealth falls here, in the London headquarters of the super-rich, that we will know we have passed the peaks of excess.

The super-poor

Data show a positive relation between aggregate income and life satisfaction across poorer regions, and then this relation turns negative for richer regions with a bliss point between $30,000 and $33,000.

ESRC Centre for Competitive Advantage in the
Global Economy[47]

The super-rich are not happy because too much money reduces life satisfaction, both for whole nations and for individuals. Too little money has the same effect, but greatly magnified. Between the two there is a range where most people have enough to get on well, to not always feel the need for more.

By 2045, the poorest people in the world are still expected to live in Africa, south of the Sahara. Demographers currently express great fears that the population increase predicted in Africa, with totals rising to as many as two billion people by 2100, will lead to an even more dire struggle than many already face. However, such concerns may not be factoring in the record-breaking recent drops in infant mortality in this part of the continent, drops which suggest that there are some very good news stories hidden among all the bad ones usually reported.

Until very recently, the fastest falls in infant mortality worldwide had been recorded in the 1960s, and improvements since then were slowing. It took just 15 years for worldwide infant mortality rates to fall from 152 babies dying per 1,000 born in 1950–55, to 100 dying per 1,000 born by 1965–70. It then took another 40 years for the rate to fall to 47 dying within a year per 1,000 born alive by 2005–11. However, today there is again an acceleration in progress being made, and that acceleration is currently projected[48] to soon result in another halving of world infant mortality rates so that by 2045–50, global infant mortality rates will be just 23 per 1,000 worldwide;[49] next they will halve again to 11 per 1,000 by 2100,[50] and this is just if current trends continue! That rate of 11 per 1,000 is the same as England and Wales enjoyed in 1968, when I was born, when 1.1 per cent of all those born that year in those two countries died before the age of one. Progress could be faster. And as always, the faster infant mortality falls, the fewer children people subsequently choose to have.

The main problem that may limit faster progress, the problem that demographers see in many countries within Africa, is geographical. Because so much of the continent is so elevated, and because rainfall without monsoon in much of Africa is lower than in Asia, there are not great river basins full of alluvial soils such as those that support other human populations of a billion.

Where there are good volcanic soils, in areas like Rwanda, population density is already quite high. The Niger and the Congo rivers are either almost fully utilized already in some parts, or in other areas the soils around them are not well suited to further exploitation.[51] Human-induced soil degradation and desertification have reduced the number of options we once had. If two billion people in Africa south of the Sahara are to be fed, much of the food might have to be grown elsewhere. Not a problem if you are rich, or are poor and still have oil reserves to sell for food, but a problem if you are poor, without oil, and human life on the planet is still valued in terms of dollars rather than souls. It will be a problem if we still trust the ethos of business in 2045 as much as some trust it today. But we have another 33 years before then to learn from our current errors and from the recent past.

In February 2012, newspaper columnist George Monbiot explained that

> David Cameron argued that those who say business 'isn't really to be trusted' do so as a result of 'snobbery'. [And according to the British prime minister] business, in fact, is 'the most powerful force for social progress the world has ever known'. Not democracy, education, science, justice or public health: business. [However, to know that David's claims are false] you need only consider the exemplary social progress in Zaire under Mobutu, Chile under Pinochet, or the Philippines under Marcos – who opened their countries to the kind of corporate free-for-all that Cameron's backers dream of . . .[52]

It was not just an environmentalist on the left who pointed out David Cameron's errors; even some of the prime minister's more senior colleagues in his own party responded with hostility to such naivety.

One leading British Tory, David Davis, was less concerned over Mobutu in Zaire and more concerned with the harm business was doing in Britain, increasing poverty as the welfare budget was cut and income from tax fell. Davis explained that it had become evident that:

> Some of Britain's 'flagship' businesses contribute little to our economy and society. In 2009 Barclays made £11.6bn pre-tax profits from its global operations, but paid just £113m in corporation tax. Our loss-making nationalised banks pay no corporation tax at all . . . The problem is not confined to banking. Senior executive and boardroom pay has outstripped share price and profit performance over the last few

decades. These problems are described by economists as 'rent-seeking behaviour' – using monopoly positions to extract wealth. Under this definition Britain has become a rentier state.[53]

When leading right-wing Conservatives begin to talk like this, using a language that their predecessors rarely if ever used, it becomes more possible to imagine a future in which the impoverishment of so many by so few global rentiers is no longer defended as 'efficient'.

There are other, more esoteric but equally valid, if optimistic, reasons to believe that times might be changing. According to the urban geographer and planner Mike Batty, if you include the hinterland in the definition of each city, then this 'remarkable pace of urbanisation clearly cannot continue, for very soon the world's population will be completely urbanised and there will no longer be any possibility of moving to the cities. We will then all be living in some kind of city and the focus will be on migrations between cities which will comprise one globally interconnected urban system.'[54] How does the author of that particular quote know this is happening – that those rural hinterlands and the poor within them are becoming so incorporated in the city? The answer lies in the current rate of change.

Our current rate of population growth within cities, as people migrate to them, is so fast that it signals a change of state. If cities were to continue to grow as they have done historically, and as they are doing now, but also people remain distant from them in the rural hinterlands, and those rural hinterlands also grow in population, then, to put it most crudely, we get far too many people. According to Mike Batty's reporting of calculations made in an older publication,[55] by 13 November 2026 the world population would reach infinity. That older publication was not some futurist magazine, but the extremely serious academic journal *Science*.

It may seem very odd to talk about the halting of population growth being related to a future decline in poverty, but the mathematics that demonstrate that we are living through exceptional times is very clear. The prediction of what was then called 'doomsday' was made in 1960 in *Science*, in which it was claimed that 'our great-great-grandchildren will not starve to death. They will be squeezed to death'.[56] The authors of that article suggested that the only route out of this inevitability was that 'man . . . himself can take control over his fate in this matter'. This they concluded was by controlling fertility, though in 1960 they were not optimistic that men would control their behaviour.

Fortunately, despite all their mathematical brilliance, and one of them being christened Patricia, the authors of that classic 1960 *Science* paper missed a key point. Human beings are not simply all men. As we now know, it was mostly women who solved the problem of human beings reproducing at a rate which would lead to them all being squeezed to death if the 1960s trends were not to abate. A half-century on, it is well worth trying to guess what it is that we now take for granted that will soon come to be seen as silly and misguided. And what new truths will we be learning that we are oblivious of today? Perhaps we will come to value the views and freedom of children more? Perhaps we will stop looking down on those with less money than us? Whatever it is, there are solutions we may be proposing now which in another half-century will turn out to be as unnecessary and fanciful as were the solutions those 1960s scientists came up with to solve the issue of a demographic doomsday appearing to be rapidly approaching.

The solution proposed in the conclusion of the 1960s scientists' paper was one-way space travel, implying that human beings should spread out to distant stars. In the nineteenth century, Europe dealt with its newly impoverished masses by sending them out to new worlds, but on sailing ships rather than spacecraft. That this suggestion has not been evoked again as a serious plan suggests that it was made in the panic caused by great and apparently not slowing acceleration. In hindsight, it is stunning that a group of such eminent men, and one woman, could have not seen even the possibility that what they were living through were unusual times. However, these scientists did have a *little* modesty. They suggested that their estimates of the end of the world might be out by 10 years or so.

Contemporary estimates that replicated the mathematics of the 1960 *Science* article put the date forward a little further than 10 years, to 2035, 2038, 2040 or 4 May 2044, to give the latest estimate of the date of what is now termed 'techno-rapture', a term a little less daunting than 'doomsday'. By the logic of these somewhat younger scientists, we will not hit nine billion by 2045, but will still reach the point where we are predicted to squeeze ourselves out of existence a year earlier, if all continues as it has done and if the expanding population of cities is also mimicked in the countryside. Of course, it isn't continuing as it has done, and it won't, but part of the reason that it won't is that rapid urbanization is now combined with rural depopulation and a consequent necessary reduction in poverty, especially super-poverty.

The author who lists those possible 'techno-rapture' dates to show how the horizon is moving away, Professor Mike Batty, concludes that 'all these trends with respect to cities and their urbanisation suggest that by the end of the century [2100] everyone will be living in cities . . . a phase transition takes place . . . but there is a sneaking suspicion that some may still not be connected to the giant cluster. The implication is that, in time, all cities will be connected, but there may remain stubborn pockets of resistance in failed states, where there are really poor, undeveloped parts of the world.'[57] Maybe, but if you are interested, take a look at Mike's paper and try to work out whether what has to happen is possible without there being a fundamental reorganization of how we live within a very short time, a reorganization that we are currently living through. The human world will not continue as it is, *mostly because it cannot*, not because we will necessarily arrange it so.

The immediate future may well be frightening, but it can also be liberating. If you doubt that great changes are afoot, try to get through just one day as people did in 1990, or as you did if you were alive then. Use no mobile phones, don't refer to the internet or use email, just for that day. It was as much the dense clustering of people as the new technology that made these innovations first possible and practical. Often their more distant origins, like that of the computer, which is behind them all, lie in great technological leaps made during wartime. All this very rapid recent change can be frightening. What will our children be needed for economically? But there are also reasons to hope. For young adults the world over, 'anonymity is what gives the crowded city its emotional excitement, its sense of new opportunity'.[58] In the very recent past only a very small proportion of people on the planet could enjoy, and suffer from, that new sense of anonymity.

Today, millions more than ever before move around the planet, into cities and out of them, most contributing to the growth of these cities while simultaneously forming multiple new webs, links and connections and maintaining old ties over social networks that are themselves changing even faster. Today, far more of the young than ever before are only-children, people who have to grow up to socialize in a different way than do those with siblings; younger people now can spend far more of their early lives with adults than most children ever did. Today, children have a better chance of surviving into adulthood than they have ever had before, not least because they are now viewed as even more precious since there are, per family (and everywhere), so fewer of them. Today, we are changing. The child born to be the eight billionth human in 2025 will be making decisions as a young adult in 2045 in such a different context to 2011 that it is hard to grasp the extent of this change. At age 20 in 2045 they will almost certainly not yet be a parent, almost anywhere in the world. How many children will they go on to have?

CHAPTER 7

10 BILLION?

> Hear, O Israel, and be careful to obey so that it may
> go well with you and that you may increase greatly
> in a land flowing with milk and honey, just as the
> Lord, the God of your fathers, promised you.
>
> Deuteronomy 6:3

In 2011, the UN predicted that there will be 10.1 billion of us by the year 2100; 10 billion by 2090, our final billion in 45 years, and then a further 100 million in 10 years, a population growth rate of only 0.1 per cent a year by 2100, a rate last experienced worldwide for any prolonged period before 1492. A few years ago the UN demographers thought it would be 9.1 billion on that same 2100 date.

Almost irrespective of whether we become nine or 10 billion, a few more billion than that, or a little less, a practical possibilist sees such numbers of people living in relative harmony on the planet as feasible. They may have milk and honey, but not too much meat, nor so many clothes that they have to throw most of their garments away before they show any signs of wear, nor will the best-off among them be able to behave with the abandonment of responsibility that the super-rich a century earlier displayed.

Milk and honey are sustainable resources. There is no limit to how much can be secured, as more can always be produced. Cattle do need to be well cared for and fewer need to be eaten so young, and bees do require flowers, not vast fields of monoculture, but we need never run out of these resources. In contrast, other elements are finite and some are very rare:

> Globally, from 1960 to 2007 production of refined copper and lead increased fourfold, lithium by nearly as much, and tantalum/niobium increased 77 fold. Consumption of fossil fuels has led to the continuous increase in CO_2 since pre-industrial times . . . Demand for rare earth elements has undergone a sharp rise in recent years. The price of lanthanum oxide has risen from US$5 per kilogram in early 2010 to US$140 per kilogram in June 2011 . . . About 15000 tons per year of the lanthanides are consumed as catalysts, in magnets and in the production of glasses.[1]

So, what happens if we need more than just milk and honey in the near future? We may be able to feed and water ourselves. We may be able to live in megacities sustained by forms of public transport that do not spew out carbon as fast as they can. We may learn to live better with one another as our growth slows and our borders become more porous. We may become smarter. But what if we run out of the minerals and chemicals that make modern living possible?

Rare earth

> Placed within the larger framework of environ-mental and resource concerns . . . global climate

change does not rank as the largest problem facing humanity, even though the changes are likely to be large. In the short term, many other environmental concerns are already more worrisome, especially major ecological changes. Over the longer term, humanity's concerns will probably shift to the gradual depletion of irreplaceable 'gifts' that Earth has freely provided . . .

William Ruddiman, a palaeoclimatologist, 2005[2]

Which 'gifts' are irreplaceable? There is a fractal pattern to the rarity of elements. If you were to look at a map of the universe where mass was drawn in proportion to the elements that constituted most of the space around us, you might at first think there was almost nothing but hydrogen and helium all around. And you would be correct. But zoom in on the earth's crust, and several other elements appear (see Figure below). Zoom in again to cracks and crevices within the crust, and what appeared rare at one scale is less rare at another. This is not to say that we should be sceptical of claims that rare elements now used as catalysts and other currently crucial ingredients for our modern way of living are finite and being depleted rapidly. It is to suggest that how we use such elements is a much greater problem than what there is. Currently there is huge waste, and even wars are fought around the acquisition of particular minerals.

Humans are capable of fighting wars over minerals of very little practical use. The rarest of all crystalline forms of the element that makes up our bodies, a particular arrangement of carbon, in its most pure form, is sought after not because it is an essential component of batteries, mobile phones and catalysing agents within car engines; it is sought after because it is associated with status, prestige and wealth. Diamonds are one of the rare minerals

The known universe and the Earth's crust drawn in proportion to their elemental constituents

Universe (known)

Earth (crust)

Source: Redrawn from Winter, N. J. (2011), 'Diffusion Cartograms for the Display of Periodic Table Data', *Journal of Chemical Education* 88, 11, pp.1507–10, http://pubs.acs.org/doi/abs/10.1021/ed1000203.

over which so many lives have been lost in recent wars (in Africa) for resources. These wars are not fought because of the practical use or value of diamonds. Diamonds mined for industrial uses are the cheapest. It is the rarest which are in most demand, purely for vanity. Just because a mineral is rare does not mean that it is always useful or that a substitute for its use might not be found in future.

Rare earth elements were only discovered in the nineteenth century and almost all of their uses have been twentieth-century inventions; mostly late twentieth century. These include catalysts in oil refining (to better clean up increasingly precious hydrocarbons), components of self-cleaning ovens, colorants for welding goggles, uses in magnets, lasers, capacitors, memory chips, and X-ray machines. In a world less reliant on hydrocarbons, one in which people discover they can live with slightly dirtier ovens, or find other ways of protecting their eyes from arc lights, in a world where computer memory is shared over the web rather than hoarded in devices, it is practical to imagine reliance reducing and other possibilities being discovered. It is far harder to imagine us learning to be less selfish, even though we are constantly being told of new evidence that although selfishness 'beats altruism within groups, altruistic groups beat selfish groups, and everything else is commentary'.[3] In other words, groups of humans who have learnt to share do better. This remains the case even if, within such groups, the more selfish still tend to rise further. But the selfish only did so well in the past when human numbers were growing and their behaviour was masked by what that continued population growth made possible – capitalism.

It takes time for new evidence to alter the main refrain. On rare earths, that refrain is that these are suddenly things we cannot do without. Suddenly it is the Chinese who have them: 'Inside every wind turbine, inside computers, phones and other hi-tech equipment from medical scanners to electric cars, are materials known as rare earths. This small group of 17 elements are in extraordinary demand – but their supply is limited, and most existing sources have been snapped up by China.'[4] But is it that simple? The newspaper story that directly followed this one, that the ice melting over Greenland might allow Europe to find other sources of rare earth minerals and of oil, elicited the following response from one anonymous reader: 'What matters is how we manage our way down. Learning to manage with less would make us look like a civilisation that deserves to continue. Frantically scrapping over the last remaining bits makes us look more like drug addicts that have just found a bag of heroin.'[5] All around us there is growing evidence that we are collectively changing the way we think, in the comments under news stories, in the cracks in the logic of old arguments, in rising scepticism that there is no alternative to ever-growing consumption.

Even the rarest and most valuable of metals, such as platinum, can be recovered by recycling catalytic converters in car exhausts. Platinum is often used in exhausts as a catalyst. Better still would be to plan to have fewer cars and hence fewer exhausts in future, or at least more cars running on electricity rather than gasoline and hence not needing such a catalytic converter. And that is happening. In many of the richest parts of the world, car use is falling fast with the economic crash, but the falls began before the turmoil became so frantic.

In Europe in 2012 it was reported that:

New car registrations in the European Union fell 10.8 per cent in September compared with the same month last year, providing a darkening consumer backdrop to another day of mounting speculation that Spain is close to seeking a formal bailout. The Eurozone's fourth largest economy was the second worst performer in figures published by the European Automobile Manufacturers' Association [ACEA],

posting a 36.8 per cent slump in sales that was sur-
passed only by Greece, with a fall of 48.5 per cent.
However, analysts said the main point of concern in
the ACEA data was the confirmation of a slowdown
in northern Europe, where the UK was the only bright
spot with a sales increase of 8.2 per cent. Elsewhere,
even the continent's strongholds are struggling with
Germany posting a decline of 10.9 per cent, followed
by a slump of more than a quarter in the Netherlands
and 18 per cent in France. Total new registrations in
the EU were just under 1.1m, compared with 1.23m
in the same period last year.[6]

It may be happening fastest in Europe, but the same
occurred in Japan in 1990, when car sales peaked at
8 million and have fallen almost every year after, to
4.6 million by 2010.[7] There is no sane reason for car sales
to ever reach their pre-slump heights in Europe again;
especially as, among all the continents, population slows
fastest and first in Europe.

Some estimates of future population growth are far
more constrained than the wide confidence limits the UN
Population Department put on their figures. The 2012
Report of the Royal Society of London suggested that the
projected sensible band of possible billions of humans for
2050 is far more limited than the UN proposes and, in
the opening paragraph of its report, that the key issues
are far more obvious: reduce consumption by the rich and
increase it for the poorest. 'The global population reached
7 billion during 2011 and the United Nations projections
indicate that it will reach between 8 and 11 billion by
2050. Human impact on the Earth raises serious concerns,
and in the richest parts of the world per capita material
consumption is far above the level that can be sustained

for everyone in a population of 7 billion or more. This is in stark contrast to the world's 1.3 billion poorest people, who need to consume more in order to be raised out of extreme poverty.'⁸ And what the rich require less of are often items that rely on rare earth elements. What the poor require more of, the rich most often take for granted.

The scenario painted so far by practical possibilists is of a world of adaptation, not of new technical solutions. It is a very old-fashioned model. Look at what has happened in countries that have undergone population growth and slowdown before, and suggest that as a default prediction. We should start by asking why it might not occur more widely.

Every country will *not* become rich and exploit every other; but after the initial shock and reaction to population growth, often resulting from outside influence, then land enclosure and consequent destitution, hardly any stable population does not work out how to live well, less frantically, and to tolerate far less the exploitation of the weak by the greedy. So, is it adaptation that we can hope for in what is predicted to be the slowest ever period we can currently expect to grow, the 45 years when we add our last billion, the 45 years from 2045 to 2090 when the UN prediction is for 10,062,090,000 people on earth? The date now predicted for the first 10 billionth simultaneously alive human to breathe?

I'm not going to see these years. My breath won't add to the carbon load any more. I'll be dead for almost all of the 2045–90 period. If I am alive for any of it, I'll probably be demented for most of those few years, so I am free to speculate widely now, as I will no longer care then if I was right or wrong. So, for once let's imagine something really good, think of these years as a possible age of achievement and look at what could change. Don't become paranoid about rare earth elements. They will soon be replaced by something else you did not know you should have been worrying about before. Think about how much progress there has been in the recent past: the formal abolition of slavery, of much child labour, and women's status rising to be seen as also humans, humans who (within living memory in most countries) could not be trusted to vote. Begin to list what could go well.

Firstly consider the move towards a world without borders. Already we have no border control within the United States and within most of the European Union. Could we not expect that to spread as it has spread in the recent past? And as borders become more porous, surely war becomes rarer? The twentieth century was the most bloody ever. It was also the century of the fastest ever population growth. Why could it not always remain the century of most war, of peak war?

Secondly consider how a majority vegetarian world might work, one in which it is rare to consume meat or fish, a world with far fewer cigarettes and much less alcohol being consumed too, a world in which people do expect to live into their seventies and eighties and begin to behave, as teenagers, as if they expect that. It could be boring – no one said it would be all good – but already, and despite a global economic recession, illicit harmful drug use is being reported as falling.[9]

Thirdly, a world is possible by 2090 in which the majority of children attend university – that is an odds-on prediction – but (and this is more daring) also a world in which universities are much more worth attending; not those awful institutions of the early twenty-first century with their pomposity but so much empty learning. Maybe there will be far less emphasis on acquiring status simply because of where you have been, and what people do will matter more.

A world with less border control, lower harmful consumption and more real education is a distinct possibility. That could be the world in which, finally, the last person dies of polio, most probably in the Congo, during a time of far more ambitious disease eradication, of increased emancipation of many groups, and a time when the wider education we once dreamed was possible – and then which we doubted was possible – occurs. But first we need to control growth, not population growth – that is being controlled – but economic growth, which is still uncontrolled.

Punctuated equilibrium

> To take growth out of its proper social context is to distort and privatize the problem. It is inaccurate and unfair to coerce people into believing that they are personally responsible for present-day ecological dangers because they consume too much or proliferate too readily. This privatization of the environmental crisis, like New Age cults that focus on personal problems rather than on social dislocations, has reduced many environmental movements to utter ineffectiveness and threatens to diminish their credibility with the public. If 'simple living' and militant recycling are the main solutions . . . the crisis will certainly continue and intensify.
>
> Murray Bookchin,
> 'Death of a Small Planet', 1989[10]

Just as the global human population acceleration began, Charles Darwin wrote that following a few 'favourable seasons', the rise in species number can be astonishing. This is what has occurred with humans. We have had a few favourable seasons, in length lasting about six human generations, and the rise in our numbers has been astonishing:

301

'we have better evidence on this subject than mere theoretical calculations, namely, the numerous recorded cases of the astonishingly rapid increase of various animals in a state of nature, when circumstances have been favourable to them during two or three following seasons. Still more striking is the evidence from our domestic animals of many kinds . . .'[11] Perhaps humans too have become newly domesticated and that domestication is moving us from one state of equilibrium to another.

Twenty years ago a theory of punctuated equilibrium was proposed as an embellishment to the Wallace/Darwin model of evolution.[12] Punctuated equilibrium is the tendency for a large dynamic system, such as global human society, to see its equilibrium trends occasionally completely disrupted. This became clear, worldwide, from the year 1851 onwards, when population began to grow most rapidly, bar four exceptions, at faster rates each year than the year before, and to carry on doing this for exactly 120 years, until 1971. The original model of punctuated equilibrium was not applied to human population growth, but it could have been. Our old equilibrium was disturbed as long ago as 1492, but it took over 350 years for that initial great disturbance to result in the final global puncturing of what had been slow steady-state growth of human numbers worldwide.

The four exceptions to continued accelerating human global population growth within the 1851–1971 period were (1) the First World War through to the end of the influenza pandemic, 1914–19; (2) the crash of 1929 through to the tail end of depression in 1936, a period which saw European fertility plummet; (3) the Second World War through to the nine months after most troops returned home (1939–45); and (4) the Great Chinese Famine (1958–61), when up to 45 million premature deaths occurred.[13]

The key question to be asked is why, barring these four epochal events, did the acceleration begin in 1851 and end in 1971? The immediate reasons are what attract most attention, but they are superficial, although we'll turn to them shortly nevertheless. What matters most are the reasons behind the reasons, so let's tell this the story in the right order, from the deepest underlying reasons first, through to what we currently consider most important.

Part of the graph below appeared in Chapter 2 of this book, but then only drawn up to the year 2000 and not with total population added or the projections forward to 2100. Look at our recent past in relation to what our near future is projected to be and you can see that we have been living through a population shock. The future will almost certainly not be as smoothly changing as is forecast. In fits and starts the slowdown could even come more quickly than this, but more on that later.

What is most important is that the deceleration has continued unabated since 1971. Currently the population growth (thin) line in the graph below is still dropping almost as quickly as it did in the 30 years up to 2000 (though you can see a slight 'hump' of baby boom just around 2010 if you look carefully). Annual global population growth was 1.27 per cent in the year to 2000; it fell to 1.03 per cent by the year to 2009. That is a continuous rapid decline in growth rates. It is made up of many slightly greater decelerations and a few slower ones (including the 2010 mini baby boom). The Netherlands saw growth rates fall from 0.67 per cent to 0.42 per cent over the same period, the United Kingdom 0.39 per cent to 0.28 per cent (although growth there has been rising in very recent years), Spain 0.16 per cent to 0.08 per cent; in Italy, growth of 0.2 per cent in 2000 has now declined so fast that it became a fall of 0.03 per cent in 2009, in Germany a 0.14 per cent rise

World Annual Human Population Growth and Level (1821–2100).

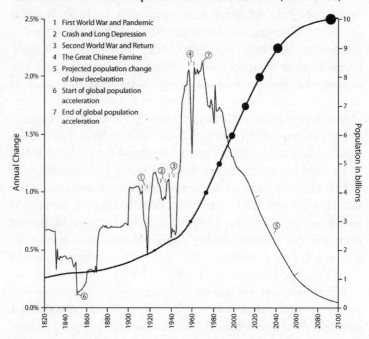

Source: Angus Maddison's estimates 1821–2000 and the UNPD 2011 based projections 2001–2100.

turned into a fall of 0.5 per cent and in Japan a 0.19 per cent rise became, in just 10 years, a fall of 0.16 per cent, all this in the years 2000 to 2009.[14]

In revised biological theories of evolution, punctuated equilibrium is used to describe whole sets of species suddenly dying out and new ones emerging. This is usually following a period of general stability before another period of quiescence establishes. In general there is equilibrium. All that changes during the quiescence are the mechanisms that tend to operate to preserve the status quo, to bring events back into line. However, occasionally, very rarely, that equilibrium is punctured and there is great and rapid change.

The theory of punctuated equilibrium can be adapted from biology, where it is being applied to many species, to concentrate on just one species: humans. The suggestion then is that the ecology of interacting groups of humans evolved after the Neolithic revolution, itself a great puncturing, to become what, in 1990s terminology, was called a self-organized critical steady state; in this case a state of gently rising population numbers interspersed with the occasional plague or famine. However, when one particular group of humans adapts, and jumps across some barrier, such as the Atlantic Ocean, that group mutates to a different kind of human society, and this eventually affects all other human groups on the planet. All their equilibria are punctured.

At first the effects of humans regularly crossing the Atlantic were hardly noticeable, if you just considered average global statistics. World population had fallen slightly in the years immediately after 1492 as deaths in the Americas spread with the introduction of Old World infections. However, globally, annual population growth rates rose to a quarter of a percentage a year from 1500 to 1600, next falling to just 0.08 per cent on average from 1600 to 1700, but then rising to just under half a percentage growth a year, on average, between 1700 and 1850, after which the puncturing of the equilibrium finally resulted in all human groups in every continent growing quickly.

Different groups are influenced at different times. The populations of the Americas were decimated many times over, from shortly after that first modern Atlantic crossing was made. The immediate effects on Japan were minuscule, although folklore has it that it did not take long for syphilis to reach Japan after Columbus's crew spread it across Europe, and, shortly after, millions of people died across Eurasia from what may have been a new disease for the Old World.[15] We will never know for sure if syphilis was new to the Old World in 1501.

Neither will we know for sure what occurred around 1851 to cause that date to be the global minimum for recent population growth. It may well have been a combination of factors. Some may have been technological, including the slow and benign spread of electricity and how that aided people to read and learn after dark. Some were political, such as the immediate and dramatic effects of the 1848 year of revolution spreading across Europe, and how that led to so many of those in power realizing that they could not continue to treat others beneath them almost as slaves. *The Communist Manifesto* was written that year.[16]

Nineteenth-century population acceleration would also partly be caused by the work that was done that resulted in understanding and then controlling diseases stemming from overcrowding, poverty, and unsanitary living, as well as preaching about the wonders of condoms (which originated in North America in the 1840s).[17] It is not impossible that just as it took a great deal of birth control to later put on the brakes, just a little birth control had earlier enabled the conditions for some (then) more sustainable growth to be established.

It is likely that we shall never quite know why all that was solid about human demography melted into the unknown around 1851. The following words were penned about innovations being made around the same time in literacy production. Franco Moretti's conclusion over what led to new ways of writing during this period is just as applicable to what led to new ways of forming families and how little we can easily explain about the nineteenth century, but how important the changes then were to how we live today: 'I no longer believe that a single explanatory framework may account for the multiple links with the larger social system: hence a certain conceptual eclecticism of these pages, and the tentative nature of many of the examples. Much remains to be done, of course, on the compatibility of the various models, and the explanatory hierarchy to be established among them. But right now, opening new conceptual possibilities seemed more important than justifying every detail.'[18]

Just as we may never quite establish why growth took off so quickly in 1851, so we might never quite get to the bottom of when that growth began to slow as it did, other than that it had to, because by the 1970s it had become too much. A little speculation is warranted about what might have caused the slowdown to begin around 1971 and to have been so sustained that it now looks as if this was not just another of those events brought on by catastrophe, but what we now see is clearly a turning point. To recall, those events were pandemic 1918–19, depression 1929–36, war 1939–45 and famine 1958–61. If you enjoy analogy, then by the colours referred to in the Old Testament,[19] the pale (plague), white (evil usurers), red (war) and black (famine) horses of the apocalypse may have already been and gone,[20] but why?

Reasons for our current slowdown can include the gradual and benign spread and multiplication of vaccines, and how this aided people's children to survive, to the immediate and dramatic effects of the 1968[21] uprising across the rich world and how that led to so many in power coming to see that there were limits to endless growth (the Club of Rome was formed that year), to the work that was done that resulted in understanding and spreading education, especially to women, to the spreading by word of mouth of the invention and availability of the contraceptive pill, widespread use of which began in North America in the 1960s, through to seeing, for the first time, the earth from the moon.

There are numerous possibilities for what it was that caused the tide to turn shortly after 1968. It is highly likely that without effective and widespread new forms of contraception, human beings would not have managed to limit their numbers once the great change began in 1851. But other factors mattered: vaccination, student uprising, limits to growth theory, women's emancipation. What all these have in common is education. And education was not just widespread by the 1970s; it was about to boom. Could it partly be that the punctuated equilibrium settling back down again to ordinary equilibrium is occurring through our collective learning, through everyone beginning to be treated as human, as educable?

By 1995, a majority of working-age people in the world, those aged 15–64, had been educated to secondary level. Less than a third had been so educated in 1970. It was only in 2007 that it became clear just how quickly educational improvements were spreading, and that these figures could be confirmed as changing so quickly.[22] The global educational improvement is remarkable and to date shows absolutely no signs of slowing down, despite, or perhaps because of, the beginnings of the deceleration in population numbers. As people all around the world have far fewer children, more and more work harder to ensure that their offspring are better educated than they were.

A recent projection of educational changes has suggested that future trends for India and China will result in numbers in any form of education in India not peaking

Men and women at university and with no qualifications, worldwide, 1970–1995

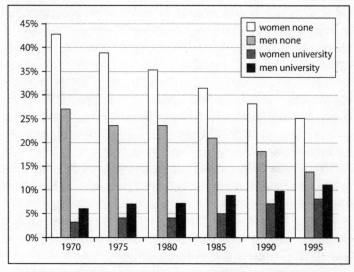

	women none	men none	women uni	men uni
1970	42.8%	27.0%	3.1%	6.1%
1975	38.9%	23.5%	4.0%	7.0%
1980	35.2%	23.5%	4.0%	7.0%
1985	31.5%	20.6%	5.0%	8.8%
1990	28.1%	18.0%	7.0%	9.7%
1995	25.1%	13.9%	8.3%	10.9%

Source: Lutz, W., Goujon, A., Samir, K. C., and Sanderson, W. (2007), *Vienna Yearbook of Population Research 2007*, pp.193–235.

until 2050, but the absolute numbers in various categories of learning falling in China from 2020 onwards. This will occur as the overall young population most likely to attend educational institutions continues to fall there even as the proportions attending higher education rise. The report accompanying the projection ends with the following salutary note: 'A historical example is provided by South

Korea. In the 1960s, based on historical growth data, the economic outlook would have been modest, but projections of its future educational attainment profile may have indicated that it was about to enter a window of opportunity combining high qualifications with low dependency ratios.'[23] When the rapid current uptake in educational opportunities is taken into account, then an even more rapid future population slowdown would appear yet more likely in both India and China. Women in particular tend to have fewer children when educated to secondary level, and fewer still if university educated.

The Figure below shows the highest level of education achieved or projected to be achieved by adults in India and China. Children are not included in these figures.

Even in countries as affluent as the United States, educational changes are still linked to fertility changes, although not all education is that enlightening:

Our current system of teaching kids to sit in straight rows and obey instructions isn't a coincidence – it was an investment in our economic future. The plan: trade short-term child-labour wages for longer-term productivity by giving kids a head start in doing what they're told. Large-scale education was not developed to motivate kids or to create scholars . . . [However today] If you do a job where someone tells you exactly what to do, he will find someone cheaper than you to do it. And yet our schools are churning out kids who are stuck looking for jobs where the boss tells them exactly what to do. Do you see the disconnect here? Every year, we churn out millions of workers who are trained to do 1925-style labor. The bargain (take kids out of work so we can teach them to become better factory workers as adults) has set us on a race to the bottom.[24]

Population by education level 1970–2050

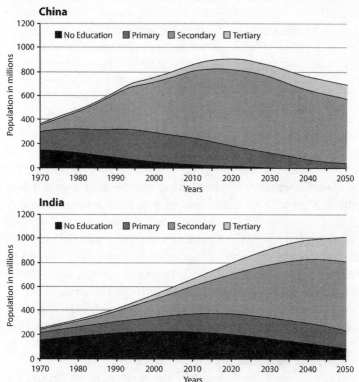

Source: Samir, K. C., Barakat, B., Goujon, A., et al. (2010, p.432), 'Projection of populations by level of educational attainment, age and sex for 120 countries for 2005–2050', *Demographic Research* 22, 383–472, http://www.demographic-research.org/volumes/vol22/15/.

So, even in the US, where so many people are now college-educated, there are calls for better, more imaginative, more useful, more creative education. As we shift globally from being village to city people, we also need to shift what and where and how we learn. And the more we learn, the fewer children we each have.

Deciding to have children

> 'At this moment, much as I want to say there's still a problem of high fertility rates, it's only about 16 per cent of the world population, mostly in Africa.' It should also be pointed out, though, that in the 17 sub-Saharan nations where birth rates are highest, life expectancy is 50 years or less.
>
> Hania Zlotnik, director of the
> UN Population Division, 2011[25]

Today, where there appears to be a problem of high fertility, there is usually an acute problem of high mortality. Some 84 per cent of the world's population do not suffer such extreme hardship that high fertility becomes an essential survival strategy. That proportion is rising. The world in 2045, the world of nine billion people, should experience even less of a problem of high fertility. The highest fertility predicted by the UNPD for 2100 is 2.13 children per couple in Africa. The lowest is 1.93. Many demographers suspect that the lowest rates will be much lower than that simply because they are lower already.[26]

Unless there is a terrible disaster, a new plague or widespread famine, examples of where whole countries experience life expectancy below 50 years should soon be relegated to the historical record, along with examples of countries where the average couple has four or five children. In many countries far more couples will have a single child than two, and far more couples and potential couples will be childless as compared to the numbers of families with three children in them.

If you factor in all we know already about how rapidly fertility is declining and then add to that the effects on fertility we should expect from forecast rises in educational achievements, what happens when literacy and numeracy improve, then long before 2100 we should no longer read statements as crude as this: 'The Optimum Population Forum judges the price of a condom to have had a nine million per cent "return on investment" when set against the cost to the planet of having a child.'[27] Children are not a cost to the planet; greedy and stupid adults are. Better education is far more important than falling fertility in preventing idiotic claims of nine million per cent returns on investments being made in this way. Is that the 'return' every time a condom is used? Would we all be infinitely rich were none of us to have children?

It is still far too easy to be alarmist over population numbers. Right now, journalists point to those parts of the world where fertility is high and often too there is war, and suggest that this is some portent of the shape of things to come. It might be what would come after a third global war. But a third global war is not commonly forecast. Our most significant worldwide baby boom occurred in 1946, following the Second World War, possibly including the boom associated with India securing independence in 1947 and Chinese revolution mostly ending in 1949. We are still seeing the echoes of that boom and are currently living through a time when its great-grandchildren are being born.

The following words should be read as a warning about why the aftermath of World War Three would potentially be even more dire than the war itself:

This is just a trailer of the horror that awaits us . . . says noted demographer Farid Midhet, referring to Pakistan's bulging population and the possibly corresponding link to rising crime, including murders, robberies, rioting and extremist activity. According to the independent Human Rights Commission of Pakistan, at least 1,257 people, including 64 children, have been murdered in different parts of Karachi alone, since the beginning of the year [2012]. Karachi, Pakistan's financial capital and the world's fifth largest city, has an estimated population of 20 million, which is increasing at the rate of six percent per year. Regarded also as one of the world's most dangerous cities, 40 percent of Karachi's population lives in squalid shanty towns. Data maintained by the Citizens Police Liaison Committee suggest that an average of 82 persons were kidnapped in Karachi per year between 2008 and 2010. Between 1997 and 2007, the average was 27 cases per year.[28]

Rising anarchy, corruption, fear, kidnap and fertility is what you get when, according to researchers based at the universities of Stanford and New York, 'from June 2004 through mid-September 2012, available data indicate that drone strikes killed 2,562–3,325 people in Pakistan, of whom 474–881 were civilians, including 176 children'.[29] But is this all set to worsen? Or might the USA move on to another country, as it has always done before? Might its leaders even learn to be less violent as its economic power dwindles? Under the article discussed above, quoting Farid Midhet, was a discussion about the birth rate in Pakistan, reported to be 'stuck' at four children per couple. This is the number the British once aimed for to 'promote the race', the number families were supposed to attain when they began to fear being bombed from the sky, cumulating in the bombing of London in 1944 and 1945 by 1,358 unmanned drones, the V-1 and V-2 rockets.[30] That was not a trailer for horror to come, but the end of one round of horror.

Recently a measure called 'wanted fertility' has been calculated where mothers are asked how many children they would wish to have. Wanted fertility turns out to be the 'single best predictor for actual fertility levels in the less developed regions . . . surveys conducted since that study reveal a 90 per cent association between wanted fertility and actual fertility levels in the 41 less developed countries for which such recent data were available'.[31] However, such a close association is not that surprising. In poorer countries women tend to have about one more baby than they say they want. In richer countries women often now have at least one child fewer than they would wish for, such as none instead of one.

The wanted fertility level usually being about one more child than the actual is an indicator of the failure rate of contraception and the failure to be able to access contraception. It may also be an indicator that in more unequal countries people have more reason to wish to be in an income group above them, and the groups just above often tend to have one fewer child. Not everyone can be in the group just above them, but when the economic distance between social groups narrows, fertility differentials also fall, and overall fertility falls faster too. Far too little has been written on fertility and inequality, but what patterns have been examined suggest that reducing economic inequalities reduces fertility even faster than the rate at which it normally fell during the period since 1971.[32]

Reports from surveys in several countries now suggest that far fewer unwanted children have been born in recent years as compared to just a decade previously, and fewer in urban as compared to rural areas, both of which could be due to better contraceptive services. The rise of HIV/AIDS may well also be implicated in these statistics. The increased availability and acceptance of contraceptive services, for individuals both with and without AIDS, will have had an effect. However, it is where disease, including AIDS, is least common that fertility is now lowest and where the fastest future falls are expected.

Across rich countries, for the first time ever in human history, people today regularly sit down to make plans to try to conceive children. Our parents had to plan and work hard *not* to conceive too many children too early. A few of our grandparents had little idea that they had much say over the process. Worldwide, for most of our great-grandparents' generation, children were conceived if and when God willed it, and it was thought that it was God that took so many of them so early. In the richest country on earth a century ago, even the wealthiest of families saw one in ten of their newborns die within a year.

None of my great-grandparents were rich enough to have servants and fall into that richest category, so it was an improbability that all four of my grandparents would have even made it to age one. People had a lot of children then, because a lot of children died. Where people have a lot of children today, it is where a lot die. If, by 2100, there is no place where many young children die, then unless the nature of being human changes, in future people will have far fewer children.

The story of why human fertility has fallen so fast across so much of the planet is a story of how human society has altered, but not of how being human has altered. The 130 years from 1971, since the deceleration began, to 2100 should be the 130 years of the beginnings of the widespread and full emancipation of women. This changes what it means to be human, and we need to consider the changing social status of women in particular if we are to see how much is possible.

From 1851 onwards, as the acceleration in our global

number began, infant mortality rates rose too. For at least the first 50 years of that acceleration we did not realize that it was not God taking the newborns, but disease, and not a great deal was done about disease and hygiene until the mothers of infants were themselves in a position to demand it.[33] That is the largely untold story of early feminism, and it is a story worth touching on to see how a revolution in thinking is possible in a short amount of time, and how, because of that revolution, we have returned to levels of fertility control under completely different conditions than those that prevailed during village life.

Fertility control has been an aspect of human life for millennia. Breast-feeding impedes conception. Recent fertility falls can be traced back to the nineteenth and eighteenth centuries in the historic records of births and baptisms in Europe. There is evidence that fertility began to fall as female emancipation first rose (ever so slightly) and infant mortality was reduced, but at the very start of this period the reductions were so slight that it was hard to ascertain from when and precisely why they occurred.[34]

In Britain, the influence of Mary Wollstonecraft's *A Vindication of the Rights of Women*, published shortly after the French Revolution began, is often seen as a mark of the tide turning. Over a century later, contraception use was widespread among middle-class women, and so it was found that by the 1920s and 1930s in England, babies 'in poorer families tended to be breast-fed for longer. One reason for this is that breastfeeding was used as a method of contraception.'[35] Breast-feeding is not a reliable contraceptive. Other far more effective means were religious laws against sex outside of marriage and the custom of refraining from sex during breast-feeding, but customs quickly change and we need to appreciate the speed of change that has occurred to see what might soon be possible.

Superficially, fertility first fell in Europe where and when it did because condoms became widespread during and after the 1880s, when the King of Belgium colonized the Congo and tapped the latex needed to make them. The pill was invented in the 1950s and entered the United States pharmaceutical market in 1960, and within two years, 1.2 million women were using it. By 1961, it was available in Germany and in the UK.[36] Fertility had fallen before without the need for the pill, but the pill made it far easier, as did the influence of all those women who had fought to become recognized as human, and what that recognition then demanded in turn from the behaviour of others.

As well as the introduction of various new physical interventions between sperm and egg, and egg and womb, there were great social changes. The setting up of systems of social security made it less vital to have children to ensure that you would not starve in old age. Because of the introduction of pensions, fertility fell in Germany 70 years before the contraceptive pill arrived. Fertility is high in parts of Pakistan now, less because contraception cannot be accessed, but rather because children remain a source of social security in old age in such an uncertain environment. Women living in times when social security is declining can have further emancipation held back. The past matters for our near future, for predictions to 2100, because it teaches us that if we lose the forms of social security we have mostly been gaining, if the emancipation of women is not continued, then we should expect to see fertility again rise in response. It can rise again in future in silence.

There is a very sparsely written record of the earliest evidence of the emancipation of women in the west of Eurasia, not because it took place a long time ago, but because, as far as we know, no one was permitted to write about it. In France and Britain during the mid to late nineteenth century, slightly more women every year said no a little more often to their husbands than they had before. Maybe more of the husbands realized the consequences of too many babies. This included many deaths of women during childbirth. What we know for certain is that slightly fewer babies were born, even before the very first contraceptive was introduced. The demand came before the supply.

As fewer babies were born, people had more time and energy to make conditions for living better, in place of concentrating so much on bringing the next generation into the world. The argument being made here is not a developmental one. It is not that some countries are more advanced than others stepping up some kind of economic ladder. Fertility in the United States is far too high given the wealth of that country. The current US fertility rate can only be explained by its high economic inequality (which in turn increases immigration). Fertility in the UK in recent years has risen also. There is no 'development' path to more or less 'developed nation' status. Globally we are all in it together, but 'in it' very unequally. A world in which population growth stops at or before 10 billion people will have to be a very much more economically equal world than the one we live in today.

During the 1980s and 1990s, it was in Iran, freed from semi-colonial despotism, and despite an initially opposing new religious leadership, where voluntary family planning reduced fertility rates from 6.6 children per woman in 1970 to 1.9 today. 'People outside Iran imagine that the family-planning program must have been coercive but it wasn't.'[37] It was part of a global tide that hit different places at different times, the precise timing often being dependent on the actions of a few. In China, fertility control became and remains coercive. In the United States, where there is still ferocious opposition to women's rights

319

(such as abortion) in many quarters, the fertility rate is still 2.06 children per couple. In contrast, in Macau and Singapore, rates of fewer than one child being born per couple were reported by 2012, 1.9 in Costa Rica in South America, and just 2.02 in Tunisia in Africa.[38]

Rates as low as those reported for Macau and Singapore are rarely achieved without coercion. In both areas there are a large number of young female domestic servants who are nationals of another country or province. Often they have no legal right to bear a child in these places, facing deportation before giving birth if they do become pregnant. They also have very restricted opportunities to become pregnant willingly. One domestic worker in Macau explains: 'There are people who sleep in the employer's living room and don't have any privacy. Our contracts say we can only work eight hours, but what happens inside the house? We usually work a lot more and don't have enough sleep . . .'[39] The same can be found in Hong Kong, and also in many Middle Eastern states.

A terrible vision of the year 2100 can be conjured up in which fertility is low but there is high economic inequality. Those who are forced through employment laws or recent customs not to give birth are a rare but growing group. Servants in nineteenth-century Britain, especially those who lived in their employees' homes, were in a similar position to the mass servitude seen today in many of Asia's economic hotspots. However, the vast majority of humankind lives elsewhere, and this form of dystopia has only ever been possible for a short length of time in those few places making abnormal short-term profits. In contrast, the vast majority of people on earth are not forced to have fewer children. They are choosing to.

Today, every evening around at least half the globe, millions of young couples sit down and have a conversation their parents will rarely have had, a conversation that their grandparents would have baulked at. They talk about when the time might be right to try to conceive their first child. Past generations talked about when the time might be right to ask permission to marry. Then, once married, childbirth was not delayed.

Today some European states are attempting to reduce the cost of bringing up children to try to encourage women to have more babies. In the 'Dr Strangelove speak' of some demographers, this translates to: 'The greater the proportion of the assistance provided (per capita) to children and young people which is borne by society at large or by the state, the higher the optimum net reproduction rate will be.'[40] Other commentating groups, including ones that used to have 'Optimum Population' in their titles, routinely suggest that no assistance should be given to encourage fertility as world human population should be reduced everywhere and in total by a precise figure, although one which is always changing. A few years ago it was by 1.7 billion.[41]

The calls to reduce population are not founded on any firm basis; what is considered to be a so-called optimum population has always risen over time, and the slowdown in population growth is gathering pace. There is also a great insensitivity in calling for faster slowdown. Already large groups of people in more affluent countries are finding that when they try, later in life than their parents did, they cannot have children.

At the heart of the densest population point on the map of Europe, Barcelona, families tend to only have one child for every couple, on average. This does not imply that such low fertility, a halving in population numbers every generation, will become widespread.[42] But the same is seen in Singapore, Hong Kong and Macau, and in many other European and Japanese cities. These places have all come to rely more and more on migration, or there will be a halving of population within a generation; that migration will accelerate the worldwide slowdown.

Constant in-migration of people born outside of Barcelona is part of the reason why people in Barcelona have so few children. Often those coming in are people choosing *not* to have children, for a while, or at all. Often those who choose to have children first leave the dense city before becoming pregnant. The growing numbers who find later in life that they cannot have children may stay in the city for longer, or come to it more readily.

By 2100, our cities and their hinterlands may become far more segregated by age, the childless living at the most dense points, smaller families a little further out, and the elderly a little further out still, and all increasingly incorporated into the city. But will we learn to age gracefully in the metropolis, or will we carry on trying to pretend we are ever youthful?

Ageing and learning to share

> I have Baby Botox every nine months, much to my mother's horror – she thinks I am too young. But another thing I inherited from my dad are frown lines, and I wanted to get rid of them. I get my nails done every two weeks, and every three months I have hair extensions made of real hair (apparently it's Russian). You can never have hair that's too big. Getting my hair blow-dried twice a week is my biggest indulgence and the one thing that I can't live without. My beauty regime is time-consuming, and my dad is horrified when I tell him how much all these things cost.
>
> Tamara Ecclestone,
> professional celebrity and heiress, 2012[43]

Tamara Ecclestone, celebrity daughter of Formula One racing car boss Bernie, thought it would be useful to tell the world about her make-up regime, about how Russian women (and perhaps men or children) sell their hair so that it can be woven into her mane, and about how she has the paralysing poison Botox injected in her face every nine months to try to keep herself looking young. If all the Tamaras of the world had the confidence to be prepared to grow old gracefully, rather than turning themselves into some permanently petrified chimera of a 21-year-old, the savings in resources would be huge, perhaps enough even to properly shock her extremely rich father.

Trying to look young is mostly about trying to look fertile and partly about maintaining esteem. The look of youth is about showing that you are still fit and able to have offspring, especially for that half of the human race who undergo the menopause. But in a world that values having many fewer children, what was considered beauty during population expansion may appear as quaint as we now consider fifteenth-century fashion to have been. Ruffs, codpieces and other uncomfortable paraphernalia were as normal then as fake tan, false eyelashes and male grooming are today. A world in which it is normal to be old cannot happily continue to try to pretend to be so much younger than it is.

One school of thought suggests that in the richest countries we are approaching the limits of human life expectancy. Overeating will increase diabetes, and even if we are careful, our bodies will wear out in future almost as fast as they do now.[44] Another school of thought suggests that the current increases in lifespan imply no necessary limits to human longevity.[45] At the time of writing, these two schools of thought are as divided as ever. In Japan, the word's longest-living country, life expectancy recently stalled for a year, and it became the second longest-living country, but the reason was not disease but disaster and all those lives lost in the 2011 tsunami. Hong Kong now enjoys the greatest longevity worldwide and also one of the lowest rates of fertility. But why, and is Hong Kong a good model for what may be far more common in 2090?

In the 1990s, making pension contributions became compulsory in Hong Kong.[46] Almost everyone is now required to be a part of the Mandatory Provident Scheme there, including casual day labourers. It was when we began to look after the old collectively that fertility first and most quickly fell. In Germany in the 1890s, the social reforms that occurred under Bismarck's rule meant that the state took more care of the old.[47] Younger adults recognized this and realized they need not have as many children to secure a little dignity for themselves in old age.

The 2003 projections which the UNPD made for their 2300 report mentioned (at the very beginning of that report) that 'females in Japan are projected to have a life expectancy of 108 years, with males having 104 years. These are the highest projected life expectancies in the world. The lowest are projected for Liberia and Mali at 88 years for females and 87 for males'.[48] However, to achieve long life, everyone, even Japanese women, will have to lead more secure lives free of even mild anxiety, worry and slight depression. As we urbanize and leave rural deprivation behind, we must also avoid entering urban anomie. We need social cohesion in the city of the future.

Even the slightest levels of anxiety are now known to be associated with an elevated mortality risk of 20 per cent; mild worry, 43 per cent; more severe anxiety, 94 per cent. Severe depression more than doubles people's chances of dying early. These are the risks after taking account of behaviours such as smoking, overeating and drinking, behaviour that tends to be more prevalent among those who are more agitated. The forms that anxiety-related premature death takes are mostly cardiovascular, but there is also enhanced risk of death from external causes such as traffic accidents and suicide. Causes such as cancer are not much elevated by mild anxiety.[49]

What is the main cause of increased poor mental health and anxiety? Richard Layte, professor at the Economic and Social Research Institute in Dublin, has recently worked with a team who have discovered that: 'Although not conclusive our results do suggest that processes rooted in social embeddedness and cohesion may be the main pathways through which inequality and mental well-being are linked. It provides evidence that status competition and inequality may have a direct effect on individual health and well-being and an indirect effect through its corrosive effects on social relationships and social capital.'[50] So, have people in Hong Kong (and Japan) lived so long recently because of the high degree of social cohesion and of feeling useful in such places? We know it is not the diet, as a similar if not even more healthy diet was associated with much lower life expectancy in this colony (and that country) when there was far higher inequality (in both places) before the Second World War.

Discussing how gaining more equality is good for ageing is a bit like talking about the benefits of taking more exercise: you can go on about what is great about exercise – the endorphins, feeling good about yourself, being able to walk upstairs – but it's hard not to end up saying, 'go out jogging now or you'll get diabetes'. Next, you end up discussing the very long potential list of negatives of not exercising. In fact it doesn't matter how you exercise, or if the way you live just means you get more exercise; what we know is that exercise is good for you. Most people know it's good for you just as most people know that greater equality is better for you, however you get it. Knowing, though, is not enough.

Increased equality under what may appear to some people to be authoritarian regimes may not seem so dire to others in similar circumstances. Supposed libertarian freedoms can appear as authoritarian diktats to all but a tiny number of economic winners in a free-market free-for-all. According to Richard Layte, 'the mechanisms through which income inequality influences mental well-being vary depending on the wealth of the country. Similarly, the overall impact of inequality appears to be lower in poorer countries. The well-known curvilinear relationship between GDP and life expectancy which shows little return to income after a country reaches roughly \$10,000 per capita wealth also seems to apply to mental well-being where the impact of inequality becomes more important to outcomes at higher levels of country wealth.'[51] It is as we become wealthier, and as our fertility falls, that equality begins to matter more and more. The young can have hope. The old need more certainty. Per capita income of the spending power equivalent of US\$10,000 is the current world mean household income. Globally we have reached the mean average at which more does not make us happier.

We now know that economic inequality is harmful to humans in the same way that we first discovered that smoking kills. It took decades to move from realizing that smoking kills to then understanding that the way this occurs is that smoking introduces carcinogens directly into the lungs, where they can cause cell mutations in the lung linings. When the relationship was first seen on a graph, we did not know what the mechanism might be. All kinds of complex ideas would have been suggested. In the end we invent a word like 'carcinogens' that helps reduce our explanation to a line of text. One day soon we will do the same to explain why humans progress so badly under inequality, especially as their fertility slows.

When the United Nations demographers first looked at ageing in that distant 2300 future, they declared that: 'At the world level, the median age is projected to rise from 26 years in 2000 to 42 years in the high scenario, 48 years in the medium . . . In the more developed regions the equivalent change is projected to be from 37 to 50 years.'[52] A median of 50 implies that half the people will live longer than age 50. A diverse market in niche nursing homes has been forecast.[53] It is hard to see how that could be possible if widespread poverty also prevails.

The final 2004 version of the United Nation's 2300 forecasts was explicit:

> Between 2100 and 2300, the proportion of world population 65 years and older will increase by one-third (from 24 to 32 per cent); the proportion 80 years and older will double (from 8.5 to 17 per cent); and the proportion 100 years and older will increase nine times (from 0.2 to 1.8 per cent). Assuming that the retirement age worldwide in 2000 is 65 years, people will retire on average only two weeks short of their life expectancy. Assuming that retirement age stays unchanged, by 2300 people will retire 31 years short of their life expectancy.[54]

Retirement ages may have to rise, although if far more of us did useful work rather than working simply for the profit of a few others, retirement age need not be raised much, but we are going to have to learn to share better.

Learning to share is hard, but it is easier to learn as we age. We often expect children to be able to do it when adults don't. We do this because we don't want our children to become distrustful and insecure. That is why we do not teach children that only the fittest deserves to do well. Put in academic criminological speak: 'The syndrome of market anomie as transferred to the individual level implies perceptions of imbalances of market mechanisms on the one hand, which are transformed into a syndrome of distrust, insecurity and specifically anomic attitudes toward legal rules on the other hand.'[55]

It is worth ploughing through the jargon to add to the mix other recent academic work, on psychiatry and psychology, which finds that:

> In contrast to the bleak hereditarian view of humans and their future, there exists a radically different perspective. Human psychological distress, to the extent that it goes beyond people's normal reactions to life events, is primarily the result of well-known and well-documented psychologically traumatic environments and events, and conditions such as racism, sexism, homophobia, unemployment, economic inequality, war, and social alienation. Future societies free of these conditions will see a dramatic reduction in human suffering, as well as a flourishing of ability and innovation, and *any possible role of genetic influences in shaping human psychological differences will be of interest mainly to historians.*[56]

All these new realizations can be daunting in aggregate, and especially when written in complex language. We are living through a very long enlightenment, a very small part of which involves realizing that the geographical balance of population will change too, along with our changing understanding.

The new world geography

> The major loser is Europe, falling from 12.0 to 6.8
> per cent, and the major gainer is Africa, rising from
> 13.1 to 23.5 per cent.
>
> John C. Caldwell, demographer,
> writing on global population shares, 2004[57]

Even in a highly urbanized world containing around 10
billion people, distance will matter. A 2009 study of the
'largest attempt to describe world knowledge in human
history' found that in all of the 22 different large linguis-
tic versions of the online mega-encyclopaedia Wikipedia,
'nearby spatial entities in this knowledge repository have
a much higher probability of having relations than entities
that are farther apart, although even entities very far apart
still have relations to each other. In other words, we have
seen that the very medium that was supposed to oversee
the "death of distance" – the Internet – has instead facili-
tated the reaffirmation of a theory about the importance of
distance.'[58] As the researchers who came to this conclusion
were looking within each language group separately, this
clustering of entries is not because those written in the same
language tend to be written about much the same places –
more French articles on France, for example. Instead they
found that wherever there was any geographical tagging
associated with an entry, that entry was much more likely
to be linked to other entries that had nearby tagging, as
compared to entries that did not.

Near things are much more related to each other in the
Slovak, then the Japanese and then the Chinese versions of
Wikipedia than within any other language block, and least
related in the more distance-impervious Dutch network.
Perhaps the existence of a series of former Dutch colonies

might be the reason? The next least geographically bound version of Wikipedia was the Portuguese version, and then the very large English version. The historical ordering of colonial expansion was Spain and Portugal, the United Provinces (the Dutch) and then the English, followed by the neo-colonial era of the United States and then, some suggest, China.

Modern forms of colonization are far more subtle than past expansions of political, social and economic influ-ence. International land investors and biofuel producers have taken over land around the world that could feed nearly a billion people. Analysis by the charity Oxfam of several thousand land deals, all completed within the last decade, show that an area eight times the size of the UK has been left idle by speculators or is being used largely to grow biofuels for either US or European vehi-cles.[59] In their report, published in 2012, Oxfam said that the global land rush was out of control and urged the World Bank to freeze investments in large-scale land acquisitions.

Many modern-day reports, such as Oxfam's recent research, evoke images of past colonial expansion and ignorance:

> More than 60 per cent of investments in agricultural land by foreign investors between 2000 and 2010 were in developing countries with serious hunger problems. But two-thirds of those investors plan to export everything they produce on the land. Nearly 60 per cent of the deals have been to grow crops that can be used for biofuels, says the report. Very few, if any, of these land investments benefit local people or help to fight hunger, said Oxfam. 'Instead, the land is either being left idle, as speculators wait for its value

to increase . . . or it is predominantly used to grow crops for export.'[60]

Such uneven development is possible in a world where China and the richer nations of the world have already put off having many children. Instead they buy up others' rights to land, in ways that in a more equitable world would be impossible.

Chinese economic expansion need not mirror that of the United States, as it is occurring in a very different context. The current context is of a rapidly contracting youth market and an expanding old-age group. The idea that free trade, where the richer partner is always more powerful, is the only way forward, known also as 'the Washington consensus', is weakening: 'For many African countries, China is now a major – and often the biggest – trading partner and aid donor. This means that deviation from the Washington consensus policies is less costly in terms of aid flows and trade preferences.'[61] During the period of American hegemony, 1948–2008, population growth rates rose and fell, ending in most continents just a fraction below where they started, though higher in Africa. That will not be the experience for the next 60 years.

The Figure above, a graph of the latest UN projections, shows how forecasts tend to be smooth and how reality is far more jagged.[62] Europe was the first continent in the world to experience net population decline since 1851. This occurred around Christmas time 1996. In 1996 there had been around 727,625,000 people in the continent; by 1997 that had fallen to 727,453,000. Numbers continued to decline in 1998, 1999 and 2000, but rose slightly after the start of 2001. Or at least this is what is thought to have occurred.

Population Growth 1950–2100

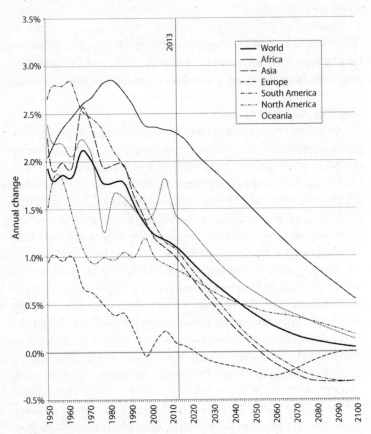

2013

——	World
——	Africa
– –	Asia
– – –	Europe
–·–·–	South America
–··–··–	North America
········	Oceania

Annual change

3.5%
3.0%
2.5%
2.0%
1.5%
1.0%
0.5%
0.0%
-0.5%

1950 1960 1970 1980 1990 2000 2010 2020 2030 2040 2050 2060 2070 2080 2090 2100

Source: UN historic estimates and projections, 1 June 2011.

We do not really know to the nearest several million how many people there are in Europe or anywhere else of Europe's size on the planet. The numbers to the nearest thousand have been given throughout this book for those pedants who enjoy spurious precision. What matters are the general trends that are being suggested. What we do know is that shortly after many of those 1960s baby-boomers welcome their slightly elevated numbers of grandchildren into the world, mostly in the decade we are in now, European population will peak for the last time – in 2022 – and then decline. Population growth rates had already peaked in 2007. This is two years after 'peak growth' in Oceania. In North America, the growth rate peaked 10 years earlier, in 1997, but because rates there were higher, the population will not decline, according to these UN models, until at least a century from now.

The Asian peak of population growth was 1985. Population is expected to first fall there by around 2050. The South American peak of growth was reached in 1961; absolute falls in human numbers are expected by 2057. The African peak of growth rates was not hit until 1981, at 2.85 per cent net growth a year. Since then that growth rate has been falling, but absolute decline in human numbers in Africa is not expected to be seen until later than in any other continent. This is simply because growth rates were highest, latest, in Africa, and because Africa is by far the poorest continent.

The children soon to be born in Africa will, some might reason, replace some of those children who have never lived because so many millions of the ancestors of their potential parents died as slaves, or en route to slavery, or were never born due to the huge disruption of African societies caused by the slave trade. Similarly, Europe will shrink in population size back to its normal share of humanity, the share before it gorged itself on so much of the goods of the world, partly as a product of organizing the middle passage (of the triangular Atlantic slave trade). However, although there might be a bittersweet sense of eventual justice in these trends, it is not for these reasons that they are occurring. Europe is not full up. Africa is not half-empty.

We are returning to an old geography. Almost all the arable land of China was deforested 3,000 years ago.[63] In recent years, however, China has been reforesting. It did so to such an extent between 1990 and 2000 that it gained an additional 181,000 square kilometres of forest in that period. Some three quarters of all the additional forest planted in the world during those 10 years was planted in China.[64] This is a very different pattern of behaviour to that which currently characterizes much thinking in the United States of America.

The United States was the first world power to become pre-eminent in a nuclear age. China, along with a spread of small city states, is now widely expected to be the first to rise up to challenge the economic dominance of the USA in a very different age, in the first age of population falls occurring outside of war, disease, famine or pestilence; in the age of planning, of ageing and of sharing. As more of the planet is reforested, as human population is mostly found again where it once largely settled, in Africa and Asia, and as we each learn to tread a little more lightly on the earth, 10 billion people can be imagined living in greater harmony than seven billion live in today. But will our numbers really ever quite reach 10 billion?

CHAPTER 8

OR NOT 10 BILLION

> The world now needs to conclude and act upon the fact that our economic, social, and environmental goals are not separate independent pillars to be pursued, but highly interdependent ones. The big picture is not one of difficult trade-offs to be overcome, as in fact many people still believe. Sustainable development goals in all three areas are in fact mutually supportive.
>
> Gro Harlem Brundtland,
> former prime minister of Norway, 2012[1]

This book is titled *Population 10 Billion*, but, at its end, I have a confession to make. I very much doubt that there will ever be 10 billion people all alive at the same time on this planet, at least not within the coming hundred years. The more I have looked into this issue, the more I have seen that it is those who are most worried who write the most about population. Perhaps this is natural, but there is very little contradicting opinion presented to the overarching thesis that population is a problem and that growth rates are too high.

Demographers who do *not* agree with the assertion that there is trouble ahead are less concerned about the future and are also more ready to question how well we understand what is happening now. In this chapter I show that it is possible that population growth is currently slowing even faster than most people think. Global economic recession would tend to exacerbate that effect. But that is not the only reason to think we may be slowing in the growth of our numbers even faster than the United Nations Population Division predicts. People in the West may find it hard to think of the cities of Macao, Singapore and Hong Kong, with their very low fertility rates, as being areas most ahead of their time; ahead in both good and bad ways. But neither Europe nor North America necessarily leads the way any more. Japan shows that low economic growth is sustainable, alongside very low fertility and very high life expectancy.

Forecasting the end of times

> Back in 1970 Ansley Coale, a demographer at Princeton, observed that the population of the United States had increased by half since 1940. At that growth rate, he calculated, the US population would reach a billion shortly before the year 2100. Within six or seven more centuries we would reach one person per square foot of land area in the United States, and after about 1,500 years our descendants would outweigh the Earth if they continued to increase by 50 percent every 30 years. We can even calculate that, at that rate of increase, our descendants would, in a few thousand years, form a sphere of flesh whose radius would, neglecting relativity, expand at the velocity of light.
>
> Joel E. Cohen, mathematical biologist, 1992[2]

We humans may not individually amount to much more than apes with a slightly overdeveloped frontal lobe, but collectively we are changing our social world in ways that no one has planned: ways that are slowing us down. Contrast the statements made in this book with the description immediately above made in 1970.

In the years immediately before 1971, at the height of the acceleration in our population, even the most celebrated of demographers could not see that the tide was about to turn. Ansley Coale died in 2002, just over a week short of his eighty-fifth birthday. During his life he was both prescient and cautionary. Between the lines he was saying that what was occurring in the 1960s simply could not continue. What was occurring was the second of two baby booms, and the second had to be smaller than the first.

Growth always slows. Undertaking calculations similar to Coale's back in 1970 would suggest that the impossibly quickly expanding sphere would begin to grow faster and faster, reaching the velocity of the speed of light in just less than 7,000 years from now. Instead deceleration began, not entirely coincidentally at almost exactly the point when Coale's prediction said that to continue would be impossible. Forty years later, we now know that we might never quite see even 10 billion people and we could live happily ever after, but will we? What could go wrong?

Even by 1920, within just the relatively recent Christian tradition, there had been 46 well known predictions that the end of the world is nigh.[3] Earlier in 2012, when I first checked the website that made this claim, the number was 44. The more people look, the more old failed claims about the end of times they find. The world keeps on not ending.

The dominant dread today is climate change, but within my short lifetime suggested reasons for an imminent end have included species extinction, especially bees dying out and not pollinating; plague; famine; material limits-to-growth;

nuclear winter; and the coming 'natural' ice age. My favourite was the less well-known 'killer bees' invasion once prophesied to be sweeping up across California. Bees are more linked to the ends of time than most other species.[4] But it won't be bees; if any species is the culprit, it'll be ourselves who'll do for humans.

People have amazing destructive powers. Over 12,000 years ago, as humans swept down the Americas, they settled the land, spreading southwards at rates of over a kilometre a year. There was almost always some group looking for a little more space, a little more land, and a little more freedom. Or there was someone who was being cast out, ostracized, or who simply got lost a little further south. Whichever way it was, once the Bering Straits had been breached, humans swarmed down into these new lands like a slow-motion plague of locusts.

As they swept down from what is now Canada, through the plains and then the isthmus, through jungle, over mountains and down to the cold tip of Cape Horn, they slaughtered to extinction almost three quarters of all mammals species on the northern American continent.[5] These were large mammals: a giant sloth that stood almost seven metres tall in height and weighed many tons; a mammoth with four-metre-long tusks; and a unique breed of sabre-toothed tiger. All are now extinct, alongside a further 30 mammal species that no longer exist in North America. Just a dozen mammals remain there today. An even higher proportion was slaughtered to extinction in South America, four fifths of that entire continent's mammalian species.[6] Humans first presided over mass extinction as they spread geographically. They do it now as they intensify demographically.

One great problem with countering the arguments that we are again at the end of times is the company that you might be keeping. There is now a niche for coming disaster deniers, and it contains men such as Dominic Lawson, who argues for us to worry less about global warming but who is better known for his sister's cooking fame,[7] and less well known for being George Monbiot's cousin.[8] Some of George's views are mentioned favourably a couple of times earlier in this book.

Other disaster deniers include Danish maverick Björn Lomborg, who sees technological fixes around every corner.[9] Björn, George, Dominic's dad (Nigel Lawson) and Canadian Green Party leader Elizabeth May memorably argued all this out in a television debate a few years ago.[10] In most things in life I agree with George and Elizabeth rather than the other two. I'd be in more convivial company predicting the end of times, so I'll have a go now and come up with one scenario that has been missed so far: what if we were to run out of people?

Population decline

> Among the 44 low-fertility countries that constitute the more developed regions, 24 are projected to see their populations drop by 2300 to less than one-tenth of their respective population sizes in 2000.
>
> 'World Population to 2300 low fertility forecast', draft UNPD report, 2003[11]

The United Nations Population Division projected that, if fertility fell a fraction lower than they expected, some 24 countries would see their populations all but disappear in the next 287 years. This was mainly because they did not include estimates for the influence of future migration into those more affluent countries. But just as doubt can be cast that such rapid population decline in these places might occur, we should also be very suspicious that in the near future there will be rapid population growth in many poorer parts of the world, especially at the higher ends of the growth estimates.

London School of Economics demographer Tim Dyson explains: 'certain aspects of the high scenario are highly questionable – even in relation to the next fifty years. Thus in this scenario between 2000 and 2050 Ethiopia's population rises from 65.6 to 197.9 million, Somalia's increases from 8.7 to 45.0 million, and Mali's rises from 11.9 to 52.6 million. Growth of this magnitude in these contexts seems unlikely.'[12] However, if we do *not* see growth of a similar high magnitude in several poorer places, we are unlikely to reach 10 billion people.

The human population may never make it to 10 billion, let alone the even higher estimates included in the 'high scenario', which would require populations in Ethiopia to triple to near 200 million, Somalia's population to rise five-fold and Mali's more than four-fold in just the space of two generations. As Tim Dyson makes clear, world human population will 'probably be less than 9.0 billion in 2300', and it may well not rise much above that beforehand. Some countries could have to cope with a much smaller population than they have now. Furthermore, the projection includes rises in life expectancies to levels no groups of humans have achieved. Without great increases in longevity, total population will fall faster than expected. Part of the reason that 10 billion is projected is that so many more of us are expected to live into extreme old age.

In 2011, in response to a deluge of often pessimistic questions concerning future population growth, the normally not especially sanguine Oxford Professor of Demography, David Coleman, was forced to explain that things were not that bad and future population growth was projected to be so muted that there was 'no need to retreat to the hills with a bag of gold and a machine-gun, I hope'.[13] In other words, there really were just a few countries left where population growth was still strong. So few that there was no need for Coleman's questioners to suggest that they needed to arm themselves and teach their children to shoot too.

Population decline is already happening in many countries and is very soon set to become the norm in most. But demographers remain unable to explain why the downturn has occurred and hence why it might continue. One suggestion has been that we humans have developed some kind of collective intelligence whereby we have somehow sensed, in the way bacteria appear to, that there are too many of us. However, scorn has been poured on this explanation applying in bacteria, let alone humans.

Even if bacteria did behave collectively for the greater good, humans are a little different, as zoologist Rosemary Redfield explains: 'We seem to be most prone to errors with those processes that most strongly distinguish us from bacteria – our sexuality and our sociality. Sex plays a central role in our lives, and we have rarely questioned whether it is also important in bacteria. Similarly, perhaps because we are social animals, we find the idea that bacteria have evolved communication and cooperation very appealing.'[14] Just because an idea is appealing, however, does not mean it is especially likely to be correct.

Thus environmentalists such as Rockefeller University's Jesse Ausubel may be misguided in evoking the idea that humans, like bacteria, might also be 'organisms [which] do try to sense limits, using something called "quorum sensing"'.[15] As explained above, and in contrast to Jesse, Rosemary Redfield (of the University of British Columbia)[16] suggests that what bacteria are actually doing is sensing their immediate environment, not their overall numbers. When locally overcrowded, they limit the diffusion of the chemicals they secrete to help them eat and survive. Her point is that even if this has a beneficial aggregate effect on the bacteria colony, it is not some kind of communal intention.

Humans behaving well because it makes local sense to behave well may benefit all humans on the planet, but such behaviour does not require awareness of all the other people on earth. Our imaginations find it hard to cope with more than a couple of hundred people (even on Facebook);[17] despite this, as has been repeatedly asserted in the chapters above, we are slowly and collectively learning to be less stupid, and so it is worth considering whether we might lower fertility even faster than is currently expected because we start to behave a little better, even if we do not have 'quorum sense'.

The United Nations Population Division's low-fertility scenario sets fertility at a quarter of a child below its medium scenario. In others words, three children would be born to two couples where the prediction had been for four. We are already at the low-scenario point in many affluent countries. Planetary demography is remarkably simple at one level. Population predictions for individual countries are most prone to errors in the estimates of future levels of migration. Future mortality rates and birth rates tend to be better predicted and less variable.

The smaller a country or the smaller an area within a country for which you are trying to forecast population, the more important are your guesses over future migration. The larger the area, the less important an influence migration has, and the more births and deaths matter. However, and this is another point repeatedly made in the chapters above, when migration occurs from poorer to richer countries, the people who migrate tend to have fewer children and grandchildren than those they leave behind. In other words, the more permissive we are of migration in the future, the more rapidly we can expect total global population levels to fall. In contrast, if we build even higher walls between us, the slowdown will take longer. As we worry about all this, however, it is important to remember that even without the possibility of migration, human beings are quite capable of living sustainably.

Easter Island (Rapa Nui) is often brought up as an example of our failure to survive when left to our own devices. The story commonly told is of an island where the overuse of wood and the exhaustion of topsoil brought about the end of a civilization. Recently an alternative explanation has emerged: the acute demand for population in Peru and the 'slave raids during the 1860s and the enforced population transfers of the 1870s [which] had a crushing impact on Easter Island'.[18] Ecologists who want to find stories of how humans are so bad at surviving will in future need to look to places other than Rapa Nui. The population pessimists also need to explain away the many examples of extremely long-lived human survival, even under the harshest of conditions.

Consider another Pacific island. For 3,000 years, humans have survived on the tiny island of Tikopia, just 4.7 square kilometres in area, but fortunate to have been formed so as to encircle a brackish crater lake. Some 400 years ago they killed all the pigs because the pigs ate too much food and perhaps were too tempting for passing sailors. The inhabitants' protein now comes from fish, and they survive cyclones by storing food deep underground.[19] For three millennia some 1,200 people have lived on this island and maintained zero population growth at a density in parts akin to twenty-first-century London. But conditions were harsh. Without contraception, survival was achieved partly through infanticide: 'The newborn is laid on its face to suffocate. There are no funerals for these children: they have not participated in life on Tikopia.'[20] Today, the greatest threat to these people is not from themselves, but from the outside world. Sea levels are rising and salt water may soon flood into the crater lake. Now they have contraceptives; next they will need desalination.

Tikopia Island, location and elevation

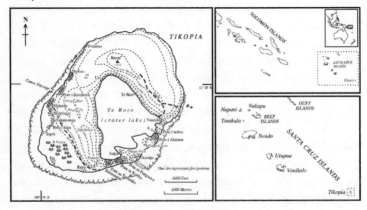

Source: Redrawn from Admiralty charts and other sources on the web.

Just as it was outside influences that appear to have most harmed human settlement on Rapa Nui, when large ships finally arrived (where before only canoes had landed), so on Tikopia what may be to blame if this civilization were to end soon could be the more rapid than usual rise in the level of the Pacific Ocean, a rise caused not by the actions of the islanders but by other humans and the enhanced melting of ice that is raising the ocean level, coupled with the thermal expansion of upper ocean layers. All this we are only just discovering. We are also only just discovering that there need be no more baby booms. The tiny fourth echo of the post-Second World War boom that we are currently living through could easily be the last baby boom experienced during our now-ending era of rising global population. With contraception we are today achieving worldwide what was only achieved through infanticide on Tikopia.

The last baby boom

> In light of progress during recent decades, there are now grounds for optimism that the human population will stabilise during this century. This will not happen automatically: investment is urgently required, and there are serious conceptual barriers to be overcome, but the costs are not great. With goodwill and prompt action, on a voluntary basis with full recognition of human rights, a plateau of perhaps 10 billion people is achievable by 2100.
>
> Paul Nurse, president of the
> Royal Society, 2012[21]

At the level of the planet, bar the improbable arrival of the occasional visitor from outer space and the exit of those few unfortunate astronauts who don't make it back to earth, net migration is zero. The future population of the planet is simply births less deaths. That is world population change. And the change in the change, the second derivative, the trend, the acceleration or deceleration: that is what matters. The second derivative is this year's births less last year's births plus last year's deaths less this year's deaths. It is shown in the Figure below for the very latest United Nations Population Division predictions, those made in May 2011.[22] These are the ones that Nobel

Laureate Sir Paul Nurse relies upon when he says that a plateau of 10 billion is possible. I think a lower number is more probable. That is because, as I was working on this book, I noticed something strange in the graph below.[23]

The scale on the left-hand side of the graph is the change in the change in population numbers worldwide between every pair of years. It is measured in millions of people. If the net increase in global population rises by a million people one year as compared to the year before, then the bar for that year will be one million people high. When the bars are above the x axis, the increase in people is accelerating. When the bars are below that line, there is deceleration in the rise in humans each year, eventually leading to population falls. The deeper the deceleration, the lower the bars are after 2013, the earlier the fall comes.

The underlying logic of any prediction is revealed by looking at the change in change that has occurred before and that which is expected in the future. Before 2011, the change in change appears erratic in the graph below – four peaks of acceleration and four dips, three dipping into actual deceleration. The greatest deceleration occurred between 1989 and 2003. That was followed by the smallest of renewed accelerations, around the year 2010, but it was that last blip that added a billion to the 2100 estimate!

So what do the United Nations demographers predict rolling forward? Continued erratic behaviour? No such thing! Look again at the graph below. They model change in change from 2011 onwards as being remarkably smooth, a repeat of the 1990s deceleration, to reach an annual decline of only just over a million people a year in population growth by 2020, then continuing through to 2059, when the deceleration slowly slows.

UN change in population change actual and projected 1950–2100 (millions)

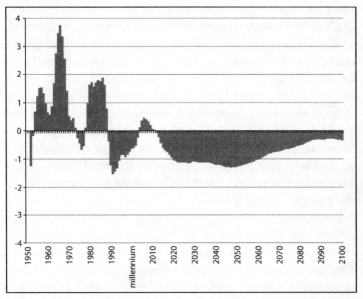

Source: UN median-variant projection, May 2011, annual change in population change.

Fools, you might think. The median-variant prediction is ridiculously optimistic. It assumes that the only period of significant deceleration in population growth we have experienced in the last six decades, the 1990s, is about to be replicated for at least 39 years. But take a look again at the Figure above. What do you notice about the gaps between the three clear peaks, the peaks in 1966, 1984 and then 2006? These peaks were 18 and then 22 years apart. Why might that be? The great clue is that we are not graphing populations of guinea pigs, humpback whales or fruit flies. These are human beings. So what is the significance of a gap of 18 years rising to 22 years?

The answer is human generations. What you see in the graph are global baby booms and echoes of baby booms, and as couples around the world control their fertility more and more, you see generation spans widening. Each peak is lower than the last and the gap between them grows as the global average age of giving birth rises from 18 to 22 years. What's next? Perhaps gaps of 26 years and then 30 years? Age 30 is where the European Union average age of motherhood is currently,[24] why should that not be the world's mean age of motherhood in two generations' time? After all, demographically, what the rest of the world has been doing recently is what happened in Europe just a couple of generations earlier. The world population boom itself began in Europe.

I've scribbled a line on the graph in the Figure below, the same graph as you saw above but now with generations of couples behaving like their parents and grandparents did. They continue to have fewer children, far fewer. In a few of the most affluent and equitable of countries it becomes normal to have none, rather than one as now. Where it was usual to have two, one becomes the norm. Rather than assume the future will simply repeat the 1990s, we are looking further back and at a more established trend.

There are all kinds of reasons why the past might not repeat itself in the way my scribbles on the graph below suggest. Famine, war, rising global inequalities, imminent climate catastrophe, or just plain old economic instability can lead to people having more children again as insurance for the future. But if disaster on these scales is not around the corner, then we may soon be dealing with more ageing and more population decline than we expect. And we'll be laughing at those early-twenty-first-century simpletons who did not recognize what was occurring in their time and were so afraid of so many other human beings,

UN change in population change actual, projected and hypothetical
1950–2100 (millions)

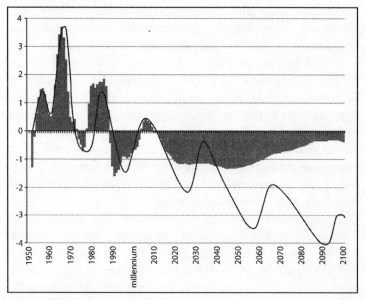

Source: UN median-variant projection, May 2011, annual change in population change
and an added hypothetical possibility.

especially afraid of those younger people, the ones who
were about to become so scarce, the population projection
ghosts that only ever lived in the demographers' models.

What if the United Nations demographers were a little
bit more imaginative? Demographers have been described
as being 'like accountants but without the charisma'.[25]
So expecting them to be more imaginative is a big ask.
However, what is needed is not creative accounting but
a recognition that something new may be occurring. The
next line added to the third version of this graph, in the
final version of this Figure shown below, is an alternative

prediction of the change in change to come when, instead of scribbling on the graph, you take the previous baby booms and map that past on to the future. Do that, and you make a very different prediction for future population levels from those most often currently bandied about.

Apply the changes shown below to the United Nations median variant and what you find is this: 'if the change in change repeats the most recent little bit of history we have enjoyed then a human population maximum is reached in 2060 at 9.295 billion, but by 2100 there would be just 7.362 billion of us, the same number as currently, officially, are projected to be alive in around five years from now'.[26] That was written in 2011. By the time you read this, 'five years from now' may soon be 'now'. New Year's Day 2016 will mark the second centenary of the most famous and optimistic speech on the future ever written, Robert Owen's New Year address in New Lanark: 'What ideas individuals may attach to the term "Millennium" I know not; but I know that society may be formed so as to exist without crime, without poverty, with health greatly improved, with little, if any misery, and with intelligence and happiness increased a hundredfold; and no obstacle whatsoever intervenes at this moment except ignorance to prevent such a state of society from becoming universal.'[27]

By 2016, the United Nations Population Division will have published a new set of projections. It will be worth studying them carefully and seeing in which direction they have moved from those published in May 2011. But the future will not be decided by graphs; what actually happens will largely depend on us, what we say and what we do. Within countries fertility has fallen fastest when equality has increased the most, particularly gender equality. It is unlikely to fall so quickly in future in those places where people do not see an increased politics of hope.

UN change in population change actual, projected and modelled
1950–2100 (millions)

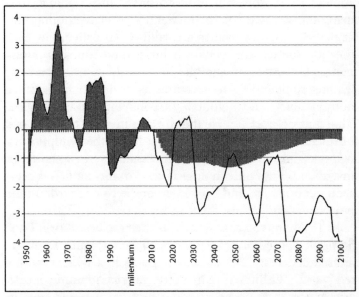

Source: UN median-variant projection, May 2011, annual change in population change
and an added model based on repeating post-war baby booms into the future.

The politics of hope

> I think that it is important as a way of embedding
> greater equality in our society to support all forms
> of economic democracy whether it is friendly
> societies, mutuals, employee-owned companies,
> cooperatives – all those systems – so that income
> differences become subject, at least indirectly, to
> some democratic force. The bonus culture has only
> been possible because people at the top have been
> completely unconstrained by not being answerable
> to other employees in the company.

Richard Wilkinson, epidemiologist, 2010[28]

351

The world is changing as we change. Epidemiologists now advocate greater equality and more grass-roots democratic control to improve our health. But the most eminent epidemiologists also squabble over the precise mechanisms at play. All human beings are fallible. To prove how even the 'top minds' can behave a little like souped-up chimpanzees, another epidemiologist recently described a third leading epidemiologist in his area as '"a lecherous wizened homunculus" and a fourth as behaving "like Margaret Thatcher on acid"'.[29] He did this to illustrate how the cult of suggesting that scientists regard each other with mutual respect while all standing on the shoulders of giants can be misguided. But epidemiologists tend to have a better press than economists, and even they are better regarded than politicians. Politicians trade in hope.

In 1974, in Rome, at what was then the first World Food Summit, United States Secretary of State Henry Kissinger announced that: 'No child will go to bed hungry within ten years.' Within ten years there was mass famine in eastern Africa. Kissinger's words are often repeated now as supporting evidence that it is almost impossible to feed billions, but they are words of optimism. They show that even Kissinger cared – for all his misguided behaviour and his government's mass-murdering action. The problem was not his intent that no one should go hungry but that the mechanism he espoused, free-market mayhem, which did not work.

Some economists still argue against self-sufficiency, and by implication against the storage of grains in case of drought. In 2009, *The Economist* proclaimed that:

> As Europeans have demonstrated over decades, pursuing self-sufficiency above all else is extremely wasteful. Self-sufficiency would also lock in patterns

of agricultural production just when climate change is affecting different parts of the world differently, making trade between them all the more important. The food-price trauma of 2007–08 is persuading some countries to say that they need to divert part of their wealth to subsidise food so they can be self-sufficient and avoid future crises. But the demands of feeding 9 billion people in 2050 tell a different story: farming needs to be as efficient as possible. That requires markets and trade.[30]

What Europeans have demonstrated over decades is that few go hungry in Europe, even during the economic crisis, as compared to the millions in the United States, where one in seven of all households had become food insecure by 2010, the highest proportion ever measured.[31]

Just three years after *The Economist*'s writers were suggesting that only the global free market would ensure all humans are well fed, the blind faith of many in the apparent efficiency of global markets has been shattered. The future of human beings is not simply a product of the accidents that happen to us, our exposure to epidemic, famine, disaster or discovery; we also have collective agency – when well organized. We are beginning to believe again that we are capable of relying on more than each other acting only out of greed to maximize our profit. Profit-seeking will not feed us. When profiteers think they can make more money by letting many people starve, they do.

The politics of hope contrasts with the politics of hype, the hype that 'a rising tide will lift all boats', that 'technology will find a substitute for oil', and that 'there is no alternative'. The politics of hope requires seeing behind 'the picture-perfect images of New York, Chicago, Miami, London and the like, showing neon lights, high-rises, malls and so on, [which] are bought and sold as ideals by the global economic powers, the global governance institutions, elites and local/national governments who benefit from the production and reproduction of such ideals. These are the very same ideals that are unfolding in the form of economic and urban development policies in places like Delhi.'[32] More and more often the bluff of those who sell hype is being called when a few profiteers in the world's most selfish of nations try to suggest that, if others were just as selfish, then they too could be as rich, could have the gilded neon cities; that everyone could be as profligate as them if only they were as selfish.

There are far better and more replicable models of the future than the megacities of the USA or London's banking and tax-exile megalopolis.[33] From the rich world take Tokyo, or Bologna, or Helsinki, cities now planned in the realization that 'Since 1960 the identification of proven oil reserves has generally kept pace with extraction, meaning that the time horizon of available oil has been within 35–50 years for several decades, but this does not alter the fact that ultimately oil is a non-renewable resource.'[34] These are cities less reliant on cars, cities whose workers are also more often their citizens, not frightened commuters living many dozens of miles out in gated estates or dormitory towns.

In Tokyo, more people are moved about with less effort than anywhere else on earth. In Helsinki, the city centre is not 'merely the location of isolated historic buildings and tourist destinations'.[35] In Bologna, 'the *Centro Storico* is an exemplar of one aspect of the European ideal: a large area of the city where walking and strolling is the natural way to move around, where streets and piazzas are not just routes to somewhere else, but meeting places and the backdrop for urban life'.[36] The contrast between the

thinking and behaviour of people in more equitable mainland Europe and Japan, as compared to the UK and USA,
is telling. But it can give hope because so many alternatives
already exist.

In 2011, in Copenhagen, an 11-mile (18 km) superhighway was built to allow distant commuters to the city to
cycle in without having to compete for space with cars.
Another 25 routes are set to be built there in the coming
months to give cyclists from all directions the opportunity
to cycle all the way from home to work and back. The
longest route will be 14 miles (22.5 km). Some $1.5 mil-
lion (€1.1m, £0.9m) from the project was not raised by
private finance, or even by the transport ministry, but by
the body responsible for public health and public hospi-
tals. Their officials explain: 'It's a common saying among
doctors that the best patient is the patient you never see.
Anything we can do to get less pollution and less traffic is
going to mean healthier, maybe happier, people.'[37]

In the spring of 2012, the government in Paris announced
its intention to return 2.5 km (1.5 miles) of the left bank of
the river Seine to pedestrian-only use. Later on in the summer it announced that a kilometre of the right bank of the
river would be turned into pedestrian corridors, walkways
by the riverside with bars and cafés. Right-wing politicians
initially vetoed the project and denied it funding. They
were voted out of office.[38]

Way back in the early 1970s, researchers in the then
West Germany concluded that there was no way of making roads safe for children when cars travelled at 30 mph
(48 kmph); that children could be taught 'kerb drill by
rote, but you will find that they do not really understand
it and cannot actually put it into practice'.[39] Across much
of mainland Europe, car speed limits in cities are now
30 kmph (18.5 mph) both to prevent children being killed

and to increase the sociability of cities. China, where children are suddenly so much rarer, is building car-free cities.[40]

The politics of hope may be never-ending, but as human growth slows, it begins to look a lot less fanciful. 'Can we do it? Yes we can!' began with the children's character Bob the Builder, but was taken up as a rallying call by Barack Hussein Obama. In November 2012, of the three top priorities Obama mentioned upon retaining his presidency, the second was reducing inequality, just after Hu Jintao, the outgoing Chinese leader, stated the same intent. From the revolutionary '*Liberté, égalité, fraternité*' to the feminist slogan 'Women bring all voters into the world', to plans for free health services to be established 'in place of fear', to Martin Luther King's 1963 pronouncement that all should say 'I have a dream', the best of politics has always been the politics of hope.

It is easy to get carried away with hope. In the year that Martin Luther King was speaking of his dream that his 'four little children will one day live in a nation where they will not be judged by the color of their skin but by the content of their character', scientists at the Mauna Loa Observatory in Hawaii were taking their sixth annual set of atmospheric carbon dioxide readings.[41] It was then, and there, that the cause of recent human-induced warming was first detected. This human-induced warming may date from much earlier than we currently think, induced by non-edible plant growth and plant decay encouraged by inefficient early irrigation for rice-growing, but in 1963, the graph of CO_2 emissions was rising.

The man who made the suggestion that CO_2 might have been rising from much earlier years, William Ruddiman, wrote that he expected it would take a great deal of time before his suggestion might be taken seriously because of herd instincts in academia and the pressures of time against reading and thinking.[42] But there are now so many more people alive who have been taught to read and told more than ever before about ways of thinking that Ruddiman may have been overpessimistic. We are collectively learning more and learning faster today than we have ever done. More people alive today may be able to read than everyone who has ever read before.[43]

We have to begin to learn that much economic growth can be harmful depending on the nature of that growth, but that other types of growth can be helpful. We must stop measuring it all in the same way. However, even the old ways of measuring economic growth can be informative and suggest that a change resulting in a reduction of per capita production and hence consumption has already taken place, and that the change date was 1971. There is a remarkable coincidence between when population first began to decelerate and when endless profiteering first began not just to appear harmful, but actually started to slow GDP growth per capita itself. Unfortunately in the UK and USA the fall in profit was initially dealt with by taking from wage rises at the bottom of both societies, which itself resulted in slower economic growth.

The current way in which we measure economic growth, Gross Domestic Product (GDP), is only just over half a century old, but estimates have been made that stretch back to two millennia ago as to what GDP might then have been and hence the long-term rate at which it has been changing.[44] GDP mirrors population growth remarkably closely, so closely in fact that dividing GDP by population shows us clearly how, as population took off, so too did GDP growth per person, and as population slows, so too is GDP per capita – either falling or only rising slowly.

The first column of data in the Figure below shows how economic growth and population kept pace with each other in the first millennia of the current era globally. Economic growth did fall a little in Western Europe, the most backward region of the planet from 1 CE to 1000 CE.[45] In contrast, from the millennium right through to the sixteenth century, economic growth was strongest in Europe. Over the entire 2,000-year period included in the table, the greatest increases in world economic growth occurred within the 30 years from 1941. In the 30 years from 1971, growth slowed in 9 of the 12 world regions shown directly below; this was an unprecedented economic slowdown.

The slowdown in economic growth rates from 1970 onwards is currently predicted to continue. On the current long recession: 'Lombard Street Research ran the numbers . . . and concluded that a tightening worth 2.6 per cent of US GDP would produce growth of just 0.4 per cent in the US in 2013, a contraction of almost 2 per cent in the Eurozone and growth of 4.5 per cent in China. "I'm not an equity strategist, but I'd suggest stock prices don't properly discount that scenario," commented Lombard's Dario Perkins.'[46] Global economic slowdown of this kind could result in a more equitable world, as it is currently the wealthiest regions that, both economically and in terms of population, are slowing the most.

We have to divide economic growth by population growth to see that economic growth per person really is slowing down. The Figure below shows that income growth per person was highest in Japan and the Middle East in the first millennium of the current era. Then, for the next 600 years, Western Europe grew a little faster, first in what is now Italy and then in what is now the Netherlands. Growth next speeded up in the United States, from a very low base; while in 1820 Britain became the highest per capita income country in the world.

World GDP per capita economic growth year 1 to 2000 by Worldmapper Regions

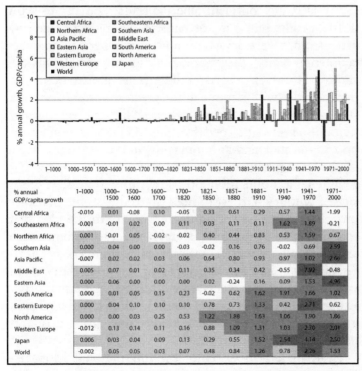

% annual GDP/capita growth	1–1000	1000–1500	1500–1600	1600–1700	1700–1820	1821–1850	1851–1880	1881–1910	1911–1940	1941–1970	1971–2000
Central Africa	-0.010	0.01	-0.08	0.10	-0.05	0.33	0.61	0.29	0.57	1.44	-1.99
Southeastern Africa	-0.001	-0.01	0.02	0.00	0.11	0.03	0.11	0.11	1.62	1.89	-0.21
Northern Africa	0.001	-0.01	0.05	-0.02	-0.02	0.40	0.44	0.83	0.53	1.59	0.67
Southern Asia	0.000	0.04	0.00	0.00	-0.03	-0.02	0.16	0.76	-0.02	0.69	2.59
Asia Pacific	-0.007	0.02	0.02	0.03	0.06	0.64	0.80	0.93	0.97	1.02	2.56
Middle East	0.005	0.07	0.01	0.02	0.11	0.35	0.34	0.42	-0.55	7.92	-0.48
Eastern Asia	0.000	0.06	0.00	0.00	0.00	0.02	-0.24	0.16	0.09	1.53	4.96
South America	0.000	0.01	0.05	0.15	0.23	-0.02	0.62	1.62	1.91	1.66	1.02
Eastern Europe	0.000	0.04	0.10	0.10	0.10	0.78	0.73	1.33	0.42	2.71	0.62
North America	0.000	0.00	0.03	0.25	0.53	1.22	1.88	1.63	1.06	1.90	1.86
Western Europe	-0.012	0.13	0.14	0.11	0.16	0.88	1.09	1.31	1.03	2.70	2.01
Japan	0.006	0/03	0.04	0.09	0.13	0.29	0.55	1.52	2.54	4.14	2.50
World	-0.002	0.05	0.05	0.03	0.07	0.48	0.84	1.26	0.78	2.26	1.53

Note: Growth rates of above 0 shaded light grey, above 1% grey, above 2% dark grey.
Source: www.worldmapper.org, in turn based on the work of Angus Maddison.

North America was playing catch-up, and the United States became the highest income per capita country in 1903. Switzerland rose economically to relegate Britain to third place by 1923. After that, the locus of faster growth per capita moved to Japan and South America between 1911 and 1940, next to the Middle East and Eastern Europe by 1941–70, and to eastern Asia, Asia Pacific and southern Asia by 1971–2000. The only regions still left to feature in the top two are found in Africa.

Africa is the continent next expected by many to grow most quickly, but it is not hard to report record growth rates from a very low base and in comparison to other economies when they appear to be on the downward slide.[47] However, the overall current global economic decline hides within it one of the greatest portents of hope. It suggests that the way we have been living, economically, has only been sustained by the 1851–1971 population boom, and that as that boom ends, so too will our current fantasy that profits can always grow.

When the population slowdown first arrives, it is the richest who try hardest to hold on to the profits that they once had. They find it hardest to adjust to the idea of a world in which you cannot simply expect to become richer as you lend monies to ever-growing numbers of naive youngsters. They cut the wages of the poor. They make young university students take out massive lifetime loans. Economists are only slowly catching on to the idea of slow growth. Many have come to realize that gross inequality hampers even slow growth.

Jonathan David Ostry of the International Monetary Fund was recently reported to have explained that: 'Income inequality in the United States has soared to the highest levels since the Great Depression and the recession has done little to reverse the trend, with the top 1 percent of earners taking 93 percent of the income gains in the first full year of the recovery . . . Growth becomes more fragile . . . in countries with high levels of inequality like the United States . . . the widening disparity since the 1980s might reduce the country's economic expansion by as much as a third.'[48] In the future, our collective fortunes may depend far more on how well we share out what we do have, rather than on trying to grow our profits ever higher.

The history of the future

> ... they had their faces twisted toward their haunches and found it necessary to walk backward, because they could not see ahead of them ... and since he wanted so to see ahead, he looks behind and walks a backward path.
>
> Dante Alighieri, *Divine Comedy*, 1555 (1321)[49]

It is the fate of seers and sorcerers who attempt to divine the future to trudge forever with their necks twisted around so that, in punishment, and in the original poetic justice, they forever circle the fourth ditch of Malebolge looking back whence they have come.[50] In Dante's eighth circle of hell, Malebolge, within its fourth ditch, you are always looking back at the past when you try to guess the future.

The *Divine Comedy* was written at the start of the fourteenth century, long before the population explosion, just before the Black Death engulfed Europe and perhaps at the point when reality felt like Dante's *Inferno*. It was first published in the sixteenth century as profits in Venice began to grow due to the lagoon's new-found geographical locus between India, China and the Americas. Someone writing following the effects of another 450 years of that geographic advantage could be far more positive over the prospects. So, by 1893, the English artist William Morris could write a fictional account of how the future might turn out. It was called *News from Nowhere*.

News from Nowhere described how children in future might play: 'They often make up parties, and come to play in the woods for weeks together in summer-time, living in tents, as you see. We rather encourage them to it; they learn to do things for themselves, and get to notice the wild creatures; and, you see, the less they stew inside houses the better for them.'[51] From fourteenth-century poetic descriptions of hell to late-nineteenth-century utopian socialism, how we see the future has always partly been a statement on the concerns of the times we are living through.

Let's look forward and risk Dante's eternity spent walking with a crick in our necks. In a world of megacities, what space is there for those who share Robert Owen's optimism of 1816, or who hanker after William Morris's vision from 1893 (his book was subtitled 'An Epoch of Rest')? Why shouldn't children play in the woods in summer? The more tightly you crowd into megacities, the more woods you have left outside. Saplings that are being planted today will provide the woods of national parks tomorrow. We already know where the woods should be in 2100. Whether they are there will depend on what is cut down between now and then.

The more you control consumption by the mega-rich, the more coastlines are left unspoilt. The very rich want to buy up the foreshore. The denser your cities, and the less sprawl and inequality you allow, the more the foothills of mountains are not crowded. We will not get children walking freely in woods, by the sea and up the hills unless we secure better control over the selfishness of a few adults. Securing greater equality for all is the principle means through which better control of the rich is won.

Modern capitalism was primarily both nurtured and sustained by the 1851–1971 population explosion. Economic growth was driven mainly not by geographical expansion but by demographic expansion. Capitalism is now transforming because it was a product of that relentless growth in human numbers. Before 1851, rapid population growth was confined to places such as London, which became the largest city in the world at that time. It was in London that Karl Marx saw capital at work so clearly. However, population growth was even more rapid in Manchester, the city to which Herr Engels sent young Friedrich to manage his mills. Karl and Friedrich were largely products of their time and their geography.

A new stability may soon be upon us, one we cannot yet see because there has been so much turmoil in the recent past. If you look at the ranking of cities in the world by population size, then from 430 BCE to the present, you see that the greatest change in city rankings has been in the most recent period, coincident with the 1851–1971 population surge. 'There are no cities in the top 50 in 430 BCE that are still there by 2000, and there are only six in the top 50 from the Fall of Constantinople in 1453. The half life of the original set of cities is approximately 200 years, which reduces to about 100 years by the 20th century.'[52] The geographical redistribution of population change has speeded up just as the rate of change itself accelerated.

For now we are still living through turbulent change. Different groups react to change in different ways. Marx and Engels wrote a manifesto. They had little faith in the elite. People tend to recommend what they are most comfortable with and what they know best. Today groups of 'high-level' scientists recommend that 'Regulation of the many commons that concern all humanity must be achieved by high level negotiations . . .'[53] The hope here is to see countries work together in ways that put their individual selfish interests aside, a bit like international science is supposed to work. However, this may not be how progress is actually won. No United Nations committee met to plan Wikipedia or to encourage thousands of scientists to publish their papers freely online in the new knowledge commons.

The billions of decisions to have fewer children were not 'high-level'. However, 'high-level' groups are now beginning to understand better what people with far less power are saying. Here is one Royal Society conclusion: 'Collaboration between National Governments is needed to develop socio-economic systems and institutions that are not dependent on continued material consumption growth. This will inform the development and implementation of policies that allow both people and the planet to flourish.'[54] If the scientific elite of a country are advocating less material consumption, and presumably a little redistribution of the wealth of those who consume too much to those who do not have enough of the basics of life, to enable that, then clearly change is afoot.

How future generations might look back on their grandparents, on us, should be a source of endless speculation. There is no need for any futurology to begin to see that population slowdown is upon us. The beginning of slowdown has been the largely untold story during my entire lifetime. Much else we have yet to see emerge.

The future might be cursed by designer babies, eugenics in test tubes, the genetic sieving out of 'smart' sperm donors. Or we may become collectively smart enough to avoid genetically modifying humans. All our long-run projections assume more equality in future, not some *Blade Runner* world. The 2300 United Nations projections allow 'fertility to converge along distinctive paths until complete equality in 2175, and permitting life expectancy alone among the components to be different between countries indefinitely, though it is forced to come close to converging'.[55]

It is not just convergence in demographics that is most commonly seen as our long-term destiny, but also convergence in wealth: 'The "problem" with global population – if there is one – is too many rich people consuming too much, not too many poor people.'[56] There are not that many rich people in the world, but there are a few rich people who consume a huge amount of our collective resources. Fortunately, this is not a long-established pattern. It has emerged alongside human emancipation from serfdom and strict hereditary rules that limited overall production, and hence consumption. And the super-rich cannot expect to see their wealth sustained in an era of slow population growth.

There are many reasons for optimism, and many of them have been long held. Nicolas de Condorcet, writing and thinking in France in the decades up to and including its revolution, could foresee a world of free and equitable provision of education to children, of growing equality in rights, of less violence and far more concordant and consolatory views. Less violence occurs as we become more equal, because it is 'dangerous competitive behavior that entails an implicit disdain for the future [and which] is exacerbated by cues that one lives in the sort of social milieu in which one's future may be cut short'.[57] The Canadian researchers who discovered this also explain that as our dangerous competitive behaviour is diminishing, so too is our collective propensity for violence.

Although it has been a long time coming, contemporary demographers writing over two centuries after the death of Nicolas de Condorcet suggest that: 'Despite various reversals and upheavals, history is tending to advance in the direction indicated by Condorcet – that is to say, towards more effective anticipation of crises and a greater capacity to react.'[58] This particular shard of optimism comes courtesy of François Héran, the current chair of the Board of Administration of the National Institute of Demographic Studies (INED) in Paris.

Condorcet was one population explosion and two centuries ahead of his time. Recently statisticians have found that 'the fall in the murder rate in England and Wales mirrors major drops in homicide rates since the mid-1990s, not just in Europe but across Asia and North America, where violent crime appears to be ebbing'.[59] Despite the general improvement now seen worldwide, those who oppose more equality suggest that we must be ever vigilant and fear feral youth. In the UK, officials now even propose spotting trouble and intervening as early as when babies start to walk. Rather like a toddler's first steps, progress occurs only in fits and starts. According to the *Telegraph* newspaper: 'Children at risk of "going off the rails" and descending into a life of crime can be spotted at the age of two, [it must be true because] the Government's adviser on discipline has said [it].'[60] The British government's adviser on 'discipline' is Charles Taylor, an Old Etonian, who says: 'Public schools are unbelievably successful. Why wouldn't you want to emulate them?'[61] Clearly the English still have a lot to learn from Condorcet, especially those made to wear fancy dress during their adolescence, every day, at Eton.

A world moving towards free and equitable provision of education to children, one that did not dress them in tail coats, could be a world in which we also learn not to try to estimate the human carrying capacity of the earth. While we still find it sensible to dress children in rigid school uniforms, we are unlikely to have progressed enough to realize that no reliable estimates of a sustainable human population for the planet exist, and that any such estimates would depend on what kind of society was thought acceptable, what kind of technology the society coexisted with and how well.

Contemporary studies of what a supposedly ideal worldwide population of humans would be usually tend to suggest a limit near to that point currently reached, and, if honest, give very wide confidence limits. One meta-analysis published in the journal *Bioscience* in 2004 suggested that: 'When taking all studies into account, the best point estimate is 7.7 billion people; the lower and upper bounds, given current technology, are 0.65 billion and 98 billion people, respectively.'[62] That is quite a wide set of confidence limits.

The authors of that 7.7 billion (give or take 90.3 billion) spot estimate suggest at the end of their paper that if they had given more weight to more recent estimates in their meta-study, estimates based on better data, they would have come up with a higher number. They also in effect suggest that if what is currently occurring is a human transformation similar to the Neolithic revolution, then it is during just such a transformation that our actual carrying capacity increases enormously. Maybe this book's title should have been *Population 100 Billion*. Only time will tell.

AFTERWORD

Of course, there has to come a point, at some point, when it is too late. Hopefully precisely when that point will be is impossible to foretell. The 4 May 2044 date of the latest estimate for 'techno-rapture', mentioned in passing halfway through this book,[1] will certainly inspire some to set that as the possible Armageddon point. For others, 2044 is simply too far away. There is always one group or another that needs to say the end is nigh, right here, right now.

If I live to 4 May 2044, I'll be 76 years old. My oldest child will be almost as old as I am now. Hopefully I'll be a grandfather, but just as you can take nothing for granted (as it is not always rational to be an optimist), so too it makes little sense to be a pessimist all your life. Be practical, be a possibilist, but be aware that whatever we worry most about today is unlikely either to greatly diminish as a concern, or to still be our greatest concern in future. We were made to worry; it keeps us safe. Here is one last thing to worry about. Better to worry about this now than later, and better to worry about the climate than about 10 billion people:

> Our impact on the climate system will change an important part of Earth's basic appearance from even the distant perspective of space: most of the north polar region that is now white will be repainted in

hues of dark blue (where sea ice melts back) and dark green (where snow-covered tundra gives way to boreal conifer forest). As satellite photos accumulated over many decades begin to show that we are repainting Earth's northern pole, the scale of our impact on climate will become obvious to all.[2]

ACKNOWLEDGEMENTS

Thanks to Leo Hollis, who came up with the title when he was at Constable, and to Andreas Campomar, Clive Hebard and Charlotte Macdonald, who saw the book through to completion. Carl Lee, Bethan Thomas, Matt Watson, Bronwen Dorling, Alison Dorling and Dimitris Ballas helped by commenting on the early flood of material. Paul Coles redrew all the graphics, while copyediting and proofreading was ably carried out by Jane Selley and Jane Donovan.

REFERENCES

Chapter 1
Introduction: stop worrying

1 Geisel, T. S. (1962, 2003), *Dr Seuss's Sleep Book*, New York: HarperCollins Children's Books.

2 UNPD (2011), *World Urbanization Prospects, the 2011 Revision*, New York: United Nations Population Division. See: http://esa.un.org/unpd/wup/index.htm.

3 The place from where the first recording was made in Dr Seuss's Plexiglas dome.

4 Canter, D. (2012, p.113), 'Challenging neuroscience and evolutionary explanations of social and psychological processes', *Contemporary Social Science* 7, 2, 95–115.

5 Golding, W. (1954), *Lord of the Flies*, London: Faber and Faber.

6 Collins, S. (2008), *The Hunger Games*, London: Scholastic Press.

7 Ridley, M. (2010), *The Rational Optimist: How Prosperity Evolves*, London: Fourth Estate.

8 Harrabin, R. (2012), 'Green groups' concern over Owen Paterson record', BBC News, 4 September, http://www.bbc.co.uk/news/science-environment-19476970.

9 Emmott's principal job is head of computational science at Microsoft Research in Cambridge. His work for Microsoft includes determining 'How to feed a global population of 10 Billion or more; How to power a planet of 10 Billion people or more; Developing the ability to predict, prevent, manage a global pandemic . . .' He's a busy man.

http://research.microsoft.com/en-us/people/semmott/ (accessed 20 August 2012).

10   Jack. I. (2012), 'The implications of overpopulation are terrifying. But will we listen to them? The Royal Court's new play about overpopulation, *Ten Billion*, could be seen as a wake up-call – or just a cry of despair', the *Guardian*, 3 August, http://www.guardian.co.uk/commentisfree/2012/aug/03/ian-jack-overpopulation-ten-billion.

11   See: http://www.vhemt.org/, where you can find 'T-shirts, caps, cups, mousepad, clock, and more' (as of November 2012 at: http://www.vhemt.org/join.htm).

12   Fukuyama, F. (1992), *The End of History and the Last Man*, London: Penguin.

13   Ruddiman, W. F. (2005, p.190), *Plows, plagues, and petroleum: How humans took control of climate*, Princeton: Princeton University Press.

14   Barford, A., Dorling, D., Davey Smith, G. and Shaw, M. (2006), editorial: 'Women's life expectancy', *BMJ* 332, 808.

15   http://www.gapminder.org/downloads/history-of-karolinska-institutet/. Note: women, perhaps sensibly, appear to strut their stuff less flamboyantly than men, for all three ideological persuasions included here.

16   Amin, A. (2012, p.170), *Land of Strangers*, Cambridge: Cambridge University Press.

17   The most well known of these biologists was Richard Dawkins; his criticism was recorded in 'Sociobiology: The Debate Continues', *New Scientist*, 24 January 1985, http://www.imamu.edu.sa/Scientific_selections/abstracts/Biology/Biology, per cent20Ideology per cent20and per cent20 Human per cent20Nature.pdf.

18   Davey Smith, G. (2011, p.556), 'Epidemiology, epigenetics and the "Gloomy Prospect": embracing randomness in population health research and practice', *International Journal of Epidemiology* 40, 537–62, http://ije.oxfordjournals.org/content/40/3/537.full.pdf. On what might also protect an individual from heart disease, the same author

posits more sex: Davey Smith, G. (2010, p.944), 'Pearls of wisdom: eat, drink, have sex (using condoms), abstain from smoking and be merry', *International Journal of Epidemiology* 39, 4, 941–7.

19   See Table 7.1 in Dorling, D. (2012), *The Population of the UK*, London: Sage, where the chances are laid out in a game for students to play so that they can determine what they themselves may most likely die of.

20   This was part of the reason for the cross-Atlantic slave trade. Mann, C. C. (2011, p.79), *1493: How Europe's discovery of the Americas revolutionized trade, ecology and life on earth*, London: Granta.

21   Known planet here means known to most people on earth, and to those who left almost all written records. As far as those in the Americas were concerned, theirs was the known planet, though it was the smaller of the two. Only now, over 500 years later, do we acknowledge it as having had its own set of civilizations that were not in some way inferior to the more germ-ridden Old World.

22   Nurse, P. et al. (2012, p.98), *People and the planet*, The Royal Society Science Policy Centre report 01/12, issued April 2012, London: Royal Society (references p.30), http://royalsociety.org/policy/projects/people-planet/.

23   Rosling, H. (2012), TED talk 'Religion and babies', filmed April 2012, posted May 2012. TED is shorthand for 'Technology, Entertainment and Design'; see: http://www.ted.com/talks/hans_rosling_religions_and_babies.html.

24   Staff reporter (2012), 'UK wind power predictable enough to keep lights on, says think tank IPPR', *Daily Telegraph*, 30 August, http://www.telegraph.co.uk/finance/newsbysector/energy/9508765/UK-wind-power-predictable-enough-to-keep-lights-on-says-think-tank-IPPR.html.

25   Magnason, A. S. (2008), *Dreamland: A Self-Help Manual for a Frightened Nation*, London: Citizen Press Ltd.

26   Gaydazhieva, S. (2012), 'Happy Earth Overshoot Day!', *New Europe*, 22 August, http://www.neurope.eu/article/happy-earth-overshoot-day.

27 Ibid.
28 Hennig, D. B. (2013, p.12), *Rediscovering the world: map transformations of human and physical space*, Heidelberg: Springer. See also this posting made on 5 March 2012: 'Mapping the Anthropocene on the 500th birthday of the cartographer Gerardus Mercator': http://www.viewsofthe world.net/?tag=anthropocene.
29 Herod, A. (2011), 'What does the 2011 Japanese tsunami tell us about the nature of the global economy?', *Social and Cultural Geography* 12, 8, 829–38.
30 Barrett, B. (2012), 'After the Nuclear Disaster, Japan Considers a Green Future', *Solutions (for a sustainable and desirable future)* 3, 1 99–103, January, https://thesolutions journal.com/node/1044.
31 Clark, N. (2012), 'Energy Policy in France Divides Governing Coalition of Socialists and Greens', *New York Times*, 14 September, http://www.nytimes.com/2012/09/15/ world/europe/energy-policy-divides-governing-coalition-in-france.html?pagewanted=2&_r=0.
32 Le Gros, C. F., and Pirie, N.W. (eds., 1951, p.5), *Four Thousand Million Mouths: Scientific Humanism and the Shadow of World Hunger*, Oxford: Oxford University Press.
33 Evans, L. T. (1998, p.116), *Feeding the Ten Billion: plants and population growth*, Cambridge: Cambridge University Press.
34 For details of John and the only academic department of demography in the USA, see: http://www.demog.berkeley. edu/~jrw/.
35 UNPD (2004, p.175) *World Population to 2300, Final Report*, Department of Economic and Social Affairs, Population Division, ST/ESA/SER.A/236, John R. Wilmoth.
36 UNPD (2003), *World Population to 2300, Draft Report*, Department of Economic and Social Affairs, Population Division, ESA/P/WP.187; 9 December 2003.
37 Ibid.
38 UNPD (2004, p.176), op. cit., John R. Wilmoth.

39   Ibid (p.167), Michael S. Teitelbaum.

40   Eberstadt, N., and Shah, A. (2011, p.24), 'Fertility Decline in the Muslim World: A Veritable Sea-Change, Still Curiously Unnoticed', *The American Enterprise Institute Working Paper Series on Development Policy*, Number 7.

41   UNPD (2004, p.145), op. cit., Tim Dyson, referring in turn to: United Nations (1995), *World Population Prospects: The 1994 Revision*, New York: United Nations Publication, Sales No. E.95.XIII.16.

42   He continued: 'Similarly, global numbers are unlikely to be allowed to go below 5.5 billion, as in the low scenario for 2100, and certainly not to the 2.3 billion given for 2300.' Notice the use of the word 'allowed' in this sentence. Who would do the allowing? UNPD (2004, p.122), op. cit., John C. Caldwell.

43   Rosling, H. (2012), TED talk, 'Religion and babies', filmed April 2012, posted May 2012; see: http://www.ted.com/talks/hans_rosling_religions_and_babies.html.

44   Bourdieu, P. (2008 translation, p. 83), *The Bachelors' Ball*, Cambridge: Polity.

45   Worldmapper map 582 (atheists) and map 136 (teenage mothers) on www.worldmapper.org.

46   Further details of the 2300 long-range population projections can be found at www.worldmapper.org and http://www.un.org/esa/population/publications/longrange2/WorldPop2300final.pdf (page 10).

47   Source: United Nations, Department of Economic and Social Affairs, Population Division (2011), *World Population Prospects DEMOBASE extract*, 'Total fertility (children per woman) – medium variant'. For further details, see: http://www.un.org/esa/population/publications/technical papers/TP2011-3_SevenBillionandGrowing.pdf.

48   UNPD (2004, p.115), op. cit., John C. Caldwell.

49   Baird, V. (2011, p.18), *The no-nonsense guide to world population*, Oxford: New Internationalist.

50   Harris, B. (2001, p.695), commentary: '"The child is father of the man." The relationship between child health

and adult mortality in the 19th and 20th centuries',
International Journal of Epidemiology 30, 4, 688–96.

51 Groves, J. (2011), 'Cameron warns Africans over the
    "Chinese invasion" as they pour billions into continent',
    Daily Mail, 20 July, http://www.dailymail.co.uk/news/
    article-2016677/Cameron-warns-Africans-Chinese-
    invasion-pour-billions-continent.html.

52 A character played by Dev Patel in John Madden's 2012
    film adaptation of Deborah Moggach's *These Foolish
    Things*, screenplay by Ol Parker.

53 Robbins, J. (1959, p.33), *Too many Asians*, New York:
    Doubleday.

54 Connelly, M. (2008), *Fatal Misconception: the struggle
    to control world population*, Massachusetts: Harvard
    University Press. See: http://www.matthewconnelly.net/
    FM_page.html.

55 Rajan, S. I., and Zachariah, K. C. (1997), 'Long-term impli-
    cations of low fertility in Kerala', Centre for Development
    Studies, Trivendrum (Kerala), Working Paper 282, http://
    ideas.repec.org/p/ind/cdswpp/282.html.

56 Bhrolcháin, M. N., and Beaujouan, E. (2012, p.13),
    'Fertility postponement is largely due to rising educational
    enrolment', *Population Studies: A Journal of Demography*,
    DOI:10.1080/00324728.2012.697569.

57 Associated Press (2012), 'Greek police failing over surge in
    hate crimes, say campaigners', the *Guardian*, 19 July, http://
    www.guardian.co.uk/world/2012/jul/19/greece-police-
    surge-race-hate-crimes.

58 Surowiecki, J. (2012), 'The more the merrier', the *New
    Yorker*, 26 March, http://www.newyorker.com/talk/
    financial/2012/03/26/120326ta_talk_surowiecki.

59 Billington, M. (2012), *Ten Billion* review, the *Guardian*,
    19 July, http://www.guardian.co.uk/stage/2012/jul/19/ten-
    billion-review-royal-court.

Chapter 2
The first half of human history

1   Barnes, J. (1984), *Flaubert's Parrot*, from Chapter 13, 'Pure Story', London: Jonathan Cape. Emphasis as in the original.

2   The detail of how many minutes to midnight we have been at at various times in recent decades can be found at: http://www.thebulletin.org/content/doomsday-clock/timeline.

3   Bulletin of the Atomic Scientists (2007), '"Doomsday Clock" Moves Two Minutes Closer To Midnight', 17 January, press release: http://www.thebulletin.org/content/media-center/announcements/2007/01/17/doomsday-clock-moves-two-minutes-closer-to-midnight.

4   See Figure at the end of Chapter 1, above, and also the many graphs of population change below in this volume.

5   Weymes, M. (2012), 'Making Inroads on Birth Certificates in East Timor', *Jakarta Globe*, 27 September, http://www.thejakartaglobe.com/home/making-inroads-on-birth-certificates-in-east-timor/546799.

6   The fall in fertility occurred long before 1979. The quotation is attributed to Hania Zlotnik, director of the UN Population Division, by Kunzig, R. (2011), 'Population 7 Billion: There will soon be seven billion people on the planet. By 2045 global population is projected to reach nine billion. Can the planet take the strain?', *National Geographic Magazine*, January, http://ngm.nationalgeographic.com/2011/01/seven-billion/kunzig-text.

7   These crew numbers are so small, it makes more sense to think of those ships like modern-day spacecraft rather than as the equivalent of ocean-going vessels today: http://www.christopher-columbus.eu/columbus-ships.htm.

8   King, F. H. (1911), *Farmers of Forty Centuries; Or, Permanent Agriculture in China, Korea and Japan*, reprinted 2004 by Dover Publications, but also available for free here: http://www.gutenberg.org/cache/epub/5350.

9   See 'Afro-Cuban History: a Time Line 1492 to 1900' at: http://www.afrocubaweb.com/history/history.htm.

10   http://www.revealinghistories.org.uk/why-was-cotton-so-important-in-north-west-england/places/cotton-mills-ancoats-manchester.html.

11   Due mostly to mass infant and early childhood mortality. See: Dorling, D. (2013), *Unequal Health: The scandal of our times*, Bristol: Policy Press, Chapter 2.

12   The song '400 years', written by Pete Tosh and sung by Bob Marley, was released on the Album *Catch a Fire* on 13 April 1973. Slavery was abolished across most of the world by 1892, in Zanzibar in 1897, but in many other places later again than that. See: http://en.wikipedia.org/wiki/Abolition_of_slavery_timeline.

13   The 12 divisions of the world are those used in the Worldmapper project (www.worldmapper.org).

14   Tufte, E. (1990, p.95), *Envisioning Information*, Cheshire, Connecticut: Graphics Press. On the quote and what it can mean, see Dorling, D. (2012), *The Visualisation of Spatial Social Structure*, Chichester, East Sussex: Wiley.

15   Schalansky, J. (2012, p.9) *Pocket Atlas of Remote Islands: Fifty Islands I Have Not Visited and Never Will*, London: Particular Books (Penguin).

16   For a brilliant description of what it might be like to see into the past in this way, and on archaeology, see: Mitchen, S. (2004, new edition), *After the Ice: A global human history 20,000 to 5,000 BC*, London, Phoenix.

17   Chronicles 21:5. For numerous versions, see: http://bible.cc/1_chronicles/21-5.htm; for references to even earlier counts see: Numbers 26: 'The Second Census': http://niv.scripturetext.com/numbers/26-1.htm.

18   As an aside, it is incidental but interesting that the Melodians recorded the anthem of the Rastafarian movement, 'Rivers of Babylon: Psalm 137:1' just as world population acceleration was about to peak in 1970. It is worth listening to again, especially if you are aged over 40: http://www.youtube.com/watch?v=o-5E6_qtXAw.

19   http://en.wikipedia.org/wiki/Doomsday_argument#We_are_in_the_earliest_5.25.2C_a_priori.

20 Dissanayake, E. (2005), 'A review of The Singing Neanderthals: The Origins of Music, Language, Mind and Body by Steven Mithen', *Evolutionary Psychology* 3, 375–80.

21 Cookson, C. (2012), 'Did Neanderthals invent graffiti?', *Financial Times*, 29 June, http://www.ft.com/cms/s/2/9fb47 24a-bfec-11e1-bb88-00144feabdc0.html#axzz1ze6jaUuJ.

22 Ruddiman, W. F. (2005, p.23), *Plows, plagues, and petroleum: How humans took control of climate*, Princeton: Princeton University Press.

23 Svante Pääbo of the Max Planck Institute for Evolutionary Anthropology, reported in: Sample, I (2012), 'Scientists reconstruct genetic makeup of 50,000-year-old girl', the *Guardian*, 30 August, http://www.guardian.co.uk/science/2012/aug/30/scientists-genetic-makeup-denisovan-girl.

24 Wilkinson, R., and Pickett, K. (2009), *The Spirit Level: Why more equal societies almost always do better*, London: Penguin.

25 Because, among many other possible reasons, English would not exist for another two millennia.

26 Ruddiman (2005, pp.71, 82 and 90), op. cit.

27 Wright, A. (2009), *Hoax! The Domesday Hide*, Leicester: Matador.

28 On Jean-Pierre Bocquet-Appel: http://fr.wikipedia.org/wiki/Jean-Pierre_Bocquet-Appel; on the centre: 'CNRS ranks fourth World (after NASA and two other American institutions) and is the European leader (before the Max-Planck-Gesellschaft and CERN)', http://fr.wikipedia.org/wiki/Centre_national_de_la_recherche_scientifique.

29 Bocquet-Appel, J.-P. (2011), 'When the World's Population Took Off: The Springboard of the Neolithic Demographic Transition', *Science*, 29 July, 333, 6042, 560–1, http://www.sciencemag.org/content/333/6042/560. See also: http://www.evolhum.cnrs.fr/bocquet/biblio.htm.

30 Vigne, J.-D., Briois, F., Zazzi, A., et al. (2012, p.8445), 'First wave of cultivators spread to Cyprus at least 10,600 years ago', *PNAS*, 29 May, vol. 109, no. 22, pp.8445–9, www.pnas.org/cgi/doi/10.1073/pnas.1201693109.

31 Wilson, D. S., and Wilson, E. O. (2006, p.18), 'Rethinking the Theoretical Foundation of Socio-biology', as submitted to *Science* magazine, http://www.cogsci.msu.edu/DSS/2006-2007/Wilson/Rethinking_July_20.pdf.

32 Amin, A. (2012, p.3), *Land of Strangers*, Cambridge: Cambridge University Press.

33 Bibby, J., Dubuc, S., Grayer, M., Kornbrot, D., Marshall, A., Simpson, L., and Norman, P. (2011, p.16), 'Moral panic about overpopulation: a distracting campaign?', web page: Radical Statistics Population Studies Group Report, http://www.radstats.org.uk/popgroup/RSPG_OPT-Oct11.pdf.

34 See Taylor, P. (2012), 'Extraordinary Cities: early "Cityness" and the origins of agriculture and states, *International Journal of Urban and Regional Research* 36, 3, 415–47, quoting Jane Jacobs and Marshall David Sahlins.

35 Recorded a few years ago as being only 1.82 children per couple; see Map in chapter 1: 'the long range forecast'.

36 Bouckaert, P., Lemey, M. D., Dunn, M., et al. (2012, p.18), 'Mapping the Origins and Expansion of the Indo-European Language Family', supplementary material, *Science*, 24 August, 337, 957, http://www.sciencemag.org/content/suppl/2012/08/22/337.6097.957.DC1/Bouckaert.SM.pdf.

37 Ibid.

38 Wade, N. (2012), 'Family Tree of Languages Has Roots in Anatolia, Biologists Say', *The New York Times*, 23 August, http://www.nytimes.com/2012/08/24/science/indo-european-languages-originated-in-anatolia-analysis-suggests.html.

39 One contemporary but still uncommon thesis sees villages as settlements that were formed around a few early cities. This is the 'thesis of cities inventing agriculture'. The suggestion is that the very earliest of small cities could only survive if ringed by villages and that the religious pronouncements from the city provided the social order necessary to maintain the villagers' obedience. The quotation is from Taylor, P. (2012), op. cit.

40 Chi, Z. (1997), 'The rise of urbanism in the middle and lower Yangzi river valley', *Bulletin: Indo-Pacific Prehistory*

Association 16, 63–7, https://journals.lib.washington.edu/index.php/BIPPA/article/viewFile/11647/10277.

41 Farid, S. (2011), Çatalhöyük Research Project – *2011 Archive Report*, http://www.catalhoyuk.com/downloads/Archive_Report_2011.pdf.

42 Bocquet-Appel, J.-P. (2006), writing on the 'The first baby boom – Skeletal evidence shows abrupt worldwide increase in birth rate during Neolithic period', 3 January, http://www.eurekalert.org/pub_releases/2006-01/uocp-tfb010306.php, open-access press release for the paper: Bocquet-Appel, J.-P., and Naji, S. (2006), 'American cemeteries data corroborate a Neolithic demographic transition on a world-wide scale', *Current Anthropology* 47, 2, pp. 341–65. Free access to the paper can be found here: http://www.jstor.org/stable/10.1086/498948.

43 Szreter, S., and Mooney, G. (1998), 'Urbanization, mortality, and the standard of living debate: new estimates of the expectation of life at birth in nineteenth-century British cities', *Economic History Review* 51, 1, 84–112.

44 Meece, S. (2006), 'A bird's eye view – of a leopard's spots. The Çatalhöyük "map" and the development of cartographic representation in prehistory', *Anatolian Studies* 56, 1–16, http://www.dspace.cam.ac.uk/handle/1810/195777.

45 Map of Manchester circa 1650: http://en.wikipedia.org/wiki/File:Map_of_manchester_circa_1650.jpg.

46 Details of the church are here: http://en.wikipedia.org/wiki/Church_of_the_Holy_Name_of_Jesus,_Manchester.

47 Ruddiman, W. F. (2005, p.56), op. cit.

48 Dorling, D. (2011, p.185) *Injustice: why social inequality persists*, Bristol: Policy Press.

49 Han Pingdi was given the posthumous name Xiaoping (孝平), 'filial and peaceful', which would become famous again in 1982: http://en.wikipedia.org/wiki/Emperor_Ping_of_Han http://en.wikipedia.org/wiki/Deng_Xiaoping.

50 For all historic figures I rely on Angus Maddison's data. File 2 here: http://www.worldmapper.org/data.html.

51 King, F. H. (1911), *Farmers of Forty Centuries; Or,*

Permanent Agriculture in China, Korea and Japan, reprinted 2004 by Dover Publications, but also available for free here: http://www.gutenberg.org/cache/epub/5350.

52 Ruddiman (2005, p.138), op. cit.

53 Walden, T. (2002, p.11), *The Spanish Treasure Fleets*, Sarasota (Florida): Pineapple Press. See also: http://en.wikipedia.org/wiki/Matthew_Boulton#cite_ref-ass_110-2, on later use of Spanish silver.

54 McGhee, G. (2011), 'Data Visualization: Journalism's Voyage West', website, http://vimeo.com/channels/newspapers and http://www.stanford.edu/group/ruralwest/cgi-bin/drupal/visualizations/us_newspapers.

55 Only a white man could introduce another white man, rather than merely announce his presence. 'There were no other white men known to be in the vicinity. As the two had not been formally introduced, it was a proper way to address Livingstone without committing a breach of etiquette': http://en.wikiquote.org/wiki/David_Livingstone.

56 Kiernan, B. (2011, p.28), 'From Irish Famine to Congo Reform: Nineteenth-century roots of international human rights law and activism', Chapter 1 in Provost, R., and Akhavn, P. (eds), *Confronting Genocide*, Heidelberg: Springer.

57 Eberstadt, N., and Shah, A. (2011, p.24), 'Fertility Decline in the Muslim World: A Veritable Sea-Change, Still Curiously Unnoticed', *The American Enterprise Institute Working Paper Series on Development*, Policy Number 7.

58 There were estimated to be about 767 million agnostics and 152 million atheists around the year 2002, when total population numbers were 6,242 million. See: http://www.worldmapper.org/extraindex/text_religion.html.

59 Schalansky J. (2012, p.137), op. cit.

60 'Radiation effects from Fukushima Daiichi nuclear disaster'. Possibly the best web page usefully collaboratively edited to date: http://en.wikipedia.org/wiki/Radiation_effects_from_Fukushima_Daiichi_nuclear_disaster.

61 Preface to second edition, p.x: http://galton.org/books/hereditary-genius/text/pdf/galton-1869-genius-v3.pdf.

62 To be found in the *Proceedings of the Royal Society*, 1912, Series B, 85, 469–76.

63 Davey Smith, G., and Kuh, D. (2001, p.701), commentary: 'William Ogilvy Kermack and the childhood origins of adult health and disease', *International Journal of Epidemiology* 30: 696–703.

64 Kermack, W. O., McKendrick, A. G., and McKinlay, P. L. (1934, p.703), 'Death rates in Great Britain and Sweden: Some general regularities and their significance', *The Lancet*, 31 March, 698–703.

65 Gordon, D., and Nandy, S. (2012, p.74), Chapter 4: 'Measuring child poverty and deprivation', A. Minujin and S. Nandy (eds), *Global child poverty and well-being: Measurement, concepts, policy and action*, Bristol, Policy Press. Referring to: Kevles, D. J. (1985), *In the name of eugenics: Genetics and the uses of human heredity*, New York: Alfred A. Knopf.

66 Huxley, J. (1926, p.ix), *Essays in Popular Science*, London: Chatto & Windus, according to http://en.wikipedia.org/wiki/Julian_Huxley#cite_note-72. The phrase appeared to be missing from the 1945 edition. If this interests you, see Dorling, D. (2010), 'The Fabian Essay: The myth of inherited inequality', *Fabian Review*, 122, 1, 19–21, http://www.dannydorling.org/?page_id=770.

67 Orwell, G. (1949), *Nineteen Eighty-Four*, London: Secker & Warburg, quotation from copy held at: http://gutenberg.net.au/ebooks01/0100021.txt.

68 Galbraith, J., quoted in Dorling, D. (2010, p.72), 'Why what I read makes me think what I think', *Radical Statistics*, issue 104, 70–3, http://www.radstats.org.uk/no103/Dorling103.pdf.

69 Galton. F. (1892 edn, p.ix), *Hereditary Genius*, London: Macmillan. The first chapter is available here: http://www.mugu.com/galton/books/hereditary-genius/pdf/genius-1.pdf.

70 Lewontin, R. C. (1974), 'The analysis of variance and the analysis of causes', *American Journal of Human Genetics*

26, 400–11. (The quote is from p.400, referenced on p.4 of the summary of Jay Joseph's *The Gene Illusion*: http://jayjoseph.net/the_gene_illusion.)

71 Richardson, K. (2000), *The Making of Intelligence*, New York: Columbia University Press (quote from this book is given on p.24 of the summary of Jay Joseph's *The Gene Illusion*: http://jayjoseph.net/the_gene_illusion).

72 Forrest D. W. (1974), *Francis Galton: The Life and Work of a Victorian Genius*, London: Elek Books.

73 Simon, B. (1978, 2nd edn, p.245), *Intelligence, Psychology, Education*, London: Lawrence and Wishart. Emphasis added to point out how vile these ideas were.

74 For the story of how the IQ tests were a fraud, see Jay Joseph, quoting Richard Lewontin, Steven Rose and Leon Kamin's conclusion, on p.25 of his summary of *The Gene Illusion*: http://jayjoseph.net/the_gene_illusion.

75 Latham, J., and Wilson, A. (2010), 'The Great DNA Data Deficit: Are Genes for Disease a Mirage?', *Independent Science News*, 8 December, http://independentsciencenews.org/health/the-great-dna-data-deficit/.

76 http://www.smithsonianmag.com/history-archaeology/Ten-Notable-Apocalypses-That-Obviously-Didnt-Happen.html; on the urban myth: http://answers.yahoo.com/question/index?qid=20110623072610AAySOe5.

Chapter 3
6 billion for the millennium

1 Davis, M. (2004), 'Planet of Slums', *New Left Review*, 26 March, http://newleftreview.org/II/26/mike-davis-planet-of-slums. See Also Davis, M. (2006), *Planet of Slums*, London: Verso.

2 The population total is of how many people are alive at any one time, simultaneously living. Note that if people live longer, the population total will be higher, even if the same number are born as before.

3 Balourdos, D., et al. (2002, p.17), *Scenarios for a sustainable*

386

society: Car transport systems and the sociology of embedded technologies, final report of EU project SOE1-CT97-1071, Ireland: Trinity College Dublin, http://www.tcd.ie/ERC/pastprojects/carsdownloads/Cars per cent20Final per cent 20Report.pdf.

4   Or 2,009,012,000 people, to be ridiculously and indefensibly exact. All these estimates rely on Angus Maddison's figures, which I used when constructing the Worldmapper time series: http://www.worldmapper.org/data.html.

5   'Perhaps the most serious flaw in *The Bomb* was that it was much too optimistic about the future,' said the authors in 2009, unrelenting to the end. Only the husband, Paul Ehrlich, was named on the book's cover. See: http://en.wikipedia.org/wiki/The_Population_Bomb.

6   Collini, S. (2011, p.9), 'From Robbins to McKinsey', *London Review of Books* 33, 16, 9–14, http://www.lrb.co.uk/v33/n16/stefan-collini/from-robbins-to-mckinsey.

7   See Worldmapper map 187: Urban Slums 2001: http://www.worldmapper.org/display.php?selected=187.

8   And in which a 'ruling class within the moneyed elite are in fact aliens managing human social affairs', harking back to old conspiracy theories: http://en.wikipedia.org/wiki/They_Live.

9   Mann, C. (2011), *1493: How Europe's discovery of the Americas revolutionized trade, ecology and life on earth*, London: Granta.

10   Baird, V. (2011, p.102), *The no-nonsense guide to world population*, Oxford: New Internationalist.

11   Evans, L. T. (1998, p.193), *Feeding the Ten Billion: plants and population growth*, Cambridge, Cambridge University Press.

12   Hughes, B. (2010), 'Too Many Of Whom and Too Much Of What? What the new population hysteria tells us about the global economic and environmental crisis, and its causes', A *No One Is Illegal* discussion paper, 13 January, http://www.noii.org.uk/2010/01/13/too-many-of-whom-and-too-much-of-what/.

13   Evans, (1998, p.85), op. cit.

14   Hughes (2010), op. cit.

15   Pearce, F. (2011), *Peoplequake: Mass Migration, Ageing Nations and the Coming Population Crash*, Eden Project Books, London: Random House.

16   Of 1950s America, but now more widely applicable. See: Jacobs, J. (1962, p.219), *The Death and Life of Great American Cities*, London: Jonathan Cape.

17   Allen, R. (2009), *The British Industrial Revolution in Global Perspective*, Cambridge: CUP 2009. The quotation can be found here: https://webspace.utexas.edu/ec22637/a/industrialrevolution.html.

18   Ravenstein, E. G. (1885), 'The Laws of Migration', *Journal of the Statistical Society of London* 48, 2, 167–235. For a summary see: http://www.csiss.org/classics/content/90.

19   Here there are echoes of Japanese 'honorary white' status as given under South African apartheid in the 1960s. Travis, A. (2012), 'Heathrow to get fast-track passport lanes for "low-risk" countries', the *Guardian*, 10 July, http://www.guardian.co.uk/world/2012/jul/10/heathrow-fast-track-passport-heathrow.

20   'If a borrower secures employment abroad and is paid abroad, Student Loans Company will ask for the name of the employer and evidence of the salary. Student Loans Company will calculate a repayment schedule based on 9 per cent of the earnings over £15,000.' The young adult then has to decide what is fair and how much they want the right to return without facing further financial threats: http://www.hmrc.gov.uk/employers/faq-sl-abroad.htm#a.

21   Hern, A. (2012), 'Chart of the day: Reduce the debt? Increase migration', *New Statesman*, 26 September, http://www.newstatesman.com/economics/economics/2012/09/chart-day-reduce-debt-increase-migration.

22   UNPD (2004, p.145), *World Population to 2300, Final Report*, Department of Economic and Social Affairs, Population Division ST/ESA/SER.A/236, Tim Dyson.

23   Ibid (p.152), François Héran.

24 Eberstadt, N., and Shah, A. (2011, p.5), 'Fertility Decline in the Muslim World: A Veritable Sea-Change, Still Curiously Unnoticed', *The American Enterprise Institute Working Paper Series on Development Policy*, Number 7.

25 Ibid (p.6). Which continues: 'Fully eighteen of these Muslim-majority places saw TFRs fall by 3 or more over those thirty years – with nine of them by 4 births per woman or more! In Oman, TFRs plummeted by an astonishing 5.6 births per woman during those 30 years: an average pace of nearly 1.9 births per woman every decade.' TFR stands for Total Fertility Rate, the average number of children born to all women in a particular place over a particular period of time.

26 Bloom, D. E. (2011), '7 Billion and Counting', *Science*, 333, 562. DOI: 10.1126/science.1209290; interview with author available at: http://www.sciencemag.org/content/suppl/2011/07/28/333.6042.562.DC1.html. It continues: 'Demographic changes have had and will continue to have profound repercussions for human well-being and progress, with some possibilities for mediating those repercussions through policy intervention.'

27 PSN (2010), *International Policy Symposium on the Connection between Population Dynamics, Reproductive Health and Rights and Climate Change*, London: Population Sustainability Network (PSN), http://www.populationand sustainability.org/941/climate-change/climate-change-sym-posium.html.

28 Pinker, S. (2012), *The Better Angels of Our Nature: A History of Violence and Humanity*, London: Penguin.

29 The source of the more calming quote at the start of this section: Bloom (2011), op. cit.

30 Ruddiman, W. F. (2005, pp.186–7), *Plows, plagues, and petroleum: How humans took control of climate*, Princeton, Princeton University Press.

31 Connelly, M. (2008), *Fatal Misconception: the struggle to control world population*, Massachusetts, Harvard University Press. See: http://www.matthewconnelly.net/FM_page.html.

32   Lilley, P. (2012, p.31), *What is Wrong with Stern? The Failings of the Stern Review*, produced by a group called CCNet, last found here: http://www.thegwpf.org/peter-lilley-what-is-wrong-with-stern-the-failings-of-the-stern-review-of-the-economics-of-climate-change/ (as of November 2012).

33   Ibid., referring to Richard S. J. Tol of the University of Sussex and Vrije Universiteit Amsterdam.

34   IMF (2010), World Economic Outlook Database, October, accessed 21 May 2012 from http://www.imf.org/external/pubs/ft/weo/2010/02/weodata/index.aspx.

35   Lawson, D. (2011), 'The population time bomb is a myth: The doomsayers are becoming more fashionable just as experts are coming to the view it has all been one giant false alarm', the *Independent*, 18 January, http://www.independent.co.uk/opinion/commentators/dominic-lawson/dominic-lawson-the-population-timebomb-is-a-myth-2186968.html.

36   Keane, B. P. (2010), 'British insult victims of An Gorta Mór, diplomats skip out on Famine Memorial', *Irish Central*, 17 May: http://www.irishcentral.com/story/ent/the_keane_edge/british-insult-victims-of-an-gorta-mor-diplomats-skip-out-fearing-reparation-demands-93994459.html.

37   Wilkinson, R., and Pickett, K. (2010, 2nd edn), *The Spirit Level: Why equality is better for everyone*, London: Penguin; http://www.equalitytrust.org.uk/resource/the-spirit-level.

38   Saunders, P. (2011), 'Academic Sociology and Social Policy Think Tanks in Britain and Australia: A Personal Reflection', *Sociological Research Online* 16, 3, http://www.socresonline.org.uk/16/3/10.html (point 1.8, page 2).

39   Bookchin, M. (1989, pp.19–23), 'Death of a small planet: It's growth that's killing us', *The Progressive*, August, http://dwardmac.pitzer.edu/Anarchist_Archives/bookchin/planet/planet.html.

40   Petit, S., and Pors, L. (1995), 'Survey of columnar cacti and carrying capacity for nectar-feeding bats on Curaçao', *Conservation Biology* 10, 3, 769–75; www.jstor.org/stable/2387099.

41 Ball, J. (2012), 'London 2012: torchbearers picked by sponsors keep flame of commerce alive', the *Guardian*, 6 June, http://www.guardian.co.uk/sport/2012/jun/06/torch bearers-nominated-olympics-sponsors.

42 Kruszelnicki, K. S. (2004), 'Lemmings Suicide Myth', *ABC Science News*, 27 April, http://www.abc.net.au/science/articles/2004/04/27/1081903.htm.

43 Mares, P. (2010), 'Monday morning in Mernda', *Griffith Review*, edition 29, http://griffithreview.com/edition-29-prosper-or-perish/monday-morning-in-mernda.

44 Donovan, S. (2012), 'Computer glitch causes Melb [*sic*] traffic gridlock', *The World Today, ABC News*, 3 October. Transcript: http://www.abc.net.au/news/2012-10-03/computer-glitch-causes-melb-traffic-gridlock/4293436?section=vic.

45 Ibid.

46 I say 'think', because the Easter Island story is partly myth. See 'Population decline', in Chapter 8 below.

47 Luis A. Avilés (2011, p.216), 'The credibility of small island overpopulation: A critique of population density maps as a proxy for overpopulation', *ACME: An International E-Journal for Critical Geographies*, volume 10, issue 2, pp. 215–31, http://www.acme-journal.org/vol10/Aviles2011.pdf.

48 See 'About the Club of Rome', which is to be found at: http://www.clubofrome.org/?p=324.

49 Baird, V. (2011, p.81), *The no-nonsense guide to world population*, Oxford: New Internationalist.

50 King, F. H. (1911), *Farmers of Forty Centuries; Or, Permanent Agriculture in China, Korea and Japan*, reprinted 2004 by Dover Publications, but also available for free here: http://www.gutenberg.org/cache/epub/5350.

51 Goodhall, C. (2011, p.20), '"Peak Stuff": Did the UK reach a maximum use of material resources in the early part of the last decade?', http://www.carboncommentary.com/wp-content/uploads/2011/10/Peak_Stuff_17.10.11.pdf, quoting in turn from a paper now published as:

A. Millard-Ball and L. Schipper (2011), 'Are We Reaching "Peak Travel"? Trends in Passenger Transport in Eight Industrialized Countries', *Transport Reviews: A Trans-nationalTransdisciplinaryJournal*,volume 31,issue 3.A copy is to be found here: http://geog.mcgill.ca/faculty/millard-ball/Millard-Ball_Schipper_Peak_Travel_preprint.pdf.

52 Zittel, W., Schindler, J., and L-B-Systemtechn (2004), 'The countdown for the peak of oil production has begun – but what are the Views of the Most Important International Energy Agency?', *Energy Bulletin*, 14 October, http://www.energybulletin.net/stories/2004-10-14/countdown-peak-oil-production-has-begun-per centE2 per cent80 per cent93-what-are-views-most-important-internati [the web address *does* end halfway through the word 'international'!].

53 BBC (2000), 'Oil reaches $30 a barrel', BBC News, 15 February, http://news.bbc.co.uk/1/hi/business/644028.stm.

54 Goodhall (2011), op. cit.

55 Dorling, D., and Thomas, B. (2011, p.128), *Bankrupt Britain: An atlas of social change*, Bristol: Policy Press.

56 Goodhall (2011), op. cit., citing in turn Ofwat figures from the annual *Security of Supply* report: http://www.ofwat.gov.uk/publications/.

57 See:http://www.defra.gov.uk/statistics/foodfarm/food/family food/ ; and Goodhall (2011), op. cit.

58 See:http://www.corrugated.org.uk/information/pages/annual _reviews.html; and Goodhall (2011), op. cit.

59 Goodhall (2011, p.15), op. cit.

60 Rosenthal, E. (2007), 'Cement Industry Is at Center of Cli-mateChangeDebate',*TheNewYorkTimes*,26October,http://www.nytimes.com/2007/10/26/business/worldbusiness/26cement.html?_r=0.

61 Bigg, G. (2012), Professor in Earth Systems Science, University of Sheffield, personal communication.

62 Smithers, R. (2012), 'UK tourist attractions suffer plunge in visitor numbers', the *Guardian*, 9 October, http://www.guardian.co.uk/business/2012/oct/09/uk-tourist-attractions-plunge-visitor.

63   Chase-Dunn, C., and Curran-Strange, M. (2012), 'Diffusion of the Occupy Movement in California', *Institute for Research on World-Systems*, University of California-Riverside, Working Paper 74, http://irows.ucr.edu/papers/irows74/irows74.htm.

Chapter 4
7 billion in December 2011

1   Ruddiman, W. F. (2005, p. 149), *Plows, plagues, and petroleum: How humans took control of climate*, Princeton: Princeton University Press.

2   On 31 October 2011: El Nasser, H. (2011), 'World population hits 7 billion', *USA Today*, 31 October, http://usatoday30.usatoday.com/news/world/story/2011-10-30/world-population-hits-seven-billion/51007670/1.

3   See the World Economic Forum website: http://www.weforum.org/issues, as accessed in October 2012.

4   Hell, I. (2010), 'Masters of the universe redesign the world at Davos', the *Independent*, 24 January, http://www.independent.co.uk/news/business/news/masters-of-the-universe-redesign-the-world-at-davos-1876926.html.

5   Kunzig, R. (2011), 'Population 7 Billion: There will soon be seven billion people on the planet. By 2045 global population is projected to reach nine billion. Can the planet take the strain?', *National Geographic Magazine*, January 2011, http://ngm.nationalgeographic.com/2011/01/seven-billion/kunzig-text.

6   UNPD (2004, p.175), *World Population to 2300, Final Report*, Department of Economic and Social Affairs, Population Division ST/ESA/SER.A/236, section by John R. Wilmoth.

7   Carlyon, P. (2012), 'Macquarie Dictionary widens definition of misogyny after Julia Gillard's putdown of Tony Abbott', the *Herald Sun*, 19 October, http://www.heraldsun.com.au/opinion/macquarie-dictionary-widens-definition-

of-misogyny-after-julia-gillards-putdown-of-tony-abbott/
story-fncw91kq-1226498914785.

8   Bucciol, A., and Piovesan, M. (2012, p.15), 'Pay Dispersion
    and Work Performance', *Harvard Business School,
    Working Paper* 12-075: http://www.hbs.edu/research/
    pdf/12-075.pdf.

9   Fisher, S., Crane, S., and Chaytor, S. (2011, p.2), *Population
    Footprints, UCL Grand Challenge Of Global Health,
    Policy briefing*, November, London, http://www.ucl.ac.uk/
    popfootprints/publications/popfoot_policybrief.

10 For some of the many possible reasons, see: Dorling, D.
    (2013), *Unequal Health: The scandal of our times*, Bristol:
    Policy Press. These reasons include doctors not living
    within the same regions as people who most need doctors,
    known as the inverse care law, where those whose needs
    are greatest receive the least health care.

11 Bookchin, M. (1989), 'Death of a small planet: It's growth
    that's killing us', *The Progressive*, August, pp.19–23, http://
    dwardmac.pitzer.edu/Anarchist_Archives/bookchin/planet/
    planet.html.

12 Gardner, L. (2012), 'Roundabout – review', the *Guardian*,
    26 September, http://www.guardian.co.uk/stage/2012/
    sep/26/roundabout-lungs-review.

13 Ibid., comment: 'Neuroticism is a good word to describe
    a couple overly worried about climate change and their
    baby's carbon footprint . . . Neuroticism is a risk factor
    for the "internalizing" mental disorders such as phobia,
    depression, panic disorder, and other anxiety disorders (tra-
    ditionally called neuroses).' By Ben T. Would, 27 September.

14 Badiou, A. (2012, p.13), *The Rebirth of History, Times of
    riots and uprisings*, London: Verso.

15 Claude Hendrickson, founder of the Chapeltown young
    people's club, the *Guardian*, speaking later, 2 July 2012,
    http://www.guardian.co.uk/uk/2012/jul/02/how-leeds-
    avoided-riots.

16 Dorling, D. (2010, p.312), *Injustice: why social inequality
    persists*, Bristol: Policy Press.

17 Nurse, P., et al. (2012, p.89), *People and the planet*, The Royal Society Science Policy Centre report 01/12, issued April 2012, London: Royal Society: http://royalsociety.org/policy/projects/people-planet/.

18 Green, T. (2012), letter, the *Guardian*, 5 March, http://www.guardian.co.uk/theguardian/2012/mar/05/tesco-housing-byron-stalin-ice-cream.

19 Flint, J., and Powell, R. (2012), 'The English City Riots of 2011, "Broken Britain" and the Retreat into the Present', *Sociological Research Online* 17, 3, p.19, http://www.socresonline.org.uk/17/3/19.html.

20 Badiou (2012, p.91), op. cit.

21 http://www.facebook.com/pages/Proletariat/109221765770188?rf=124729370934918.

22 Davies, J. B., Sandström, S., Shorrocks. A., and Wolf, E. N. (2008, p.7), *The world distribution of household wealth*, Helsinki, UNU-WIDER: http://www.wider.unu.edu/publications/working-papers/discussion-papers/2008/en_GB/dp2008-03/.

23 Dorling, D. (2012, p.285), *Fair Play, a reader on social justice*, Bristol: Policy Press.

24 Capgemini 16th annual world wealth report (2012), p.11, http://www.capgemini.com/services-and-solutions/by-industry/financial-services/solutions/wealth/worldwealth report/wwr_archive/.

25 These are people with over $25,000,000 in 'investable assets' where 'the average wealth of those surveyed had net assets of over $100 million'. Ro, S. (2012), '10 stats about how people with over $100 million invest', *Business Insider*, 11 August, http://www.businessinsider.com/ultra-high-net-worth-100000000-invest-2012-8.

26 Pow, C.-P. (2011), 'Living it up: super-rich enclave and transnational elite urbanism in Singapore', *Geoforum* 42, 382–93.

27 Hickman, L. (2012), 'James Lovelock: The UK should be going mad for fracking', the *Guardian*, 15 June, http://www.guardian.co.uk/environment/2012/jun/15/james-lovelock-interview-gaia-theory.

28 Neumayer, E. (2004), 'The super-rich in global perspective: a quantitative analysis of the Forbes list of billionaires', *Applied Economics Letters* 11, 793–6, http://www2. lse.ac.uk/geographyandenvironment/whoswho/profiles/ neumayer/pdf/article per cent20in per cent20applied per cent20economics per cent20letters per cent20(forbes).pdf.

29 http://en.wikipedia.org/wiki/Forbes_list_of_billionaires.

30 Beaverstock, J. V., Hubbard, P., and Short, J. R. (2004), 'Getting away with it? Exposing the geographies of the super-rich', *Geoforum* 35, 401–7, http://www.lboro.ac.uk/ gawc/rb/rb93.html

31 Badiou (2012, p.60), op. cit.

32 Schuetze, C. F. (2012), 'Norway Increases Carbon Tax on Domestic Production', *International Herald Tribune*, 15 October, http://rendezvous.blogs.nytimes.com/2012/10/ 15/norway-increases-carbon-tax-on-domestic-production/.

33 MacLeay, I., Harris, K., and Annut, A. (2011, p.44), *Digest of United Kingdom Energy Statistics*, Department of Energy and Climate Change, London: TSO: http://www. decc.gov.uk/assets/decc/11/stats/publications/dukes/2312- dukes-2011-full-document-excluding-cover-pages.pdf.

34 Dorling (2010, p.242), op. cit.

35 A. Millard-Ball and L. Schipper (2011), 'Are We Reaching "Peak Travel"? Trends in Passenger Transport in Eight Industrialized Countries', *Transport Reviews: A Transnational Transdisciplinary Journal* 31, 3, 1–26. A copy is to be found here: http://geog.mcgill.ca/faculty/ millard-ball/Millard-Ball_Schipper_Peak_Travel_preprint. pdf.

36 Rao, L. (2012), *Clothing Swap Startup Tradesy Wants To Turn Every Woman's Closet Into Currency*, techcrunch.com, 24 October, http://techcrunch.com/2012/10/24/clothing- swap-startup-tradesy-wants-to-turn-every-womans-closet- into-currency/.

37 Schuetze (2012), op. cit.

38 Goodhall, C. (2011), *'Peak Stuff': Did the UK reach a maximum use of material resources in the early part of*

the last decade?, http://www.carboncommentary.com/wp-content/uploads/2011/10/Peak_Stuff_17.10.11.pdf.

39 Dorling, D. (2011, p.217), *So you think you know about Britain?*, London: Constable. See graph of waste versus inequality for the world's most affluent 25 countries. A copy is here: http://www.dannydorling.org/books/britain/.

40 Care, L. (2012), 'Extracting the truth about peak oil', letter, the *Guardian*, 5 July, http://www.guardian.co.uk/business/2012/jul/05/extracting-truth-peak-oil and see: http://lucycare.net/.

41 Ruddiman (2005, p.162), op. cit.

42 As Joan MacNaughton, 'a former top UK civil servant and vice chair of the high level panel, told the *Guardian*'. See: Harvey, F. (2012), 'Global carbon trading system has "essentially collapsed"', the *Guardian*, 10 September, http://www.guardian.co.uk/environment/2012/sep/10/global-carbon-trading-system.

43 Business Spectator (2011), *Banks look to capitalise on carbon tax*, 13 July, on-line report from Australia: http://www.businessspectator.com.au/bs.nsf/Article/Banks-look-to-capitalise-on-carbon-tax-report-pd20110712-JPQRL?OpenDocument&src=hp9.

44 To be found on the website of actress Jane Fonda: http://janefonda.com/too-many-people/, 7 May 2011.

45 Ruddiman (2005, p.105), op. cit.

46 Hill, A. (2012), 'Children's books reflect harsh reality', the *Guardian*, 6 July, http://www.guardian.co.uk/books/2012/jul/06/childrens-books-reflect-harsh-reality.

47 Roaf, S. (2012), letter to the *Guardian*, 14 March, http://www.guardian.co.uk/environment/2012/mar/14/carbon-targets-renewables-atomic-risks.

48 Edwards, R. (2012), 'UK nuclear sites at risk of flooding, report shows', the *Guardian*, 7 March, http://www.guardian.co.uk/environment/2012/mar/07/uk-nuclear-risk-flooding.

49 Lynas, M. (2012), 'Without nuclear, the battle against global warming is as good as lost', the *Guardian*, 14

September, http://www.guardian.co.uk/environment/2012/sep/14/nuclear-global-warming.

50   Jungjohann, I. A. (2011), *Get the Facts Right: Germany has seen a Boom in Green Jobs*, Heinrich Böll Stiftung, 15 March, http://boell.org/web/139-735.html.

51   Eddy, M. (2012), 'A higher cost for German energy switch', *The New York Times*, 16 October, http://www.nytimes.com/2012/10/17/world/europe/energy-price-increases-pose-challenge-for-merkel.html.

52   Staff reporter (2012), 'Npower and British Gas price rises fuel fears of "cold winter" for households', *Daily Telegraph*, 12 October, http://www.telegraph.co.uk/finance/personalfinance/consumertips/household-bills/9604907/Npower-and-British-Gas-price-rises-fuel-fears-of-cold-winter-for-households.html.

53   Syal, R., and Carrington, D. (2012), 'Wind farms on the bog of Ireland could provide UK electricity', the *Guardian*, 8 October, http://www.guardian.co.uk/environment/2012/oct/08/wind-farms-ireland-uk-electricity.

54   Ryall, J. (2012), 'Nearly 36pc of Fukushima children diagnosed with thyroid growths', *Daily Telegraph*, 19 July, http://www.telegraph.co.uk/news/worldnews/asia/japan/9410702/Nearly-36pc-of-Fukushima-children-diagnosed-with-thyroid-growths.html.

55   Halperin, C. (2012), 'Changing Cities: A Wind Turbine That Creates Fresh Water Out of Thin Air', ABC News, 26 August, http://abcnews.go.com/blogs/technology/2012/08/changing-cities-a-wind-turbine-that-creates-fresh-water-out-of-thin-air/.

56   Bookchin, M. (1989), 'Death of a small planet: It's growth that's killing us', *The Progressive*, August, pp. 19–23, http://dwardmac.pitzer.edu/Anarchist_Archives/bookchin/planet/planet.html.

57   Jubbal, J. (2009, p.2), 'The future sustainability of human population in the light of climate change and depleting fossil fuels', MSc dissertation, by LSE (London School of Economics and Political Science) Masters student in

operational research, http://populationmatters.org/documents/future_sustainability_full.pdf.

58 Ibid. (p.12).

59 Ibid. (p.24).

60 Bradsher, K. (2012), 'For China, unfamiliar anguish over unsold goods', *The New York Times*, 23 August, http://www.nytimes.com/2012/08/24/business/global/chinas-economy-besieged-by-buildup-of-unsold-goods.html.

61 Ruddiman (2005, p.184), op. cit.

62 Godin, S. (2012), *Stop stealing dreams*, http://www.sethgodin.com/sg/docs/stopstealingdreamsscreen.pdf.

63 Bourdieu, P. (2008 translation, p. 83), *The Bachelors' Ball*, Cambridge: Polity. See pp.79–80 on the 1880s, and pp.84–5 on the demeanour of peasants.

64 Hagell, A. (2012), *Changing Adolescence: Social trends and mental health*, Bristol: Policy Press.

65 Collishaw, S., Maughan, B., Natarajan, L., and Pickles, A. (2010), 'Trends in adolescent emotional problems in England: a comparison of two national cohorts twenty years apart', *Journal of Child Psychology and Psychiatry* 51, 8, 885–94. I have suggested in an earlier publication – Dorling (2010, pp.272–6), op. cit. – that part of this fall might be due to the inclusion of more equitable countries in the dataset in recent years. Hopefully I was wrong.

66 Nuffield Foundation (2012, p.5), *Social trends and mental health: introducing the main findings*, London: Nuffield Foundation, www.nuffieldfoundation.org.

67 Yusoff, M. S. B., Rahim, A. F. A., and Yaacob, M. J. (2010), 'The sensitivity, specificity and reliability of the Malay version 12-items general health questionnaire (ghq-12) in detecting distressed medical students', *ASEAN Journal of Psychiatry* 11, 1, 1–8, January–June, http://www.aseanjournalofpsychiatry.org/pdf/ASEAN_3_11_Shaiful.pdf.

68 Montazeri, A., Harirchi, A. M., Shariati, M., Gararoudi, G., et al. (2003), 'The 12-item General Health Questionnaire (GHQ-12): translation and validation study of the Iranian

version', *Health and Quality of Life Outcomes* 1, 1, 66, http://www.hqlo.com/content/1/1/66.

69   Oswald, A. J. (2010), 'Emotional Prosperity and the Stiglitz Commission', *IZA Discussion Paper* number 5390, http://ftp.iza.org/dp5390.pdf.

70   Scores appear to be out of 36 in the original paper, scaled to be out of 12 here; see Figure 1 of: Oswald, A., and Powdthavee, N. (2007), 'Obesity, Unhappiness, and The Challenge of Affluence: Theory and Evidence', *Warwick Economic Research Papers* no. 793, http://www2.warwick.ac.uk/fac/soc/economics/research/workingpapers/2008/twerp_793.pdf.

71   Hagell, A. (ed., 2012, p.1), *Changing Adolescence: Social trends and mental health*, Bristol: Policy Press.

72   Pevalin, D. J. (2000), 'Investigating Long-term Re-test Effects in the GHQ-12', *ISER Working Paper* 2000–20, https://www.iser.essex.ac.uk/publications/working-papers/iser/2000-20.pdf.

73   Tung, J., Barreiroa, L. B., et al. (2012), 'Social environment is associated with gene regulatory variation in the rhesus macaque immune system', *PNAS Early Edition*, www.pnas.org/lookup/suppl/doi:10.1073/pnas.1202734109/-/DCSupplemental.): 1-6.

74   Wilkinson, R. (2010, pp.134–5), 'Inequality and social outcomes – the journey to the spirit level and beyond: an interview', *International Journal of Management Concepts and Philosophy* 4, 2, 126–36.

75   Zink, C. F., Tony, Y., et al. (2008), 'Know Your Place: Neural Processing of Social Hierarchy in Humans, *Neuron*, 24 April, 58, 2, 273–83. DOI: 10.1016/j.neuron.2008.01.025, http://www.ncbi.nlm.nih.gov/pmc/articles/PMC2430590/.

76   Sapolsky, R. M. (2004, p.412), 'Social status and health in humans and other animals', *Annual Review of Anthropology* 33, 393–418, http://academic.reed.edu/biology/professors/srenn/pages/teaching/2008_syllabus/2008_readings/9_sapolsky_2004_stress.pdf.

Chapter 5
8 billion by the quarter century (2025)

1 And 'shrugging off jet lag with the indifference of some-one who, when asked where she lives, replies: "Oh, on a plane"...': Aitkenhead, D. (2012), 'Dambisa Moyo: "The world will be drawn into a war for resources"', the *Guardian*, 24 June, http://www.guardian.co.uk/global-development/2012/jun/24/natural-resources-and-develop ment-china.

2 Ibid.

3 To quote from the bibliography on her website: http://www.dambisamoyo.com/biography/.

4 Aitkenhead (2012), op. cit.

5 Bibby, J., Dubuc, S., Grayer, M., Kornbrot, D., Marshall, A., Simpson, L., and Norman, P. (2011, p.5), *Moral panic about overpopulation: a distracting campaign?*, Radical Statistics Population Studies Group Report: http://www.radstats.org.uk/popgroup/RSPG_OPT-Oct11.pdf.

6 See the last section of Chapter 1, 'Lessons from "Coconut Land"', referencing the book *Too Many Asians* and dis-cussing how wrong it turned out to be about Kerala.

7 Now at:http://www.youtube.com/watch?v=dN06tLRE4WE, original shown on BBC4 on Friday, 25 November 2011. Details can be found here: http://www.bbc.co.uk/pro-grammes/b00pdjmk.html.

8 Jägerskog, A., and Jønch Clausen, T. (eds, 2012), *Feeding a Thirsty World: Challenges and Opportunities for a Water and Food Secure Future*, Report Number 31, Stockholm International Water Institute, Stockholm.

9 According to what is reported at http://en.wikipedia.org/wiki/Maplecroft, although it is somewhat harder to work out what they are if you read only their own web pages: http://maplecroft.com/about/who_we_are/.

10 Nurse, P., et al. (2012), *People and the planet*, The Royal Society Science Policy Centre Report, 01/12, issued April 2012, London: Royal Society (references p.30): http://roy-alsociety.org/policy/projects/people-planet/.

11 Walpole, S. C., et al. (2012), 'The weight of nations: an estimation of adult human biomass', *BMC Public Health* 12:439, http://www.biomedcentral.com/1471-2458/12/439.

12 Cohen, Joel. E. (1992), 'How Many People Can Earth Hold?', *Discover Magazine*, 1 November 1992, http://discovermagazine.com/1992/nov/howmanypeoplecan152/.

13 Carrington, D. (2012), 'Fish to shrink by up to a quarter due to climate change, study reveals. Scientists predict 14–24 per cent reduction in fish size by 2050 as ocean temperatures increase', the *Guardian*, 30 September, http://www.guardian.co.uk/environment/2012/sep/30/fish-shrink-climate-change. The wider research group was led by Prof. William Cheung from the University of British Columbia in Canada. For more details of his work see: http://www.fisheries.ubc.ca/faculty-staff/william-cheung.

14 Once you could read almost everything about a subject. I did this for my very narrow PhD thesis in 1989/1990. But now that so many thousands more people are able to write and research; now that we have the World Wide Web to write on and read from, how can you ever know what is most comprehensive? All we can do is our best.

15 Parfitt, J., Barthel, M., and Macnaughton, S. (2010), 'Food waste within food supply chains: quantification and potential for change to 2050', *Philosophical Transactions of the Royal Society B*, 365, 3065–81, http://rstb.royalsociety-publishing.org/content/365/1554/3065.full.

16 Staff reporter (2012), 'How to stop fishermen fishing', *The Economist*, 25 February, http://www.economist.com/node/21548240, referring in turn to a 'new study (under peer review for the journal *Science*)', http://www.economist.com/node/21548212.

17 Goar, C. (2012), 'Venerable Economist sounds alarm over growing inequality', the *Toronto Star*, 18 October, http://www.thestar.com/opinion/editorialopinion/article/1273939-venerable-economist-sounds-alarm-over-growing-inequality-goar.

18 Nurse et al. (2012), op. cit (references p.49).

19 Gibbons, A. (2012), 'Raw Food Not Enough to Feed Big Brains', *Science Now*, 22 October, http://news.sciencemag.org/sciencenow/2012/10/raw-food-not-enough-to-feed-big-.html.

20 Ruddiman, W. F. (2005, p.191), *Plows, plagues, and petroleum: How humans took control of climate*, Princeton: Princeton University Press.

21 Ibid. (p.194).

22 Clark, R. N., and Brauer, D. (2010, p.3), 'Overview of Ogallala Aquifer Program', *Proceedings of the 5th Decennial National Irrigation Conference*, 5–8 December, Phoenix, Arizona. Paper Number IRR10-10034, ASABE, St Joseph, Michigan: http://www.cprl.ars.usda.gov/wmru/pdfs/, then scroll to Clark and Brauer, 25-Jan-2011 10:11.

23 Six papers on that aquifer alone can be found here: http://www.cprl.ars.usda.gov/swmru-publications.php.

24 Jägerskog, A., Jønch Clausen, T. (eds, 2012), *Feeding a Thirsty World: Challenges and Opportunities for a Water and Food Secure Future*, Report Number 31, Stockholm: Stockholm International Water Institute (SIWI).

25 Ghassem-Fachandi, P. (2012), *Pogrom in Gujarat: Hindu Nationalism and Anti-Muslim Violence in India*, New Jersey: Princeton University Press, http://press.princeton.edu/titles/9755.html.

26 Varis, O., and Kummu, M. (2012), 'The major Central Asian river basins: An assessment of vulnerability', *International Journal of Water Resources Development*, 28, 3, 433–52.

27 Giordano, M., Shah, T., de Fraiture, C., and Giordano, M. (2012, p.22), 'Innovations in Agricultural Water Management: New Challenges Require New Solutions', Chapter 2 in Jägerskog and Jønch Clausen (eds, 2012), op. cit.

28 Nurse et al. (2012, p.68), op. cit. (references page 30).

29 Wallace, A. R. (1858), *On the tendency of varieties to depart indefinitely from the original type*, essay written in Ternate, February, copy here: http://people.wku.edu/charles.smith/wallace/S043.htm.

30 Nurse et al. (2012, p.77), op. cit., referring in turn to Royal Society (2009), 'Reaping the benefits: science and the sustainable intensification of global agriculture', *Royal Society Policy Document* 11/09, Royal Society: London.

31 Institute of Mechanical Engineers (2011, p.37), *One planet, too many people?*, London: IME, http://www.imeche.org/Libraries/2011_Press_Releases/Population_report.sflb.ashx.

32 Agrimonde (2009, p.24), *Scenarios and Challenges for Feeding the World in 2050*, summary report, Paris: Institut National de la Recherche Agronomique and Agricultural Research for Development, http://www.international.inra.fr/the_institute/foresight/agrimonde.

33 Generally favourably here, but look down to the end: http://en.wikipedia.org/wiki/Comparative_advantage. For more on Ricardo, often portrayed as one of the originators of modern economics, see the very start of Chapter 4 above.

34 Foresight (2011, pp.10–11), *The Future of Food and Farming, Foresight Report's Implications for China*, London: Government Office for Science, http://www.bis.gov.uk/assets/foresight/docs/food-and-farming/12-898-the-future-of-food-and-farming-implications-for-china.pdf.

35 See Figure on page 67 and the note in that graph of the Great Chinese Famine of 1958–62.

36 Foresight (2011, p.37) op. cit., http://www.bis.gov.uk/assets/foresight/docs/food-and-farming/11-547-future-of-food-and-farming-summary.pdf.

37 No, you couldn't make it up: http://en.wikipedia.org/wiki/Caroline_Spelman, referencing in turn *The New Statesman* (2009), 'The new ruling class', 1 October, http://www.newstatesman.com/uk-politics/2009/10/oxford-university-wealth-school. Note that she was replaced by Matt Ridley's brother-in-law, Owen Paterson, who makes a brief appearance in the first chapter of this book and who is even more disliked by environmentalists than was Caroline.

38 Hockridge, E. (2012), 'GM cotton problems' (letter), head

of policy, Soil Association, the *Guardian*, 20 June, http://www.guardian.co.uk/environment/2012/jun/20/gm-cotton-problems.

39 Staff reporter (2012), 'Maharashtra bans Bt cotton seeds', *The Times of India*, 9 August, http://articles.timesofindia.indiatimes.com/2012-08-09/india/33118430_1_cotton-seeds-bt-cotton-cotton-growing-states.

40 These comments can be found beneath the story: Carrington, D. (2012), 'GM crops good for environment, study finds', the *Guardian*, 13 June, http://www.guardian.co.uk/environment/2012/jun/13/gm-crops-environment-study.

41 Monbiot, G. (2012), 'Must the poor go hungry just so the rich can drive?', the *Guardian*, 13 August, http://www.guardian.co.uk/commentisfree/2012/aug/13/poor-hungry-rich-drive-mo-farah-biofuels?commentpage=2#comment-17668876.

42 Dorling, D. (2008), 'Supplementary memorandum from Professor Danny Dorling, pages (evidence) 323–4', House of Commons Transport Committee: *Ending the Scandal of Complacency: Road Safety beyond 2010*.

43 Dorling, D. (2011), *Roads, Casualties and Public Health: the Open Sewers of the 21st Century*, Publication of PACTS' 21st Westminster Lecture, ISSN 1740-0368, London: Parliamentary Advisory Council for Transport Safety.

44 Grescoe, T. (2012, p.60), *Strap Hanger: Saving our cities and ourselves from the automobile*, New York: Times Books.

45 See details of the Global Forest Disturbance Alert System, which, among much else, charts the extent to which trees are being cleared to grow biofuels. Interestingly it is produced '. . . in partnership with Cal State Monterey Bay and NASA Ames Research Center', both also in the USA: http://rainforests.mongabay.com/deforestation-tracker/.

46 Bookchin, M. (1989), 'Death of a small planet: It's growth that's killing us', *The Progressive*, August, pp. 19–23, http://dwardmac.pitzer.edu/Anarchist_Archives/bookchin/planet/planet.html.

47   Dorling, D. (1995, p.37), *A New Social Atlas of Britain*, Chichester: John Wiley and Sons. A copy of the book can be found here: http://www.dannydorling.org/?page_id=81.

48   Evans, L. T. (1998, p.222), *Feeding the Ten Billion: plants and population growth*, Cambridge, Cambridge University Press. The Commonwealth Scientific and Industrial Research Organization (CSIRO) is Australia's national science agency. For more information: http://www.csiropedia.csiro.au/display/CSIROpedia/Evans,+Lloyd+Thomas.

49   http://www.guardian.co.uk/theguardian/2012/apr/03/correctionsandclarifications-editorialsandreply. Corrected figures to original article, the original article being by Eric Klinenberg and referenced next below.

50   Klinenberg, E. (2012), 'I want to be alone: the rise and rise of solo living', the *Guardian*, 30 March, http://www.guardian.co.uk/lifeandstyle/2012/mar/30/the-rise-of-solo-living.

51   Ibid.

52   UNPD (2004, p.95), *World Population to 2300, Final Report*, Department of Economic and Social Affairs, Population Division ST/ESA/SER.A/236, section by Alaka Malwade Basu: 'Towards an Understanding of the Emotions in the Population of 2300'.

53   Bourdieu, P. (2008 translation, p.12), *The Bachelors' Ball*, Cambridge: Polity. See p.15 for the inheritance formula. Where there were two children, the elder received two thirds; with three children the eldest had one half.

54   For the stories of emigration behind the legend, see: http://en.wikipedia.org/wiki/Pied_Piper_of_Hamelin.

55   Kavoussi, B. (2012), 'Birth Rate Plunges, Projected To Reach Lowest Level In Decades', *Huffington Post*, 26 July, http://www.huffingtonpost.com/2012/07/26/birth-rate-economy_n_1705744.html.

56   Note that it was lower from 2007 to 2011 but rose when the tsunami killed so many people. Sudden increases in mortality tend to be followed by temporary rises in fertility: http://www.indexmundi.com/g/g.aspx?c=ja&v=31.

57　The fertility rate in Singapore in 2012 is here: http://www.indexmundi.com/g/g.aspx?v=31&c=sn&l=en.

58　So those very high fertility rates for the UK may well be revised downwards in future years as it becomes apparent that there were far more women aged around 30 in the country than had been estimated.

59　Staff reporter (2011), 'Census: US marriage rate at a record low', *USA Today*, 14 December. A copy of the text is available here: http://usatoday30.usatoday.com/news/health/wellness/marriage/story/2011-12-14/Census-US-marriage-rate-at-a-record-low/51921584/1.

60　Staff reporter (2011), 'Asian demography: The flight from marriage', the *Economist*, 20 August, http://www.economist.com/node/21526329

61　UNPD (2004, p.148), op. cit., Tim Dyson.

62　Nurse et al. (2012, p.99), op. cit., referring in turn to Royal Society (2009) *Reaping the benefits: science and the sustainable intensification of global agriculture*, Royal Society Policy document 11/09. Royal Society: London.

63　'The PRESIDENT remarked . . . in all the years he had had the honour of being connected with the Society, he had never heard a paper read of a more luminous character, and which so bound together in the most perfect forms all the branches of the science of natural history, more particularly as it developed the truths of geography upon what he considered to be its soundest basis, that of geological observation and analogy.' Remarks following the reading of Wallace, A. R. (1863, p.10), 'On the Physical Geography of the Malay Archipelago', *Journal of the Royal Geographical Society*, 33, 217–34, http://wallace-online.org/content/frameset?pageseq=20&itemID=S078&viewtype=text.

64　Dorling, D. (2010), 'The Darwins and the Cecils are only empty vessels', *Environment and Planning A*, 42, 1023–5. An open-access copy is to be found here: http://www.env-plan.com/epa/editorials/a43114.pdf.

65　Myerson, A. (1925, p.23), *The inheritance of mental*

diseases, Baltimore: Williams & Wilkins; referenced on p.1 of the summary of Jay Joseph, *The Gene Illusion*: http://jayjoseph.net/the_gene_illusion.

66   Hodson, G., and Busseri, M. A. (2012, p.190), 'Bright minds and dark attitudes: Lower cognitive ability predicts greater prejudice through right-wing, ideology and low inter-group contact', *Psychological Science* 23, 2, 187–95. originally published online 5 January 2012. DOI: 10.1177/0956797611421206.

67   Keiller, S. W. (2010), 'Abstract reasoning as a predictor of attitudes toward gay men', *Journal of Homosexuality* 57, 914–27.

68   Dean, G., and Nais, D. (1997), 'Professor H. J. Eysenck, in memoriam 1916–1997', *Correlation* 16, 1, 48–54, http://www.astrology-and-science.com/h-eyse2.htm.

69   Goldstein, H. (2012, p.154), 'Francis Galton, measurement, psychometrics and social progress', *Assessment in Education: Principles, Policy & Practice* 19, 2, May, 147–58: http://www.bristol.ac.uk/cmm/team/hg/full-publications/2012/Galton.pdf.

70   Ibid. (p.156).

71   Canter, D. (2012), 'Challenging neuroscience and evolutionary explanations of social and psychological processes', *Contemporary Social Science* 7, 2, 95–115; quoting on p.106: Joseph, J. (2002), 'Twin studies in psychiatry and psychology: Science or pseudoscience?', *Psychiatric Quarterly* 73, 1, 71–82.

72   Wright, L. (1997, p.33), *Twins: and what they tell us about who we are*, New York: John Wiley & Sons (quote referenced on p.4 of the summary of Jay Joseph, *The Gene Illusion*: http://jayjoseph.net/the_gene_illusion).

73   Ghose, T. (2011), 'Heritability of Intelligence: A new study of thousands of people in Europe quantifies the genetic underpinnings of intelligence, finding that some 50 percent of smarts stems from genes', *The Scientist*, 9 August, reporting in Davies, G., et al. (2011), 'Genome-wide association studies establish that human intelligence is highly heritable

and polygenic', *Molecular Psychiatry* 16, 996–1005. DOI: 10.1038/mp.2011.85, 2011.

74   Davey Smith, G. (2012), 'Epigenesist for epidemiologists: does evo-devo have implications for population health research and practice?', *International Journal of Epidemiology* 41, 1, 236–47. See discussion before the quote on: 'Fuck off and Die': http://ije.oxfordjournals.org/content/41/1/236.full, quoting copiously from Pearl, R. (1927), 'Differential fertility', *Quarterly Review of Biology* 2, 102–18.

75   Taylor, P. (2011, p.472), 'Rehabilitating a biological notion of race? A response to Sesardic', *Biological Philosophy* 26: 469–73.

76   Morris, R. (2012), 'LA riots: How 1992 changed the police', BBC News, 29 April, US and Canada, http://www.bbc.co.uk/news/world-us-canada-17878180.

77   Graham, M., Hale, S. A., and Stephens, M. (2011), *Geographies of the World's Knowledge*, London: Convoco: http://www.oii.ox.ac.uk/news/?id=680.

78   Haldane, A. G., and Nelson, B. (2012), 'Tails of the unexpected', paper given at The Credit Crisis Five Years On: Unpacking the Crisis, conference held at the University of Edinburgh Business School, 8–9 June, http://www.bankofengland.co.uk/publications/Documents/speeches/2012/speech582.pdf.

79   Galton believed that monkeys were just below Negroes on the 'normal' curve. He may have seen them as being at the top of another normal curve lying just below humans. As the last section of Chapter 2 explained in some detail, Francis Galton wrote that the greatest mental superiority was to be found in the 'modern European' and the lowest in 'the lowest of the Negro races'. He though he was among the most superior of all.

80   UNPD (2004, p.122), op. cit., John C. Caldwell.

81   Pakulak, E., Yamada, Y., Hampton Wray, A., Isbell, E., and Neville, H. (2012), 'Effects of childhood socioeconomic status on cognition and related neural systems in adulthood',

Neuroscience 2012 annual conference, 17 October, abstract: http://www.abstractsonline.com/Plan/ViewAbstract. aspx?sKey=734b1ccd-cfcf-4394-a945-083ca58f8033&c Key=707aae9d-766c-4309-8368-9f4d37117bf1&mKey= per cent7b70007181-01C9-4DE9-A0A2-EEBFA14CD9F1 per cent7d.

82 Leader writer (2012), 'True Progressivism: A new form of radical centrist politics is needed to tackle inequality without hurting economic growth', *The Economist Magazine*, 13 October, http://www.economist.com/node/21564556.

83 Gordon, D. (2008), 'Children, policy and social justice', in Craig, G., Burchardt, T., and Gordon, D. (eds), *Social Justice and Public Policy: Seeking fairness in diverse societies*, Bristol: Policy Press. On a loving god, see Haldane's namesake (note 78 above), 'an inordinate fondness for beetles', http://en.wikiquote.org/wiki/J._B._S._Haldane.

84 Gordon, D. and Nandy, S. (2012, pp.63–4), Chapter 4, 'Measuring child poverty and deprivation', in Minujin, A., and Nandy, S. (eds), *Global child poverty and well-being: Measurement, concepts, policy and action*, Bristol: Policy Press.

85 If you doubt that humans are becoming more clever, consider Nelson's namesake (note 78 above) giving some remarkably stupid advice in 1793 to his midshipmen: 'There are three things, young gentlemen, which you are constantly to bear in mind. Firstly, you must always implicitly obey orders, without attempting to form any opinion of your own respecting their propriety. Secondly, you must consider every man your enemy who speaks ill of your king; and thirdly, you must hate a Frenchman, as you do the devil': http://en.wikiquote.org/wiki/Horatio_Nelson.

Chapter 6
9 billion by 2045

1 Quoted in Cave, D. (2012), 'Cuba will make it easier to travel abroad', *The New York Times*, 16 October, http://

www.nytimes.com/2012/10/17/world/americas/cuba-lifts-much-reviled-rule-the-exit-visa.html.

2   UNPD (2004, p.36), *World Population to 2300, Final Report*, Department of Economic and Social Affairs, Population Division ST/ESA/SER.A/236.

3   Amin, A. (2012, pp.163–4), *Land of Strangers*, Cambridge, CUP, quoting from Sloterdijk, P. (2010, p.229), *Rage and Time*, New York: Columbia University Press.

4   Ibid.

5   A key reason why there are fewer cross-border immigrants in Tokyo, people from outside of Japan, is that you have to travel a lot further out of Tokyo than you do from London to cross an international border.

6   Bakewell, O. (2011, final page), 'Migration and Development in Sub-Saharan Africa', in Phillips, N. (ed.), *Migration in the Global Political Economy*, Boulder, Colorado: Lynne Rienner, http://www.imi.ox.ac.uk/pdfs/migration-and-development-in-sub-saharan-africa.

7   Ibid., quoting European census data reported by Katseli, L., Lucas, R., and Xenogiani, T. (2006), 'Policies for Migration and Development: A European Perspective', Policy Brief no.30, Paris: OECD Development Centre. See: http://en.wikipedia.org/wiki/Louka_Katseli.

8   Nurse, P., et al. (2012), *People and the planet*, The Royal Society Science Policy Centre Report, 01/12, issued April 2012, London: Royal Society, quoting in turn from de Beer, J., Raymer, J., van der Erf, R., and van Wissen, L. (2010), 'Overcoming the problems of inconsistent international migration data: A new method applied to flows in Europe', *European Journal of Population* 26, 459–81.

9   Tobler, W. (2012), *Lee's Migration Theory: Pluses and Minuses*, prepared for the Western Regional Science Association meeting, Santa Barbara, February 2013: Lee, E. (1967), 'A Theory of Migration', *Demography* 3, 47–57.

10 Baird, V. (2011, p.76), *The No-Nonsense Guide to World Population*, Oxford: New Internationalist. See also: *Daily Express* article by Alison Little, headlined 'Let Christian

migrants in first, demands Carey', and *Times* opinion piece by the former archbishop entitled 'Migration threatens the DNA of our nation' (7 January 2010), both referenced in http://www.ekklesia.co.uk/node/10956 on 8 January 2010.

11   '. . . what author and feminist activist Betsy Hartmann has called . . .': Angus, I., and Butler, S. (2010), 'Should Climate Activists Support Limits on Immigration?', *Monthly Review*, 25 January, http://mrzine.monthlyreview. org/2010/ab250110.html.

12   Royal Commission on Environmental Pollution (RCEP) (2011, p.80), *Twenty-ninth report: Demographic change and the environment*, Cmd 8001, London: TSO: http:// webarchive.nationalarchives.gov.uk/20110303145146/ http://www.rcep.org.uk/reports/29-demographics/29-demographics.htm.

13   Schalansky, J. (2012, p.99), *Pocket Atlas of Remote Islands: Fifty Islands I Have Not Visited and Never Will*, London: Particular Books (Penguin).

14   Note, however, that the British Broadcasting Corporation still titles its stories on this misleadingly: BBC (2012), 'Mau Mau torture court ruling awaited by Kenyans', 5 October, http://www.bbc.co.uk/news/uk-19832502.

15   Hatherley, O. (2012), 'Rebel Cities: From the Right to the City to the Urban Revolution by David Harvey – review', the *Guardian*, 12 April, http://www.guardian.co.uk/ books/2012/apr/12/owen-hatherley-rebel-cities-harvey.

16   Amin, A. (2012, p.55), *Land of Strangers*, Cambridge: Cambridge University Press.

17   N. J. Habraken, 1972, quoted in Ward, C. (1985), *When we build again: let's have housing that works!*, London: Pluto Press.

18   Batty, M. (2011), 'When all the world's a city', *Environment and Planning A*, vol. 43, pp.765–72.

19   See Worldmapper Map 7: Population year 1, at www. worldmapper.org, and the poster at: http://www.world-mapper.org/posters/worldmapper_map7_ver5.pdf (relying on Angus Maddison's estimates). However, some cities on

the old silk route and other bypassed places have almost disappeared.

20 Grescoe, T. (2012, p.185), *Straphanger: saving our cities and ourselves from the automobile*, New York: Times Books.

21 Although woe betide anyone thinking of calling it Greater Sydney, as it would encompass New Zealand!

22 See the City Population website maintained by Thomas Brinkhoff, professor in the University of Applied Sciences, Wilhelmshaven/Oldenburg/Ostfriesland, Institute for Applied Photogrammetry and Geoinformatics (IAPG): http://www.citypopulation.de/world/Agglomerations.html.

23 The world city hierarchy is given by Peter Taylor's brilliant 'The World according to GaWC 2004'. See: http://www.lboro.ac.uk/gawc/world2004c.html. Note that Tehran is the city that is displaced most in this map.

24 Lent, A., and Nash, D. (2011, p.52), *Surviving the Asian Century: Four steps to securing sustainable long-term economic growth in the UK*, New Era Economics Report, Institute of Public Policy Research, August, http://www.ippr.org/images/media/files/publication/2011/08/surviving-the-asian-century_Aug2011_7872.pdf.

25 Albertson, K., and Whittle, R. (2012), 'To hell with neo-liberalism: Back with Liberalism', Manchester. Personal communication associated with that draft article, from Albertson, September 2012.

26 Dorling, D. (2012), *The no-nonsense guide to equality*, Oxford: New Internationalist.

27 Hennig, B., and Dorling, D. (2012), 'London-mapper an online social atlas of London', Introduction, http://www.londonmapper.org.uk/features/inequality-in-london/ Referring to http://eprints.lse.ac.uk/28344/.

28 Ross, N., Dorling, D., Dunn, J. R., Henriksson, G., Glover, J., Lynch, J., and Weitoft G. R. (2005), 'Metropolitan Income Inequality and Working-Age Mortality: A Cross-Sectional Analysis Using Comparable Data from Five Countries', *Journal of Urban Health: Bulletin of the New York Academy of Medicine* 82, 1, 101–10.

29   'Capgemini Consulting and HMRC benchmark the performance of tax administrations in ten countries', http://www.uk.capgemini.com/insights-and-resources/by-success-story/hmrc-identify-further-step-change/?ftcnt=10031, 27 June 2012.

30   'Offering the wealth management industry over 20 years of insights into the investment needs of High Net Worth Individuals . . . We help clients to accelerate their strategies for growth in the wealth management market by optimizing customer/market-facing initiatives and advisor/distribution channel-facing initiatives.' 3 November 2012, http://www.capgemini.com/services-and-solutions/by-industry/financial-services/solutions/wealth/.

31   Figures drawn from the Capgemini (2012) *16th Annual World Wealth Report*: http://www.capgemini.com/services-and-solutions/by-industry/financial-services/solutions/wealth/worldwealthreport/worlds_wealth/.

32   My favourite Stephen King quote is his description of a conservative commentator as 'Satan's mentally challenged younger brother'. See: Von Drehle, D. (2009), 'Mad Man: Is Glenn Beck Bad for America?', *Time* magazine, 17 September, http://www.time.com/time/magazine/article/0,9171,1924495-3,00.html. However, the slightly less colourful quote used here is from Flood, A. (2012), 'Stephen King: I'm rich, tax me', the *Guardian*, 1 May, http://www.guardian.co.uk/books/2012/may/01/stephen-king-tax-the-rich.

33   Goldberg, D. T. (2009, p.238), *The threat of race: Reflections on racial neoliberalism*, Oxford: Blackwell.

34   Blair, T. (2012), 'Tony Blair in the Huffington Post: In Favour of Philanthropy', The Tony Blair Faith Foundation, 16 April http://www.tonyblairfaithfoundationus.org/news/2012/04/16-0.

35   Comments to be found beneath the article: ibid., http://www.huffingtonpost.co.uk/tony-blair/in-favour-of-philanthropy_b_1426932.html.

36   Capgemini (2009), *13th Annual World Wealth Report*: http://

www.capgemini.com/services-and-solutions/by-industry/
financial-services/solutions/wealth/worldwealthreport/
wwr_archive/.

37 Capgemini (2010), *14th Annual World Wealth Report*: http://
www.capgemini.com/services-and-solutions/by-industry/
financial-services/solutions/wealth/worldwealthreport/
wwr_archive/.

38 Capgemini (2011, p.12), *15th Annual World Wealth
Report*, http://www.capgemini.com/services-and-solutions/
by-industry/financial-services/solutions/wealth/world
wealthreport/wwr_archive/.

39 Badiou, A. (2012, p.12), *The rebirth of history, times of
riots and uprisings*, London: Verso.

40 Brennan, J., and Flynn, F. (2012), 'Quinn gets nine weeks
for contempt of court', the *Independent*, 3 November,
http://www.independent.co.uk/news/world/europe/quinn-
gets-nine-weeks-for-contempt-of-court-8280145.html.

41 Source: Capgemini research on 'Lorenz curve analysis',
November 2012: http://www.capgemini.com/services-and-
solutions/by-industry/financial-services/solutions/wealth/
worldwealthreport/wwr_archive/.

42 He is said to have changed his name by deed poll after he
fell out with his mother. This can be found in the small
print of an article listing some of the many family spats:
The Australian, report of 9 March 2007: http://www.
theaustralian.com.au/news/nation/billion-dollar-war/
story-e6frg6pf-1111113121768.

43 Rourke, A. (2012), 'Gina Rinehart: from mining magnate
to Australia's newest media mogul', the *Guardian*, 19 June,
http://www.guardian.co.uk/business/2012/jun/19/gina-
rinehart-mining-magnate.

44 Schalansky (2012, p.24), op. cit. (See note 13 above).

45 Kay, R. (2012), 'Aga Khan sails into eco storm over purchase of tropical island in Bahamas', *Daily Mail*, 3 January,
http://www.dailymail.co.uk/news/article-2081533/
Aga-Khan-sails-eco-storm-purchase-private-tropical-
island-Bahamas.html.

46   Anonymous (2012), 'Every summer the Greek and international press publish stories that a celebrity is about to
buy the island', Wikipedia, http://en.wikipedia.org/wiki/
Skorpios, accessed November 2012.

47   ESRC (2012), press release: 'Too much money reduces
life satisfaction', Economic & Social Research Council,
23 August, http://www.esrc.ac.uk/impacts-and-findings/
features-casestudies/features/23180/too-much-money-
reduces-life-satisfaction.aspx. Proto, E., and Rustichini, A.
(2012), 'A Reassessment of the Relationship Between GDP
and Life Satisfaction', Centre for Competitive Advantage
in the Global Economy, Paper #94, University of Warwick,
http://www2.warwick.ac.uk/fac/soc/economics/research/
centres/cage/research/wpfeed/94.2012_proto.pdf.

48   UN Data (2008), *UN median variant projection*, United
Nations Statistics Division (UNSD) of the Department of
Economic and Social Affairs (DESA): http://data.un.org/Data.
aspx?d=PopDiv&f=variableID per cent3A77 November
2012.

49   For further details of current known rates, as of 2012, see:
http://en.wikipedia.org/wiki/Infant_mortality.

50   UN Data (2010), *UN revision of projections*, United
Nations Statistics Division (UNSD) of the Department
of Economic and Social Affairs (DESA): http://data.
un.org/Data.aspx?d=PopDiv&f=variableID per cent3A77
November 2012.

51   UNPD (2004, p.115), *World Population to 2300, Final
Report*, Department of Economic and Social Affairs,
Population Division, ST/ESA/SER.A/236, John C. Caldwell.

52   Monbiot, G. (2012), 'Britain is being rebuilt in aid of
corporate power. Trust business, Cameron tells us, self-
regulation is a force for social good. Silly me – I thought it
was an invitation to disaster', the *Guardian*, 27 February,
http://www.guardian.co.uk/commentisfree/2012/feb/27/
britain-rebuilt-in-aid-corporate-power.

53   Davis, D. (2012), 'Crony capitalism', *Prospect Magazine*,
22 February, http://www.prospectmagazine.co.uk/economics

/crony-capitalism-david-davis-attacks-big-business-poli-cies/.

54   Batty, M. (2011, p.765), 'When all the world's a city', *Environment and Planning A*, 43, 765–72.

55   Ibid., referring to von Foerster, H., Mora, P. M., and Amiot, L. W. (1960), 'Doomsday: Friday November 13 AD 2026', *Science* 132, 1291–5, http://www-ee.stanford.edu/~acfs/vonFoersterArticle.pdf.

56   Von Foerster et al. (1960, p.1295), op. cit.

57   Batty (2011), op. cit. The quote is a collection of phrases taken from pp.768, 770 and 771.

58   UNPD (2004, p.92), op. cit., section by Alaka Malwade Basu, 'Towards an Understanding of the Emotions in the Population of 2300'.

Chapter 7
10 billion?

1   Nurse, P. et al. (2012), *People and the planet*, The Royal Society Science Policy Centre Report 01/12, issued April 2012, London: Royal Society (references on p.56): http://royalsociety.org/policy/projects/people-planet/.

2   Ruddiman, W. F. (2005, p.178), *Plows, plagues, and petroleum: How humans took control of climate*, Princeton: Princeton University Press.

3   David Sloan Wilson, biologist, quoted in van der Zee, B. (2012), 'Biologist wants to "make the world a better place"', the *Guardian*, 6 March, http://www.guardian.co.uk/society/2012/mar/06/david-sloan-wilson-make-world-better-place.

4   Harvey, F. (2012), 'The rare earth riches buried beneath Greenland's vast ice sheet', the *Guardian*, 31 July, http://www.guardian.co.uk/environment/2012/jul/31/rare-earth-greenland.

5   Response at 11.51 p.m. on 31 July by 'Reinroch' to the story: Harvey, F. (2012), 'Europe looks to open up Greenland for natural resources extraction', the *Guardian*,

31 July, http://www.guardian.co.uk/environment/2012/jul/31/europe-greenland-natural-resources.

6 Milmo, D. (2012), 'European car sales fall for 12th month', the *Guardian*, 16 October, http://www.guardian.co.uk/business/2012/oct/16/european-car-sales-fall-new-car-registrations.

7 Grescoe, T. (2012, p.194), *Straphanger: saving our cities and ourselves from the automobile*, New York: Times Books.

8 Nurse et al. (2012, p.7), op. cit.

9 Travis, A. (2012), 'Illicit drugs "going out of fashion". Latest Home Office figures record a decline in illicit drug use in England and Wales, including of mephedrone and Spice', the *Guardian*, 27 September, http://www.guardian.co.uk/society/2012/sep/27/illicit-drugs-out-of-fashion.

10 Bookchin, M. (1989), 'Death of a small planet: It's growth that's killing us', *The Progressive*, August, pp.19–23: http://dwardmac.pitzer.edu/Anarchist_Archives/bookchin/planet/planet.html.

11 Darwin, C. (1859, 2010, p.20), *The Origin of Species*, Bibliolis Classics extract edition, London: Bibliolis Books Ltd.

12 Bak, P., and Sneppen, K. (1993), 'Punctuated Equilibrium and Criticality in a Simple Model of Evolution', *Physical Review Letters*, 71, 23, 4083–6.

13 Akbar, A. (2010), 'Mao's Great Leap Forward "killed 45 million in four years"', the *Independent*, 17 September, http://www.independent.co.uk/arts-entertainment/books/news/maos-great-leap-forward-killed-45-million-in-four-years-2081630.html.

14 Angus Maddison, *Historical Statistics of the World Economy: 1–2008 AD*, updated to 2009, http://www.ggdc.net/MADDISON/oriindex.htm, and kept up to date by his colleagues after Maddison died.

15 Harper, N. K. et al. (2008), 'On the Origin of the Treponematoses: A Phylogenetic Approach', *PLOS neglected tropical diseases*, http://www.plosntds.org/article/info per cent3Adoi per cent2F10.1371 per cent2Fjournal.pntd.0000148.

16   A copy of which is here: http://www.marxists.org/archive/marx/works/1848/communist-manifesto/, which explains: 'The discovery of America, the rounding of the Cape, opened up fresh ground for the rising bourgeoisie.'

17   Collier, A. (2007), *The humble little condom: a history*, New York: Prometheus Books.

18   Moretti, F. (2007, p.92), *Graphs, Maps, Trees*, London: Verso.

19   Revelation 6:2–8, King James Version: '. . . behold a white horse . . . another horse that was red . . . and lo a black horse . . . and behold a pale horse: and his name that sat on him was Death, and Hell followed with him. And power was given unto them . . .': http://www.biblegateway.com/passage/?search=Revelation+6&version=KJV.

20   http://en.wikipedia.org/wiki/Four_Horsemen_of_the_Apocalypse. (This is to be hugely optimistic.)

21   On which Zhou Enlai correctly pointed out that it was too early to tell what the outcome of 1968 might be. See: Cowen, T. (2011), 'It is too soon to tell – the real story, China fact of the day', *Marginal Revolution Blog*, 11 June, http://marginalrevolution.com/marginalrevolution/2011/06/it-is-too-soon-to-tell-the-real-story.html.

22   Lutz, W., Goujon, A., Samir K. C., and Sanderson, W. (2007, p.222), *Vienna Yearbook of Population Research 2007*, 193–235.

23   Samir, K. C., Barakat, B., Goujon, A., et al. (2010, p.432), 'Projection of populations by level of educational attainment, age, and sex for 120 countries for 2005–2050', *Demographic Research* 22, 383–472, http://www.demographic-research.org/volumes/vol22/15/.

24   Godin, S. (2012), *Stop stealing dreams*, http://www.sethgodin.com/sg/docs/stopstealingdreamsscreen.pdf.

25   Baird, V. (2011, p.16), *The No-nonsense guide to world population*, Oxford: New Internationalist, quoting Hania Zlotnik, director of the UN population division, speaking in 2011.

26   As fertility already is lower in so many countries, it becomes

lower as people move to cities. For the source of these estimates see: United Nations, Department of Economic and Social Affairs, Population Division (2011), *World Population Prospects DEMOBASE extract, total fertility (children per woman)* – medium variant.

27 The Forum is presumably the Trust: Hind, J. (2009), 'Twenty other reasons not to have a baby', the *Observer*, 8 February, http://www.guardian.co.uk/lifeandstyle/2009/feb/08/motherhood-children-babies2.

28 Note, Karachi is the eighth largest city by other measures used in this book. Ebrahim, Z. (2012), 'Pakistan Faces a 'Youth Bomb', Inter Press Agency, 3 August, http://www.ipsnews.net/2012/08/pakistan-faces-a-youth-bomb/.

29 CNN news website (2012), 'Drone strikes kill, maim and traumatize too many civilians, US study says', 26 September, CNN News, http://www.cnn.co.uk/2012/09/25/world/asia/pakistan-us-drone-strikes/index.html.

30 Of the 1,402 that fell on Britain, those aimed at London numbered 1,358, Norwich saw 43 and Ipswich 1. However, many fell short in Kent, thankfully often in countryside. See: http://en.wikipedia.org/wiki/V-2#Operational_history.

31 Baird (2011, p.19), op. cit., referring in turn to: Pritchett, L. H. (1994), 'Desired Fertility and the Impact of Population Policies', *Population and Development Review* 20, 1, 1–55.

32 Dorling, D. (2012, pp.49–63), *The no-nonsense guide to equality*, Oxford: New Internationalist.

33 Dorling, D. (2013), *Unequal Health: The scandal of our times*, Bristol: Policy Press (first section of book).

34 Woods, R. (2006), *Children Remembered: responses to untimely death in the past*, Liverpool, Liverpool University Press.

35 O'Tierney, P. F., Barker, D. J. P., et al. (2009, p.424S), 'Duration of Breast-feeding and Adiposity in Adult Life', *The Journal of Nutrition* 139, 2, 422S–425S, http://jn.nutrition.org/content/139/2/422S.full.pdf+html.

36 Watkins, E. S. (2012), 'How the pill became a lifestyle drug:

the pharmaceutical industry and birth control in the United States since 1960', *American Journal of Public Health* 102, 8,1462–72, DOI: 10.2105/AJPH.2012.300706.

37   Baird (2011, p.36), op. cit.

38   By the *CIA World Factbook*, as reported on the highly accessed Wikipedia page that compares reported rates: http://en.wikipedia.org/wiki/List_of_sovereign_states_ and_dependent_territories_by_fertility_rate.

39   Cindry Poernasari, representing the Peduli Indonesian Migrant Workers Concern Group, as quoted by Azevod, T. (2011), 'ILO passes landmark treaty on domestic workers', *Macau Daily Times*, 16 June, http://www. macaudailytimes.com.mo/macau/26345-ILO-passes-land- mark-treaty-domestic-workers.html.

40   UNPD (2004, p.104), *World Population to 2300, Final Report*, Department of Economic and Social Affairs, Population Division ST/ESA/SER.A/236, section written by Herwig Birg.

41   Baird (2011, p.10), op. cit.

42   '. . . the fertility rate of the city of Barcelona has stabilized at 1.1 children per woman, but can what is true of an urban environment that is constantly renewed by migra- tion also be applied at the global level and be sustainable for hundreds of years?' UNPD (2004, p.156), op. cit., sec- tion written by François Héran.

43   Ecclestone, T. (2012), 'What I see in the mirror, I wish my eyebrows were thinner . . .', the *Guardian*, 29 June, http://www.guardian.co.uk/fashion/2012/jun/29/tamara- ecclestone-beauty-routine. Her charity work can be read about here, as can details of her UCL and LSE educational achievements: http://www.tamaraecclestone.com/.

44   Olshansky, S. J., Carnes, B. A., and Désesguelles, A. (2001), 'Prospects for longevity', *Science* 291, 1491–2.

45   Oeppen, J., and Vaupel, J. W. (2002), 'Broken limits to life expectancy', *Science* 296, 1029–31.

46   Employers are obliged to enrol even their casual workers regardless of how few days they might work for them. See:

http://www.mpfa.org.hk/eng/mpf_system/system_features/coverage/index.jsp accessed November 2012.

47 'Germany became the first nation in the world to adopt an old-age social insurance program in 1889', http://www.ssa.gov/history/ottob.html. Note that the retirement age was initially 70, later *falling* to 65.

48 UNPD (2003, pp.5–6), *World Population to 2300, Draft Report*, Department of Economic and Social Affairs, Population Division, ESA/P/WP.187, 9 December.

49 Russ, T., et al. (2012), 'Association between psychological distress and mortality: individual participant pooled analysis of 10 prospective cohort studies', *British Medical Journal* 345, DOI: 10.1136/bmj.e4933 (published 31 July), http://www.bmj.com/content/345/bmj.e4933.

50 Layte, R. (2012, p.509), 'The Association Between Income Inequality and Mental Health: Testing Status Anxiety, Social Capital, and Neo-Materialist Explanations', *European Sociological Review* 28, 4, 498–511.

51 Ibid. (2012, p.509).

52 UNPD (2003. p.7), op. cit.

53 Albeit only by my colleague Carl Lee, who kindly read a draft of this book and proclaimed that he would like to end his days in a home that catered for people with his particular eclectic taste in music, literature and culture.

54 UNPD (2004, p.2), op. cit.

55 Karstedt, S., and Farrall, S. (2006), 'The Moral Economy of Everyday Crime: Markets, Consumers and Citizens', *British Journal of Criminology*, DOI:10.1093/bjc/azl082.

56 Conclusion of Joseph, J. (2004), *The Gene Illusion: Genetic Research in Psychiatry and Psychology Under the Microscope*, New York: Algora Publishing. See p.25 of summary at: http://jayjoseph.net/the_gene_illusion (emphasis added).

57 UNPD (2004, p.115), op. cit., section written by John C. Caldwell.

58 Hecht, B., and Moxley, E. (2009), 'Terabytes of Tobler: Evaluating the First Law in a Massive, Domain-Neutral

Representation of World Knowledge', *Proceedings of the 9th international conference on Spatial information theory*, Heidelberg: Springer, 88–105, ISBN:3-642-03831-X 978-3-642-03831-0,http://www.brenthecht.com/papers/bh echt_cosit2009_tolberslaw.pdf.

59 Oxfam (2012), *World Bank must freeze investments to protect poor people from land grabs*, Oxford: Oxfam, 4 October: http://www.oxfam.org/en/grow/pressroom/press release/2012-10-04/land-sold-last-decade-could-grow-enough-food-feed-billion-people.

60 Vidal, J. (2012), 'Land acquired over past decade could have produced food for a billion people', the *Guardian*, 4 October, http://www.guardian.co.uk/global-development/2012/oct/04/land-deals-preventing-food-production.

61 Chang, H. J. (2012), 'Africa needs an active industrial policy to sustain its growth. African countries will be better off with a more activist development strategy than with the failed Washington orthodoxy', the *Guardian*, 15 July, http://www.guardian.co.uk/commentisfree/2012/jul/15/africa-industrial-policy-washington-orthodoxy.

62 The graph is drawn using United Nations, Department of Economic and Social Affairs data, from the Population Division, a World Population Prospects DEMOBASE extract, using data last revised in 2011.

63 Ruddiman (2005, p.141), op. cit.

64 See Worldmapper map 107: http://www.worldmapper.org/posters/worldmapper_map107_ver5.pdf.

Chapter 8
Or not 10 billion

1 Puschra, W., and Burke, S. (2012, eds), *Sustainability in an Unequal World: How Do We Really Get the Future We Want?*, FES International Policy Analysis, Friedrich-EbertStiftung, New York office, September 2012, http://library.fes.de/pdf-files/iez/global/09371.pdf.

2 Cohen, Joel E. (1992), 'How Many People Can Earth

Hold?', *Discover Magazine*, 1 November, http://discover-magazine.com/1992/nov/howmanypeoplecan152/. Cohen is currently head of the Laboratory of Populations jointly at the Rockefeller University and Columbia University, New York.

3   Religious Tolerance (2012), '46 failed end-of-the-world predictions that were to occur between 30 & 1920 CE, but didn't', website accessed in November 2012: http://www.religioustolerance.org/end_wrl2.htm.

4   The 1974 film titled *Killer Bees* starring Edward Albert and Kate Jackson was followed by *Swarm* in 1978, and most recently *1313 Giant Killer Bees* in 2011: http://www.dreadcentral.com/reviews/1313-giant-killer-bees-2011.

5   This particular story, like all stories of human history, is not universally agreed. For an alternative see: http://realhistoryww.com/world_history/ancient/Misc/Ancient_American_affinities/American_affinities.htm.

6   Ruddiman, W. F. (2005, pp.57–8), *Plows, plagues, and petroleum: How humans took control of climate*, Princeton: Princeton University Press.

7   Lawson, D. (2011), 'The population time bomb is a myth', the *Independent*, 18 January, http://www.independent.co.uk/opinion/commentators/dominic-lawson/dominic-lawson-the-population-timebomb-is-a-myth-2186968.html.

8   On Mr Dominic Lawson see: http://en.wikipedia.org/wiki/Dominic_Lawson, and on his cousin George see here: http://www.whocomments.org/wiki/George_Monbiot. Both were accessed in November 2012.

9   Lomborg, B. (2007), 'An inconvenient peace prize', the *Guardian*, 12 October, http://www.guardian.co.uk/commentisfree/2007/oct/12/aninconvenientpeaceprize.

10 Alter, L. (2009), 'Let's Do The Time Warp Again: Monbiot and May vs Lomborg and Lawson', TreeHugger blog, 2 December, http://www.treehugger.com/clean-technology/lets-do-the-time-warp-again-monbiot-and-may-vs-lomberg-and-lawson.html.

11   UNPD (2003, p.14), *World Population to 2300, Draft Report*, Department of Economic and Social Affairs, Population Division, ESA/P/WP.187, 9 December.

12   UNPD (2004, p.147), *World Population to 2300, Final Report*, Department of Economic and Social Affairs, Population Division, ST/ESA/SER.A/236, section written by Tim Dyson.

13   Coleman, D. (2011), 'David Coleman on population and the environment – live chat', the *Guardian* blog, 23 August, one of many of Coleman's replies to comments. This one made on 24 August 2011, 1.01 p.m., to be found below here: http://www.guardian.co.uk/environment/blog/2011/aug/23/david-coleman-population-environment-live.

14   Redfield, J. R. (2002, p.369), 'Is quorum sensing a side effect of diffusion sensing?', *Trends in Microbiology* 10, 8, 365–70, http://mollycat.ucdavis.edu/pdf/redfield_quorum.pdf.

15   Baird, V. (2011, p.130), *The no-nonsense guide to world population*, Oxford: New Internationalist. Here she is quoting Jesse Ausubel.

16   In Canada, and with one of the best websites in academia: subtitled: 'Do bacteria have sex? (We know you care!)' See: http://www.zoology.ubc.ca/~redfield/.

17   In this we do much better than chimpanzees, who tend to cope best with knowledge of up to 60 others. See Mithen, S. (1998), *Prehistory of the mind*, London: Phoenix; and also Dunbar's number, which is well referenced here, including with reference to Facebook: http://rationalwiki.org/wiki/Dunbar's_Number.

18   Peiser, B. (2005, p.542), 'From Genocide to Ecocide: The Rape of Rapa Nui', *Energy and Environment* 16, 3–4, 512–39, http://www.uri.edu/artsci/ecn/starkey/ECN398 per cent20-Ecology, per cent20Economy, per cent20Society/RAPANUI.pdf.

19   Smith, A. (2003), *Background to the story of Tikopia – An essay prepared for BBC, by the Archbishop of Honiara, Adrian Smith*. See: http://www.kevinbates.com.au/index.

php?option=com_content&task=view&id=41&Ite
mid=39.

20   Schalansky, J. (2012, p.209), *Pocket Atlas of Remote
      Islands: Fifty Islands I Have Not Visited and Never Will*,
      London: Particular Books (Penguin).

21   Nurse, P., et al. (2012, p.98), *People and the planet*, The
      Royal Society Science Policy Centre Report 01/12, issued
      April 2012, London: Royal Society (references p.30):
      http://royalsociety.org/policy/projects/people-planet/.

22   UNPD (2011), 'Total population thousands by country –
      medium variant', *World Urbanization Prospects*, http://
      esa.un.org/unpd/wup/index.htm.

23   Dorling, D. (2011), 'We're all . . . just little bits of history
      repeating (Part 1 – History)', *Significance Magazine* website,
      13 June, http://www.dannydorling.org/?page_id=2254.

24   To be precise, it was 29.8 years in the year 2009, rising
      at a rate of about one month a year since 2003. See Table
      2 on this web page: http://epp.eurostat.ec.europa.eu/statis-
      tics_explained/index.php/Fertility_statistics.

25   Baird (2011, p.12), op. cit.

26   Dorling, D. (2011), 'We're all . . . just little bits of history
      repeating (Part 2 – Future)', *Significance Magazine* website,
      14 June, http://www.dannydorling.org/?page_id=2255.

27   Extract from the industrialist Robert Owen's *Address to
      the Inhabitants of New Lanark* given on New Year's Day
      1816, at New Lanark on the river Clyde. See: http://www.
      robert-owen.com/.

28   Richard Wilkinson (2010, p.129), 'Inequality and social
      outcomes – the journey to the spirit level and beyond: an
      interview', *International Journal of Management Concepts
      and Philosophy* 4, 2, 126–36.

29   Davey Smith, G. (2012, p.305), 'Epigenetics for the
      masses: more than Audrey Hepburn and yellow mice?',
      International Journal of Epidemiology 41, 303–8,
      DOI:10.1093/ije/dys030.

30   Staff reporter (2009), 'How to Feed the World', *The Economist*,
      19 November, http://www.economist.com/node/14915144.

31 World Hunger Education Service (2012), *Hunger in America: 2012 United States Hunger and Poverty Facts*: 'In 2010, 17.2 million households were food insecure, the highest number ever recorded in the United States': http://www.worldhunger.org/articles/Learn/us_hunger_facts.htm.

32 Ahmed, W. (2011, p.179), 'Neoliberal Utopia and Urban Realities in Delhi', *ACME: An International E-Journal for Critical Geographies* 10, 2, 163–88, http://www.acme-journal.org/vol10/Ahmed2011.pdf.

33 Brooks, R. (2013), *The Great Tax Robbery: How Britain Became a Tax Haven for Fat Cats and Big Business*, London: One World.

34 Balourdos, D., et al. (2002, p.3), *Scenarios for a sustainable society: Car transport systems and the sociology of embedded technologies*, Final Report for EU project SOE1-CT97-1071, Ireland: Trinity College Dublin: http://www.tcd.ie/ERC/pastprojects/carsdownloads/Cars per cent 20Final per cent20Report.pdf.

35 The capital of Finland: ibid. (p.42).

36 In Italy: ibid.

37 Regional councillor Lars Gaardhoj explaining the rationale for health bodies funding the project: McGrane, S. (2012), 'Commuters Pedal to Work on Their Very Own Superhighway', *The New York Times*, 17 July, http://www.nytimes.com/2012/07/18/world/europe/in-denmark-pedaling-to-work-on-a-superhighway.html?pagewanted=1&_r=1.

38 Chrisafis, A. (2012), 'Paris to return Seine to the people with car-free riverside plan', the *Guardian*, 2 August, http://www.guardian.co.uk/world/2012/aug/02/paris-seine-riverside-expressway-pedestrian.

39 Ward, C. (1990, new edn, p.107), *The Child in the City*, London: Bedford Square Press.

40 Rolfsen, E. (2012), 'City of 80,000 planned for China will eliminate need for cars', *Calgary Herald*, 30 October, http://www.theprovince.com/City+planned+China+will+eliminate+need+cars/7471279/story.htm.

41 According to David Keeling. See: http://scrippsco2.ucsd.edu/program_history/early_keeling_curve_2.html.

42 Ruddiman (2005, p.114), op. cit.

43 See Worldmapper maps 195–8: http://www.worldmapper.org/display.php?selected=195.

44 See Worldmapper maps 159–64: http://www.worldmapper.org/display.php?selected=159.

45 CE, meaning Current Era, is used because *Anno Domini* means very little outside of Europe, both then and now.

46 Pratley, N. (2012), 'Shadow of the "grey swan" looms darker over the economy', the *Guardian*, 25 October, http://www.guardian.co.uk/business/nils-pratley-on-finance/2012/oct/25/shadow-grey-swan-looms-darker-economy.

47 Clarke, D. (2012), 'Africa: how to be an expert', the *Guardian*, 12 November, http://www.guardian.co.uk/world/2012/nov/12/africa-expert-celebrity-madonna.

48 Quoted in Lowrey, A. (2012), 'Wealth disparity a drag on economic growth', *The New York Times*, 16 October, http://www.nytimes.com/2012/10/17/business/economy/income-inequality-may-take-toll-on-growth.html?pagewanted=all.

49 From the *Divine Comedy*, published 1555, Dante's *Inferno*, Canto XX, lines 13–15 and 38–9, Mandelbaum translation. For the full quotation, see: http://en.wikipedia.org/wiki/Divine_Comedy#cite_ref-14.

50 Malebolge is the eighth circle of hell. The word means 'evil ditches', Malebolge itself being a large, funnel-shaped cavern, divided into 10 concentric circular trenches. See: http://en.wikipedia.org/wiki/Malebolge.

51 Morris, W. (1893), *News from Nowhere or, an Epoch of Rest: being some chapters from a utopian*, serialized first in the *Commonweal* newspaper, http://www.gutenberg.org/files/3261/3261-h/3261-h.htm.

52 Batty, M. (2010, p.8), 'Visualizing Space–Time Dynamics in Scaling Systems', *Complexity* 16, 2, 51–63. DOI: 10.1002/cplx.20342http://onlinelibrary.wiley.com/doi/10.1002/cplx.20342/abstract.

53 Nurse, et al. (2012, p.105), op. cit. (references p.30), http://royalsociety.org/policy/projects/people-planet/.

54 Ibid. (p.106).

55 UNPD (2004, p.83), op. cit.

56 Baird (2011, p.75), op. cit.

57 Daly, M., and Wilson, M. (2005, p.59), 'Carpe Diem: Adaptation and devaluing the future', *The Quarterly Review of Biology* 80, 1, 55–61, http://psych.mcmaster.ca/dalywilson/d&w per cent20qrb per cent202005.pdf.

58 UNPD (2004, p.157), op. cit., section written by François Héran.

59 Travis, A. (2012), 'Falling murder rate linked to decline in domestic violence', the *Guardian*, 19 July, http://www.guardian.co.uk/uk/2012/jul/19/falling-murder-rate-domestic-violence.

60 Patton. G. (2012), 'Future criminals "can be spotted at age of two"', *Daily Telegraph*, 8 March, http://www.telegraph.co.uk/education/educationnews/9129539/Future-criminals-can-be-spotted-at-age-of-two.html.

61 O'Hara, M. (2010), 'Head teacher Charlie Taylor's unconventional approach pays off', the *Guardian*, 23 August, http://www.guardian.co.uk/education/2010/aug/23/pupil-behaviour-headteacher-interview.

62 Van Den Bergh J. C. J. M., and Rietveld P. (2004, p.195), 'Reconsidering the limits to world population: meta-analysis and meta-prediction', *BioScience* 54, 3, 195–204. An open-access copy can be found here: http://life.bio.sunysb.edu/~spgp/2004_03_16/reconsidering per cent20world per cent20pop per cent20growth.pdf.

Afterword

1 Or, to be a little more precise, in the final section of Chapter 6 above: 'The super-poor'.

2 Ruddiman, W. F. (2005, p.168), *Plows, plagues, and petroleum: How humans took control of climate*, Princeton, Princeton University Press.

INDEX